AUDIO
POSTPRODUCTION
for DIGITAL VIDEO

Jay Rose

Published by CMP Books
an imprint of CMP Media LLC
Main office: 600 Harrison Street, San Francisco, CA 94107 USA
Tel: 415-947-6615; fax: 415-947-6015
Editorial office: 1601 West 23rd Street, Suite 200, Lawrence, KS 66046 USA
www.cmpbooks.com
email: books@cmp.com

Technical editor: David Moulton
Acquisitions editor: Dorothy Cox
Copyeditor: Lydia Linker
Managing editor and layout design: Michelle O'Neal
Cover layout design: Damien Castaneda

Distributed to the book trade in the U.S. by: Distributed in Canada by:
Publishers Group West   Jaguar Book Group
1700 Fourth Street   100 Armstrong Avenue
Berkeley, CA 94710   Georgetown, Ontario M6K 3E7 Canada
1-800-788-3123   905-877-4483

For individual orders and for information on special discounts for quantity orders, please contact:
CMP Books Distribution Center, 6600 Silacci Way, Gilroy, CA 95020
Tel: 1-800-500-6875 or 408-848-3854; fax: 408-848-5784
email: cmp@rushorder.com; Web: www.cmpbooks.com

Printed in the United States of America

02 03 04 05 06   5 4 3 2 1

ISBN: 1-57820-116-0

CMP**Books**

Table of Contents

To my cat, again

Introduction

Acknowledgments

While mine is the only name on the cover, it took a lot of people to put this book together. CMP Books publishers Matt Kelsey and Paul Temme helped bring the concept together, Managing Editor Michelle O'Neal made the pages actually happen, and Lydia Linker gets credit for polishing up the language. I'm particularly grateful to Senior Editor Dorothy Cox for her help organizing the book and then her patience with my total revision of its scope. This was supposed to be a slim volume of basics. It's turned into a compendium of just about every professional audio technique that can be adapted to desktop post.

David Moulton, a Grammy-nominated engineer, highly respected audio educator, creator of the *Golden Ears* CDs, and author of *Total Recording*, took the time to look for technical flaws and sloppy writing. I thank him for finding lots of both. Thanks also to Dr. Barry Blesser, the inventor of studio digital reverb, for vetting my history of delay-based effects. And I owe a lot to my son Dan, assistant chief engineer at NPR powerhouse WBUR. He was always available to talk technical and help me discover ways to explain important concepts.

Boston-based producers Rob Stegman of Bluestar Media, Marc Neger of Creative Media Group, Francine Achbar of High Impact Marketing and Media, and Mike Kuell of Jetpak Productions graciously provided material for the tutorials. Special thanks to Mitchell Greenspan of the DeWolfe Music Library for the dozens of musical examples, to John Moran of Hollywood Edge for the sound effects, and to busy PBS narrator Don Wescott for some narration.

The female on the CD is my wife Carla, a former actress (and one-time spokesperson for Howard Johnson Hotels) who now writes popular books about Photoshop and digital graphics. In fact, she wrote two of them while holding my hand through the creation of this manuscript. I thank her for everything.

Introduction

There's a funny thing about the work I do. When there's good cinematography, lighting, editing, or special effects, you can see it on the screen. But good audio postproduction is mostly invisible. You can't tell what was done to fine-tune an actor's dialog. You don't know which noises were caused by on-screen action, and which were added later. A good piece of music editing sounds like the music was played that way in the first place. Equalization, dynamics control, noise reduction, and all the other processes discussed in this book are usually used as subtle corrections, not special effects. When we do the job right, you don't know we've been there at all.

This makes it nearly impossible for filmmakers to teach themselves how to do audio post. Even if you've got the best ears in the world, you won't spot most of the techniques. In fact, relying on your ears alone can be a mistake. If you don't know what to listen for, or how a process actually changes a sound, you can be led to do things that might sound good temporarily but damage the finished track.

I wrote this book for two different groups of people, both of whom probably have an idea of what they want their track to sound like but aren't sure how to get there. Students and beginners can use the book to understand what options are available to improve a soundtrack, even after the actors have gone home. Experienced producers can learn the techniques that audio professionals use to solve technical and creative problems quickly.

This book is full of tutorials, practical examples, and cookbook recipes. But don't worry about having a technical background. Everything is in plain English, with plenty of demonstrations and visual analogies. I believe you're an intelligent person—after all, you bought my book—but you might not have much training in the sciences. Grade school math, ordinary common sense, and a CD player are all you'll need to follow the technical explanations.

How this Book is Organized

- Chapter 1 provides quick help for the most common audio problems. If the solution can be explained in a couple of sentences, you'll find the answer here; otherwise, you'll be directed to the appropriate chapter.

The next few chapters are the basics. While Chapter 2 is essential, you might not need to read the next three.

- Chapter 2 explains what sound actually is, and how digital audio works. It's the basis you'll need to get the most out of the rest of the book. If you think you already know this stuff, glance through these pages anyway. You could have been misled by some of the myth and marketing hype that surrounds audio.

- Chapters 3 through 5 are for people who want to build an efficient and reliable audio post setup, whether it's a single desktop computer or a fully professional suite. It includes guidelines, technical tips, and time- or money-saving shortcuts. The separate chapters deal with practical acoustics, equipment, and software.

The next chapters are about working on the track itself.

- Chapter 6 helps you plan and budget a good soundtrack, and understand the steps necessary to create it.

- Chapters 7 and 8 are about getting audio into your NLE—what settings to use when transferring from a camera or video deck, how to maintain sync, how to record studio narrations and replacements for on-camera dialog, and what to do when things go wrong.

- The next three chapters are about the three principal sound sources: voice, music, and effects. Chapter 9 will teach you a better and more efficient technique for editing voices than you'll find in any NLE manual. Chapter 10 covers the best ways to choose and find music for a production, and then allows you to practice a totally different kind of editing—the one music editors use on feature films. Chapter 11 covers the full range of sound effects issues: where to find them, how to record your own, and how to fit them to picture.

- Chapters 12 through 17 are about shaping sounds with processes like equalization, reverb, and noise reduction. This may be the most critical part of creating a track, and it's the one that seems to be most misunderstood by filmmakers. Even if you've had experience in a music studio, read these chapters. The processes are often used differently in film and video.

- Chapter 18 is about mixing. It's a big chapter. There's more to a mix than you probably think.

- Chapter 19 covers what to do after the mix, including ways to test the final product and what's necessary for Web, theatrical, and DVD audio. Along the way, you'll learn how compression schemes like Dolby Digital and mp3 really work—and how to make them sound their best.

A glossary and information about the book's CD follows Chapter 19.

About the cookbooks

The processing chapters, 12 through 17, include recipes: step-by-step instructions for common operations. Most are also demonstrated on the CD.

While the recipes provide specific settings for each process involved, it's almost certain they won't be exactly right for your track. Every recording is different, and a tiny difference in how you used a microphone or set a recording volume can make my settings inappropriate. Read the entire chapter, so you'll know how to fine-tune things.

Additional recipes   The Cookbooks are works in progress. If you need a recipe that isn't in the book, read through the chapter again; it'll probably give you enough insight to solve the problem. But if you're still lost—or you think I've missed something important that applies to other filmmakers—write to cookbook@dplay.com. Explain what you're trying to do. I'll try to come up with specific steps. Also write to me if you've come up with a unique recipe you want to share (with appropriate credit, of course).

I'll publish the new recipes at www.dplay.com/cookbook from time to time. I'll also include them in a second edition of this book, if there is one. But two caveats: don't expect me to solve a problem on your deadline; my studio clients have priority. And don't send me unsolicited audio files. If they're necessary, I'll give you uploading instructions.

About the CD

This book comes with a CD that has about an hour's worth of diagnostics, demonstrations, and tutorial tracks for you to practice on. It's an audio CD, rather than a CD-ROM, so you can play it through the best speakers you own. But none of it's copy protected, so you can load it into your NLE as well.

Despite the lack of copy protection, most of the tracks are covered by copyright. Buyers of this book may transfer the tracks to their hard drive to practice techniques or run the diagnostics. But any other use requires specific written permission. If you hear a piece of music or sound effect that would be perfect for your production, check the text for licensing information.

About this book and *Producing Great Sound for Digital Video*

In early 2000, we published *Producing Great Sound for Digital Video*, one of the first books in CMP Books's DV Expert Series. It's been a tremendous success, staying at the top of its category at Amazon.com. By the time you read this, there'll probably be a second edition available.

I've tried to keep this book, and the second edition of the other one, as different as possible. A lot of this is in response to reader comments, email, and postings at the DV.com Audio Solutions Forum.

Some readers complained that *Producing Great Sound* didn't go into enough detail on technical setups, processing and mixing. I simply didn't have room. That's one reason why CMP Books gave me so many more pages to discuss it here.

Others wanted more about location audio. So the second edition of *Producing Great Sound* has expanded sections on choosing and using microphones, boom and lav technique, wireless, and the various challenges of recording professional sound in a prosumer camera.

Of course, the theory of sound and principles of digital audio are the same in both books. But I've tried to explain them using different approaches. If you don't understand a topic in one book, you'll have a second chance in the other.

Software agnostic?

CMP Books's marketing department introduced me to this term. Prior to that, I'd only heard of agnosticism in its dictionary definition: a philosophy that says you can never understand first causes or truly know the Ultimate Being.

I happen to understand and believe in software. But this book isn't about a specific platform, program, or version. In a few cases, I've used specific applications because they're uniquely good for demonstrating certain functions. Otherwise, I've tried to cover both Mac and Windows solutions.

By and large, the techniques in this book work on any system, from a laptop NLE to a million-dollar post facility. They've been developed over 75 years of radio, talking pictures, and television. And they'll continue to apply, even as new software and hardware is developed. You should be able to use these pages for a long time.

Chapter 1

Help!

It's possible you bought this book because you're trying to solve an immediate problem. Think of this chapter as Frequently Asked Questions, addressing the most common concerns in postproduction sound.

Many sound problems can't be resolved in a couple of sentences, so you'll be directed to relevant chapters of this book. A few can't be resolved at all; the best I can do in those cases is suggest ways to create a substitute track.

Use this chapter to solve the immediate problem. But please, go on to read the rest of the book. It'll teach you the techniques professionals use to improve marginal sounds, and to make well-recorded ones jump out of the speakers. These are the secrets behind a great soundtrack.

Problems with Understanding Technical Terms

We all use jargon to save time. I'm assuming you've got some video experience—though not necessarily with its audio aspects—and are familiar with the language of shooting and editing. If not, most of the terms are defined in a Glossary at the end of this book.

Some audio jargon is inevitable in a book about sound, of course. Don't let it frighten you. It's there so you can use audio equipment and processes efficiently. Every time I introduce an audio term, I'll explain it in everyday language (and use visual analogies if possible). Audio terms are also defined in the Glossary, and the Index will point you to fuller discussions.

Problems with Sound Quality

This is a quick guide. There's a lot more about troubleshooting at the end of Chapter 7.

1. Tracks Are Too Soft in My NLE

We're talking about too soft to *hear* properly, not that the waveforms are too small to see their tiny details on the timeline. There's usually no reason to see those details—in chapters 9 and 10 you'll learn how to edit by ear, which is faster and more accurate. But if you really need to study a waveform, open the clip in its own window.

FireWire, i.Link, or IEEE 1394 setup[1]

If you transferred from the camera digitally using a FireWire connection, the levels you have were those on the tape. The scene was shot too softly. Next time, check the camera's instructions about setting volume, or check the discussions about camera audio in *Producing Great Sound for Digital Video*—if you have a copy.

Your track might still be savable. Open the clip in an audio editing program and apply the *Gain* or *Amplify* command, set to bring the loudest sound in the clip to about –6 dBFS. Or use a *normalize* command, if it lets you apply a similar –6 dBFS or 50-percent setting. Save the result.

- Read about *dBFS* in Chapter 2.

Bringing the clip to –6 dBFS, instead of to the maximum 0 dBFS, leaves some room for equalization and other processing. Many NLEs will distort if you attempt to process a file that's too loud. If you're not planning any processing at all, you can make the clip louder, but it's usually best to wait until you're finishing the project.

Since the original footage was shot too softly, there's a strong chance raising its level will also boost hiss and other electronic noises from the camera. While you can't totally remove hiss, you can make it less objectionable with an expander or noise reduction software.

- Read about expanders in Chapter 13.
- Read about noise reduction in Chapter 16.

Mic distance problems

If increasing the clip's volume also increases room noise and echoes, the microphone was too far from the subject. *This seems to be the most common problem with DV sound.* It's usually because a camera-mounted mic was used.

In real-world interior spaces, there is no way a camera mic can do as good a job as a properly placed boom or lav. It doesn't matter what brand or type of microphone you use. Distance is the enemy, and basic physics dictates that any mic more than a couple of feet from the speaker's mouth won't pick up sound cleanly. Professionals use camera mics only for breaking news and

---

1. They all mean the same thing. See Chapter 7.

events, when there's no time to rig up something else; or for in-your-face interviews where both camera and mic are close to the subject. Chapter 8 of this book talks about mic technique in postproduction audio. There's a large section on production miking in *Producing Great Sound for Digital Video*.

You may be able to improve intelligibility with equalization and reduce apparent echo level with an expander. Unfortunately, you can never make a distant mic sound like it was close.

- Read about equalization in Chapter 12.
- Read about expanders in Chapter 13.

Analog transfer from camera to NLE

If you've digitized by connecting the camera's audio output to a soundcard or NLE pod with analog cables, any of the above situations might still be true. But there's also a chance that problems were introduced during digitization, and these can be completely fixed.

Play some sample footage in your camera using good monitor speakers or headphones. If the camera sounds better than what's in your computer, you should redigitize. Before you do, calibrate your system so you can transfer at a proper level.

- Read about analog calibration in Chapter 7.

If you've already done large amounts of editing, it may be faster to digitize only the audio. Sync the new audio files to what's already in the timeline. If you're just starting the project, it's faster to redigitize sound and picture simultaneously, and then delete the original clips.

2. Tracks Are Too Loud in My NLE

If audio is so loud that waveforms extend from top to bottom of a clip window, it probably also sounds distorted or has a crackling noise at the loudest spots. If you transferred into the computer via FireWire, the likelihood is the camera audio is also distorted or crackling, and most of these problems can't be fixed. Check the original footage to make sure.

Certain kinds of distortion can be made less offensive with equalization. You may be able to replace individual words with ones from alternate takes; or rerecord the dialog in a studio using ADR techniques.

- Read about equalization in Chapter 12.
- Read about dialog editing in Chapter 9.
- Read about ADR in Chapter 8.
- An occasional click from too loud a waveform can be repaired in an audio program, either by applying a *declicking* process or by drawing a smoother waveform with a pencil.

If you transferred through an analog connection and the camera track sounds fine, follow the redigitizing advice in the previous section.

Once this kind of distortion and noise gets onto a track, lowering the volume won't make it go away. But there is a slim possibility the track is just loud enough to be causing distortion in the computer's sound card or your amplifier, and the actual audio data is fine.

- Try lowering the volume on the timeline. If that fixes things, export to an audio program and knock the gain down about –2 dB.

If individual tracks on the timeline are fine, but things get too loud and distorted when you mix them, paying attention to the master mix volume will help.

- Read about mixing in Chapter 18.

3. Sound Is Distorted

Distortion refers to a fuzziness in the sound, making dialog hard to understand. Noise, thin sound, or boominess are different problems, which are addressed in the next section.

In most cases, distortion happens because sound was recorded or digitized too loudly. See the previous section. If sound is distorted but the volume isn't too loud, there are two likely causes. Listen to the original tapes in your camera, using good speakers or headphones, to find out which one applies.

Sound is distorted when you play it in the camera

Something went wrong at the shoot. This could be defective equipment, a weak battery in a microphone, or levels that were set badly in the camera or a mixer or preamp. These problems are beyond the scope of this book, but are covered in *Producing Great Sound* so you can avoid them next time.

You may be able to improve intelligibility with equalization, or replace the on-camera dialog with studio voices in an ADR session.

- Read about equalization in Chapter 12.
- Read about ADR in Chapter 8.

Sound is okay when you play it in the camera

Either your computer's system-level audio controls are misadjusted, or you've got a problem in how a mixer, preamp, or other equipment has been set up. Fix it and redigitize.

- Read about analog wiring in Chapter 4.
- Read about calibrating analog transfers and making the necessary adjustments in Chapter 7.

4. Tracks Are Too Noisy

Decide what kind of noise you're hearing, because the cures are different. Noise may be acoustic and environmental, picked up at the shoot. Or it can be electronic, including steady hisses and whines, steady hums and buzzes, occasional beeps, or periodic pops and clicks.

Acoustic noises

The best way to eliminate very short noises is to substitute syllables from elsewhere in the scene or an alternate take.

- Read about dialog editing in Chapter 9.

If traffic, air conditioner, or similar noises are softer than dialog, the track can be improved with a combination of equalization, expansion, and noise reduction. This kind of combination is almost always more effective and does less damage than using noise reduction software alone.

- Read about equalization in Chapter 12.

- Read about expansion in Chapter 13.

- Read about noise reduction software in Chapter 16.

If acoustic noise is louder than dialog, the above techniques can also be of help. But they're also likely to leave metallic-sounding artifacts because of the extreme processing involved.

If tracks are very noisy, you'll have to do what Hollywood does and replace the dialog in a studio session.

- Read about ADR in Chapter 8.

Noise reduction is as much about hiding noise as eliminating it, and some noises never really go away. That's why postproduction noise removal isn't as effective as proper mic placement and noise control at the shoot.

Wind noises　When wind hits a microphone, it often creates a low rumbling that can overpower the voice. The rumbling can be removed with a filter. But if the rumble has overloaded the mic or recording equipment, it can cause distortion that makes that part of the track unusable. The only solution is to edit replacement syllables from alternate takes or rerecord the dialog as ADR.

- Read about filtering in Chapter 12.

- Read about dialog editing in Chapter 9.

- Read about ADR in Chapter 8.

Noise combined with echo   The microphone was too far from the subject. The camera's volume control might have been turned up to compensate, but the situation is identical to the one discussed in "Tracks Are Too Soft in My NLE" (page 2).

Electronic noises

Hisses and whistles   Treat them as you would acoustic noise, mentioned previously. Whistles and other constant-pitched high frequency noises can be controlled with a parametric equalizer.

- Learn how to tune a parametric equalizer in Chapter 12.

Hums and buzzes   Comb filtering can be surprisingly good at eliminating moderate dimmer noise or ground-loop buzz.

- Read about comb filtering in Chapter 14.

Really strong buzzing from a disconnected ground at the shoot can't be fixed. Use some of the replacement techniques in the previous section.

Occasional beeps   If there's a beeping in digitally captured tracks that isn't on the camera footage, the problem is most likely either a driver issue or a timecode break.

- Check the manufacturer of your FireWire card, and Apple's or Microsoft's Web sites, for driver updates that have anything to do with the FireWire or audio capability in your computer.

- If the camera was wound forward between shots and the tape was new, the internal time-code and control tracks may have dropped out between takes. Attempting to capture from this non-recorded area can cause problems, including occasional beeps. Do two separate captures, manually winding the tape between them to assure each has continuous control tracks. Or redigitize the audio with an analog connection.

Timecode breaks can happen even when you do something as innocuous as reviewing a take. Some NLE manufacturers recommend you prerecord the tape with black, from start to finish, before shooting. That will eliminate the dropped timecode.

Periodic pops and clicks   If this kind of noise is in the computer but not on the original footage, there are two likely culprits: either a sample rate issue or dropped frames.

- Read a lot about solving pop and click problems in Chapter 7.

Sample rate issues   If popping or clicking occurs in a FireWire transfer, it can be from incompatible sample rates. Digital video uses 32 kHz or 48 kHz sampling. The timeline and capture sample rate should match what was used at the shoot.

- Read about sample rates in Chapter 7.

- Even if the file is good, popping or clicking can occur during NLE playback if there's a sample rate incompatibility. Open the file in an audio program and listen for clicks. If it sounds okay there, use that program to convert the file's sample rate to match the NLE's setting.

- If the footage is at 32 kHz, it may not be possible to capture at that rate, and you may have to use an analog transfer for the audio.

Clicking and popping can also occur when an audio CD, which uses 44.1 kHz sampling, is ripped and the file is put in an NLE timeline running at 48 kHz.

- Open the 44.1 kHz file in an audio program and convert its sample rate. Some audio programs will let you rip a CD directly to a 48 kHz file.

If popping or clicking occurs when transferring audio over s/pdif or AES/EBU digital wiring, the culprit can be a lack of audio word sync.

- Make sure the recording program and audio input card are set to synchronize from the card's input.

- Read about digital wiring in Chapter 4.

Dropped frames   Processor overload can cause both audio and video frames to be lost, but the video ones are often less noticeable unless there's very fast motion on the screen. Dropped audio frames, on the other hand, can cause an easily heard jump in the waveform. The problem can occur during both FireWire and analog captures.

Dropped frames can also cause lipsync problems, but in some footage you might notice the popping before you notice a sync error.

- Avoid processor overload by turning off any nonessential function in the computer and disconnecting it from the network before starting a capture.

- In Windows, create a user profile with the simplest possible setup. In Macintosh, create a startup set with as few extensions as possible. Making a mistake here can lead to other computer problems. Before you begin, be sure you know what you're doing, or consult your local operating system guru.

- Real-mode drivers can slow a Windows machine down. If there are any running, they'll show up as "MS-DOS compatibility" in the System Properties dialog. Removing them is a guru-level adjustment.

- Windows TSRs and Mac Inits may be running in the background and cause dropped frames. Remove any you don't need.

- Excessive monitor depth makes the CPU work harder. In Windows, select "High Color" in the Display control panel's Settings. On a Mac, select "Thousands of Colors" in the Monitors control panel. DV's color range isn't as subtle as the higher computer settings, so you won't be missing anything.

- Virtual memory affects system performance. In a Mac, turn it off and restart. In Windows, have your guru set up a 4 MB virtual memory cache.

- Defragmenting the hard disk can also help.

- In a marginal computer, even monitoring the capture is enough extra work to cause dropped frames. You may have to turn off on-screen and audio monitoring while capturing.

5. Audio Is Thin, Boomy, or Hollow

These are usually caused by bad mic technique at the shoot, and may not be fixable. But some conditions can be improved.

Thinness   Thin sound—a lack of low frequencies—can be a problem in the original tracks or be due to wiring problems in your setup. It usually can't be fixed with an equalizer because the low frequencies aren't on the track to be equalized. Attempting to boost lows, in this case, just results in noise and distortion.

Check the camera footage. If it's good and you're doing analog transfers, suspect the wiring between camera and computer. If everything coming out of the NLE sounds thin, there's probably a problem between the computer and your monitors.

- Read about postproduction wiring in Chapter 4.

If the footage sounds bad, either the mic was defective or there was a wiring problem between mic and camera. This can also happen when some transformer-equipped XLR adapters are used improperly. It can't be fixed in postproduction, but monitoring on good isolating headphones can help you spot it at the shoot.

Boominess   A boomy sound is usually caused by low-frequency resonances in the room. It can often be improved by setting a parametric equalizer exactly to the boom frequency, and lowering about –12 dB.

- Read how to tune a parametric equalizer in Chapter 12.

Hollowness   Hollow sound can be caused by two nearby mics being mixed together.

- If the mics are on separate tracks in your NLE, audition them separately. If they sound good individually, pick just one or edit between them as different characters speak.

- If the mics are on a single stereo track in your NLE, use the Take Right or Take Left command to listen to each separately.

If the mics were mixed together at the shoot, it can't be fixed.

Hollowness can also be caused by too great a distance between mic and subject. You can't fix this in postproduction. Read about mic distance in the first section of this Chapter, so you'll know how to avoid this problem next time.

Lipsync Problems

Some audio and video cards have known issues with particular NLEs. Check the manufacturers' Web sites and the Community section at DV.com for the latest information.

- There is a large section about lipsync problems in Chapter 7. If the quick tips here don't help, you may find an answer there.

The key to diagnosing lipsync problems is to analyze how they occur. Are things consistently out of sync by the same amount? Does the error grow larger over time? Or is it variable and sporadic?

6. Consistent Errors

This is usually an incompatibility between camera and the capture setup. Check the audio and video card manufacturers' Web sites for updated drivers. If you're capturing via FireWire, also check the FireWire card maker's site as well as Apple or Microsoft.

- Try capturing or playing the clip in another application.

- Turn off any audio data compression in the capture settings.

7. Cumulative Errors

If sync gets progressively worse as the film goes on, the cause can be a tiny sample rate issue.

- Make sure the project and capture settings match the footage's sample rate.

Some cameras cheat and don't output at exactly 48 kHz. This isn't an adjustment or tuning problem; it's the result of cost-sensitive design and can't be fixed. It can cause cumulative errors in FireWire transfers.

- Transfer the audio as analog instead of FireWire. Some NLEs let you select a different audio input while capturing video over FireWire; this will maintain picture quality. Others may require separate passes for audio and video if you want to keep the picture digital. Be aware that audio quality can suffer in an analog transfer; it depends both on your setup and how well you calibrate things. Read Chapters 4 and 7 for advice.

- If that doesn't help, suspect the video frame rate isn't accurate either. (Cost-sensitive design, again.) Redigitizing the picture instead of transferring it over FireWire can help, but the quality will depend on your video input card. If that's an issue, try the next two suggestions.

- Measure how many frames out the end of the film is, and apply a clip speed adjustment to compensate. This may sacrifice quality. If you're changing speed in an audio program, *don't* use pitch correction; it can hurt quality even more.

- Use cutaways in the video or tiny edits during audio pauses to correct sync. This doesn't harm the sound or picture quality.

8. Sporadic Errors

If sync drifts in and out, or errors seem to happen unpredictably, suspect dropped frames.

- See the previous section ("Electronic noises") regarding dropped frames.

This can also happen because of problems in a particular section of the footage. An analog transfer may help.

Edit and Mix Problems

9. Problems with Dialog

If the sound quality is generally good but specific words are garbled, they can often be fixed by replacing syllables from elsewhere in the scene or alternate takes. When done right, this doesn't cause noticeable lipsync problems.

- Doing this kind of microsurgery in an audio program is always more precise, and often faster, than using an NLE. That's because you're not limited to cutting on frame lines.

- Read about dialog editing in Chapter 9.

Individual words can also be replaced with studio recordings. This isn't as complex as ADR, but the same mic techniques should be used.

- Read about ADR recording in Chapter 8.

10. Musical Issues

- Read about finding music, copyright, and related issues in the first half of Chapter 10.

- Read about easy ways to trim music to precisely fit video in the second half of Chapter 10.

- Read about controlling how music competes with voice in Chapters 12, 13, and 18.

11. Problems with the Mix

Matching dialog

If a character's voice quality changes during a scene because different camera angles were miked differently, split the dialog onto multiple tracks, one track for each miking situation. Apply equalization and reverberation to make them sound the same.

- Read about equalization in Chapter 12.

- Read about reverberation in Chapter 14.

If all the recordings are good quality, process the shorter clips to match the unadjusted longest clip. If some of the recordings were badly miked or have other problems, you'll have to sacrifice the quality of better clips to match.

Disappearing elements

If you could hear a sound when you mixed the project but not when you play the final tape, and the playback system is mono, the most likely cause is a polarity[2] inversion.

If just one element is gone, there's a problem with its clip. Either it was recorded incorrectly, or it was processed through a badly designed stereo simulator.

- Use an audio program to invert the phase of one channel. Or use a Fill Left or Fill Right command on that sound in an NLE.

- Read about stereo simulation in Chapter 17.

- Read about mono compatibility in Chapters 6 and 18.

If dialog or narration is missing but music or sound effects seem to remain, there was a problem in the connection between NLE and VTR. This happens most often when a stereo cable is inadvertently plugged into a balanced jack on a mixer or NLE pod.

- Change the connection and dub the tape again. Read about wiring in Chapter 4.

---

2. Often called *phase inversion*.

Most stereo VCRs become mono when you connect their antenna output to the antenna jack of a TV. This can cause polarity problems to show up on a client's set and not on your monitors.

- In an emergency, use the RCA audio output jacks on the back of the VCR to feed a stereo signal to an amplifier.

This doesn't fix the basic problem, and the tape won't sound good under many playback conditions. Go back and apply one of the other cures as soon as you get the chance.

Music is too loud or soft compared to voice

If it sounded right when you mixed it and not when you play it on a different system, it's a monitoring issue. This often happens when you mix or process using the speakers bundled with most NLEs, which are notoriously poor, and then play the tape in a home theater system or auditorium.

Either get new speakers, or take the project to a sound studio, and remix. Headphones are not a cure—even good ones—unless your viewers will be using them as well. Headphones present a very different impression of a track, and mixes done on them often have effects or music too soft to play well on normal speakers.

- Read about choosing a monitor in Chapter 3.
- Read about taking tracks to a studio at the end of Chapter 18.

Mix, or individual elements, alternate between too soft and too loud

You need to apply compression.

- Read about compressors in Chapter 13.

Mix doesn't sound good when encoded for the Web

Data compression processes work best when the source material was mixed with awareness of the processes limitations. This can be totally nonintuitive: things that make a track sound better in the studio can seriously hurt the compressed version. Extreme equalization and level compression are the worst offenders.

- Read about data compression in Chapter 19. Then remix.

Random Strangenesses

If a program is behaving unpredictably, quit it and start again. If that doesn't help, restart your computer. In extreme cases, it often helps to delete the program's preferences files. This can cause other problems and almost always require that you re-enter a serial number and other information, so don't take this step unless you understand what you're doing.

12. NLE Audio Drops Out When Playing from the Timeline

This can happen if clips with different sample rates are playing together. The NLE can't convert them fast enough.

* Check the sample rate of each clip. Use an audio program to convert any that don't match the project's settings.

13. Speed or Pitch Has Changed for No Apparent Reason

Some part of your setup is using the wrong sample rate. This can happen at the system level, or it can be an incompatibility between two programs.

* Exit or quit nonessential programs. An audio application may have taken over the computer's sound hardware.

* Restart the computer.

* If your computer is connected to a digital audio sound source via s/pdif or AES/EBU, check the source's sample rate. It may be forcing the computer to the wrong rate.

* Some digital audio cards occasionally have trouble recognizing the connected rate and need to be manually reset in their control panels.

Some NLEs send the wrong information to encoding systems when converting a project for the Web.

* Save the project from the NLE with no audio data compression. Then open it manually in the compression software.

14. DV or DAT Deck Won't Record Audio

If you're using a digital connection and the deck won't go into record mode, it's probably a sample rate sync issue. This is different from lipsync.

* Make sure the recorder is set to the same sample rate as the project.

Professional recorders such as Digital Betacam won't accept a digital audio stream unless it's also locked to the video's blackburst. This is a facility setup issue.

* Read about digital audio wiring in Chapter 4.

* In an emergency, use an analog audio connection. This may compromise the quality.

15. VHS Dub Has Static, Noise, or Poor Audio

VHS Hi-Fi depends on accurate tracking of the video heads, and the playback machine might not match the recorder. This can cause the deck to keep switching between Hi-Fi and linear mode, which has more hiss and distortion. Or it can shut down the track entirely.

- Adjust the tracking on the playback set.

- A head cleaning cassette might help.

- In an emergency, manually set the deck to Standard, Linear, or Mono audio. It won't sound as good as Hi-Fi, but you won't have noises or dropouts as the deck switches modes.

- Have the deck professionally serviced.

It Just Doesn't Sound as Good as What I Hear at the Movies

- Read the rest of this book.

Vibrations to Volts to Bits

Remember this:

- We hear the world in ratios, not absolute numbers. Both volume and pitch work this way. The everyday math that works with measurements or money can lead you completely astray when it's applied to audio.

- Sound exists only in time; there is no such thing as an "audio stillframe." This affects everything you do with a track.

- Although sound itself is analog, there are good reasons to keep a soundtrack in the digital domain while you're working on it. But some of the rules for digital audio are different from those for analog.

A Tree Falls in a Forest...

Jokes and koans aside, we'll assume it makes a sound. Let's also assume you're doing a film about timber logging and the sound is part of a title sequence. You need to record the crash; edit, process, and mix it for maximum impact; and do these things in a way that lets the viewer hear what you intended.

You probably bought this book to help accomplish goals like that. If you're impatient, you can go back to the Table of Contents, find the tasks you want to accomplish, and follow the suggestions that make up most of this book. They're based on years of experience and really do work.

But I believe you'll get a far better track—and ultimately be a better filmmaker—if you read this introductory chapter. It describes how sounds come about, how they travel through the air, and how they become analog and then digital audio signals that can be taped or broadcast. When you understand this process, good sound becomes intuitive and creative, rather than something mechanical to look up in a book. Then what I've written can serve as guidance, inspiration, and shortcuts based on professional techniques—things you can build on, rather than rules to blindly follow.

This isn't rocket science, just grade-school physics and math. But because it isn't visually intuitive, many filmmakers surround the process with myth and hype that can ultimately hurt their tracks. Taking a few minutes now to logically think about how audio works will help you avoid expensive and time-consuming mistakes.

To the tree.

> ⚠️ **Gotcha** _____
>
> In this book, you'll find a bunch of *Gotchas*—audio myths, misapplied principles, and other audio mistakes that can affect your track. They're based on real-world confusions I hear from filmmaking friends, read on Internet forums, or even find in the tutorials of well-known software!

How Sound Works

If our tree fell on the Moon, no one would hear it. Sound requires air,[1] which surrounds us with tiny, independent molecules. Anything that moves in the air reacts with them.

- As the tree's leaves fly by, they scatter molecules aside (a soft *woosh*).

- As branches and limbs break, they vibrate. The vibration is transferred to nearby molecules (*crackle*).

- When the thick trunk gets close to the ground, it squeezes a lot of molecules in a hurry (*bang*).

- When the trunk lands, the ground vibrates and moves molecules next to it (*thud*).

All that movement eventually transfers to our ears, and we hear the tree come down. Let's concentrate on just one aspect of the sound: the tree approaching the ground.

Before things start happening, air molecules surround the tree somewhat evenly. Their individual positions may be random, but the overall density is the same on all sides of the trunk. If we could enlarge and see them, they'd look like the black specks in Figure 2.1.

As the tree falls, it pushes molecules directly in front of it and squeezes them together (right side of Figure 2.2). At the same time, it forms a partial vacuum behind it—where there was tree, now there's nothing. The vacuum pulls nearby molecules into it, spreading them out (left side).

---

1. Unless you're making a science-fiction film. It's an accepted movie convention that explosions, rocket fly-bys, and other events make noise in the vacuum of space. Sci-fi filmmakers also generally ignore another fundamental rule of physics, as you'll learn in a couple of pages.

The squeezed air molecules in front of the tree have to go somewhere, so they push against those farther out. Those newly-pushed molecules in turn push others even farther, and so on. This creates a wave of *compression,* or higher air pressure, moving out from the tree. Meanwhile, the partial vacuum behind the tree forms a wave of low pressure, or *rarefaction.* It also moves out from the tree and draws nearby molecules toward it.

Despite my drawing, trees are not two-dimensional blobs. Air molecules can flow around the trunk and branches. So as our waves spread out, molecules rush in to equalize the pressure behind them. The result is a growing bubble of compression and rarefaction that constantly spreads out from the tree. If you could freeze it, it would look like Figure 2.3 (below).

2.1 Air molecules evenly distributed around a standing tree.

2.2 The falling tree squeezes molecules in front, and spreads out those behind.

2.3 The result is a growing bubble of compression and rarefaction, spreading out from the tree.

The Speed of Sound

If air were solid, you could push one end and the other would immediately move. But molecules in a gas are independent. Push one, and it takes a moment for pressure to build up enough to move its neighbor. Our pressure bubble spreads from the tree at about 1,100 feet per second[2]. That might seem pretty fast, but sound is a slowpoke compared with light.

---

2. Actually, sound travels 1,087 feet per second at 32 degrees Farenheit, gaining about 1.1 foot per second per degree, with very minor variations based on pressure and humidity. Calling it 1,100 feet per second is good enough for filmmaking.

When a sound is being picked up by two mics, differences in the length of time it takes to reach each can affect sound quality. We'll deal with that in Chapter 8.

⚠️ *Gotcha* _____

Twelve yards is a frame!   A video frame is roughly 1/30 second, and sound travels only about 36 feet in that time. If you've got footage of a subject across a street, and your audio sources are a camera-mounted mic and a lav on the subject, the two tracks will be one frame out of sync. If you see someone shoot a gun on the other side of a football field, the bang will reach you five frames after you see the barrel flash!

If you've got a good eye, you can see sync errors of half a frame. Large film and TV mixing suites are big enough that this becomes an issue because a director may be sitting 18 feet from the screen. It takes half a frame for sound coming from the front of the room to reach them. You have to decide where to stand when evaluating lipsync. Giant movie theaters such as Radio City Music Hall often play a soundtrack two or three frames early so it'll be in sync for someone in the middle of the room. In a room that size, sync can never be accurate for everyone in the audience!

Frequency

A tree falls just once, so our example creates a single pressure wave—something you're as likely to feel as to hear. But most things making sound have continuous vibrations. Consider the imaginary guitar string in Figure 2.4. When it's pulled back (2.4a), it stores energy. When it's let go, it snaps forward quickly and creates a pressure wave. But since it snaps past its resting position (2.4b), tension draws

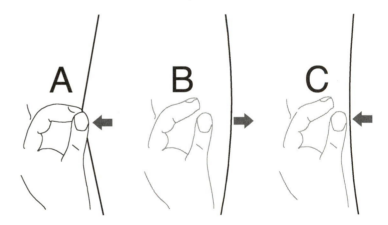

2.4   The guitar string vibrates back and forth after you let go.

it back, creating rarefaction. The process repeats (2.4c) until all the energy from the pull is absorbed by the air.

The result is a regular, constant series of compression and rarefaction bubbles—a *sound wave*—spreading out from the string. If we could freeze it, it would look like Figure 2.5. When the wave hits our ears, it vibrates our eardrums, moves the tiny bones inside, and is carried to the fluid in our inner ears. There it activates a few of the specialized nerves and we hear a *ping*.

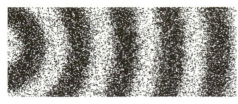

2.5 Sound waves are a regular pattern of compression and rarefaction.

Which nerves get activated is determined by how frequently the pressure peaks hit our eardrum,[3] which is how fast the string was vibrating. We call this the string's pitch. Hi-fi books often say we can hear pitches between 20 and 20,000 peaks per second, though the term is *hertz* (Hz) and it's called a *frequency range* of 20 Hz–20 kHz. Some people say sounds as high as 30 kHz are important.

A few exceptional humans can hear 20 kHz. Many young people can hear up to 17 kHz or so. But even the best high-frequency hearing deteriorates with age and can be destroyed by prolonged exposure to high-level sound (at the workplace, in a club, or because of overdriven headphones and car stereos). Very few adults hear specific, quiet sounds above 15 kHz, though trained ears can often sense a sort of openness when higher frequencies are present.

Fortunately, even though 15 kHz–20 kHz may be a quarter of all the frequencies humans can hear, there's not much going on up there. That's because, with very few exceptions, we perceive frequency as a ratio between two pitches, not as an absolute number of hertz. You can see how this works in Figure 2.6, a piano keyboard with three major thirds (a common musical interval) highlighted. I've written the frequencies above each note:

- Middle C is at 261.6 Hz (rounded to the nearest tenth). The E above it is 329.6 Hz, a difference of 68 Hz.

- The C two octaves below is 65.4 Hz and the E above that 82.4 Hz—only 17 Hz higher.

- The C two octaves above is 1046.5 Hz and its E is 1318.5 Hz—272 Hz higher.

Yet the size of the jump from C to E sounds the same in each case, as you can hear on track 1 of this book's CD. It's also always the same ratio, about 1:1.25.

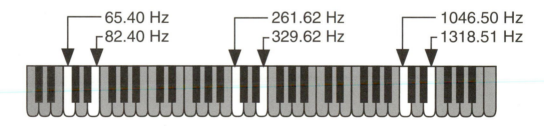

2.6 Musical thirds sound like the same interval, even though the absolute frequency difference varies.

---

3. And by how much pressure the peaks have. This pressure component is the secret behind perceptual encoders like mp3, as you'll learn in Chapter 17.

⚠️ **Gotcha** _____

The misplaced middle. This nonlinear way we hear means that lower frequencies contain more information per hertz than upper ones. Many filmmakers—and quite a few NLE programmers—get this wrong.

Since the range of most DV equipment is 20 Hz–20 kHz, the uninitiated might think the middle of the
audio band is halfway between those points: 10 kHz. Logically, anything above that frequency should sound
high, and anything below it low. Programmers (who, of course, are logical people) have chosen 10 kHz as the
center of the parametric equalizer in some popular NLE software, as you can see in Figure 2.7.

When you think in terms of ratios, 1 kHz is about the middle of the band: 50 Hz to 1 kHz is a ratio of 20:1,
and so, of course, is 1 kHz to 20 kHz. And if you listen to the series of tones on Track 2, you'll probably decide
that 1 kHz is nicely centered between high and low.

Want more proof that we're hearing ratios rather than absolute numbers? Track 1 continues with
a half-step jump from our lowest note—C (65.4 Hz) up to C# (69.3 Hz, a difference of 3.9 Hz).
It then plays the same numeric difference at the top of the orchestral range: first 4186 Hz (a C),
then 4189.9 Hz. The difference between the first two sounds will be obvious. But unless you've
got very good ears, the second two will seem to be the same note.

 Hear for yourself _____

Track 1 of this book's CD plays all of the above examples, with voice identification.

_____

By the way, we've thrown the term octave around a lot in the preceding paragraphs. You've
probably already guessed that an octave isn't a precise number of hertz. It's simply another name
for the frequency ratio 1:2.

 Hear for yourself _____

Track 2 of the CD consists of a short series of pure tones, played at the same volume. Take a guess at each frequency. Then listen to Track 3, the same tones with voice announcements. Still think 10 kHz is in the middle?

Learning to identify approximate frequency ranges is one of the most important steps to using an equalizer
properly. It's worth practicing with these two tracks a few times[4].

_____

_____

4. If you want to *really* hone your perceptions, spend a few months doing the exercises in David Moulton's
Golden Ears CDs (www.moultonlabs.com).

If your software has an equalizer with 10 kHz in the center, be careful! It will tempt you to mess with very high frequencies when what you're trying to solve is probably a midfrequency problem. This not only wastes time but can lead

Parametric Equalization

Band 1

☒ Enable

Frequency: 10000 Hz

Bandwidth: 4

Boost/cut: 50

Frequency Response

+12 dB
+6 dB
0 dB
−6 dB
−12 dB

0   22050

2.7 Some popular NLEs' equalizers put 10 kHz in the middle of the audio spectrum, like this. It's just wrong.

you to overequalize and boost distortion and noise. Read how to use an equalizer properly in Chapter 12.

Harmonics

We've described the CD examples so far as "pure tones." They sound electronic because real-world sounds are seldom pure. In this case, purity has a precise meaning: a pure tone is energy at a single frequency. Engineers call it a *sine wave* because a graph of its pressure over time looks like a graph of the mathematical sine function.

Remember our imaginary guitar string vibrating at one pitch? For a given string and tension, the pitch is determined by what size wave fits exactly from one fixed end of the string to the other. The frequency of this pitch is called the *fundamental frequency*. But guitar strings are flexible and bend in the middle, so multiple instances of shorter waves at higher pitches can also fit neatly from end to end. These are called *harmonics*, and they're in precise mathematical ratios to the fundamental. Figure 2.8 shows a fundamental, along with harmonics at twice and four timesthe fundamental pitch.

Because fundamental and harmonics happen simultaneously, they force the vibrating string into complicated, constantly-changing wiggles. You can see them with oscilloscope, which displays changing voltages

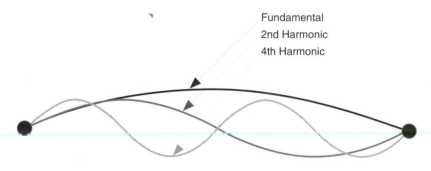

Fundamental
2nd Harmonic
4th Harmonic

2.8 A fundamental and two harmonics of a vibrating string.

over time. (Normally, you'd use a microphone to convert changing air pressure to voltage for the scope. But since we're dealing with an imaginary string, I used software to create its wave.)

2.9 Figure 2.8's complex wave, shown on an oscilloscope.

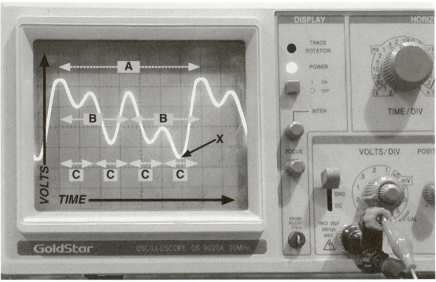

Figure 2.9 is a scope photo of what Figure 2.8's combination of fundamental and harmonics looks like.

- The area A is the fundamental, measured from one compression peak to the next.

- B is the second harmonic. We see exactly two of them for each fundamental wave, meaning its frequency is exactly twice as high.

- Note how the compression phases of both A and B add together at the start of the wave.

- C is the fourth harmonic, exactly four times the frequency of the fundamental.

- Rarefaction phases of all three waves coincide at point X. They add together, giving this point the lowest voltage of the entire wave.

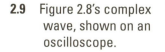 *Hear for yourself* _____

Track 4 includes two sounds: a pure tone at 200 Hz, and one adding just the two harmonics shown in Figure 2.8 (400 Hz and 800 Hz). Even though this is a very simple sound, you should hear a difference. The first tone will sound electronic. The other is more like a pipe organ.

There's no theoretical limit to how many harmonics can exist for any fundamental (though you might not hear the highest ones). In these examples, I've shown only even-numbered harmonics; real-world sounds can also have odd-numbered ones. Additionally, I've shown the fundamental and harmonics as having the same strength. But real harmonics' strengths are determined by mechanical properties of the vibrating element, resonances in the instrument body, and even where you plucked or hit it. The strength of each harmonic changes over time. That's why a classical guitar, a classic rock guitar, and a classroom guitar all sound different when the same note is played.

Frequency Range

Without harmonics, instruments playing the same note would sound virtually the same. You wouldn't be able to tell the difference between a violin and a flute. That's why it's important for a sound system to carry frequencies above the 5 kHz fundamental of the highest orchestral instruments.

> ### ⚠ Gotcha
>
> **Few sounds have just one frequency!** Real-world sounds are rich, moving tapestries of harmonics that extend across the audible spectrum—far more than the two in our simple example. So don't expect to find a magic frequency in an equalizer that will emphasize only violins in the orchestra or separate male voices from female.

But the system doesn't have to extend much higher. Most instruments pack a lot of harmonics below 10 kHz; a good thing because most real-world playback systems are useless half an octave above that limit. Despite how speaker manufacturers may brag about "20 Hz–20 kHz ranges," most computer, multimedia, and consumer-level stereo speakers fall far short of that goal. The advertising relies on fudged numbers or unspecified qualifiers. Test your system (and your ears) with Track 5 of the CD.

💿 Hear for yourself

Track 5 consists of a few repeating musical selections[5] that alternate between being played at full fidelity and through a filter that cuts off at specified high frequencies. If your speakers (or ears) are capable of handling that frequency, you'll be to able hear when the filter switches in and out. But if the highs aren't making it through your system anyway, the filters won't make any difference.

Try playing these tests through your best hi-fi speakers and note how high you can hear. Then try loading it into your NLE and listening to it there. You may be shocked at how much you're missing through typical computer monitors. But also notice that even when I apply a fairly low cutoff filter (7.5 kHz), enough harmonics come through that the music is still recognizable, if somewhat dull.

(This track was produced with very high quality digital filters, far sharper than those provided with most NLEs or audio programs. If you create similar tests, be sure your filter isn't lowering sounds below the specified cutoff. It'll make your speakers appear better than they are.)

---

5. "Swing Out Brother" (J. Trombey, DWCD219/10), "Queen of the Night" from *Magic Flute* (Mozart, DWCD142/2), "Rock Hits" (R. Hardy/B. White, DWCD293/11). All from the DeWolfe Music Library, protected by copyright and used by permission. You'll learn more about this versatile library, as well as a lot more about working with music, in Chapter 10.

Unpitched Sounds

Some sounds don't have regular vibrations. Our falling tree trunk, a gunshot, or the clap of a film slate create a single pressure wave of no particular frequency—though resonances in the surrounding space can add a sense of tonality. Many continuous sounds don't have a frequency either; the crunch of breaking branches, the hiss of the phoneme /s/, or the fizz of a glass of soda are sounds caused by collections of essentially random movements. The best we can do is describe their predominant frequency ranges. When we talk about the low pitch of rumbling thunder, we're not talking about a specific pitch but about how this random noise centers around low frequencies.

⚠️ **Gotcha** _____

Hiss doesn't have frequency. Unpitched sounds are virtually impossible to remove with an equalizer, unless you don't mind doing serious damage to dialog. This includes a lot of the noises that plague DV shoots: ventilation systems and computer fans, traffic, and the electronic hiss from wireless mics and poor camera preamps. The best you can do is make these sounds less annoying; see Chapter 16 for some tips.

Loudness

Our falling tree will move a lot more molecules with more force than the guitar string; that's why we hear it as "louder." The human ear has mechanical compensation to handle an amazingly wide range of loudness; the sound of a nearby jet plane hits your eardrum with about

⚠️ **Gotcha** _____

How high is enough? While 20 kHz is the standard upper frequency limit for DV tape, don't assume any soundtrack must extend that high:

• The upper limit for U.S. analog television and FM Stereo is 15 kHz. Frequencies higher than that cause transmission problems. Knowing this, TV manufacturers don't worry about building higher-frequency capability into their products.

• Even digital broadcasting may be limited to near 15 kHz for a while. Station hard-disk servers and satellite links often cut off at that frequency to conserve resources.

• Most Hollywood films made before the '70s—including most popular musicals—stop around 12.5 kHz, the limit for optical soundtracks. Outside of major cities, you'll find a lot of theaters still don't go much higher.

• Acoustic and orchestral music has suprisingly little energy above 15 kHz, though a good ear can certainly hear when it's missing. (Heavily processed pop music sometimes emphasizes very high frequencies electronically, often to the point of harsh distortion.)

10,000,000,000 more molecular movements than the quietest tones used in a lab to test your hearing. We cope with this range by hearing it as ratios rather than absolute intensities—just as we do with frequency. The *difference* in loudness between one tuning fork and a pair of them sounds the same as that between one tuba and two.

So in the technical world, we use ratios to gauge the strength of a sound; we compare it to a standardized loudness and use the resulting fraction. The fastest way to deal with complex fractions is to use a math shortcut, *logarithms*. You don't have to know how logarithms work. Just remember that they're fractions. Adding two logs actually multiplies the numbers they represent. Subtracting them divides the numbers. Logs 1 + 2 = log 3—but if the base is 10, this really means 10 × 100 = 1,000.

Decibels

The common measurement to express the level of both sounds and electronic audio signals, the *decibel* (dB), is a logarithm. Unlike a watt or a degree Fahrenheit, which are measurable quantities, decibels are fractions of something else. They're mostly meaningless until you know what they're fractions *of*.

When we talk about the loudness of a sound in air, we're almost always referring to the fraction formed by it and a theoretical "softest sound a human can hear," the *threshold of hearing*.[6] Log 0 means a fraction of 1/1, so something at exactly that threshold would be written as 0 dB SPL (sound pressure level). Few things are that soft. The quietest recording studios are about +30 dB

⚠️ **Gotcha** _____

A sound can't have "so many decibels." Decibels make sense only when you know their reference. We've talked about dB SPL for sounds in air because SPL is a standard reference. Sounds in a digital signal chain are almost always measured as dBFS (defined later this chapter); those on an analog wire may be dBu, dBm, or dBV (Chapter 4). But decibels without extra initials—just plain dB—are simply fractions, useful only when talking about how much a sound should be boosted or lowered... or when you want to impress a novice with meaningless audio jargon.

SPL. A good shooting stage would be around +40 dB SPL. Average dialog level at a boom mic may be around +65 dB SPL. Average playback level in the a movie theater is supposed to be 85 dB SPL, but is usually much higher, particularly during coming attractions. A jackhammer close up, would be around +125 dB SPL.

---

6. A pressure fluctuation of 0.0002 microbars, which is an energy of 0.0002 dynes per square centimeter. It may be theoretical, but it's set by international standard.

The Inverse Square Law

Remember how the falling tree created a spreading bubble of compression and rarefaction? As the bubble gets farther from the tree, its surface area necessarily grows (think of the skin area of an expanding balloon). But the energy it carries can't change unless you threw down another tree at the same moment in time. When the bubble was small, its energy was directed at only a few molecules. When the bubble is bigger and there are more molecules around it, it can't push each one as hard.

This is a long way of explaining what you already know: a falling tree sounds louder when it's nearby and softer when it's far away. But few people appreciate *how much* the volume changes based on distance. The effect is geometric because the surface of a sphere grows so much faster than its diameter.

Each time you *double* the distance from a sound source, the power of the sound is one fourth as much. Each time you *halve* the distance, it's quadrupled. And these effects multiply. If you quadruple the distance, the sound's power is one-sixteenth. It's called the inverse square law because power changes as the square of the change in distance.

Sound also gets weaker as it travels because some energy is lost to air friction. This effect is insignificant compared to the inverse square law, and in small rooms you can usually ignore it. In large halls or outdoors, high-frequency energy can be absorbed by the air enough to be audible when the air is extremely dry.

⚠ *Gotcha* _____

Closer is better. A lot of videographers never consider how many ways the inverse square law applies to their work. A camera mic at four feet will pick up only half the volume as a boom at its usual distance of around two feet, but you may be able to raise the input control to compensate. Unfortunately, room noises and echoes are all around, and getting farther from the actor doesn't mean you're getting farther from the problem sounds. In practical cases, doubling the distance from desired sound can make acoustic noises and echoes twice the volume by comparison. Unless you're dealing with ideal acoustic circumstances, there's no way a camera mic at six to eight feet can sound anywhere near as good as a properly used boom or lav.

The same principle affects postproduction setups, though we're dealing with speakers and ears instead of actors and a mic. When you listen to monitor speakers, you also hear reflections off of nearby walls. Unless you're in a perfectly tuned acoustic space, the reflections subtly change what you hear, affecting mix and processing decisions. Move the speakers closer to your ears, and you'll hear that much less of this interference. Result: better decisions.

Volume Changes Over Time

While the fundamentals of a violin and piano playing the same note may be identical, you can tell them apart if you pay attention to their *envelopes*.

Very few nonelectronic sounds are absolutely constant. Their volume can vary over time frames ranging from a few hundred milliseconds to many seconds. For example, a violin string starts vibrating slowly as the bow begins to move across it, builds strength, and then continues to sound as long as the bow keeps scraping. A piano string, on the other hand, is violently struck by the hammer and starts making noise immediately. But because there's no other source of energy, it starts to fade down almost immediately. How a sound's volume changes over time is its envelope.

Figures 2.10 and 2.11 compare envelopes of a violin and piano (shown in an audio program's waveform display because envelopes are too slow to display on a scope). Each picture represents about two seconds. I've drawn heavy black lines along the tops to trace the envelopes. The jaggy bits you see on the bottom are individual soundwaves.

The envelope of human speech depends on what's being said but doesn't necessarily follow individual words. Figure 2.12 shows an actress saying, "John, I think you should know I've been seeing…". She's speaking smoothly, but some words are jammed together and others are slowed down. I've added text above each individual sound so you can see how uneven the envelope is.

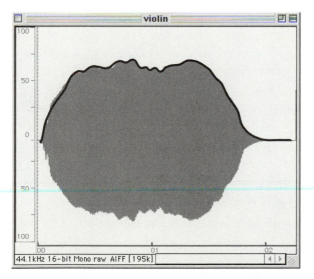

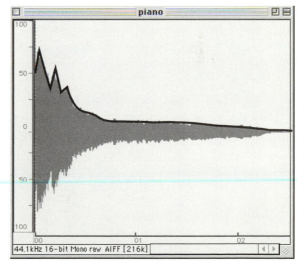

2.10   A violin sound grows slowly but continues as long as it's bowed.

2.11   A piano note starts suddenly but starts to fade almost immediately.

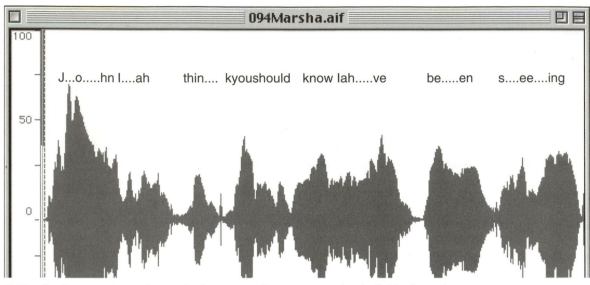

2.12 Spoken-word envelopes don't necessarily correspond to individual words.

Hear for yourself

Track 6 is the sounds whose envelopes we've just studied: violin and piano (both with and without harmonics), and Marsha's speech.

Analog Audio

So far, we've examined sound mostly as variations of air pressure. Electronic equipment deals with electrical pressures (voltages) and currents, not air pressure changes. The basic way to turn

⚠️ *Gotcha*

When envelope and frequency overlap. The *j* sound that starts "John" is about 1/20 of a second long,[1] but as we've discussed, frequencies around 20 Hz can be audible. So is the *j* sound part of the envelope or a soundwave by itself?

In this case, it's part of the envelope, both because Marsha's natural voice doesn't go down as low as 20 Hz and because it's nonrepeating. This issue becomes important when you're dealing with dynamics processing to automatically control levels. If the system isn't set properly, you'll hear a kind of muffling. Learn to avoid it Chapter 13.

---

1. Actually, the sound *j* consists of a very fast "d"—about 1/60 of a second long—followed by a drawn out ZH "zh" (say it slowly and you'll hear what I mean.) This kind of analysis is important for serious dialog editing, and is covered in Chapter 7.

sound into electricity is to create a changing voltage that corresponds exactly to the sound wave: When there's compression, the voltage is positive; when there's rarefaction, it's negative. The amount of voltage at any moment reflects the strength of the wave. In other words, the electric voltage is an *exact analogy* of the sound.

You may be working with digital cameras and computers, but this analog audio is still at the heart of the process. Microphones and speakers are analog devices—even if they have digital connections—and most postproduction studios have a lot of analog wiring. But analog signals are fragile. Things can change the voltage, adding distortion or noise. If you don't understand what's going on with analog audio, bad things can happen to your track.

Pressure to Voltage and Back

Microphones and speakers work like tiny generators and motors. The dynamo at a power plant uses a rotating turbine to spin a coil inside a magnetic field; this creates a changing voltage. The dynamic mics used for handheld interviews and voice-overs work exactly the same way, except the coil doesn't rotate. Instead, it's attached to a thin diaphragm that flexes in response to air pressure.

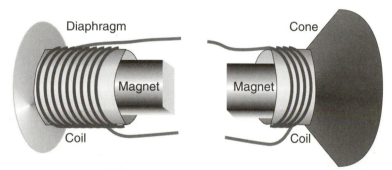

2.13 A dynamic mic (left) and a speaker (right) work on the same principle.

A speaker is a microphone in reverse. Instead of a diaphragm, it has a large paper cone attached to the coil. Changing voltage—the audio signal—is applied to the coil, making it move back and forth inside a magnetic field. This vibrates the cone, which then pushes and pulls against air molecules.

Dynamic mics and speakers are so similar that their functions can be interchangeable. Most intercoms use a speaker both to radiate and to pick up sound. Conversely, radio station engineers have been known to play tricks on air talent by momentarily connecting a mic to a talkback feed. Done right, the mic will start to whisper back at the announcer right before a broadcast.[7]

---

7. Okay, I did this when I was a young engineer. But if you don't understood the electronics thoroughly, this prank may end up frying your microphone.

The electret elements in most DV mics don't have magnets and won't work as speakers. But their function is the same: turning changing air pressure into changing voltage. There's a deeper discussion of mics in Chapter 8.

Balanced Wiring

You may think you work in television, but the analog cables you use are actually little radios. When you connect a mic to a camera, or an NLE to a mixer or audio input, those wires pick up nearby electric fields. Video monitors and data cables broadcast high frequencies; power cords and the wiring in the walls radiate low-frequency noise. Since you can't avoid these fields, the trick is keeping them from mixing with your track.

As you probably remember from grade school or model trains, any electric circuit requires two conductors. Most consumer line- and mic-level wiring accomplishes this with a single conductor for each audio channel, surrounded by a foil or braid shield that serves both as the return conductor and a barrier to high-frequency noise. This scheme, *unbalanced wiring*, is cheap and moderately effective. Unfortunately, the shield isn't very good at stopping power-line hum, timecode, or crosstalk from other audio channels.

The solution is to have two separate but identical wires, twisted very close to each other, inside the shield. While one wire is carrying current in one direction, the other's current is going the opposite way. Analog audio constantly changes polarity to reflect the compression and rarefaction of the sound waves. But at any given instant, the voltage on one wire will be positive while the other is negative. That's why it's called *balanced wiring*. It's connected to an input circuit that only pays attention to the voltage difference between the wires. Figure 2.14 shows how it works.

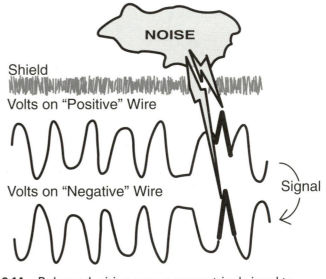

2.14 Balanced wiring uses a symmetrical signal to reject asymmetrical noise.

Since the wires are physically identical and very close together, any noise that bursts through the shield is picked up by both. The voltage that results from the noise is the same on both wires, so subsequent equipment doesn't detect it. Some simple math can help you understand this phenomenon (Table 2.1).

Table 2.1   Simple math explains why balanced wiring can reject noise.

Conductor	Original signal	Noise	Total on wire
A	+1.0 v	+0.5 v	+1.5 v
B	−1.0 v	+0.5 v	−0.5 v
Difference between A and B	2.0 v	0 v	2.0 v

Balanced wiring does not require XLR connectors, nor do these connectors guarantee a circuit is balanced. But the alternative, unbalanced wiring, doesn't have to be noisy if you plan it properly. Chapter 4 discusses practicalities of both wiring schemes and how to connect between the two.

⚠️ **Gotcha** _____

Balanced wiring requires balanced equipment. Balanced wires don't actually reject the noise; that magic happens in whatever the wires get plugged into. Both the signal source and the destination need special circuits for balancing. These circuits can be expensive and are usually left out of prosumer equipment.

Digital Audio

Those bugaboos of noise and distortion in analog audio are cumulative. Each time a signal goes through a different processor or is stored on another generation of analog tape, it gets slightly noisier or more distorted. In the days before digital recording, a movie soundtrack could go through dozens of processing circuits and as many as six magnetic or optical generations between mic and moviegoer. Finding the best compromise between noise and distortion was a constant battle.

But computer signals don't deteriorate that way. The words I'm typing now are captured flawlessly to RAM, written to hard disk, and e-mailed to a publisher. There, three editors and a designer will work on successive copies before the printer's negatives are made. Yet, no data errors are introduced by these multiple computer generations.[8] A single pass through the printing press is more likely to make a word or image unusable than all the computing. This is because digital ones and zeros are unambiguous and easy to copy, and computer media includes safeguards that can correct many errors.

If we turn an analog audio signal into digital data, it should be just as robust. Of course the process of turning constantly changing analog voltages into ones and zeros and back has its own pitfalls. Twenty-five years ago when the technology was new, these problems gave digital a bad

_____
8. And probably none by my capable editors. Thanks, guys.

reputation among audio purists. But today we've learned to deal with all of them. Digital, when done right, is the best recording medium we've got. For professional TV and film purposes, its advantages outweigh analog so much that the older method has been virtually abandoned.

Digitizing

The process of turning analog to digital is easy to visualize with an oscilloscope. For any moment, you can see exactly what the voltage is. Scopes have grids printed on their displays to track time and voltage; the values depend on how you set the controls. In Figure 2.14, I've assigned the grid very simple numbers: each vertical unit represents one volt, and each horizontal is one millisecond. The wave is the dual-harmonic we examined earlier.

When children first learn to count, they do it in whole numbers: *1 apple, 2 apples, 3 apples.* Their math skills don't yet include the concept of "half an apple." Neither does a computer's. One bit is the smallest possible unit, and there can be no such thing as half a bit. But we can assign that smallest bit any unit we want. It can be something whole, like a penny. Or it can be a fraction of a whole unit, like a hundredth of a volt.

These values may be tiny, but if you string bits together to make words, you can express much bigger numbers. A one-bit digital word has two possible values, 1 or 0. A two-bit word has four possible values: 00, 01, 10, 11. Word processing typically uses *bytes*, or 8-bit words. Modern computers frequently string multiple bytes together into a single word. Using two bytes for a 16-bit word, you get 65,536 possible values.

Let's keep things simple. For our first digital audio, we'll use three-bit words, which have eight possible values. We'll count in volts, scaled from −3 to +4 on our scope screen. Digital 000 would be −3 volts, digital 001 is −2 volts, and so on. The wave fits nicely in that range.

Using the grid, let's turn our wave digital. Once per millisecond (that is, once per horizontal unit) we'll read the voltage. Since our counting unit is a volt, we round to the nearest whole one:

```
At 1 ms…    +2 volts
   2 ms…    +1 volt
   3 ms…    +1 volt

   …etc.
```

This string of analog numbers, …+2, +1, +1,… could be recorded on digital tape as the three-bit words 101, 100, 100… . I've marked the value for each millisecond with a black dot on the screen. You can see in Figure 2.15 how the dots follow the sound wave.

To play this string of numbers back as sound, we create an analog wave that has the right voltage at the right time. Visually, this is as easy as connecting the dots (the principle isn't much harder in audio circuits). But the result—the light gray line in Figure 2.16—doesn't resemble the original much. What went wrong?

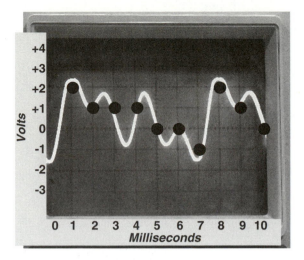

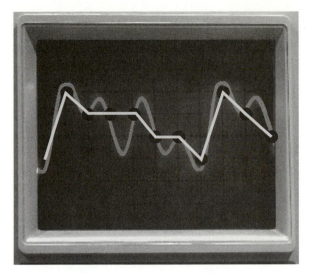

2.15 Sampling our soundwave's voltage, once per millisecond.

2.16 Our low-resolution recording isn't very accurate.

Actually, two things are at fault. Those rounded whole volts—the best we can do with our three-bit words—are too far apart to accurately record the wave. And a sample rate of once per millisecond isn't fast enough to accurately capture an 800 Hz harmonic. Both problems are easy to fix.

Each time you add one more bit to the word length, you double the number of possible values. So let's bump up to four-bit recording: instead of just eight possible values between –3 and +4, we now have 16, letting us count in half volts. Let's also double the speed and take a fresh sample every half millisecond (you'll learn why that's sufficient in the next few pages). Figure 2.17 shows these new samples as smaller black dots: twice as many as in Figure 2.15, now rounded to the nearest half volt.

We haven't added much data—four bits would be considered a very low-resolution system,[9] and 2000 samples per second (usually known as a *2 kHz sample rate*, or *2 kHz s/r*) is regarded as only fast enough for bass effect channels. But the reconstructed wave is a lot more accurate. Figure 2.18 shows how well it follows the original. Even more important, CD Track 7 lets you judge the result: an actual four-bit, 2 kHz s/r recording of the multi-harmonic wave from Track 4. It was converted back to CD standard so you could play it, but that process didn't restore the lost data. You're hearing what four bits at 2 kHz s/r really sounds like!

Hear for yourself

Track 7 lets you hear the actual wave produced by Figure 2.17, along with the original wave for comparison.

9. Typical of cheap hand-held voice memo recorders.

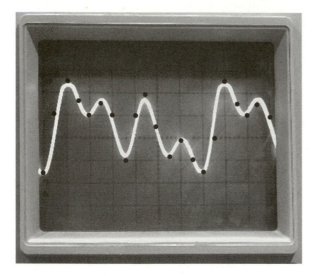

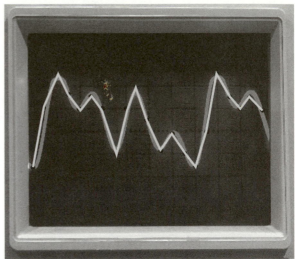

2.17 Doubling the bits lets us mark half volts. Doubling the speed gives us twice as many samples.

2.18 Figure 2.17's recording is a lot more accurate.

Bit Depths

Track 7 sounds as good as it does because even low-bit systems can handle simple waves recorded at the right level. CDs and most digital video systems use 16-bit audio words for considerably more accuracy and volume range. When the signal has to be converted to or from analog, circuit designers choose a maximum possible voltage (when all 16 bits are ones, or *full scale*). The smallest bit is then defined as 1/65,536 of full scale, or about 0.00013 dB of it.

Some rounding off is still necessary because even a bit that tiny isn't the same as a constantly changing wave. The worst case is when a signal is halfway between two minimum bits for a maximum error of about 0.00007 dB of full scale—far less than humans can hear. But we need that precision. Each time you manipulate the signal by changing volume or adding a processor, you're actually telling the computer to do some math. Since the result isn't likely to fall perfectly on a whole-bit value, it's rounded off again. These errors are cumulative. Do enough processing, and the result will be audible distortion or noise. For that reason, audio professionals now use 24-bit words, for a possible error of 0.00000026 dB. They do as much as possible in that domain, and then reduce the final output to 16 bits for compatibility with CD and digital video.

There's another way to consider bit depth. Each bit doubles the possible number of values, increasing the ratio between media noise and full scale by 6 dB[10] (that ratio is often called *signal/noise*, or *s/n*). An eight-bit signal, common in early computers, has 48 dB s/n. Sixteen-bit DV

10. Actually, 6.0205999 dB. But you can round it off. What's a few hundredths dB among friends?

Digital signals have no relation to voltage. The digital audio values on a CD or stored on your hard drive represent fractions of full scale. But the actual value of full scale depends on the analog circuits: it might be 0.01 volts at a camcorder's mic input, 3.5 volts unloaded on a balanced line connector, 8 volts in a hi-fi speaker, or whatever the equipment designer prefers.

This is a good thing. It means while the signal is in the digital domain, you don't have to worry about absolute values at all. The software doesn't care whether a track is destined for a thousand watt transmitter, the Internet, or your own headphones.

For this reason, digital audio levels are always expressed as *dBFS*, a decibel ratio to full scale. Full scale is the absolute maximum, so a ratio of 1:1 (0 dBFS) is the loudest you can get. Because no voltage changes can be recorded above full scale, if the original analog voltage exceeds the design limit, the digitized result has an absolutely flat-topped waveform: total (and very ugly) distortion.

Circuit designers frequently flash the "overload" light when a signal approaches –1 dBFS to avoid this distortion. But there really isn't a digital overload. That would require a digital signal greater than 0 dBFS, which is impossible.[1]

_____

1. Except in the case of one particular and ugly-sounding test signal, which never occurs in a soundtrack.

and CDs have a theoretical 96 dB s/n, though the analog circuits are seldom that good. Twenty-four-bit signals have 144 dB s/n—well beyond the range of the most golden-eared humans, as well as most electronics—but it provides significant margin for error.

Many DV cameras also support 12-bit recording, at a reduced sample rate, to double the number of audio tracks on a videotape. Twelve-bits are 72 dB s/n, which is a wider range than traditional broadcast television. But 12-bit recording is frequently noisy since it's almost impossible to set the level accurately enough to take full advantage of the range.

Dither

Humans can't hear a single sample's worth of rounding error, but a bunch of them in a row produce a distortion that's annoying because of the way it follows the signal. The solution is to add analog noise—*dithering*—at about one-third the level of a single bit. This randomizes the error so it doesn't sound like distortion any more. The ear is good at tracking desired sounds even when they're obscured by noise, so dithering can effectively extend the dynamic range. Dithering can also be *noise-shaped*—the random signal is equalized to be stronger at frequencies where the ear is less sensitive. Its randomness continues to hide distortion, but we don't hear the noise as much.

⚠️ *Gotcha* _____

What signal to noise? When measuring s/n in the analog world, it's customary to refer to a nominal signal level, typically 0 VU. That's because while analog circuits start distorting once you reach that level, you can still record a louder signal. Momentary peaks 6 dB higher than 0 VU can sound fine, even though longer sounds that loud would reveal the distortion.

Since digital recording has an absolute limit of 0 dBFS, that level is usually used for digital s/n measurements. But the usually operating level is −12 dBFS or lower, to leave room for peaks. When comparing digital s/n to analog, you must take that safety margin into effect. So while 16-bit digital has 96 dB s/n, a 16-bit miniDV isn't capable of sounding better than an 80 dB analog s/n.[1]

_____

1. That's a theoretical maximum. No miniDV camera comes even close.

Audio programs may give you some choices for dithering when you need to reduce bit depth. If your program does this, use dithering and play with the noise-shaping options. The effects may be too subtle for most media production, unless you're translating a 16-bit signal to eight bits. Most NLEs' audio capabilities aren't sophisticated enough to use dithering at all.

Sample Rates

Sound exists only as pressure changes over time. Eliminate the time component, and you've got steady air pressure—useful for weather forecasts, but not soundtracks. So it makes intuitive sense that how frequently you sample a signal's level influences how accurately you've recorded it.

In fact, this principle was known long before practical digital recording was invented. In the 1920s a Bell Labs engineer, Harry Nyquist, proved mathematically that the highest frequency you can faithfully reproduce has to be less than half the sample rate. Sounds above the *Nyquist Limit* start to mix with the sample rate itself. The resulting data implies additional frequencies, which aren't harmonics of the original wave. When you play back the data, those frequencies are re-created as well as the desired one. What you get is a horrible squeaking or whistling overlaid on the original.

To avoid this, analog-to-digital conversion circuits use *antialiasing* filters to reject high frequencies; the filters are often set to just under half the sample rate. Digital-to-analog circuits have similar *reconstruction* or *smoothing* filters at the same frequency.

Because of the Nyquist Limit and practical limitations in filter design, digital audio systems are usually set to reject any frequency higher than about 45 percent of the sample rate.

- CDs are set at 44.1 kHz s/r so they can carry a 20 kHz audio signal, generally accepted as the minimum requirement for high fidelity.

- Computer media often use a 22 kHz s/r to save data. This implies an upper audio limit of 10 kHz, about the same as AM radio.

- Analog TV and FM Stereo cut off at 15 kHz because the transmitters put control signals above that frequency. So broadcasters often use 32 kHz s/r in their storage systems and satellite links.

- U.S. telephones traditionally cut off at 3.5 kHz. So when switching networks and long-distance lines were converted to digital, a sample rate of 8 kHz was chosen.

- Our example in Figures 2.16 and 2.17 has a second harmonic at 800 Hz. This puts it safely below the Nyquist Limit of our 2 kHz sampling. That's why Track 7 can accurately play the harmonic.

There are exceptions. Professional video is standardized at 48 kHz sampling. But most NLEs that handle 48 kHz s/r also support 44.1 kHz s/r and use the same filters for both. That means there's no advantage to the higher rate. Some professional equipment uses 96 kHz sampling, but very few engineers believe we can hear as high as 40 kHz. The higher rate was chosen to keep filter artifacts—which increase as you reach their cutoff frequency—far from critical audio.

Digital vs. Analog

Many music producers like a kind of distortion created by overloaded analog tape and will dub their digital masters through a 1980 vintage studio recorder just to get it. Then they'll redigitize for CD release. This practice strikes me as completely reasonable, even though I've virtually eliminated analog in my own studio (except for microphones, monitors, VHS and BetaSP decks,... and a telephone).

But arguments about the superiority of one medium over the other can be as intense as Presidential elections. Some people insist that audio hit its peak with vinyl records and has gone downhill since; they point to awful mp3s on the Internet as proof. Others assert that digital is inherently "steppy" or can't reproduce certain waves. Both of those last assertions are absolutely true. But they ignore the fact that it's easy to demonstrate how analog circuits suffer from problems that are exactly equivalent.[11]

It's not worth fighting about. If you're doing any desktop or professional video production, digital audio will be part of your life. What's important—particularly if your background is analog—is understanding some fundamental differences between the two media.

---

11. See my book, *Producing Great Sound for Digital Video,* second edition (CMP Books, 2002) or my Web site for some of these demonstrations.

Analog Handles Overloads More Gracefully

When an analog mixer, processor, or recorder receives a signal that's too loud, it starts to distort. The distortion is gentle at first and increases as the input gets louder. If it persists, of course you turn down the volume. But if an unexpected signal peak causes a sudden overload, the distortion may be tolerable and there's no reason to change anything.

That's not true for digital. Anything louder than full scale—even for a single sample—gets badly distorted. This often shows as a crackling that can obscure the signal and in most cases can't be fixed. This distortion often occurs in the original digitizing. It also seems to happen mostly with field recordings that can't be easily replaced, not just because of Murphy's Law, but because studio sessions allow more time for setting levels accurately.

But watch out. This distortion can also happen within the digital domain, when an otherwise perfect signal is boosted by a processor or multiple signals are added in a mixer. In some systems, you won't spot the distortion until after things are rendered. The only cure is to review everything and be prepared to redo it if there are problems.

Digital Conceals Errors, Then Fails Utterly; Analog Lets Each Error Hurt the Signal

In a digital system, an error is missing or inaccurate data. In an analog system, it's usually a burst of noise. Neither medium is particularly prone to errors, but either can have them because of malfunctioning equipment, dirty tapes, noisy environments, and other problems.

It sometimes seems like digital has more things to go wrong. Problems like unsynchronized clocks (Chapter 4) can cause clicking or hiccups that are hard to trace, and there's no equivalent error in the analog realm. But the fact is, analog has its own unique array of problems. We've simply been dealing with them longer.

Digital systems have two kinds of safeguards against problems. Small errors can be corrected perfectly, with mathematical techniques. Larger ones are detected but can't be corrected; instead, missing parts of the waveform are interpolated from the surrounding good data. Usually, this error concealment is undetectable. Very large sections of bad data cause the system to either produce noise or mute automatically. In practice, if a digital signal is getting progressively worse, you can keep hearing clean audio through much of the damage and not even know there's a problem. Then it disappears entirely.

Analog systems have no such safeguards. Once noise mixes with the signal, it's there to stay. But the signal's there too, and you'll probably still hear it. In practice, as analog signals get progressively worse, you hear the changes and know something's wrong.

Analog Degrades with Each Process; Digital Doesn't Have To

Even the best analog equipment adds a tiny amount of noise and distortion when you go through it. Knowledgeable recording engineers strive for as simple an analog signal chain as possible, and avoid extra tape generations except for special effects. But good digital recorders don't degrade the signal at all, and good digital processors do so little damage that you'd have to string hundreds of them together before you'd notice anything.

However, you still have to be knowledgeable if you want digital good sound. Processors can be misused. Each conversion from digital to analog and back adds some generation loss. Avoiding these problems isn't hard, once you're armed with some basic understanding and the proper techniques. This chapter's been about the understanding. The rest of this book is about the practicalities.

Chapter 3

The Studio: Acoustics and Monitoring

Remember this:

- The shape and wall treatment of a room can have a big effect on what you hear in a track, and can lead you to make bad decisions.

- Soundproofing has nothing to do with egg crates or foam tiles. If you want to keep noise away, you have to follow some rules about mass, decoupling, and sealing.

- The most important sound gear you can buy is monitor speakers. Choose them wisely.

My first audio post suite was a shelf in the living room. It had three consumer tape decks, a PA system mixer, a graphic equalizer, and a home brew patch bay. I used my stereo amp and speakers for monitoring.[1] This ragtag assembly should have sounded awful. But I'd engineered at three radio stations and spent a couple of years working in film sound, so there were a couple of tricks up my sleeve. Careful wiring and constant tweaking kept the equipment at its peak. My marginal setup, when used correctly, certainly sounded better than pro gear used wrong.

3.1 My current studio, the Digital Playroom.

---

1. Projects from that rinky-dink setup included a couple of national radio spots, some federally funded PSAs, and audio for a museum show. I had a lot more nerve than equipment.

My current suite is considerably nicer (Figure 3.1), and is good enough for the projects I do for Disney and CBS. But it was built on a low budget, and I used ideas similar to those from that first studio (plus a few decades of additional experience). Call it guerilla engineering—knowing when you have to follow the rules, and when it's okay to cheat.

This section of the book describes acoustic treatments, wiring, and equipment for both audio-only rooms and video rooms where sound is considered important. While sound studios are frequently built to higher audio standards than video editing rooms, there's absolutely no difference in the principles involved. The advice here works equally well for both, and it can also be applied to a garage studio where your band hangs out.

Facility Goals

Before investing in construction or equipment, take a minute to figure out how you'll use them. You might be able to save some money.

- Are you planning to edit here but then take tracks somewhere else for cleanup and mix? This may be the most cost-effective strategy if you're making only a few short films. You won't need much more than a NLE and a small speaker.

- Are you planning to record narration or replacement dialog? Obviously, you'll need a mic. But take care of the acoustics first: a couple of hundred dollars spent in this area can help more than a thousand dollar microphone.

- Planning to mix your videos yourself? If you want to be reasonably sure of how the track will sound on viewers' sets or in a theater, good monitors are the most important component. But they might not be ones you'd choose for listening to or mixing music. Acoustic treatment also influences how a monitor will sound.

- Planning to make a living in this room with clients showing up to supervise? They'll expect a high level of acoustics and also some space to spread out. If you're going after ad agency or high-end corporate work, you'll need glitz as well: a lounge area, refreshments, and lots of pretty, winking lights.[2]

It's most likely your needs fall somewhere in the middle; you want a room where you can accurately edit and mix your own tracks with an occasional voice-over recording. You don't want outside noises to interfere, and you don't want to annoy other people in the building. And your budget is limited.

---

2. A former boss once told me, "people hear with their eyes." He'd insist I consider the knob-to-light ratio when specifying new equipment (the more lights, the better). His audio suites certainly looked better than the room I've got now, even though they sometimes didn't sound as good. They also made more money, so maybe he was right.

If you know what you're doing, none of this is a problem.

Acoustics

I was visiting a friend, an Avid editor at a TV station that had recently built new, luxurious offices. The facility was beautiful: every surface was either pastel enamel or oak, and the large square rooms had sparse furniture so people wouldn't feel cramped. His new edit room—designed to impress local advertisers—was designed to match. It even featured a giant TV on the wall opposite the client chair. Figure 3.2 shows the approximate layout.

He couldn't understand why his mixes sounded okay in the NLE but were virtually unintelligible when clients watched them on the TV. If you read the previous chapter, you can probably guess what was going on:

- The hard walls and empty bookcase reflected all the sound energy that hit them. The room was actually an echo chamber.

- When he was sitting at the NLE, he was much closer to his tiny monitor speakers than to the back wall, so the returning echoes were a lot softer than the direct speaker sound (because of the inverse square law).

- When clients sat in their chairs, the direct sound traveled eight feet from

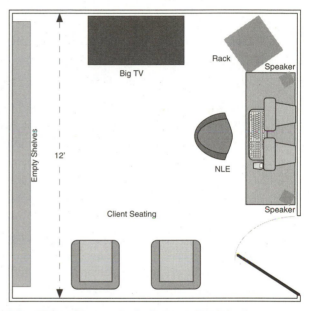

3.2 This edit room looked great, but it had problems.

the big TV's speakers. The echo from behind them traveled about 10 feet and was almost as loud. The echoes from the clients' sides traveled about 13 feet, so these were still significant. Since these various paths were all different lengths, the sound got to the clients at slightly different times, blurring what they heard.

Vibrating air between two parallel hard walls works like the string of a guitar. It resonates at a frequency based on the distance between the walls and resonates at harmonics of that frequency. This resonance makes echoes stronger at those frequencies than at others. In nontechnical terms, the space is *boomy*.

In this case, the 12-foot-wide room resonated around 47 Hz[3]—too low to do much damage to the track—but it also resonated at harmonics of 94 Hz, 141 Hz, and 188 Hz, well within the speech range. Contributing to the unintelligibility, these resonances emphasized parts of some vowels and made them last longer than consonants. Since the room was also 12 feet in the other direction, reflections between those walls had exactly the same resonances.

 Gotcha _____

A square room won't sound cool. Parallel walls are almost always a problem, and the more energy the wall reflects, the worse things will sound. A perfectly square room with hard walls can't sound good because resonances in both directions will be the same.

Also, his tiny personal monitors at the NLE weren't very efficient at those low frequencies where the room rang. So he tended to turn up the bass in his mixes. When he played them on the big TV, the mixes were too bassy. This further excited the room resonances, making the booming worse.

There was no perfect fix short of knocking the walls down and trying again. I suggested he fill the bookcase with randomly-sized tape boxes, which would break up at least some of the reflections, and hang as many fiberglass or foam panels as possible on the walls to absorb echoes. He could also move the client chairs a lot closer to the TV set so the clients would hear more direct sound and less echo. And if he got better monitor speakers for his NLE, he wouldn't overemphasize the bass.

Fighting Resonance: Build a Crooked Room

Changing the room's shape wasn't an option for my friend. It may be for you, if you're carving out new space or modifying an existing one. The first way to avoid problems is to make sure the walls aren't parallel. Nonparallel walls spread the resonances out over a lot of frequencies instead of having them build up at just a few. Crooked rooms can sound better than rectangular ones.

These angles don't have to be extreme. In Figure 3.1, you can hardly tell that my audio suite isn't square. But in Figure 3.3—the room's plan—you can see there are no parallel walls: the corners are 92 degrees. Figure 3.3 also suggests how to fit a crooked room into a straight building without wasting too much space. It shows one long angled wall placed against an existing straight one, and the other long angled wall backing into a crooked closet.

---

3. The formula is Frequency = 565 / Length (in feet) for the fundamental, with significant harmonics at 2×, 3×, and 4× that frequency. There are other directions these resonances can form, but the path between perfectly parallel walls is the worst.

Even though the room is crooked, it should be symmetrical. When you're seated at the listening position, the size and shape of the room to your left should match the size and shape to your right as closely as possible. The room in Figure 3.3 is aligned to the center of the wall opposite the announce booth—where the "16.5 feet" dashed line appears. (In Figure 3.1, the picture monitor, two computer monitors, and audio workstation control surface are centered on that wall.)

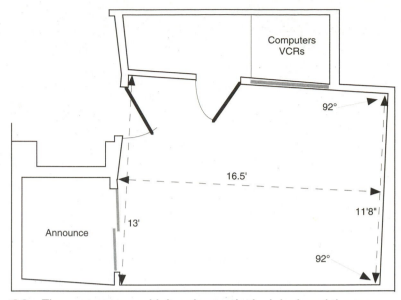

3.3 The contractor couldn't understand why I designed the room this way, until he heard it.

If you don't have the luxury of building new walls, try to find a room where width, length, and ceiling height aren't exact multiples of each other. This keeps resonances from ganging up in a single group of frequencies. If possible, work across a corner so the sound source faces the longest diagonal dimension of the room, while maintaining that symmetry on both sides. The most important thing is to add wall treatments that absorb the reflections. But if you need soundproofing—as opposed to echo control—you should soundproof first.

Fighting Sound Transmission

Most modern construction is virtually transparent to sound; the most isolation you can expect from a standard sheetrock wall is about –30 dB reduction in the middle of the band—subjectively about an eighth of the original volume and still audible. Sound reduction at low frequencies is much worse.

Whether you're building from scratch or improving an existing room, there are only two practical ways to keep sound out: make the walls massive or make them springy (also called *decoupling*). When sound hits one side of a conventional wall, it's carried through the studs and vibrates the wallboard on the other side. If you make one or both sides heavier, they won't vibrate as much and can stand up better to low frequencies. If you build the wall so the sides aren't rigidly connected by a stud, vibrations won't carry as well.

One common solution is to add a second layer of wallboard on one or both sides. This adds mass. You can use different thicknesses of board to give the sides different densities, so they can resonate at different frequencies. Double 5/8-inch board on one side and a combination of 5/8-inch and 1/2-inch on the other, is a usual construction.

> ⚠️ **Gotcha** _____
>
> **_Soundproofing happens inside the walls._** Ask most people what soundproofing is and they'll describe foam tiles, egg crates, or other treatments on the walls. While foam tiles or other treatments can control reverberation, they don't stop sound. Egg crates are only good for storing eggs.

A different approach is to isolate one of the wall's surfaces from the studs entirely. This was traditionally done with sound-deadening board, a kind of spongy, brown panel laid between the studs and the drywall. A newer and more effective method uses resilient RC-1 steel channels (shown in Figure 3.4) running horizontally along the length of the wall every two feet or so. The lower, flat surface has holes for screwing to studs or an existing wall. Another layer of drywall is laid against the channels' upper surface and is attached with special screws that aren't long enough to reach the studs or existing wall. You can get these RC-1 steel channels at big lumber yards or acoustic suppliers, and—other than knowing to use the short screws—they don't require any special skills to install.

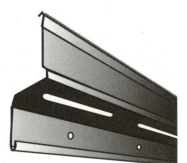

3.4 Resilient channels act like springs to isolate the studs and wall surface.

Remember that sound travels vertically as well as horizontally; resilient channels and extra drywall work just as well on ceilings as they do on walls. Channels and drywall aren't appropriate for floors; instead, use hard rubber cubes and 5/8-inch plywood. The cubes are sold for the purpose of sound control and are already mounted in fiberglass batts.

If you've got the space, a wall can be built with double studs, staggered from each other on a wider plate. This works like the resilient channels; they disconnect one surface of the wall from the other, with the added advantage of more air space between the surfaces. Sound insulation can be woven between the studs for additional isolation. Using a combination of these techniques, you can bring a wall's attenuation up to about 60 dB—as good as the best recording studios.

To prevent sound leaks, caulk all wallboard to the floor and ceiling. Weatherproofing materials and techniques are perfectly appropriate. If you're using double wallboard, stagger the joints and tape both layers. Completely seal any penetrations, including plumbing and electrical. Use surface-mounted boxes so you don't have to cut into the wall for outlets and switches, and make sure the other side of the wall is also free from cutouts.

Gotcha _____

Sound is sneaky stuff. Walls don't stop much if they have holes in them. Vibrating molecules can get through the tiniest holes. Any soundproofing technique will be useless if the wall isn't also air-proof.

I once had to soundproof an existing room because of a clacking teletype machine on the other side of the wall. I decided to add mass by lining the walls with lead, to be covered with thin wallboard. When the lead was almost completely up, I worried it was a bad choice: the teletype was still very audible. But as we closed those last few inches, the sound went completely away. It was as if the machine had suddenly been turned off!

To keep an HVAC system quiet, use flexible ducting connected to commercial HVAC silencers mounted in the wall. The silencers are metal cylinders with baffles inside and are about two feet in diameter and three feet long. If it's not possible to mount silencers, put right angles in the duct. HVAC will also be quieter if you specify a low velocity fan and large ducting. It's a good idea not to use standard diffusers on the vents; when they spread air around, they also generate a lot of noise. In my studio, the 8-inch ceiling ducts are terminated with normal metal ceiling vents, but I took the diffusers off with a pliers. It's a high-tech look and a much quieter than normal installation.

Doors need significant mass as well as a sealing mechanism to stop sound. If you can't afford expensive soundproof door systems, specify solid-core doors. Then add a layer of 1/2-inch plywood on each side for more mass. You might need special hardware and a steel frame to support the heavier door. Caulk the frame to the wall and use tubular weather stripping on all four sides for sealing.

 Gotcha _____

The missing upper wall. Modern office buildings are often built with large open spaces. A suspended tile ceiling is installed across the entire space, and then walls are built to break the large space into rooms. Unfortunately, these walls only stretch up to the tile. The tiles themselves and the space above are transparent to sound.

You can get a reasonable improvement by adding fiberglass batts, made for this purpose, above the false ceiling. The batts are denser than normal thermal insulation and available at acoustics suppliers. This technique is effective at voice frequencies but not for bass notes.

Fighting Echoes

Small rooms have echoes, even though you probably can't hear them. If a room is less than 12 feet wide, early reflections are too fast to hear as separate sounds.

- If the echoes are frequency selective, like in my friend's edit room, they can add a boominess to everything.

- Even if you angled the walls or broke up their surfaces, echoes can still combine with existing sounds to reinforce some frequencies and cancel others. This makes mixing or equalizing difficult.

- If you're recording in a small room like this, the mic won't pick up directional and visual cues that help you ignore echoes. The track will sound echoey on playback, even though it didn't when you recorded it.

Fortunately, echoes are the easiest sound problem to cure. Auralex, SDG, and Sonex all make wedge-surfaced two- to four-inch-thick foam tiles designed to absorb sound reflections. They cost between $2.50–$16.00 per foot at broadcast suppliers. The different brands will sound the same for most purposes; make your choice based on appearance and price. But don't just tack them on the wall. With a few simple additions, you can build absorbers that look better and are more effective, with fewer tiles.

Turn back to Figure 3.1 (page 41) to see a couple of these absorbers in my studio; they're the things toward the top of the photo and on both sides of the console. There are plenty more on the walls you can't see. About one quarter of the wall surface is covered with these things. The absorbers' surface is 2-inch grooved foam

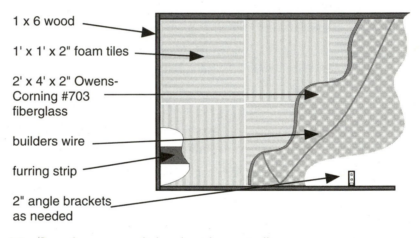

1 x 6 wood

1' x 1' x 2" foam tiles

2' x 4' x 2" Owens-Corning #703 fiberglass

builders wire

furring strip

2" angle brackets as needed

3.5   One of many sound absorbers in my studio.

tiles. The two secret ingredients are fiberglass and air. The fiberglass isn't the pink stuff sold for attics, which isn't very good for sound. Instead, use 2-inch-thick Owens-Corning 703, a semi-rigid yellow panel made specifically for its acoustic properties. It's available at acoustic suppliers or large lumber yards in bundles of 40 square feet for about a dollar a foot.

Figure 3.5 shows how the absorber gets put together. Build a frame out of 1×4 boards (pine is fine, but oak looks better) and attach it to the wall. Press to fit the fiberglass into the frame—you can trim the fiberglass with a knife and compress it slightly to make it stay in place—and secure it with builder's wire stapled to the frame. Then cement the foam tiles onto the 703 panel with construction adhesive. Since 1×4 lumber is actually about 3.5 inches wide, the tiles' grooves will stick out half an inch for a nicely finished appearance. If you don't mind the grooves sticking out a little more, mount 1×2 furring strips (also known as *strapping*) on the wall to put an airspace behind the 703 panel.

You can make the frame any size you want, but it's most convenient to keep the inside dimensions multiples of your particular brand tiles' size. How much absorber do you need? There are complex formulas to answer that precisely (check my Web site for some good books on the subject). But you can get good results by covering about one-third of the wall area with fiber and tile, or you can cover one-quarter of the wall with the airspace version; that should be enough to make any hard-walled room sound good for editing and mixing. Mount the panels so their centers are about ear level. Use a little more coverage if you'll also be recording voice-overs.

If you're going to be mixing music or theatrical tracks with a lot of bass, be aware that low frequencies can be hard to control even when speech and higher frequencies are being absorbed nicely. The common solution for this is a *bass trap*, a fairly large kind of absorber usually mounted in the corners of a room. The best ones are designed for specific frequencies and are built into the space; but if you're hearing boominess, you may be able to get by with triangular foam ones costing about $60 each. If the room is a good size and you're not dealing with extreme bass, and you don't hear a problem, then save the space and don't worry about trapping.

Monitoring

When choosing loudspeakers, many new filmmakers turn into misers. They buy the cheapest ones they can get away with and figure they'll upgrade as their skills and budgets improve. It may make sense to purchase a computer this way because they keep getting faster and cheaper. But it's a bad idea for monitors.

Speaker designs don't change very quickly. Today's "improved" versions might benefit from new materials or slight tweaks in philosophy, but the differences are minor. Monitor systems that would be ancient in computer terms—15 years old or more—are still in daily use at professional studios. So it makes sense to buy a little more quality than you think is appropriate now. With inflation, you'll pay more tomorrow for what you could have bought—and been using—today.

The speakers you choose have a profound effect on the quality of your soundtrack. They're the lens through which you judge everything else. No matter how good your ears are, they can't compensate for bad speakers. Unfortunately, a lot of the powered desktop speakers bundled with NLE systems are totally wrong for making mix decision. These speakers are chosen by dealers to be checklist items—a complete package *has* to have speakers—and size and wholesale cost are more important to dealers than sound. Unless you're using the setup strictly for editing and never equalize or mix on them, they're a waste of money.

Nearfield and Small Speakers

We've talked about how reflections from nearby walls can color what you hear from a monitor. Fortunately, the inverse square law can help. If you sit closer to a speaker than to reflecting surfaces, echoes will be comparatively softer. This kind of *nearfield* monitoring became popular about two decades ago and works when the speakers are three times closer than the nearest hard surface. But the technique by itself doesn't guarantee good sound. It just means that a good speaker won't appear worse because of the room.

Today, the market is flooded with so-called nearfield speakers. The term refers to size: a speaker has to be pretty small to sit on an editing desk and be in that magic nearfield. Unfortunately, it's hard to build a very small speaker that sounds good. You have to move a lot of air molecules to get decent low-frequency performance, and that takes either a large cone or one that can handle extended movement. High frequencies require a specialized driver, which takes up more space.

One solution is to integrate small, individual components with an amplifier tuned to make up for the nearfields' deficiencies; professional systems taking this approach can sound excellent. But good components and precisely calibrated electronics are expensive—the better nearfield systems typically cost a few thousand dollars, which is more than a large speaker of equivalent quality. More modestly priced small speakers, costing a few hundred dollars, are often full of compromises. Manufacturers choose cheap components and apply a *lot* of tuning in the electronics. This results in uneven response with plenty of distortion across the band. The speakers can boast an impressive frequency range, but none of those frequencies sound good.

The bottom line is accurate nearfield monitoring is expensive. It's more cost-effective to treat the room so that bigger speakers can be used at a slightly farther distance.

⚠️ *Gotcha* _____

Real-world speakers aren't. Some people claim small, cheap speakers are better because they're like the ones in cheap TV sets. The reasoning is that these speakers will give a more accurate picture of what most people will hear. If a viewer does have better speakers than most people, things can only improve.

The fact is cheap speakers are bad in random ways. What improves sound on one can make it worse on another. What *is* consistent is that most cheap speakers miss an octave or more on both ends of the spectrum. This affects how you balance voice and music because music has more energy at those extremes. And the restricted range can hide serious problems with hum, boominess, and noise.

Make your mix decisions on good speakers, so you know what's actually going to be on the track. Then check it on bad ones to see if it's still intelligible under the worst conditions.

If you use nearfields, be aware that the area where they sound best can be very small. Beyond that range, reflections will start to color the sound. A producer, editor, and client sitting at a typical edit setup will each hear mixes slightly different, unless they're in each others' laps.

Subwoofers

Another philosophy is to use small, high-frequency speakers—sometimes only a few inches across—and couple them with an extended bass speaker somewhere out of the way. The logic is that high frequencies are more directional than low ones—true—so you can still get an effective stereo image without the bulk of low-frequency drivers. These systems are popular among computer gamers who surround themselves with the small speakers for an immersive experience. They're also sold for unobtrusive, background music systems because the small speakers are easy to hide.

Most of these systems are horrible for dialog. The thumping bass they provide can be nice for music and game environments but have nothing to do with what people will hear on TV or in a well-designed auditorium. Furthermore, most of these systems sacrifice the lower mid-range to achieve small size at a reasonable price. Frequencies between 125 Hz and 500 Hz or so—where vowels live—are either missing or heavily distorted.

Having a speaker concentrate on just the lowest frequencies isn't necessarily a bad idea. Theatrical sound systems use subwoofers and they're the 0.1 in surround schemes like 5.1.[4] But these systems also have full-size speakers for the main channels. The subs deal only with extreme bass notes, and the entire voice range is carried by the mains.

Choosing a speaker

If you want to hear what you're mixing or equalizing and can't afford a top-notch set of nearfields, you need full-size monitors. (You also need acoustic treatment, which is why we covered it first.) The best place to buy these speakers is often a broadcast, studio supplier, or high-end audio dealer. The worst may be an electronics chain, music store, or over the Internet.

The problem is that consumer speakers are designed to be impressive with music. This often means unrealistically loud bass and very bright highs aimed at a relatively small area. They're great if you want to be entertained in a living room, but they're nowhere near accurate for dialog. Fortunately, there are ways to sort out the best speakers for production.

Read the specs. Some manufacturers brag about *frequency ranges*—alleged limits the system will reach. But frequency ranges are meaningless unless you know how much the volume can vary from one frequency to another. Because it's a ratio, it's expressed in dB. If speaker A is rated sim-

---

4. So named because the bass, which will never exceed a low Nyquist Limit, is often sampled at 1/10 the rate of the other channels.

ply as having a 40 Hz–20 kHz range, and speaker B claims 60 Hz–18 kHz ± 4 dB, speaker B probably sounds a lot better—its manufacturer is taking more care in the precision of the specification and also, we can hope, the actual performance of the loudspeaker. The best speakers include a graph showing precisely how the sensitivity varies across the band. The best speaker manufacturers give you distortion specs as well, often also displayed as a graph over the frequency range.

Be leery of specs for low-cost, self-powered speakers. Manufacturers often cheat, and publish claims for the amplifier but not for the whole system. Compare the kinds of data you get from respected studio speaker companies like JBL (www.jblpro.com) and Genelec (www.genelec.com), with what's published for consumer hi-fi or prosumer music speakers. Even if you can't interpret all the information without an engineering degree, the mere fact of its presence should be reassuring.

Check a speaker's weight specification. Better speakers usually are heavier. Magnets have to be bigger to generate stronger fields. Amplifiers have bigger transformers for more current. And the cases are made out of denser, more rigid materials.

Learn to trust your ears. Assemble a CD with some well-recorded but unprocessed dialog in various voices, some music typical of the kind you use in productions, and a few sections of good voice-music mixes from well done productions. If possible, spend a few dollars to listen to this CD in a well-equipped sound studio until you know what it really sounds like. Get very familiar with the ratio of voice to music in the premixed pieces.

⚠ *Gotcha*

Louder sounds better. Most people have a hard time separating loudness from quality. A subtle boost in level gives one speaker a definite edge. Sneaky dealers sometimes do this intentionally, setting a slightly higher volume for the more profitable models. Make sure that volumes match before comparing quality.

Then go to a dealer who lets you audition by switching between different speakers while playing the same material. Start with two models near the top of the dealer's range, adjust them for about the same volume, and switch back and forth between them while listening to your CD. Knock the *better* speaker out of the running. (If they both sound the same, discard the more expensive one.) Pair the remaining model with the next model down in price. Keep comparing, working your way down in model and price until you notice that the CD doesn't sound like it did in the studio. Then go back up one notch: that's your speaker. If it's a little more expensive than you planned, remember that these things don't wear out or become obsolete. Think of it as an investment in your art. You'll be using it for years.

If a dealer won't let you adjust the volume, won't let you bring your own CD, or won't let you compare multiple brands in the same listening session, go somewhere else.

Hear for yourself

Track 8 is a frequency sweep to help you test individual speakers. Listen to it at a moderately loud level. The sine wave should sound smooth for the entire track. Watch out for a thickening at some frequencies or for a second note added an octave above the tone; this is a sign of distortion. Listen for rattles at any frequency; this indicates loose components which are a sign of sloppy manufacturing.

Don't rely on this track to judge a speaker's frequency response, even if you're using a sound level meter. Room acoustics can reinforce some frequencies and suppress others, making the measurement inaccurate.

Self-powered or separate amplifier?

It may be more convenient to install a speaker system with a built-in amp; all you have to do is run an audio cable and plug the speaker into the wall. (It might not be as convenient if there isn't an outlet handy.) Keeping the amp and speaker in the same box means you don't have to worry about heavy-gauge speaker cables. But before you choose a self-powered speaker, make sure you've considered these points:

- Some large systems use the same cheat as those minimonitors by using an amp that sacrifices distortion for wide response. This may be a legitimate compromise in a midlevel music speaker, but this speaker can add hurt dialog. Make sure both voice and music are perfectly clear.

- USB or other digital speaker systems aren't anything special; they just have another circuit tacked inside. There's no reason why they should sound any better than an analog-input speaker, using either an internal or separate amplifier.

Make sure a separate amplifier is powerful enough. Professional rackmount or high-end hi-fi amps are usually conservatively rated. They can actually deliver the continuous power they promise. Look for one rated at least 50 watts per channel. Be wary of *peak* power ratings on consumer amplifiers; these typically include a lot of distortion. In this case, distortion is worse than annoying: it can create high-frequency harmonics that damage the speaker. If you do use a consumer amplifier, leave the tone controls in their neutral position and turn any loudness or extended-bass switches off.

Power also requires heavy-gauge cable. With high resistance, thin wires waste watts and limit the amplifier's ability to control speaker movement. For most installations, 16-gauge unshielded copper wire should be sufficient. It doesn't have to be anything special; ordinary wire from a hardware or chain electronics store will do the job.

It's critical that connections to both the left and right speaker match. If they're reversed, one speaker will be pushing molecules while the other will be pulling on them, which can seriously reduce low frequencies and cause other problems. Use cable where each wire is a different color or has other definite marking. The amp and speaker terminals will also be coded—one red and one black, or one + and one − . Make sure terminals and wires are matched consistently on both sides of the room. If you have any doubts, use Track 9 to check the installation.

Hear for yourself

Track 9 helps you test speaker phasing. It has two short bursts of simultaneous low- and high-frequency narrow-band noise on both channels, with voice announcements about the bursts phase. Sit in a good position (see Figure 3.6) and listen to the entire track. If the bass seems louder in the first half, the speakers are properly wired. If it seems louder in the second half, swap the two conductors at one speaker only. Leave the other speaker and the amplifier alone.

Room Equalization

Just like self-powered speaker systems that have tailored amplifiers to make up for deficiencies in the speakers, you can add an equalizer ahead an amp to compensate for problems in the room and problems in unpowered speakers, in theory. When this technique is done subtly by a knowledgeable engineer with good test equipment, it can make a near-perfect room and great monitor system slightly better. But it's never a good idea to use equalization to fix a problem room or compensate for poor speakers. You're just trading one sound problem for another.

Speaker Placement

While the actual distances involved depends on your setup, most experts say you and the speakers should form an equilateral triangle (Figure 3.6). It's not supercritical, and a little variation shouldn't make much difference. But if accurate stereo monitoring is important, you should be centered between the speakers—no closer than 2/3 the distance between them, and no farther than 4/3 their distance. Get much closer, and sounds in the center won't be correct. Get much farther and you start to lose a sense of stereo. But how close or far you should be depends on the room. Good acoustics give you a lot more flexibility.

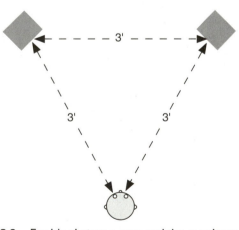

3.6   For ideal stereo, you and the monitors should form an equilateral triangle.

The high-frequency drivers (the smallest speaker element you can see) should be pointing towards you and at about ear level. There shouldn't be anything between the speakers and you—the back of a video monitor or tape deck can reflect high frequencies away. Ideally, there shouldn't be anything even *close* to the path between them and you because anything could cause reflections that reinforce different frequencies unevenly.

Monitoring for Surround

If you're mixing surround productions, things get a bit more complicated. Ideally, all of the room's walls should be treated with exactly the same absorption materials.

In standard 5.1 surround, the main left and right monitors should form an equilateral triangle with your listening position, just as the speakers do in stereo. The rear, or surround, speakers should be 90 degrees from the mains, which places them more over your shoulder than behind you. Ideally, their height should be the same as the mains'. In the real world, rear speakers often don't end up in a theoretically perfect position; there's usually too much else going on in the room. Depending on obstructions, you can put the rear speakers as much as 10 degrees from the ideal horizontal position and somewhat higher than the front speakers. Just try to keep the speaker arrangement symmetrical symmetrical.

In theory, the center speaker should be directly in front of you and at the same distance from you as the mains and centered between them, but that space is probably already occupied by the main picture monitor. A magnetically shielded speaker sitting on top of that monitor and angled slightly downward is the best compromise in most cases.

> ⚠ **Gotcha** _____
> **Should "tabletop" speakers be on the table?** The small speakers bundled with NLEs usually aren't very good in the first place. But most editors set them down on a crowded tabletop, which can make them sound even worse because of reflections from the desk surface and objects on it.
>
> Do the speakers a favor, and elevate them to ear level. This usually means putting them on the same shelf as the picture monitors.

> ⚠ **Gotcha** _____
> **Magnetically shielded speakers aren't.** Good loudspeakers have large magnets that can interfere with the sweep of a nearby TV picture tube when they get too close. If this happens, the result is an area of distorted colors on the part of the screen closest to the speaker. For this reason, many manufacturers make shielded speakers with reduced magnetic fields around them.
>
> Actually, shielding isn't used. An effective magnetic shield would be too big, heavy, and expensive. Instead, smaller magnets are strategically placed around the main one. The smaller magnets cancel the main magnet's field in directions where stray magnetism could cause problems.

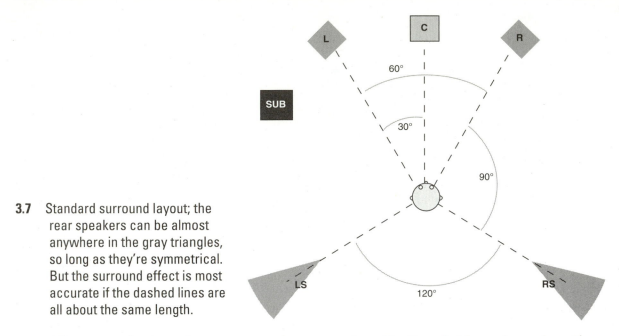

3.7 Standard surround layout; the rear speakers can be almost anywhere in the gray triangles, so long as they're symmetrical. But the surround effect is most accurate if the dashed lines are all about the same length.

The surround subwoofer can go anywhere convenient. You'll probably get better bass if you locate it in a corner of the room. Figure 3.7 shows placement for all six speakers.

There are other surround schemes, but this is the one recommended by the International Telecommunications Union. Actually, the whole idea of surround is still very new and is just starting to enter desktop production. Other arrangements may become popular.

How about Headphones?

Headphones let you deal with bad acoustics by ignoring them; this creates a private world for your ears. This can be helpful when editing because you'll be able to hear things that might otherwise be missed. But in my experience, headphones aren't a good idea for the mix. They emphasize subtle details, tempting you to mix music and sound effects too softly for the nonheadphone wearing viewer.

Headphones are necessary, of course, when you're recording narration or sound effects in the room. You have to monitor what you're getting, and using a speaker would interfere with the mic. Headphones come in two types:

- Closed-cup headphones surround the ear and create tiny, sealed air chambers. These headphones can do a good job of blocking the outside world and are the preferred type for location recording. It's hard to create good bass in a small sealed area, so they seldom are very accurate in the low end. But they're great at revealing problems during a voice recording.

These headphones have to be fairly large and press against the head tightly, so they're usually not comfortable for longtime use.

- Open, or vented, headphones have soft, porous foam pads that rest against the ear. Air molecules are free to flow around the pads, so the headphones can produce much more accurate sound. This also makes them fairly transparent to outside noises. Announcers generally prefer this type because a little of their natural voice can be heard in the room, along with their amplified voice from the mic. Announcers also like these headphones because they're more comfortable during long sessions. Sizes vary from the tiny ones sold with portable players—even earbuds have an open design because they don't seal themselves in the ear canal—to very large models preferred by studio musicians.

Monitor Switching

Any good studio recording console has a mono test switch, which temporarily combines the stereo channels and routes them to both speakers. This is essential because phase problems can make parts of a mix sound hollow, or even disappear completely, for mono listeners. While it would be easy to add this function to software, I don't know of any mainstream program—audio or video—that does.

You can buy elaborate switching matrixes that include mono test buttons, but they're expensive. Or you can build one with a little bit of soldering and about $10 worth of parts. Use the circuit in Figure 3.8. When the switch is up, the stereo output of your NLE or mixer goes directly to

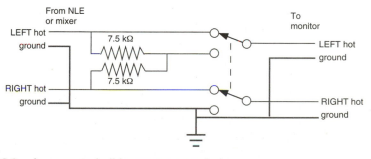

3.8   An easy-to-build stereo test switch.

the monitor amplifier. When the switch is down, the signals are combined through 7.5 kΩ resistors and are routed to only one side of the monitors; the other side is silenced. The resistors present a high enough impedance that there's very little leakage between channels in stereo mode.

Telephone Monitoring

It's often convenient to play a music selection or interview edit over the phone to clients. The quality won't be wonderful, but they can judge content and discuss it with you in real time. Holding your phone next to a monitor speaker is awkward and unprofessional. Unless your studio has perfect acoustics, a speakerphone will pick up more echo than track; the result can be unintelligible. The best solution is a direct connection from your mixer or NLE to the phone system.

You can buy a simple phone coupler from a broadcast supply house for about $100. Or you can build one with the simple circuit shown in Figure 3.9. The transformer is a Radio Shack #273-1069, which costs less than three dollars. It adapts a unbalanced headphone feed to the balanced phone system and isolates the phone line from your local ground to prevent noise. The capacitor keeps the phone line's DC component out of the transformer. Most headphone feeds are just the right voltage to work well in this circuit; adjust your equipment's volume control to get a reasonable level without distortion.

If you want to record something over the phone, this circuit works just as well in reverse. Simply plug the circuit into an unbalanced line input on a mixer or recorder. Your voice, breathing, and any noises in the room will be about 20 dB louder than the caller's—that's how the signal actually appears on the phone line. For best results, use a phone with a mute button and turn your end off while the other person is speaking.

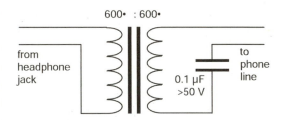

3.9 An even easier-to-build phone coupler.

Or buy a phone *hybrid* for about $500; it uses a phase-inversion circuit to balance both ends of the conversation.

Metering

Good speakers will tell you a lot about spectral balance, noise, and distortion. But human beings aren't good judges of volume, and your perception of it can change from moment to moment. Metering is particularly important if you're producing for broadcast. TV stations are very strict about the volume they send to their transmitters. Networks even insist on specific ranges in their program contracts. Broadcasters have automatic equipment to regulate loudness, but nonstandard tapes often end up distorted or noisy. If you're producing for home VHS or the Web, there's a little more flexibility, but you still want to verify that signals are loud enough to avoid noise, while you stay away from overloads during the mix.

While the metering in current NLEs is much better than it used to be, some programs still don't have a way to accurately gauge what you're digitizing or to tell if a mix is too hot. Other programs may have meters, but they're not reliable or easy to use because of hardware limitations or sloppy programming. One major issue is that NLE designers often don't understand meter response time.

Back in analog days, distortion was proportional to volume. Equipment was designed so that nominal levels didn't distort too badly. Overloads would start to distort more, but if they weren't too loud and were over quickly, the distortion wouldn't be too noticeable. This worked nicely with the way we hear: it takes a moment for us to judge volume, and very fast sounds don't seem as loud as they really are. *VU* (volume unit) meters were invented with both these facts in mind. They had mechanical provisions to limit how fast the needle could move: a proper VU meter would take 0.3 second to move from one side of the scale to the other. The scale was calibrated with 0 VU at the nominal level and then calibrated in decibels above and below zero. Distortion wasn't a problem for signals below that level, so a good mix would stay at zero as much as possible.

But digital signals max out at 0 dBFS. If a signal reaches that level for even a single sample, the waveform may be distorted. If there are three or four samples above 0 dBFS (they're called *overs*) in a row, there's a good probability[5] it's unusable. The only way to deal with this is with a meter than can respond instantly. Good digital meters go from zero to full scale in a matter of microseconds and are described as *peak-reading* rather than VU. Peak-reading meters are designed to fall back more slowly, on the order of one-tenth of a second, so you can actually see the peaks. The best ones will leave the top light on for a few seconds (so you can read its level) while the rest of the column goes back to normal operation.

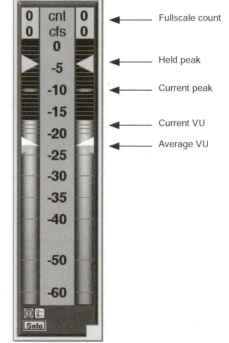

3.10 A good level meter combines peak and VU functions.

Unfortunately, response time isn't how we hear isn't how we hear. You need peak-reading to catch overloads and something like VU ballistics to judge perceived volume. Good audio level meters combine these functions and use multiple colors or brightness to show average, peak, and maximum levels simultaneously. Figure 3.10 shows the level meter in SpectraFoo, an audio analysis system for the Mac.

Unfortunately, NLE meters are seldom designed with this kind of sophistication, and you might not have the processing power to run a separate metering program while using mixing. A reasonable solution can be an external meter like the Radio Design Labs RU-SM16 in Figure 3.12. It's

5. *May* be distorted? *Probability* there's a problem? By definition, a digital signal can't be even the teeniest slice of a decibel over 0 dBFS, so there's no way for the software to know when there's been an overload—it could be just a very loud, but undistorted, signal. However, real-world waveforms almost never have flat tops or bottoms that would keep the signal that loud for longer than a sample or two. So if there's a series of readings at 0 dBFS, we make the assumption something is wrong.

about $200 and can be switched between VU and peak mode. Hook it up to your computer or tape deck output and calibrate it to your normal working level. A more comprehensive solution, but still cheaper than devoting a separate computer to metering, is the simultaneous peak/loudness/maximum Dorrough unit in Figure 3.13. The manufacturer developed its own algorithm for determining the relationship between loudness and time, which is similar to a VU meter's but more accurate. These products cost money, but like loudspeakers, are an investment that'll be usable for decades.

3.11 Cheap voltmeters disguised as VU meters.

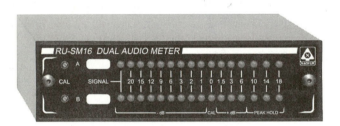

3.12 A relatively low-cost but accurate external meter.

3.13 A comprehensive but more expensive external meter.

⚠ *Gotcha*

Most VU meters aren't. Very few companies make mechanical meters with true VU ballistics any more, and they charge a lot for their product if they do. These precision instruments are usually found only on high-end studio equipment.

More often, the things that *look* like VU meters are cheap voltmeters with random time characteristics. This happens even in serious professional video gear costing thousands of dollars (see Figure 3.11). These toy meters are too fast to indicate loudness but too slow to catch peaks that could overload a digital system. Don't rely on them.

Chapter 4

The Studio: Equipment and Wiring

Remember this:

- There are specialized gadgets you can add to your system, to improve both your sound and your working life. Many of these gadgets don't appear in video catalogs.

- Audio comes in a lot of different voltages and signal formats and often use the same connectors. Just because a plug *fits*, don't assume it'll work right. Consult this chapter whenever you're not sure.

- It's hardware. It will break. But many hardware problems can be fixed without a soldering iron.

Hardware for Audio

Aside from the computer, a basic postproduction system doesn't need more than the accurate monitoring described in the last chapter. But some other gadgets can be helpful, even in simple setups, and may be essential as your work gets more sophisticated.

In Chapter 3, we discussed how monitor systems don't become obsolete the way computers do. Moore's Law—capacity doubles and cost halves every 18 months—doesn't apply. The same rule works for other audio hardware. Many microphones outlive the studios that originally bought them. Even relatively high-tech items like CD players and digital mixers don't depend on cutting-edge technology; they'll stay productive until their mechanical parts break down. The bottom line? This stuff is an investment. Choose accordingly.

⚠ **Gotcha** _____

So what brand and model should I buy? This chapter describes hardware that can make your projects easier and sound better. With some guidelines regarding price, I've tried to describe what's available and what features to ask for. But I can't predict which units will be best for your purposes on the day you're ready to buy. Check an impartial source like *DV* magazine or DV.com for current information and reviews.[1]

_____
1. Full disclosure: I write for *DV*. But I can attest its reviews are impartial.

Audio Input /Output

You could probably create a complete film without ever plugging an audio cable into your computer. Dialog can be imported with picture via FireWire; music and sound effects can be ripped from CDs or downloaded from the Web. This is good because the audio inputs on many PCs are of dubious quality. Some don't have any at all.

But most filmmakers will also need sound from sources that aren't computer friendly, like microphones or an analog video deck. You could use your camera as an audio-to-FireWire converter, but its mic preamp probably contributes significant noise, and automatic level controls will destroy a sound's dynamics. It's far better to install a high-quality way to get sound into the computer.

If you're making mix or processing decisions, you also want a high-quality way to take analog sound *out*. Otherwise, you may not be able to trust your monitors. Many generic sound cards are noisy, have high-frequency problems, or distort on loud but otherwise clean signals. Track 10 of this book's CD is designed to reveal some of these issues.

Hear for yourself

Track 10 contains voice, music,[1] and test signals designed to reveal deficiencies in a digital audio output. Instructions in the track tell you what to listen for. Play it through your computer's CD-ROM drive (or use a ripped file version). It may help to also play it as a reference with a good CD player connected to the same monitors.

The analog audio outputs on most FireWire cameras are even worse than generic sound cards; don't even think about using a camera for critical monitoring. Fortunately, it's easy—and relatively inexpensive—to add studio-quality inputs and outputs (I/O) to any modern computer. The traditional way is to install a third-party sound card with driver software. Excellent-sounding internal PCI cards start around $400 at music and broadcast supply stores and can include features like XLR balanced audio, AES/EBU or s/pdif, and MIDI or SMPTE timecode support.[2] You can even get them with multiple outputs, which work with multitrack audio programs to feed simultaneous tracks to a mixer. If you're editing on a laptop, look for an analog I/O adapter in PC card format.

But the industry is moving away from cards, and toward small boxes or rack panels that connect via USB and FireWire. These boxes offer the same features, sometimes for less money. They can

---

1. "Finding Your Way" (C. Glassfield, DWCD226/2), "Elizabethan Fantasy" (F. Silkstone/N. Parker, DWCD128/38). From the DeWolfe Music Library, protected by copyright and used by permission. More about this library in Chapter 10.

2. All these connection standards are described later in this chapter.

have higher sound quality because they're away from the electrically noisy motherboard of a computer. The simple connection makes the boxes easy to install or switch between computers.

> ⚠️ **Gotcha** _____
>
> **When good I/O goes bad.** These audio I/O devices don't wear out, and their connection schemes are more or less universal. So you can keep using the same one when you upgrade computers.
>
> Driver software, on the other hand, can become obsolete overnight. A CPU change or even an operating system upgrade may cause problems ranging from occasional static to complete failure. Audio hardware manufacturers try to keep on top of these issues. Check their Web sites any time you upgrade your system.

A few USB devices combine analog and digital audio I/O with remote controls for mixing and editing, offering physical (rather than virtual, on-screen) volume faders, jog/shuttle knobs, and transport buttons. While they require compatible software—some are bundled with multitrack audio editors—the extra controls are considerably faster to use than a mouse and they are worth the investment.

Reading the specs

There are serious differences in analog quality among the various audio I/O devices on the market. Check the specs, particularly for:

Frequency response.[3]   Look for three separate numbers: upper and lower frequency limits, and a volume range in dB. A spec like 20 Hz–20 kHz ± 2 dB is good for an audio I/O system running at 48 kHz s/r. Be sure the spec refers to the complete chain from analog to computer and back; it's useless if it just refers to one side or the other. Frequency response is dependent on sample rate; make sure you're reading it for the one you'll be using most. If the rate isn't specified, assume the manufacturer used the highest one the card supports.

Distortion.   Again, the spec should include the complete chain. The analog side should be running at its rated nominal level. Distortion is usually expressed as a percentage (less than 0.01 percent is very good; as low as 0.003 percent is common in pro systems) and may be specified at a single frequency like 1 kHz.

Oversampling is a technique that increases high frequency accuracy and lowers high-frequency distortion; you'll find it in the best cards.

Signal to noise ratio or dynamic range.   16-bit audio is theoretially capable of 96 dB between full scale and noise, and this is sometimes referred to as *dynamic range*. *Signal to noise* (s/n)

---

3. Not the same as frequency *range*, which is a meaningless marketing term.

refers to the difference between the nominal signal and the noise floor in decibels. In digital video, the nominal level is –20 dBFS for pro equipment and somewhere around –12 dBFS for consumer; if you subtract that from the dynamic range, you get the s/n. The difference between nominal and 0 dBFS (or full scale less a safety margin) is the *headroom*. A dynamic range of 90 dB is considered very good for 16-bit systems. One of 70 dB is marginal.

Many I/O systems today are designed for 24-bit audio, which can achieve a theoretical dynamic range of 144 dB on the digital side. But analog circuits haven't caught up and even the best 24-bit cards rarely exceed 100 dB from input to output. 24-bit audio is pretty much reserved for professional applications. As of this writing, even the high-priced NLEs used to cut feature films don't support 24-bit audio.

Digital I/O

In theory, there shouldn't be any difference between how two I/O systems handle a s/pdif or AES/EBU digital audio stream. That's usually true in the lab. The real challenge is how well the unit does with less than perfect digital in the studio. If your other equipment has problems—or even if you use the wrong kind of cable—the digital information can be compromised. Well-designed circuits can pull a signal out anyway and produce perfect audio. But many midlevel digital input systems can't; the result can be subtle damage to the stereo field, periodic clicking or high-frequency hash mixed with the signal, or total silence.

Unfortunately, you won't find any specs to compare digital I/O performance. The best you can do is look at the analog specs: Assume a device without good analog numbers is digitally sloppy as well.

Mixer

Most DV filmmakers who do their own mixes, do it in software. But a low-cost hardware mixer can still be useful:

- It lets you select among multiple analog sources like a MiniDisc portable, VHS deck, or synthesizer, and lets you adjust levels prior to digitizing.

- It can provide balanced XLR inputs that work with professional mics for narration recording and dialog replacement.

- It can let you adjust NLE output levels, and can provide gentle equalization before dubbing to an analog deck, without having to re-render.

- You may even decide to use it as a mixer! When you're auditioning music, put a CD player on one set of inputs and your NLE timeline or source footage on another. That way, you can hear how well the proposed music works with your video—without wasting the time to transfer or render anything.

Analog mixers with a couple of balanced mic and a few unbalanced line inputs are available at music stores and start around $100. As the price goes up, expect more flexibility, cleaner sound, and varying degrees of field-worthiness, which might make the costlier mixers useful for production audio.

Digital mixers always have both digital and analog audio I/O. Starting around $1,000, they cost more than analog mixers. Most offer programmability—you can store libraries of configurations or equalization settings which saves setup time and makes the sound easier to match if you rework a project. If you're going to mix multiple tracks in hardware, look for a digital mixer with automation and built-in processors like compressors and echo. These digital mixers can save time and money.

Analog and digital mixers are rated with the same kind of specs as audio I/O cards, and the information in the previous section applies.

Selecting and Routing Signals

As you gather more equipment, keeping the right pieces connected can get complex. Reaching behind the gear and replugging every time you change functions is more than time-consuming; it can wear out the connectors. A mixer large enough to handle every signal combination can get expensive.

Patchbays

These panels, found in every recording and broadcast studio, simply extend the various equipment connections and keep them in one convenient place. Even low-cost ones (often under $70 at music stores) can have rugged 1/4-inch jacks, which last longer and provide a better connection than the miniature or phono jacks on your equipment. Low-cost patchbays usually have jacks on both front and back, so they can be installed easily with premade cables. Studio versions may use solder or data-style punchblock connections for higher reliability. Matching patchcords to connect the front jacks are usually only a few dollars each—less in multiple packs.

Most consumer patchbays *normal* their connections. When no cord is plugged in, vertical pairs of jacks are connected internally. As soon as you plug in the patchcord, this connection is broken. An example appears in Figure 4.1; the NLE's output is on the top row and monitor amp's input right below it; normally, the editor's signal is directed to the speakers. If you need to make a VHS copy, you could run a cord from NLE output to tape in—breaking the normal—and another from tape output to monitor in. Figure 4.1 shows how it works.

Most patchbays include *half normals* that break the connection only when you plug into one jack of the pair. The other jack lets you tap the signal, sending it to both the patchcord and the normalled device—highly useful if you're dubbing to two analog decks simultaneously. Because modern equipment generally has much higher impedance at the input than the output, the two

4.1 Internally normalled connections *(top)* disconnect when you use a patchcord *(bottom)*. Often, all the upper/lower pairs in a patchbay are internally normalled.

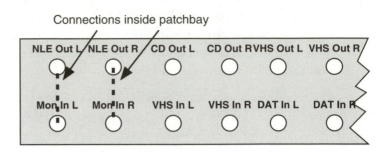

Connections inside patchbay

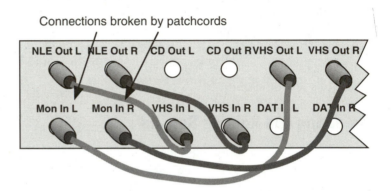

Connections broken by patchcords

devices won't interfere. You can also do the same thing with a Y-connector, or in some cases, with a simple, molded dual-headphone adapter; engineers call this function a *mult*. You'll get distortion or signal loss if you try to mult two outputs to a single input, or mult older transformer-coupled audio devices.

Watch those half normals! If you plug a signal into a jack that doesn't break a connection, you could be inadvertently multing two outputs: the intended one, and the unbroken normalled one. Even if the unintentional device is silent, it'll still drag signal levels down or cause distortion. Plug a cord into the other jack in that pair—it doesn't matter where the other end goes—to break the normal.

> ⚠ **Gotcha** _____
>
> **Normally howling.** When you're setting up a normalled patchbay, don't put any device's input and output on the same vertical row. It may look neater that way, but the normals will cause feedback. Instead, offset them as I did in Figure 4.1.

Digital router

Digital audio signals operate at very high frequencies and won't work reliably in a standard patchbay. They also require matched impedance, so standard multing is impossible. The usual solution to both problems is a digital audio router, which uses internal buffers to feed any input to any combination of outputs. Routers start around $300 for six input and output channels.

Digital audio puts both channels of a stereo signal on a single wire, so a 6×6 router actually handles 12 simultaneous audio streams.

Generators

Digital audio is a serial signal where each bit of the audio and some control information is transmitted sequentially. The boxes on each end have to agree which bit means what. Many devices today will delay an incoming signal until it matches the internal clock, but if bitstreams get too far out of sync, clicking can result. Most equipment lets you select the input as an actual clock source; this prevents clicking, but any time variation (*jitter*) in the incoming signal can cause distortion. A better solution, found in most professional audio setups, is to distribute a more reliable *word clock* signal on a separate wire. This is a constant heartbeat at the sample rate, or occasionally 256× the sample rate (*superclock)*. Word clock generators vary from a few hundred to a few thousand dollars, depending on their precision and ability to work with high-resolution audio formats. They can also be free—some devices have a word clock output along with their digital audio connections. If the word clock generator's internal crystal is reliable enough, it's worth calling it the Master and distributing its signal.

Most professional digital video decks need the audio sample rate to be synchronized with the frame rate. If a serial audio word doesn't start at exactly the right time relative to a frame, the deck won't record. Good word clock generators have a video reference input for this reason. Connect it to the same blackburst or house sync as your video equipment, or to the sync reference output of the video deck.

A separate SMPTE timecode generator used to be an essential in audio post, but isn't any more. Most devices that read or sync to timecode can also generate it. But if you're going to be using a timecode generator to keep audio and video together, be sure it's also locked to a video sync signal, otherwise the timecode words will drift relative to the frame rate, causing massive problems down the line. This possibility rules out using most MIDI equipment as a timecode source for digital video.

A few *synchronizers* such as MOTU's Digital Timepiece have the ability to generate word clock, SMPTE timecode, MIDI timecode, video reference, and special sync signals for digital multitracks, locked to either an internal clock or an input signal in any of those formats. This kind of versatility may be necessary if you're trying to connect digital audio, music software, and video decks together in complex post suites. These devices have little in common with older timecode synchronizers, which kept analog tape recorders in sync with video and are now largely obsolete.

An audio tone generator also used to be considered essential to create pure and steady signals at different frequencies for equipment testing and level calibration. These days, most desktop audio programs can generate tones as files and then play them. Fully-equipped audio post suites will have tone generators built into their mixers or effects units. If all you need is a 1 kHz tone for color bars, check your NLE's documentation; it may be built into the Print to Video function. Test tones on audio CDs are also useful and this book's disc provides a few.

Hear for yourself

Not really for your listening pleasure. Tracks 11 through 13 are steady tones, 30 seconds each, at –20 dBFS (network standard lineup level): 100 Hz, 1 kHz, 10 kHz. Track 14 is a 1 kHz tone at –12 dBFS, which may be more appropriate if you're producing for Web or CD-ROM.

Recorders and Players

Many desktop filmmakers use DAT or MiniDisc in the field. But miniature consumer portables often have poor analog output circuits, and you can lose quality just by dubbing from recorder to computer. If you're using this kind of recorder, consider investing in a full-size AC-powered deck only for playback. Or get a higher-quality portable that can connect to your computer digitally and use it in the field as well.

DAT, MiniDisc, and CD speed is usually locked to an internal crystal, which makes it stable enough to use for sync sound over the short term without timecode. Crystal quality varies, but it's reasonable to expect no more than one frame of error over 15 minutes. (Low-cost portable CD recorders are starting to appear on the market as this is being written, and I can see them becoming standard for event and high-quality dialog recording.)

Audio cassette and most open-reel tape decks are useless for sync sound because their speed isn't stable and very few of them sound as good as a modern MiniDisc recorder. You may need a cassette deck to make audio-only copies for transcribing interviews or client review, though burning an audio CD in a CDR drive is certainly faster.

Timecode DAT and DTRS Digital 8 track (also known as DA-8) are the current standard formats for audio interchange in video and film production. If you're doing high-end work with other studios or supplying alternate-language mixes for networks, you'll need to support them; expect to pay more than $10,000 for the two. ADAT Digital 8 track is used by many music studios (and is considerably cheaper); you may need one of these decks if you're working a lot with musicians. But if you don't have an immediate and long-term need, put off buying any tape-based audio format.

24-track hard drive recorders are becoming a standard in music studios and may soon work their way into video post. These work like a tape recorder in that all the tracks are available for recording or playback at once, they have tape transport controls, and most will sync to SMPTE timecode. But the hard drive recorders primarily use computer components which bring the price down. Some let you copy their drives to low-cost DVD media for backup and interchange.

Multitrack portable hard drive recorders are the latest thing in feature film sound. They use standard file formats and can output DVDs. But even if you're doing high-end post, you probably won't need one.

Other Hardware

MIDI interfaces connect a computer to music equipment which let you play musical notes or sound effects precisely or edit a keyboard performance on-screen. The interfaces are frequently connected to *samplers*, audio recorders designed for precise manipulation and playback of very short sounds. This kind of equipment is seldom found in desktop audio post setups, but is considered essential in creative audio post suites.

Test equipment such as oscilloscopes or distortion analyzers are worthwhile only if you know how to use them. But there are two pieces of low-cost electronic test equipment worth considering for any facility:

- A volt/ohm meter with a continuity buzzer (such as Radio Shack's #22-802, $25) will let you check cables, batteries, and wall-wart power supplies easily. Replace these things when they go bad, and you'll eliminate a lot of expensive service calls.

- A sound level meter (Radio Shack #33-2050, $35) will keep your monitoring honest by checking the sound pressure level (see Chapter 2) while you work. There's a tendency to start pushing speakers louder and louder as the day wears on, changing how you hear the audio spectrum and making good equalization or mix decisions harder. Use a meter to check the volume of typical home setups, kiosks, or however your mixes are heard and set your monitors to match. If you're mixing for theatrical or auditorium release, standard level is 85 dB SPL at the mix position, for a single speaker playing a test tone at nominal level.

Wiring for Audio Post

The computer world has come a long way. Our first home machine used identical DB-9 connectors for mouse and printer, and you could find that same plug on a videogame's joystick, some modem cables, and the VTR control interfaces where I worked. Nobody could tell just by looking at a plug what kind of circuit it would work with.

What a change in less than two decades! Today you can take just about any FireWire- or USB-equipped peripheral—camera, disk drive, printer, mp3 player, or anything else—plug it into a matching jack on a computer or hub and be pretty sure it'll work.

Audio is still in the dark ages. Physically identical connectors can be used for widely different kinds of signals. Connecting them the wrong way can result in damaged equipment, missing audio, and mysterious other problems that are hard to diagnose. You sometimes can't even tell, looking at a jack, which of several varieties of plug it's designed for. Occasionally the only cure is to examine the equipment manuals. But there is some rationality. If you learn to identify the various connectors, understand the different electrical standards involved, and apply some common sense based on the kind of equipment, there's a good chance you'll connect with success.

Common Connectors

Prosumer gear usually has small connectors because they're cheap. Pro equipment has bigger ones because these are more reliable and make a better connection. Here's a hierarchy of connectors, with some tips about each.

Mini-plugs

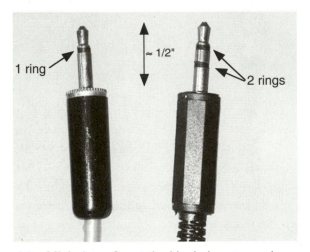

1 ring

≈ 1/2"

2 rings

4.2   Mini-plugs. Count the black rings to see how many conductors.

Mini-plugs come in 2- and 3-conductor versions. You can tell the difference by counting the insulation rings: there'll be just one on a 2-conductor plug, and 2 on a 3-conductor plug (Figure 4.2). Unfortunately, 2- and 3-conductor jacks look identical from the outside.

The 2-conductor versions are invariably used for mono, unbalanced signals. The 3-conductor ones are often used for stereo—the tip and ring carry left and right, and the sleeve is a common signal return. But some wireless mics and transformer adapters used in the field have balanced connections on 3-conductor minis. Plugging an unbalanced stereo signal into a balanced input can cause strange anomalies, including low-frequency loss or even the disappearance of a musical soloist in a recording. But if you plug a *2-conductor* unbalanced signal into a 3-conductor balanced input, things will probably work fine: the jack's ring contact presses against the plug's sleeve, completing the circuit.

Mini-jacks are not very reliable. The electrical contact area isn't very big to begin with, and when the tiny springs begin to loosen, the jacks can fail utterly. Unless a piece of equipment and its cables are absolutely not going to move, it's a good idea to provide some kind of strain relief. A wire tie to a convenient bracket or a piece of tape holding the cable in place can prevent stresses that wear out the springs. Mini-jacks on field equipment can be extra-vulnerable because the springs get stressed every time you plug in for a new setup. A short extension cable with a mini-plug and mini-jack more or less permanently attached to the equipment, can be a lifesaver. When the extension cable's jack wears out from constant use, throw it away and attach a new one.

Mini-plugs are nominally 3.5 mm in diameter. This is slightly larger than 1/8 inch, which a few manufacturers use instead. While the two varieties are usually interchangeable, when a 3.5 mm jack starts to wear out you'll notice it sooner if you're using 1/8-inch plugs.

You may come across 2.5 mm minis. This is a different standard rarely used for audio.

For most of the 90s, Apple Computer used a modified mini-jack on their audio inputs; it had a third conductor, beyond the reach of a normal plug. Its PlainTalk microphones had an extra-long plug and used that contact for power.

Phono or RCA connectors

RCA connectors have a spring shell about 3/8 inches in diameter, and a single pin (Figure 4.3). They're used for shielded, unbalanced connections where the shell continues the shield. While they're more reliable than mini-plugs, phono jacks use a bent steel inner conductor which wraps around the pin. If the steel weakens at the bend, the connection can become intermittent, and there's no way to repair it from outside. Phono plugs shouldn't be used in situations that require constant replugging.

Unlike mini-plugs and phone plugs, the shielding on phono plugs makes them suitable at frequencies far above the audio range. They can be used for consumer video and s/pdif digital audio.

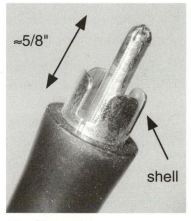

4.3 Phono plug.

1/4 inch or phone plugs

The 1/4 inch is the mini's big brother. They look similar but are twice the diameter and slightly more than twice as long (Figure 4.4). Phone plugs also come in 2- and 3-conductor versions. The 3-conductor ones are used for unbalanced stereo signals and balanced mono ones; the mini-plug warning about plugging balanced into unbalanced applies here too. Some mixers use 3-conductor jacks in a bidirectional mode as insert points for connecting effects to individual channels. The tip sends a signal to the effect, and the ring returns it. When no effect is attached, an internal normal completes the circuit.

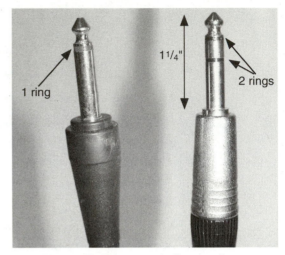

4.4   Phone plugs have a similar conductor arrangement.

The larger size makes a big difference in their reliability and 1/4 inch plugs are appropriate for almost any application that doesn't require a latch to keep plug and jack together. They rarely fail after repeated connections, which is why most prosumer patchbays use them.

Somewhat smaller *Bantam* plugs, 0.173 inches in diameter, are sometimes used in professional patch bays because you can fit more in the same area. You may also come across 0.206-inch jacks on obsolete equipment. A broadcast supplier or electronics wholesaler can sell you matching connectors.

XLR

XLR plugs have shells 3/4 inches in diameter and can be three or four inches long including their strain relief. A plug or jack can be male (pins) or female (sockets). Most female versions have a latching arrangement to keep it from being accidentally disconnected; you have to squeeze a button on the plug, or depress a tab on the jack, to remove the male. See Figures 4.5 and 4.6.

XLRs provide a secure and conductive connection and are preferred for almost all professional applications. The most common configuration is 3-conductor, for balanced wiring with a shield. Socket 1 of the female is slightly raised to engage first, so pin 1 is always used for the shield. Most modern equipment uses pin 2 for the "hot" side of a balanced pair or the main conductor of an unbalanced connection; older gear might not follow this arrangement. It usually doesn't matter. Similarly, males are almost always used for outputs and females for inputs, but that wasn't always the case.

4.5 XLR male and female plugs.

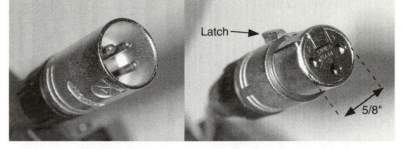

4.6 XLR panel jacks: latching female *(left),* non-latching female *(middle),* and male *(right).*

⚠️ *Gotcha* _____

XLR does not mean balanced analog audio. Catalogs sometimes treat the two terms as synonyms, but unless you're talking about microphones, it's not the case. Some manufacturers install XLR connectors to make their equipment look more professional but charge extra if you actually want balanced circuits. Other manufacturers use 3-conductor phone jacks for balanced audio to save space on the panel. AES/EBU, the standard professional format for digital audio, uses balanced XLR connectors to move very high-speed data.

XLRs are sometimes called *Cannon* connectors after the company that first made them. They're available with more than three pins for stereo, intercom, and power use.

BNC

Just as professional video uses the more reliable BNC connector instead of phono plugs, many audio pros use BNCs for s/pdif digital audio. Pros will either replace the phono jacks with BNCs or permanently crimp BNC adapters onto the equipment.

Toslink and mini-plug optical

Digital audio can use fiber optics instead of wire to transmit a signal. Toslink and mini-plug optical connectors are frequently found on consumer stereo equipment and some prosumer multitracks. Toslink plugs have a black plastic shell that sticks into the jack and keeps things secure; a short pin with a clear end protrudes and transmits the light. You can get cheap adapters to convert a Toslink cable to an optical mini-plug.

Computer connectors

Some multichannel analog or digital connections use DB-25 plugs to save money and space. Wiring specs are at the whim of the manufacturer. Consult the manual or buy manufacturer-approved adapter cables which fan out to phone or XLR plugs. Since the wiring scheme will be different for analog and digital, make sure your adapter is for the right application.

Cross-Connecting Balanced and Unbalanced Audio

Balanced wiring won't do any good unless the equipment at both ends is designed for it. If either end is unbalanced, the noise resistance goes away. If most of your equipment is already balanced, or your facility is very complicated or includes long cable runs, it makes sense to keep things the way they are and adapt the nonbalanced devices. This will keep the sound as clean as possible, preventing line-borne noise and ground loops. The most common solution to balancing nonbalanced equipment is an electronic adapter; thse also compensate for the voltage difference between consumer unbalanced and professional balanced gear (described in the next section). Ask for something called a *balancing*, *impedance*, or *level matching* adapter—it goes by all three names.[4] Good ones cost between $50–$150 per channel, depending on features and whether it has XLR connectors or screw terminals. More expensive units aren't necessary.

But if wiring runs are short and the studio isn't very complicated, you can usually mix balanced and unbalanced devices just by wiring them correctly. This unbalances the entire cable, so you may need to route it away from power and video lines to prevent noise. This kind of direct connection also doesn't compensate for level differences; to do this, see the next section. Tables 4.1 and 4.2 explain the wiring.

Table 4.1   Feeding an unbalanced output to a balanced input.

Unbalanced Output	Balanced Input		
	Wire	XLR Plug	3-conductor Phone
Signal (pin or tip)	+ (red or white)	pin 2	tip
Ground (sleeve)	– (black or clear)	pin 3	ring*
No connection	shield	pin 1	sleeve

> * Most balanced phone jack inputs are designed so this connection happens automatically when you plug in an unbalanced 2-conductor plug.

---

4. Even though impedance usually has nothing to do with it, as you'll learn in a few pages.

⚠ **Gotcha** _____

The case of the occasionally disappearing signal. A weird situation can come about when a balanced mono signal is sent to a stereo unbalanced input. If the adapter is not wired properly, both sides of the stereo pair will hear the signal perfectly—except one side will be inverted with a negative voltage when the other side is positive. Casual monitoring over stereo speakers or headphones won't show that there's anything wrong. But if the stereo track is played in mono, the signal will cancel itself and disappear!

This may seem unlikely, but I get at least half a dozen emails a year asking me to explain where a track went, or why the music stayed, but the announcer went away. The usual culprit is a premade adapter or cable with a 3-conductor phone or mini-plug on one end, and either a similar plug or two RCA plugs on the other.

Don't assume that just because an adapter *fits*, it's doing the right thing to your signal. And always check stereo tracks in mono (see Chapter 3).

In Table 4.1, ground on the balanced input is not connected to ground on the unbalanced output. Most adapters are not wired this way, but this provides a *telescoping shield* with a little more noise immunity (also discussed in "Guerilla Problem Solving," starting on page 80).

Table 4.2   Feeding a balanced output to an unbalanced input.

	Balanced Output		Unbalanced Input
Wire	XLR Jack	3-conductor Phone	
+ (red or white)	pin 2	tip	Signal (pin or tip)
– (black or clear)	pin 3	ring	No connection*
shield	pin 1	sleeve	Ground (sleeve)

* This is appropriate for modern, electronically balanced outputs. Transformer-balanced outputs might not show any signal unless its conductor is connected to ground.

Voltage and Impedance Standards

Line-level voltages

Line-level voltages started back in the heyday of radio broadcasting. The national networks had to agree with the telephone company, who actually carried network programming cross-country, exactly how much power a signal should have when it left the studio. Too much and the phone company's equipment would distort the signal. Too little and the signal would get noisy. Exactly 1/1,000 watt was chosen as a convenient standard. Audio power levels could now be specified as *dBm* (decibels compared to a milliwatt).

Wattage is a function of voltage and impedance and is difficult to read directly. But phone lines and radio equipment had a standard 600Ω impedance, which always produces 0.775 volts at 1 milliwatt. So *Volume Unit* meters were designed to read 0 VU when they saw 0.775 volts at 1 milliwatt. If a program hovered just under 0 VU, with only occasional peaks over, broadcasters knew they were delivering both a consistent loudness to their audience and a safe milliwatt to the phone company.

The new meters were nifty. But broadcasters soon discovered that when they connected the meters directly across a line, the internal rectifiers distorted the signal. The meters had to be isolated by a resistor, which also dropped the signal 4 dB. Instead of getting meters that were 4 dB more sensitive, broadcasters announced that in *their world* +4 dBm = 0 VU. This became the pro audio standard until the early 1970s. VU meters were always hooked up with that resistor and almost all equipment was designed with 600 Ω connections to match.

About 30 years ago, modern circuits that didn't need careful impedance matching became popular. 600Ω wiring was abandoned in most studios—meaning that a milliwatt could be almost any voltage. But those VU meters were both an investment and a way of life. They still worked fine, but nobody could say they were calibrated exactly to +4 dBm. So rather than design a new meter, the standard was changed slightly to consider only the voltage. The measurement couldn't be called dBm any more—milliwatts aren't involved—so now we have *dBu* (*decibels unterminated*). The historical standard of +4 dBm at 600Ω equals exactly 1.228 volts, so that's what oday's pro equipment kicks out when the meter reads 0 VU. The original weird voltage became the +4 dBu standard, or simply *line level*—but only for professionals.

But while pro equipment originally used 600Ω transformers, hi-fi and other consumer equipment saved money by connecting directly to the electron tubes, which had much higher impedances. The dBm spec wasn't relevant to consumer equipment, so there was no reason to keep its reference. Instead, the more rational *dBV* was created—decibels referred to exactly one volt. As it happens, tubes work best with an input around one-third volt, 10 dB less than the standard. −10 decibels referred to one volt became the consumer line level: first for hi-fis, then for home tape recorders, then VCRs, then miniDV.

These two voltage standards evolved in parallel. Neither has any particular advantage in modern equipment, but there's a big installed-base for both, and manufacturers had to keep them both alive. And *that's* why, when you plug a pro deck into a computer or other prosumer input, it usually dis-

> ⚠️ **Gotcha** _____
>
> *−10 dBV and +4 dBu aren't 14 dB apart!* The two standards for 0 VU are based on different decibel references, so you can't directly compare one to the other. But they both use the same physics and math, so there's a definite relationship. I crunched the numbers for you in Table 4.3.

torts. Or why when you dub directly from a miniDV camera to BetaSP, the track is 11.78 dB too soft.

Table 4.3   Comparing prosumer dBV and professional dBu.

	Prosumer/ Consumer World	Voltmeter	Professional World	
	+6 dBV	2.0 v	+8.2 dBu*	
	+4 dBV	1.6 v	6.2 dBu	
	+1.78 dBV	1.228 v	+4 dBu	(Pro 0 VU)
	0 dBV	1 v	+2.2 dBu	
	–2.2 dBV	.775 v	0 dBu	
	–6 dBV	.5 v	–3.8 dBu	
(Consumer 0 VU)	–10 dBV	.316 v	–7.8 dBu	
	–20 dBV	.01 v	–17.8 dBu	

* Or dBm at 600Ω.

A quick glance at Table 4.3 shows you a couple of other handy rules—cutting any voltage in half changes it by –6 dB, doubling it is +6 dB, and changing it by 10 dB means a voltage ratio of about 3:1.

Cross-connecting consumer and pro line-level

Along with the differences in voltage, pro line-level connections are almost always balanced, and consumer ones are unbalanced. So the easiest way to deal with both incompatibilities at the same time is to use a level-matching adapter, described previously. But if you don't really need balanced wiring, you may be able to save some money.

Professional gear might have enough range to handle the –10 dBV signal without too much noise. Connect it according to Table 4.1, turn up the input volume, and see if you can get a decent meter reading. Resist the temptation to turn up unbalanced devices' *output volume* to compensate. This will almost always cause distortion. If you don't get appropriate levels by adjusting only the pro gear, use a level-matching adapter.

The pro-to-consumer connection is a little trickier. You need a couple of resistors to create a 6 dB loss—you lose another 6 dB throwing away half the balanced signal—and then either use the volume control to make up that missing 0.22 dB, or don't worry about it. Get two 1 kΩ resistors (Radio Shack #271-1321) for each

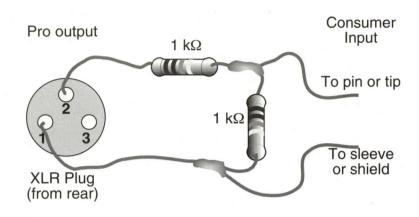

4.7 A couple of common resistors can convert +4 dBu balanced to an almost perfect −10 dBV unbalanced.

channel. Follow Figure 4.7, which should work for most modern equipment. But if the pro gear has an output transformer, you might not hear anything at all. Add a jumper from XLR pin 3 to pin 1 and change the top resistor to 3.3 kΩ (Radio Shack #271-1328).

SMPTE timecode

Timecode, when carried on a standard cable, or when it's on a VTR's address track—*longitudinal timecode*[5] or *LTC*—is actually digital data imposed on an analog carrier, so I'm including it with other analog wiring. The format is biphase squarewave around 2.4 kHz, which makes it sound like a fax machine signal. Since this is close to the middle of the audio band, and squarewaves are rich in harmonics, SMPTE code loves to leak into unbalanced audio wiring. Keep its cables far away from others.

SMPTE timecode appears on just about any kind of audio connector or BNC, at the whim of the manufacturer. It's usually unbalanced. There is no standard voltage for it. Devices made specifically for timecode, such as window generators, generally output around 1 v and can read anything from about 10 millivolts to 10 volts. Devices that have a different primary purpose, such as recorders, often keep timecode at the same level as its other audio: either −10 dBV or +4 dBu. Because almost all modern devices look at zero crossings rather than absolute level, today's gear is very forgiving of mismatches. But if you're feeding +4 dBu timecode to a prosumer audio device, the extra level could cause leakage. Build the pad in Figure 4.7 using the 3.9 kΩ resistor described in the text.

Three other versions of timecode exist but don't travel on audio cables. *Vertical interval timecode* or *VITC* is superimposed on the video itself. Many DV cameras put timecode data on

---

5. So named because the track is parallel to the tape edge, instead of slanted like an analog video track.

FireWire along with the picture. MIDI timecode runs on dedicated MIDI cables and doesn't follow the SMPTE format. So-called RS-422 code isn't timecode at all but a bidirectional series of where-are-you queries and answers between an edit controller and video deck.

Digital Wiring Standards

In a world that cares only about ones and zeros, it's not necessary to worry about noise pickup or absolute voltage levels. But there's another concern: digital audio uses very high frequencies. At high frequencies, digital signals act more like radio than like audio. If impedances aren't precisely matched, these signals can bounce back and forth inside the wires between input and output. These data echoes are often strong enough to make a signal unusable. (All high-speed data has similar concerns. That's why you have to worry about terminating a SCSI chain. FireWire and ethernet devices have the termination built-in.)

Fortunately, there are only two common electrical standards for digital audio, and they use different connectors, so manufacturers can build the right impedance termination into the equipment, based on which connector is used. To avoid problems, you have to use the right impedance wire as well. Also, you can't mult or split a digital audio signal; that changes the impedance. Instead, use a distribution amplifier or transformer.

AES/EBU digital audio

The AES/EBU standard[6] is found on virtually all pro digital equipment. It uses 5-volt squarewaves and 110Ω impedance, is balanced for noise immunity, and almost always has 3-pin XLR connectors wired the same way as analog audio ones. Standard XLR cables can be used for AES/EBU digital audio, but only for less than 20 feet or so. Most cable manufacturers make 110Ω balanced wire specifically for digital audio. It's only a bit more expensive than audio cables; you should use it any time reliability is important.

Some facilities use RG-59 75Ω video wire for AES/EBU because it's cheaper than 110Ω balanced. This is cost-effective only for long runs because you need a $40 transformer at each end to unbalance the signal and convert the impedance. The transformers are made by Neutrik and Canare and are available at pro audio suppliers. In cases where word clock is distributed, it's generally carried on RG-59 with BNC connectors.

s/pdif digital audio

The s/pdif standard[7] is found mostly on consumer and prosumer gear. It uses 1/2-volt squarewaves and 75 Ω impedance, usually on phono connectors. This happens to be the same as con-

---

6. The initials stand for Audio Engineering Society and European Broadcast Union, who set the standard. It's also known as AES3.

sumer video, and video cables from a chain electronics store are perfectly acceptable for s/pdif. Or if you're making your own, use RG-59 video wire.

Toslink

Toslink is an optical format that uses glass fibers and special connectors found only on consumer equipment. Some MiniDisc recorders will accept an optical input through what appears to be a standard mini-jack. Toslink signals are a serial pattern of light, following the AES Consumer format.

⚠️ *Gotcha* _____

AES/EBU as consumer? s/pdif as pro? We've discussed wiring standards for the electrical connection between devices because at digital audio frequencies, wiring can get tricky. But AES has also specified two *data* standards for what's on these wires: consumer and professional.

In general, the differences between the data formats are minor. Most have to do with things like copy protection (ignored in pro equipment) or pre-emphasis (obsolete). One specifies the number of bits in the audio sample—pro can handle 24-bits, consumer only 16-bits—but other than bit depth, there's no difference in audio quality. A 16-bit signal will sound exactly the same in both data formats.

Fortunately, the formats are so close that for 16-bit audio, most equipment will accept either bitstream.

Guerilla Problem Solving

Generally, audio wiring problems show up with three kinds of symptoms: hum, other noises, and intermittent audio. Once it's there, none of these can be eliminated from a track without affecting dialog.

Hum

The dreaded 60 cycle hum is inaccurately named. It's actually more of a buzz—a distorted wave that can have lots of harmonics much higher than 60 Hz—extending through voice and music frequencies and almost impossible to remove. It's most common in unbalanced setups where the shield and equipment grounds are part of the signal path. Ground loops form when there are multiple ground paths carrying tiny audio currents, and virtually every cable connected to audio equipment can contribute to them. The loops act as antennas, picking up the low-frequency noise radiated by the building's wiring. Even worse, the standard 3-prong AC plugs on most gear

---

7. Sony/Philips digital interface format is always abbrievated lowercase (s/pdif). Also known as IEC958 or IEC60958 when an equipment manufacturer doesn't want to promote Sony's or Philips' name.

tie that antenna to hundreds of more feet of ground wire inside the walls and run next to some very noisy high-current power cables.

So the first step in cleaning up hum is to unplug everything that has any contact with audio. That includes the video cables in your audio/video editor, data cables on CD-ROM drives that also have audio connections, and even shielded RS-422 control cables on a video deck. (Before you start unplugging, make sure the wires are labeled with their corresponding jacks.) Go all the way back to your monitor amplifier. Then reconnect the wires one at a time, starting at the monitor amplifier and working down the signal chain from output to input. Listen for hum after each connection. When you hear it, you'll know which cable is causing the loop and you can apply some of these cures.

⚠ **Gotcha** _____

Ground loops without wires. Sometimes loops form because two grounded equipment chassis are making electrical contact. This can be hard to diagnose if the equipment is mounted in a rack, where the metal screws and rack rails complete the circuit. But if nothing else seems to be the culprit, suspect this.

It's easy to cure. Large audio dealers can sell you low-cost kits with fiber tabs that wrap around the equipment's mounting holes, or the kits can have insulated shoulder washers and nylon screws. These isolate the gear while still providing support.

Two of the most common hum culprits are cable TV feeds and grounded power cords. If a VCR or monitor/receiver is connected to both cable TV and your audio system, you can get giant ground loops, even when the video equipment is turned off. It's easy to diagnose; you can just unscrew the cable TV and listen. To diagnose power-cord ground problems, use a three- to two-prong molded AC adapter from a hardware store. Don't connect its metal grounding foot to anything. Use this as a temporary diagnostic procedure only, because it defeats an important safety feature and makes any line noise filtering less effective. There are better permanent solutions.

Once you've located the offending connection, you have to break its loop. You can often do this by disconnecting one of the grounds in an audio, video, or control cable. Turn your monitor down before trying this with audio cables—while breaking the ground may fix the hum, it might also raise it to speaker-rattling levels. If an audio cable uses RCA connectors, just pull the plug partway out so the center pin connects but the outer shield doesn't. If the cable has phone plugs, use clip leads or plug a short phone-to-phone patch cord into the jack and touch the tip of its other end to the cable being tested. If this eliminates the hum, rig up a more permanent way to disconnect the ground—by cutting the cable, or building a small adapter in an insulated box—and you're done.

You may also be able to reduce ground loop noise by providing a better, lower-resistance audio ground. Run a heavy cable—such as both conductors of a 14-gauge speaker wire twisted together at both ends—from a grounding point on each device to one central point in your studio (often a mixer or computer audio input). For just this purpose, most audio equipment has a screw on the back marked with one of the icons in Figure 4.8. If you don't see a ground screw, the best place for one is usually the sleeve of an

4.8 Look for one of these icons near an equipment screw to find a good place for connecting a ground.

unbalanced input: connect your ground wire to the exposed metal shell of an input plug. While providing a better ground is a classic way to reduce noise, I've found it's not as effective as actually breaking the ground loop.

Of course, some grounds can't be cut. Power line third-pin grounds are there for safety reasons. Cable TV systems won't function without their ground. In these cases, you'll need a transformer to pass the signal while not letting the grounds through, in effect, balancing a tiny part of the unbalanced wiring. If the loop is on a TV cable, the cure is trivial: get a pair of 75Ω/300Ω antenna transformers and wire both its 300Ω sides back-to-

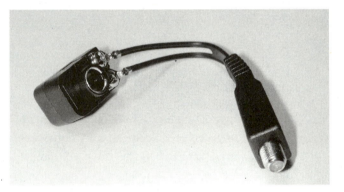

4.9 A cheap cable TV hum eliminator.

back. Figure 4.9 shows how to do this with $6 worth of Radio Shack parts: #15-1140 and #15-1523. At the back of your VCR, connect the assembly in series with the cable and then wrap the whole thing with electrical tape. If you start seeing ghosts on local channels, the transformers are leaking: put the whole thing in a metal box grounded to the VCR or use a better prebuilt assembly available from large video suppliers for about $50.

Ground loops in audio cables can be broken the same way. Radio Shack's #270-054 ($15), designed for car systems, couples a stereo line-level signal through a pair of small transformers. It's not really hi-fi, but it's surprisingly good for the price and may be all you need. If you want better sound, high-quality, ground-isolating transformers are available at pro audio dealers for about $35 per channel. Ground loops can also affect video and usually appear as a darkened horizontal band that slowly crawls up the screen. If that video cable is also forming an audio ground loop, you can fix both problems at the same time with a video hum-stopping transformer—about $150 at pro video houses.

The ultimate solution is to use balanced wiring exclusively. When done right, ground loops can't form.

Random noise

You might also encounter some mystery hummers that sound like they could be loops but aren't. The audio heads in an analog VCR or cassette deck can pick up hum, particularly if there's a big power transformer nearby. All dynamic and some condenser mics have tiny transformers that can pick up hum from other equipment (or even building wiring, if you're unlucky). Moving things a few inches—or turning them 90 degrees—usually helps, but you might learn that certain mics just can't be used in certain places. Defective or badly designed AC supplies in AC/battery equipment can also cause hum: run the equipment on batteries until things get fixed.

These transformers can also pick up high-frequency noise from video monitors. Turn off the monitor if you think this is the culprit. The only long-term cure is to move the transformer a few feet away, or use an LCD display. If you must use a microphone next to a conventional monitor, make sure it's transformerless.

Sporadic high-frequency noise can leak from building wiring into audio cables, particularly microphone and unbalanced line-level ones. Because the problem frequently has to be cured at the source, it can take some detective work and a licensed electrician to sort out. Large, old electric motors in elevators and oil burners can have tiny sparks that get picked up in their own windings and radiate through the building power. Common wall-mounted light dimmers work by slicing up low-frequency electric power and create nasty harmonics throughout the audio band. Replace dimmers with low-noise versions. The radiation is the worst when you get closer to the dimmed circuit but disappears when the lights are fully on. So the easiest cure, if dimmers in an edit suite are causing problems, is to replace all the bulbs with lower-wattage ones and stop dimming.

For the best noise immunity, replace unbalanced wiring with balanced circuits. This is a major overhaul—you need to change more than the cables—and best left for facility rebuilds.

Sudden death

Your room has been working perfectly. Then you start hearing clicking, bursts of static, or nothing at all. First do a little deductive reasoning:

- Have you changed anything? New software might require new drivers for your hardware. If you used borrowed equipment on the last job or patched in a client's camera, have you returned everything to its normal condition?

- Can you isolate it to one piece of equipment? Are some meters bouncing even though you don't hear anything from the speakers? Work backwards from your monitors or forwards using headphones. If you've got a patchbay, it's a great diagnostic tool; patch around suspect equipment until you determine which is causing the problem.

- Can you isolate it to one place in the project? If a certain part of your mix always has static, it's probably an overload or bad media. Lower the levels or work around it.

- Did it fail overnight? Something that worked last night but not this morning probably died on power-up. It could be as simple as a user-replaceable fuse—but if the fuse is good (take it out and test it with your continuity meter) or a replacement fuse immediately fails, call for service.

- Are any tiny buttons in the wrong position? Pressing the wrong solo on a mixer can turn off the output. Selecting the wrong reference in a piece of digital audio gear can create clicking mixed with the sound.

One of the most common failure points in prosumer equipment is the input and output connection. Mini-jack springs stop making contact, and the inner sleeves in phono jacks start to let go. If you suspect this is the problem, try wiggling the plug in its jack and listen for anything. A bad jack will frequently respond to manhandling, if only for a moment. If this seems to work, you can often temporarily fix things by flexing the cable in different directions until you find a position that produces sound. Then tape or tie the cable to keep it there. Ultimately, you or a technician will have to take the unit apart and replace the jack.

Modular power supplies—wall warts—can be subject to sudden and inexplicable failure. A fuse or rectifier inside the wall wart decides to burn out. If you suspect that's the problem, unplug the supply from the equipment and check its output with your voltmeter. It should be at or somewhat higher than the rated voltage because the output goes down under load. Most of these units aren't fixable. Contact the manufacturer or take a trip to your local electronics store for a replacement.

One of the best pieces of problem-solving advice I ever heard was, "Walk the dog." Get away from the problem, ideally out of the room, for a few minutes. A fresh outlook always helps.

If you've determined that something is broken beyond your ability to fix—or possibly even diagnose—it's time to call a tech. But first, write down everything you know about the problem: when it developed, what the symptom is, any unusual meter or panel readings, and what you've done so far to fix it. Gathering that information when you first try to deal with the problem can save hours of repair time.

Chapter 5

The Studio: Audio Software

Remember this:

• NLEs are powerful software. But they're not great places to edit or mix a track. A few accessory programs can make your project sound better.

• Moving sync elements from one program to another—even on separate computers—is painless if you follow some simple rules.

• The Internet can replace tapes and overnight couriers, but look beyond e-mail for the best results.

Nonlinear is nothing new. Hollywood was doing it almost a century ago, long before computers existed. When you're cutting film, you can add or delete shots in whatever order you prefer. The rest of the movie will ripple[1] automatically. Movies are random-access as well: when you're working on a scene, you first hang all the selected shots in a trim bin, a large cloth-lined barrel with tiny hooks suspended across the top. Then you grab whichever ones seem appropriate, try them in different orders, and generally juggle until you're happy.

Audio editing used to be done the same way. Because I came from a film background, my first sound editing studio (Figure 5.1) had a trim bin for tape. Audio tape doesn't have sprocket holes to hang it from, so I used plastic clips instead. The editing itself was as nonlinear and random-access as today.

---

1. Editor-speak for having later scenes automatically move to accommodate the earlier ones. It's an issue when cutting videotape, but you might not even have to deal with it in an NLE.

Today's editing programs have kept some of the film techniques. You put selected clips in *bins*, even though any other software would call it folders. Your timeline shows strips of still frames—it sure *looks* like film—which you can cut with a razor tool. But in many programs we've lost one of analog tape's most valuable audio editing features: automatic cross-fades.

5.1 "Confurring" with a studio colleague, circa 1970. Note the tape trims—most likely individual phrases—hanging from clips behind the cat.

Splices Were Cross-fades

Audio used to be cut in a splicing block, shown in Figure 5.2. You'd lay two strips of magnetic tape in the long shallow channel, with the tapes' edit points lined up with the deep diagonal groove. Then you'd pull a razor blade through the diagonal groove, cutting both strips identically. You'd discard the scrap, and join the

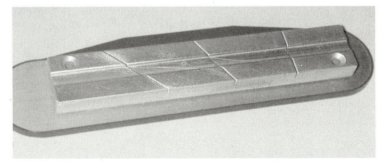

5.2 A well-worn audio splicing block. Note the long shallow groove for tape pieces, and the three angled ones for razor blades.

remaining pieces with sticky tape. I did this a few thousand times a week for two decades.

The angle of the groove is no accident. It slows down the transition from one sound to the next. When you join two waveforms, there's a good chance the voltage won't match at the cut point—creating the jump in the middle in Figure 5.3. A vertical rise like that has infinite harmonics, which creates a click. But you can avoid the click by cross-fading, so the middle of the edit is actually an average of the two waves[2].

Compare the two spliced tapes in Figure 5.4 (if you saw recorded tape in a magnetic viewer, it would look a lot like the drawing). The tape head is sensitive to magnetism only at its gap, the thin white vertical line. As the splice moves past the gap, it picks up less magnetism and gradually sees less of one side and more of the other. The upper splice, a 45 degree angle, creates a 16 milli-second cross-fade,[3] short enough to sound like a cut while avoiding the click. This angle was the most used, and you can see that the 45 degree groove in Figure 5.2 is the most worn. Professional blocks frequently had steeper angles, like the ones in the picture, for cutting slow-speed tape. But there are times you want a slower transition, like the one in the bottom of Figure 5.4. If you look closely at my old block in Figure 5.1, you'll notice some long razor blade scratches down the middle. Editors would often create their own cross-fades at very shallow angles. The 1.5-inch scratches on my block were equivalent to 3-frame audio dissolves.

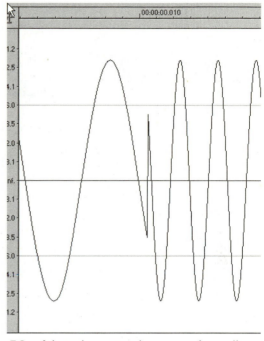

5.3 A jump in a wave because of an edit.

⚠ **Gotcha**

Clicking with your NLE. Almost every NLE does a hard cut when you join two clips in the timeline. If you want to edit where there's no silence—such as in a an interview or piece of music—there's a chance of a click. On most setups with limited monitoring, you might not even notice that click until the piece is mixed.

One way around this it to make checkerboard edits on multiple tracks by manually applying cross-fades. But this wastes time. For serious work, you need a program that specializes in audio.

---

2. You can also avoid the click by cutting only where the waves match. Since every wave goes through zero, some programs automatically snap their edit marks to the closest zero crossing.

3. Feel free to do the math—professional broadcast production used tape with a mono track 1/4-inch wide, moving past the head at 15 inches per second.

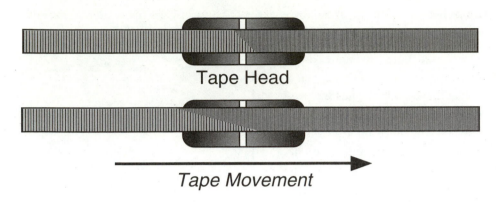

Tape Head

Tape Movement

5.4 The angled splice between pieces of tape created a cross-fade when it went past the heads.

Audio Software

Nonlinear Video Editors

Today's NLEs come with basic audio capability. Almost all are suitable for track layouts and simple mixes. Trying anything more complex can range from being a time-waster to a disaster. Even if a program has a pretty on-screen mixer, the audio filters[4] supplied with most NLEs are often clumsy, lack important controls, or don't let you tune them while listening. You can get third-party plug-ins for some editors, but the most sophisticated ones are generally in formats that NLEs don't support. Even a good compatible one can suffer in the NLE environment because of limited bit depth or short preview memory. And many NLEs appear to have been written by programmers who don't understand audio. There are user

> ⚠ **Gotcha** _____
>
> *A single frame can be too long.* One of the biggest barriers to sophisticated audio editing in a NLE is their insistence that edits snap to the frame line. This makes sense for video, but 33 ms—one frame—is a very long time for sound. Critical consonants like /t/ or /d/ can be only a third that length. In fast-paced music, a frame can be almost 1/32 note—not a lot of time but certainly enough to make an edit sound wrong.
>
> Even video editors that let you mark audio with better than one-frame resolution limit the clip length to whole frames, so you can't mark both the in- and out-points accurately. And the clip itself must be positioned on a frame line[1].
>
> _____
>
> 1.   Hollywood never had this problem. 35 millimeter magnetic stock has four sets of perforations per frame, for a resolution of about 10 ms.

_____

4.   In the audio realm, a filter is a specific kind of equalizer, as you'll learn in Chapter 12. Calling a reverb or compressor a filter is silly.

interface errors like the badly scaled equalizer shown in Chapter 2; algorithms for critical things like sample rate conversion are frequently compromised to speed up rendering time.

For serious audio post, you've got to move beyond a NLE.

Audio-Centric Programs

A few years ago, you'd just call these audio programs. They had no video capability. But now, almost every sound editing program shows QuickTime or AVI in sync with the track and displays timing in SMPTE frame rates as well as bars and beats. In these sound-and-picture programs, audio is definitely the main interest, as opposed to NLEs where it's usually an afterthought. Among the audio-centric features you'll find in most of them:

- Smooth audio scrolling and marking down to the single sample (1/1600 frame). While you're not forced to pay attention to this kind of resolution, it makes precise editing possible when you need it.

- 24-bit files with as much as 56-bit processing. DV source files are invariably 16-bit, but the more precise processing means cleaner effects like compression and equalization.

- High-quality algorithms for things like time compression and sample rate conversion.

- Tighter integration with a wider range of processing plug-ins than you'll find in a NLE. Most plug-ins are tunable while you listen to long previews or even jump around the file. Many plug-ins are real time and don't require any rendering.

- The ability to use MIDI or USB hardware controllers for scrolling and mixing.

- Automatic or easy-to-apply cross-fades at edit points.

About scrubbing

A sound is not a blob on a screen. In Chapter 2, you saw how words are seldom related to a sound's envelope. The editing technique in most NLE tutorials—you look for a spike or dip in the waveform and then mark it—is only a rough guide when you start doing sophisticated editing.

Most NLEs provide some form of slow-speed audio scanning in their clip window so you can hear where an edit should be marked. Good ones let you choose between *jogging*, with which you directly control clip motion by moving the mouse from side to side, and *shuttling*, which changes speed in response to mouse movement. A few NLEs don't provide audio jog or shuttle at all. Having jog and shuttle control seems to depend on platform and sound card as much as the programmers' intentions.

In the audio realm, this scanning is usually called *scrubbing*. On the best audio workstations, scrubbing is smooth and precisely related to controller movement: it feels like you're rocking a reel of tape or scratching a DJ's turntable. Some programs offer alternative scrub modes. Fixed slow-speed playback may be handiest for seeing the relation between sound and waveform. Variable-speed motion, similar to shuttling, lets you navigate through a long sound quickly and then slow down to find the edit. Stutter scrubbing repeats very short sections of the sound—as small as 10 ms—to find transitions quickly. Stutter scrubbing is often the only way to find where two vowels join or mark where a note changes in some music.

◉ *Hear for yourself* _____

Track 15 lets you hear and compare different scrubbing options with dialog and two kinds of music. You'll hear tape-like scrubbing, slow scanning, variable motion, and stuttering with various sized chunks between 10–300 ms.

Few audio programs support more than one or two kinds of scrubbing; when you're selecting a program, check to make sure it has the scrubbing most appropriate for your work.

Some popular audio programs don't scrub at all and expect you to edit visually. For more precise marking, set a short loop around the edit point and play the loop while slowly moving its boundary. This is a time-consuming workaround, but it does the job. Check the software's manual for specific instructions.

Multitrack software

These usually have unlimited audio tracks arranged along a timeline similar to the one in a NLE. They usually doesn't have anything equivalent to a clip window for scanning and marking edit points; instead, audio files are imported onto the timeline and *regions* can be selected from the timeline waveforms. The regions can then be trimmed, split, or dragged around the timeline, just

⚠ *Gotcha* _____

What you see isn't what you get. Even though audio professionals had been doing perfectly acceptable edits by ear for half a century, computerized sound editing evolved as a visual medium because that's all early desktop machines could handle. But don't swallow some programmers' and marketers' assertion that it's the *best* way to edit.

You have to hear what you're marking. Except for the convenient examples in NLE tutorial files, the spike of a drumbeat rarely matches the bar line, and lots of music doesn't have loud drums at all. It may be easy to cut on pauses in scripted dialog, but interview and other real-world voices frequently continue without a pause beyond a desired out-point. Some audio transitions, such as individual notes in a smooth musical line or the seven distinct phonemes in the word trial,[1] don't change the envelope at all.

---

1.   You'll learn how to manipulate phonemes—and do impossible edits—in Chapter 9. Meanwhile, the phonemes are /t/, /r/, /ah/, /ih/, /y/, /uh/, /l/.

as you would in a NLE. Some multitrack programs let you import edited audio directly from a compatible NLE; clips show up as regions on the proper track at the right time. Like NLEs, multitrack programs are generally *nondestructive*: files that have been cut into regions aren't really changed. Instead, a database is built showing where each part of a file should appear on the timeline. There is no capture window; if you want to add something new, select a track and record directly onto the timeline. You can listen to any combination of tracks and watch synchronized picture while recording.

Unlike NLEs, you don't have to edit on frame lines. You can turn on a grid that constrains edits to any convenient unit—including frames—or edit totally freely. Using a multitrack to fine-tune and mix gives you other advantages such as the following.

- Tracks don't have to be stereo. A voice-over can be mono and centered; sound effects can be *panned* wherever appropriate between left and right. This makes complex track layouts easier.

- Almost all programs have a mixing panel with virtual faders, routing switches, and extensive metering. Fader movement usually can be controlled by hardware MIDI or USB controllers with real faders—a big time-saver—and the only way to fade one track up and another down while listening. Mixers also have extensive automation capability.

- Transport controls usually include multiple locate points and loop play, and can also be remoted to hardware controllers.

- Mixing is real time for any number of tracks and effects without rendering.

Figure 5.5 (page 92) shows some of the windows in one multitrack program.

Music software

MIDI sequencers evolved in the mid-80s as a way to record and edit keyboard performances. The musical sounds themselves weren't recorded; just instructions about which note to play and when, how loudly, and on what instrument. The files could then be played on external synthesizers, creating a perfect musical performance. Today sequencers are the standard tool for music composition and creation, and often play through samplers to create new songs from recordings of nonelectronic instruments or voices, or a sequencer can print full scores for orchestral performance.

As computer capability grew, many sequencers started adding digital audio features. Today's programs combine multitrack sound editing and mixing with simultaneous MIDI tracks and video playback. While they're most often used with external MIDI instruments, notes can be entered with a mouse, and software-based synthesizers and samplers can be run on the same computer. I consider them an essential sound design tool. If you've got musical talents and like to score your own films, one of these programs will probably be more useful than an audio-only multitrack.

5.5 A multitrack audio program.

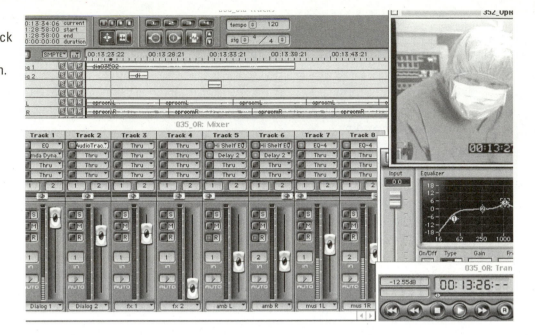

 Note

Note the individual tracks at the top of Figure 5.5, along a timeline calibrated in timecode. You can zoom in on any audio element in this section for more precise editing. A mixer window, below the tracks, lets you plug real-time effects as well as control level and stereo panning into any track. At the bottom of that window, you can see how tracks are named to make mixing simpler. Each fader also has a volume meter to show instantaneous track levels; dialog and music are currently active, and the other tracks are quiet. Along the right is a video viewer that moves in sync as you scrub audio, a precise equalizer, and transport controls.

Check a music store for books, magazines, and plenty of software and hardware toys devoted to MIDI. Figure 5.6 shows a typical window, with audio on one track and piano-roll notation of musical notes on another. The menu shows some of the note editing functions.

Editing software

Sometimes you need to make multiple edits in a single sound file, as when you want to rearrange a voice-over narration or trim music to length. Doing this in a region- or clip-based editor could make you deal with dozens of tiny sections. It would be a lot easier to edit word-processor style, where you could select, delete, copy or paste freely in a single file. It would also involve far fewer mouse clicks. *Editors* are the word processors of the audio world. They're often called *two-track editors* because multitrack programs are also capable of editing, but it is a misnomer. Editors work on files. They can be mono or stereo.

Like word processors, editors let you open more than one file at a time and copy and paste between them. Unlike multitrack programs, editors make permanent changes to a file. If you're not sure you like that idea, work on a copy. On the other hand, once you've finished a sequence you're done: there's no need to render or mix anything. Editors have other advantages in the audio workflow:

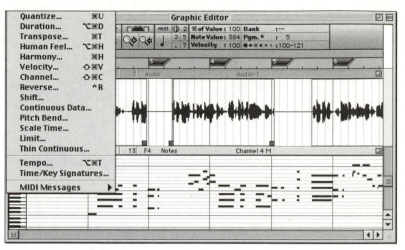

5.6 Most music sequencers now support simultaneous audio and MIDI.

- Edit resolution is often higher than a multitrack and can be as fine as a single sample.

- Editors usually have more extensive built-in effects.

- They're usually more flexible and do a better job of converting file standards, sample rates, and bit depths.

- Some let you preset conversions or effects and then batch-process multiple files at once.

- Most provide a pencil tool that lets you redraw the audio waveform, smoothing over occasional clicks or rounding out an overload.

In general, editors are great timesavers. If I already had video software and could buy only one other program, I'd specify an editor (and mix in the NLE). Figure 5.7 shows a typical one.

Audio Utilities

Here are some additional programs to make audio post easier. This section doesn't cover specific processors like reverbs or noise reduction, which have full chapters devoted to them later in this book. Self-editing music library software is covered in Chapter 10.

Effects shells

NLEs have limited plug-in capability. If it accepts any at all, it's usually limited to the ActiveX or Premiere format. A standalone shell lets you run other plug-ins as applications on your desktop, you can open a file in one, preview and process through the plug-in, and then save a processed

5.7 An editor is better and faster than a multitrack for manipulating complete files. Along with saving edit time, there are often more processing options that can be applied either to a whole file or to a selected area.

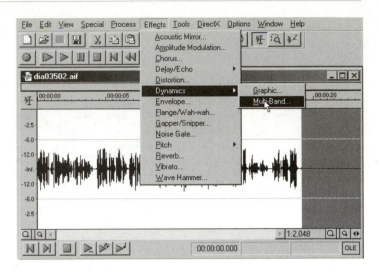

version. While most audio programs can also do this, it can be a needless expense if all you want to do is process.

One commercial shell, Bias's Vbox (Mac/Windows), gives you access to the whole world of VST.[5] There are hundreds of plug-ins in this format, ranging from high-quality professional processors to hacker-developed, freeware sound manglers in every imaginable style.

Other shells may be available from plug-in manufacturers to let you use their products in different environments. Arboretum Systems (www.arboretum.com) is offering its Hyperengine shell with some of its more basic processors as a free download.

_____

5. Virtual Studio Technology, a plug-in format invented and trademarked by Steinberg Media Technologies, is now an open standard.

Conversion software

NLEs can be flexible about accepting different sample rates and bit depths yet still do a poor job of actually converting the file. Periodic clicking is the most common symptom. It's almost always better to convert in a program designed for sound. If you don't have an audio editor, consider a separate conversion utility. Many are available as shareware, though quality varies. A reliable option is Apple's QuickTime Pro for Mac or Windows, a very low cost upgrade to its free Quick-Time Player.

Most converters can import and export multiple file formats as well as different audio standards, but few are licensed to convert audio to mp3, the most common Web audio compression standard. To do that, you may need a separate mp3 encoder. Quality varies, but generally the commercial encoders which include both the official licensed Fraunhofer[6] engine and the open-source LAME one do the best job.

Search software

It can be hard to find a specific sound in a large library. Commercial music and sound effect publishers often come with their own databases or let you search on the Web (see Chapters 10 and 11). But if you've assembled your own large collection, you may want software that lets you search by keyword and then audition a sound. SfxSearch (www.gefen.com, Mac/Windows, about $100) is specifically designed for this function. Some audio programs come with templates for mainstream database managing software, so you can cobble your own.

Macintosh versus Windows

I put this section last because conventional wisdom insists that you choose software first and then buy whichever platform it requires. Don't be confused by software that's supposed to be cross-platform; some features may be supported on one computer but not on another. Allegedly cross-platform hardware can also have differences: FireWire or USB may be more difficult to configure on Windows machines. But a particular device might not have Mac drivers.

Chances are you've already got a computer for your NLE, so this is a nonissue. Get audio software that runs on its platform. Mac users can also run most Windows software by using the VirtualPC emulator, but the emulation itself steals computing power so programs won't run as quickly as they would on a comparably rated PC. The other combination—Mac emulation under Windows—still isn't practical at all.

---

6. Fraunhofer IIS-A invented MPEG Layer-3 (mp3) and MPEG-2 AAC, an emerging standard.

File Exchange and Networking

Large facilities frequently have audio and video editors sharing storage over high-speed dedicated local networks, so many people can work on the same project. This requires expensive servers and additional tweaking, and usually needs the help of a computer specialist.

> ⚠ **Gotcha** _____
>
> **When networking gets in the way.** Some system-level utilities periodically check local networks, which ties up your CPU for a few moments at a time. Generally, this isn't a problem. But it can interfere with audio capture or recording processes. Turn off or disconnect networking before you start.

In smaller facilities, audio files can be shared over a standard office network, using the peer-to-peer networking built into most computers these days. (Because there isn't a central server, you can end up with a condition where multiple copies of a file—each slightly different—exist on separate computers. Make sure you're using the right one.) But even if you've got only one computer, you may still want to share files between NLE and audio software. If both programs are using 16-bit uncompressed audio at the same sample rate, there won't be any loss of quality—even if the files have to be converted between WAV, AIFF, QuickTime, or other formats.

Synchronizing Shared Files

The good news: maintaining lipsync in shared files isn't too hard. Digital audio is self-clocking, so both programs will expect a precise number of samples per second. The only real challenge is keeping individual elements lined up as you go from one program to another.

Countdowns and 2-pop

Ever watch a film leader? A clock-like pattern rotates once per second, with numbers counting down inside it. When the number *two* appears, you hear a blip and the screen goes black. Exactly two seconds later, the film starts.

That blip is a 1 kHz sine wave lasting exactly one frame, affectionately named a *2-pop*.[7] It's the best brute-force way to get things in sync. While you're in the NLE, count two seconds back from the start of program and insert an all-white frame. Or find a clip of film leader—some NLEs come with one—and put it at the head of your timeline. Put a pop on *every* audio track, directly under the white frame or number two. Video editors frequently put the pop at timecode 59:58.00 so the program can start at exactly one hour.

---

7. Not to be confused with 2-pop.com, an excellent informational site dedicated to nonlinear editing with an emphasis on Final Cut Pro.

When you're ready to move to an audio program, export entire individual tracks as files that include the pop, and save a reference copy of the video with the flash frame. Load the files onto different tracks of an audio program, and they'll probably sync up by themselves, since you're inserting them at the same start time. But if they don't, just slide tracks until the pops match. Then tweak the video, using the program's video offset or start time function, so the flash or 2 lines up with the pop.

Keep the pop when you mix in the audio program; you'll probably want to mute the pop on some tracks so it doesn't get too loud. Import the mix back into your NLE, drop it on a track, and slide the pop back into sync. Now you can delete the original audio clips on other tracks.

If you have any doubts about your system's ability to hold sync long-term, put a pop and flash at the end of the film as well. After you've re-imported the mix to your NLE and synced its front, see if the end lines up. If not, you can calculate the error and apply a speed correction.

A variation to the 2-pop is to put a beep at each number on a countdown leader. It can be hard to spot tiny errors from a single pop when watching at normal speed so this method gives you eight more chances to catch sync problems.

5.8 Approaching the 2-pop in a timeline and viewer. The audio pop starts exactly in sync with the frame that has a big *2*.

When you're taking tracks to an outside facility for mixing, 2-pops are reliable enough that you can use them for sync. Burn your files to removable media or CD-ROM, or save them in your computer as a standard audio CD. Verify that the facility will be able to lock its equipment to the format you provide.

Hear for yourself

Track 16 contains a 9-blip countdown ready to line up against visual leaders. The first eight tones are at 1 kHz, for numbers *10–3*. The last is at 2 kHz as an audible warning the program is about to start. Or use just the first 1 kHz blip as a 2-pop.

Time-stamped files

The disadvantage of using 2-pops as a sync reference is that you have to export entire tracks. If a track is mostly silent, you'll be creating large files needlessly. This generally isn't a problem for short-form videos, but can be a real waste of time and space[8] over the length of a film.

⚠ *Gotcha* _____

Sync slip. Some multitracks use timecode numbers to fire off regions on their timeline and trust the common sample rate to keep things in sync once started. This generally works fine, unless you change the project's timecode format. This changes the number of samples between the start of one region and the start of the next. If there's a long time between starts, the second region will be noticeably out of sync with the first.

Sophisticated audio software and dedicated workstations map every audio event to an internal, sample-based timeline. The software and workstations translate these numbers to timecode as needed.

Open Media Framework (*OMF*) was invented by Avid and is now supported by a number of NLE and multitrack manufacturers. It lets you transfer a project's timeline, along with all its clips and cross-fades as one large file. Depending on the program, handles may be specified. *Handles* are extra audio before and after a clip for cross-fades and a source of room tone. OMF files can get very large; you may want to break the project into sections for convenient handling and storage. In most situations, it's a one-way street: you can transfer OMF from video software to audio but not from the audio program back to NLE. But if you're mixing in the audio program, all you'll probably need to re-import to video is the final stereo track. A standard file with 2-pop is adequate for that.

Some standard audio file formats, including EBU Wave,[9] support internal timestamps. Some software uses these stamps to line up elements when you transfer them from one project to another. Theoretically, you will also be able to use them to transfer from NLE to audio program, but no program is currently doing this.

Audio via Internet

I own two timecode DAT decks. When I bought them (the youngest one is about four years old), this was the standard interchange format for professional video sound. I'd finish working on a project, dub a timecode DAT from my audio workstation, and courier it to the video post house. Now, weeks go by without either DAT deck moving an inch of tape. My courier now is a broadband data connection. Mixes leave my workstation via ethernet, hop across our router onto the Internet, and are at the post house's server in a matter of minutes. Quality is identical to a DAT—16-bit 48 kHz s/r audio—and sync is a simple 2-pop. Those expensive tape decks are now only used for long-form projects (when the client doesn't request a CD or CD-ROM instead) or for tracks going to facilities stuck in the twentieth century.

_____

8. Fortunately, you can save some space by using a compression utility like PKZip or StuffIt. These usually aren't very effective on audio files, but they do a great job compressing silence!

9. An enhanced version of the PC file format standardized by the European Broadcast Union.

I've also pretty much abandoned the analog audio cassette. This used to be the only way you could get a client to listen to talent or music auditions or to review a mix. Now, clients get their tracks instantly, electronically. They don't need the full quality and huge files of 16-bit audio, but the much smaller mp3 format is a universal standard and—when done right (Chapter 19)—sounds better than cassettes.

Email

Attaching an mp3 file to an e-mail is the easiest, most casual way to send a short sound file. It's also the least reliable:

- Some Internet services limit incoming file size. Long tracks can get bounced, without even a "mailbox full" message.

- Some services seem to have filters to reject anything with ".mp3" in the filename, possibly to avoid record company lawsuits. Zip or stuff the file, delete the three offending letters from the name, and send it that way.

- Because the mp3 format doesn't include the kind of error correction found in other files, sounds can become corrupted and unplayable when sent as attachments. Zipping or stuffing won't make the file much smaller, but it will help guarantee it gets there in one piece.

Email can also be inconvenient for your client. Verify the client has a fast connection and doesn't mind getting large files. Or use the Web or FTP to solve all these problems. Post the material to a server at your convenience and let the client know when it's up there. The client downloads at his or her convenience. The transfer protocol is more reliable than e-mail attachments, and if a downloaded file is corrupted, the client can go back and get it again.

Web transfers

Many clients prefer the simple interface of the Web. If you've got a Web site and basic HTML skills, set up separate directories for your clients. Give each client an index page with links to whatever you want to send him or her—along with contact information, ads for your services, or whatever else you think appropriate. This is the most convenient way to let a client compare mp3s of potential voice talent or music selections—clients can also pass the URL to colleagues to get a group consensus—and Web transfers are robust enough to handle full-fidelity final mixes. Figure 5.9 shows a recent view of one of the client directories at my site. This one includes mp3s of progressive mixes of a project, plus the final high-resolution track for dubbing to DigiBeta. It's not beautiful Web design, just down-to-earth useful.

If you have a registered domain name (such as www.jayrosesound.com), you can buy full Web hosting services for under $200 per year. The hosting company maintains the Web server, its high-speed Internet connection, and full help and tech support; you upload pages and files using your existing Internet account and Web browser or other software. Because you're paying for the service, you control every aspect of the site. Options often include streaming audio and video servers, e-mail accounts at that domain, chat or mail list functions, and shopping carts. If you've got an Internet connection with a fixed IP address, you can set up your own server with these functions. But that can become a major undertaking for someone without an IT department.

If you don't have a domain name, look into the advertising-supported free sites. You provide the content, which can include files; they force your users to look at banner ads. A Web search for "free hosting" will give you dozens of them. But check the rules before signing up: some sites specifically prohibit mp3 uploads.

5.9 A password-protected client page at my studio's site.

FTP

Web transfers require that you set up an HTML page with links to the files, and it's impossible for clients to upload files to your site. FTP transfers are more like accessing a networked hard drive: you see a directory of available files, grab the ones you want, or save new ones from your computer. You or your client will need an FTP server, but most Web-hosting packages include this service for free. You'll both also need FTP client software. Some popular Web browsers have commands that let you upload and download files to FTP sites. Or use one of the powerful freeware programs dedicated to this purpose.

Password protection

Most FTP and Web directories can be password-protected (though the free services don't provide this function). It keeps your clients' material confidential and makes them feel special. I recommend it. Check with your Web host or IT department to see how to do it on your site.

Chapter 6

Planning the Track

Remember this:

- The most critical, technical specification is how the film will be heard. This is often up to the viewer, not you.

- You can create a track so that everything gets heard the way you want. It just requires a little planning in terms of spectrum, time, and soundstage. With a little more thought, you can create a track that adds interest to your film.

- An important part of postproduction should happen before you start editing. That's when you plan technical and budgetary details, and decide how the track will get done.

Communication is a two-way street. Some theorists say the meaning of a message isn't its words but how someone acts when hearing it. According to theorists, that's the best way to account for factors like nonverbal cues, feedback, and existing ideas about the subject. So if I walk up to you and say, "Nice day," and you smile, it's because we both know I was really saying, "Good to see you." But even if that's what *I* meant, you could frown and say, "Nah, it's not warm enough." Clearly, the meaning of my message got lost.

Enough theory. For DV filmmakers, the practical side is that a soundtrack—whether it's commercial, corporate, theatrical, or event—doesn't have a life of its own. It and the visuals only exist to elicit a response from the viewer.[1] Unless you understand how the viewer will hear your track, you can't know what should go into it.

Different Media Are Heard Differently

I'm not saying they *sound* very different. The technical differences between broadcast television, DVD, and most videotape formats are fairly small. They all do a reasonable job of carrying

---

1. Even if the response is only, "Wow, what a great film!"

80–15 kHz stereo with little noise. The only real distinctions are in how many channels the formats carry and how much distortion accompanies the signal.

Unfortunately, what viewers hear is seldom the best a medium can do. It's limited by realities of playback equipment, room acoustics, and everyday psychology. Because of the way we listen to video, a track can work beautifully in one medium and fall flat in another.

Broadcast

Don't expect much from conventional analog TV. While the transmission system is capable of reasonably good stereo, few viewers ever hear it that way. The majority of sets—even large-screen ones—have limited-range speakers and considerable distortion at typical listening levels. Low-cost sets often have resonant peaks as well.

Manufacturers don't bother putting better speakers in sets because few consumers will pay for—or even notice—the difference. The average living room or office has the kind of acoustics that hurts intelligibility and destroys musical balance. Background noise is usually fairly high. Both these problems are compounded by viewing positions that are often closer to reflective surfaces than to the set. Savvy commercial and program producers try to counter this with processing to make their tracks seem louder. Broadcasters use different processing to keep their stations' average loudness constant. The result of these physical realities and processing games is a total loss of subtlety.

> ⚠ **Gotcha** _____
> ***Stereo tracks in a mono world.*** A significant part of the TV audience hears both channels mixed together, in mono. Unfortunately, some mono-to-stereo processors, musical instruments, and sound effect libraries that have been hyped to sound extra-wide in stereo depend on polarity reversal tricks that aren't compatible with mono listening. When the channels are mixed, sounds can completely disappear!
>
> If you're preparing a track for TV, always check the mix in mono.

Stereo also gets lost in the broadcast world. Even if a show is produced in stereo, you have to assume most of the audience will hear it in mono. Low-cost color sets, even the ones with two speaker grills, are mono. VCRs record in stereo, but their antenna outputs are almost always mono, and that's how most people hook them up. Cable networks might be stereo on the satellite, but it's up to local cable systems whether to use more expensive stereo equipment to rebroadcast. Add the echoey environment of most living rooms, and what folks hear has little to do with what you mixed.

Surround can make things worse. Techniques used in some desktop audio programs to enhance stereo actually confound a surround decoder. Effects that seemed stretched across the front of your studio when you mixed, can get squeezed into the rear of the room if a viewer has a surround setup.

A few practical tips to help TV tracks survive this hostile world:

- Start with elements that are noise-free and undistorted because station processing will emphasize flaws.

- Don't plan for more than two or three layers of sound: dialog and important sound effects (centered and loud); ambiences and background effects (stereo and medium loud); and music (stereo and variable).

- Don't make accurate stereo a part of the plot; most people will never hear it. Forget about notions of left and right; these won't exist for many viewers.

- Be careful any time voice is mixed with wide-range music. Few viewers will hear the ratio between voice and music the same way because speakers and acoustics vary so much. Often, music will seem lower in the field than it did when you mixed. Multiband compression (Chapter 13) can help keep things predictable.

Subtlety is wasted on TV. Many viewers won't be in a position to pay attention to what you've done. Broadcast TV is often accompanied by conversation, chores, and background noises—or is the background itself.

Educational Video

Classroom playbacks can sound worse than living room ones. It's not strictly the medium's fault. Schools can have VHS hi-fi and good presentation monitors—usually with better sound than mass-market TVs (of course, school players see harder use than home sets and might not be well maintained). The real problem is acoustics. Very few classrooms sound good. Hard parallel surfaces are the norm and ceilings are often low and hard. The resulting echo hurts intelligibility.[2]

> ⚠️ **Gotcha**
>
> **But what about quality?** When conditions are just right—good equipment and acoustics, no competing noises, and a station that uses little processing—TV sound is capable of subtlety and beauty. If you're of an artistic bent, you may prefer to design a track just for those lucky viewers who might actually hear it all, and not worry about the rest.
>
> It's your choice. Personally, I consider it a greater art to create a track that sounds interesting while respecting the limitations of a mass medium.

---

2. And has become a cliché: if you want to make dialog sound like it's in a classroom, add hollowness and reverberation. I wonder how many children have trouble in school just because it's hard to hear what Teacher is saying.

Educational films generally have simpler tracks than entertainment ones, both to keep the message clear and to save money. Often there's just a dialog or narration track, a few key sound effects, and sparse music. Slowing down the narration can help compensate for poor acoustics.

Fortunately, most classes can be expected to quiet down while a film is being shown. And the threat of a quiz may force students to pay attention.

Home Theater and Auditorium Presentation

Things start to get a little better here. Systems are wired to take advantage of stereo or even surround, which can present a very detailed sound field. Speaker quality is often much higher than that in consumer TVs, though it too can vary widely. Department store surround setups frequently compromise high-frequency response and distortion to cut costs. Those very small, easy-to-mount speakers with subwoofers popularized by a few manufacturers have problems at dialog frequencies. Auditorium systems are usually designed for voice, but many sacrifice high frequencies for high power—some don't extend much beyond 12 kHz.

Acoustics are also variable. Home theater setups range from hard-walled living rooms to mini theaters. Large auditoriums can be designed for intelligibility, but architects usually have other constraints. General-purpose meeting rooms and hotel ballrooms often don't have any acoustic treatment other than a fissured tile ceiling.

On the other hand, viewers are usually motivated to pay attention. If they've paid for a home theater system, there's a good chance they actually like to watch movies. If they're in an auditorium, it's probably part of a social or work-related event they care about. This attention also raises the "shh!" factor; audience noises and other distractions are minimized.

A good home theater or auditorium track can have a wide dynamic range and take advantage of stereo or surround spread. Dialog can vary in loudness and position. You can have many layers of effects going on and still hear the music. For best results, plan to mix with speakers at about the same volume as the audience will hear—usually just below 85 dB SPL for average dialog.

Theatrical Soundtracks

Ahh. Every now and again I get to work on one of these. Count on reasonably good acoustics, reliable stereo (usually with surround), and—in a well-maintained theater—wide-range speakers with low distortion and little electronic noise. There's very little environmental noise as well, though multiplexes frequently have low-frequency rumbles from the auditorium next door. Once the movie starts, people usually pay attention.

So you can plan for a rich, dynamic track with multiple layers of sound coming from every direction and music recorded in surround formats. Theatrical mixes and sound systems are supposed to be standardized with an average dialog level projected at 85 dB SPL—but producers

> ⚠ *Gotcha*
>
> **Wide screen, narrow dialog.** Theaters want to sell as many tickets as possible. So seats extend the full width of, and can be very close to, the screen. This creates problems if you try to spread dialog realistically across the screen. For front-row viewers sitting at the sides of the theater, the inverse square law dictates that dialog on their side of the screen will be too loud and dialog on the other will be too soft.
>
> The standard practice is to keep dialog centered, or only slightly off center, no matter where actors appear on the screen. This solves the side-seating problem and also makes the track easier to follow for everyone in the room. (If audio positions jumped every time the camera position changed, the result would be disorienting.) Off-camera characters and crowds can come from any direction that makes dramatic sense.

and theater managers keep pushing this to raise audience adrenaline levels. Yes, movies are getting louder. Plan to mix accordingly.

Internet and CD-ROM Audio

The only rule is there aren't any. Streaming audio quality varies from worse than telephone (because of swooshy artifacts) to better than FM radio. The quality depends on what choices you make in data-compression method and settings. CD-ROM audio is capable of CD quality, but can be limited to 10 kHz to save disc real estate.

What is much worse is that there's absolutely no control over how the track will be played. It could be played on a laptop with speakers that are nearby and in stereo but barely cover 200 Hz–6 kHz. It could be played in a tower with a loud fan and single small speaker, located underneath the viewer's desk. It could be played on small nearfields which are designed for gaming, not dialog. Nearfields can come with or without a subwoofer and are either wired properly or have left and right channels reversed. Or the track could be played through high-quality headphones, but it may also have its channels reversed. Forget about trying to predict noise and other potential distractors. You have no way of knowing whether a track will be played in a quiet office, a noisy family room, a quiet carrel, a busy classroom, or on an airplane.

The only solution I've found is to plan tracks with nothing critical outside the midrange and no more than two things going on at once. If you want complexity, make the elements sequential instead of simultaneous. Just as with broadcast TV, Internet and CD-ROM elements must be free of noise and distortion; you know the quality will get much worse before it's heard. But a wide frequency range isn't important, and extensive highs can even hurt you by robbing bits from the midrange during Web encoding.

All this will probably change as computer, TV, and home theater converge. But the above formula has worked reliably on projects from early CD-ROMs to current Webisode theater.

Putting It Together

Of course, these categories aren't absolute: a corporate piece may be shown in an auditorium at the home office, then over the Web to branch managers; theatrical features with historic themes have been cut down for classroom use. You have to use your own judgement about the potential audience and what they'll hear. The rules summarized in this chart are just a starting point.

Table 6.1   Technical and human factors influence how different media are heard.

	Broadcast TV	Educational	Home Theater and Auditorium	Theatrical	Internet
Speaker quality	narrow frequency range, distorting, often peaky in mids	consumer TVs or slightly better	quality varies: some full-range, some lack mids	usually very good	often lacking bass; subwoofer-equipped systems often lack mids
Dynamic range	very little	very little	medium to high	very high	depends on codec
Room acoustics	poor	poor to horrible	poor to good	good to very good	poor but usually nearfield
Tracks	up to 4, but most people will hear mono	mono or stereo	up to 5.1	up to 6.1, almost always shown as mixed	can be stereo, but plan for a large mono audience
Consistency	none	none	slight	medium to high	none
Competition	life continues while TV is on	little to none	most people concentrating on screen	just a few inconsiderate patrons	computer fans, office distractions
Viewer attention	depends on content	somewhat high	motivated	high	variable
Track layers	few	few	medium	many	few

Spread Things Around

The best Hollywood tracks are planned so that sounds don't compete in space (the *soundstage*). Sound effects may come from the left, right, or behind you. But you rarely hear them in the center of the screen when there's dialog going on. That area belongs to the voices.

Simultaneous sounds usually have different frequency ranges as well. Composer John Williams chose low notes for the ominous theme in *Jaws*, so ocean sounds would also be heard. But he felt free to use the full orchestra in *Star Wars* to underscore the Death Star, which didn't make its own noise in space. Leonard Bernstein learned this the hard way some years earlier with his score for *On the Waterfront*. He composed a beautiful orchestral crescendo, timed perfectly to the peak of an important scene. But the scene's emotion was based on dialog, so the crescendo had to be turned down as it went along. The final mix preserved the voices and killed the musical value.[3]

Spreading things out in the frequency spectrum makes sense for sound effects as well. If there's going to be a car crash, don't have a woman screaming at the same time the tires squeal. One of those sounds will surely get lost.

Or spread sounds out in time. If you hold her scream until after the crash, it can still make dramatic sense and not compete with other sounds. Or have her scream in anticipation of the crash—then squeal those tires and follow it up with a child crying. While all that high-pitched stuff is going on, you can still use a low-frequency crash or fireball. And the midrange is wide open for shouts or musical stabs.

And if the medium supports it, you can spread things around in space. That's what stereo and surround are for. Don't forget the dimension of distance as well; it can translate better to the small screen. Plan to move some elements farther back by using a combination of volume, equalization, and reverb. Manipulating distance should usually be saved for postproduction; with few exceptions, field recording should be done with the mic as close to the subject as possible.

About Stereo

Most people have been exposed to the idea of stereo through consumer electronics, radio, and TV. But I've found many filmmakers don't really know what it means or appreciate how it can vary.

Stereo doesn't have to mean two tracks. The first Bell Labs experiments (and most early stereo film epics) used separate channels for left, center, and right. It wasn't until the format reached home listeners that two channels became the norm because that's all a vinyl record could deliver. But the point of stereo isn't how many speakers are used; it's the ability to reproduce an infinite number of points between speakers. Stereo relies on localization mechanisms that evolved as part of human hearing. It creates an artificial space that's different from the room you're listening in.

---

3. Bernstein followed 1954's *Waterfront* by writing hit Broadway shows, a third symphony, an opera, a mass, numerous smaller pieces, and four books. He also had time to lead the New York Philharmonic and perform as a concert pianist. But he never attempted another film.

Listen to the music in Track 17 on a pair of good speakers at fairly close range and forming an equilateral triangle with your listening position. This track was properly produced in stereo. You'll hear piano in the center, violins to the middle left, and woodwinds to the middle right. The percussion enters in the center. Then you will hear brass on the far left. All this from only two speakers.

 Hear for yourself _____

Track 17 is true stereo in an orchestral recording from the DeWolfe Music Library.[4] You'll hear piano in the center, violins to the middle left, and woodwinds to the middle right.

⚠️ *Gotcha* _____

If that's right, then what's left? It's possible you'll hear directions reversed in the above example. They were correct when I mastered the disc, but computer and NLE speakers sometimes have their wires crossed. This is a good opportunity to fix things.

Your brain supplies these phantom locations—sounds from places where there aren't any speakers—because the volume and timing of each instrument is slightly different in each of the channels. This reflects the acoustics of the recording studio. For contrast, play Track 18. It's also a two-channel recording of the same music, and looks almost the identical in a waveform display (see Figure 6.1). But those critical timing and volume differences have been eliminated, and every instrument appears in the center. Even though the CD track's format is stereo, the sound is *monaural* (single ear) or mono. Engineers call this kind of track *dual mono* because the same information is on two tracks. If it were a computer file, 50 percent of its data would be redundant. In an NLE, mono audio should stay in mono file formats, panned to the center[5] or set to play through both tracks. This saves disk space and make the system run smoother.

 Hear for yourself _____

Track 18 is the same musical recording as Track 17 but with all the directional information removed.

In film and video, the distinction between mono and stereo is primarily a postproduction issue. Field-recorded dialog is almost always mono because that's how it'll be mixed; if two channels are used for dialog, they're to give the sound editor a choice between microphones. Events and ambiences are usually recorded in stereo. Now, while you're planning the track, is the best time to decide whether to use mono or stereo for each element:

---

4. "Voyage of Destiny" (F. Talgorn) DeWolfe CD 272/1, protected by copyright and used by permission.

5. Depending on software, the function may be called *pan*, *fill*, or *take*: in each case, the idea is to have a single track play equally from both speakers, so it appears in the center.

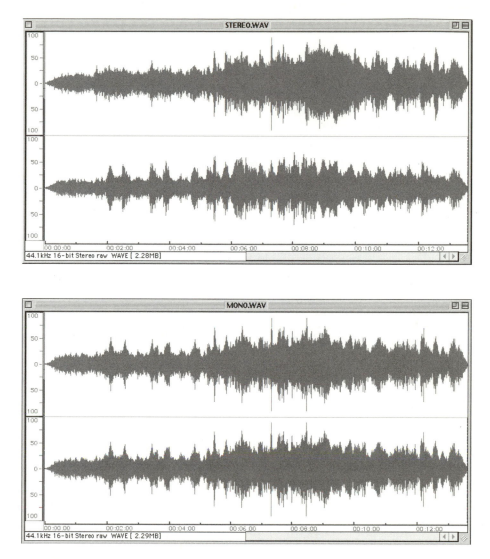

6.1 True stereo from Track 17 *(top)*, and dual mono from Track 17 *(bottom)*.

- Many CD sound effects and even some music cues are actually mono and don't need to tie up two tracks in your NLE.

- Voice-overs should always be mono for a single announcer; there's no point to using two microphones on a single mouth. If two people are having a conversation in voice-over, it's often a good idea to record them to separate channels so you'll be able to process their voices separately. But unless you're looking for a special effect (which won't survive broadcast), don't plan to leave those voices separated that way in the mix.

- Foley sound effects (Chapter 11) should be mono and placed where appropriate.

- Walla crowd sounds (Chapter 8) should usually be recorded and mixed in stereo.

When it's time to mix, you'll have to choose where each mono sound (other than dialog) gets placed across the stereo field. You can also turn mono into simulated stereo using various techniques, most of which are fairly simple and some of which are appropriate for film tracks. We'll discuss and demonstrate them in Chapter 17.

Using Different Elements for Texture

Some of today's action films have nonstop tracks. Everything is loud. When there's no excuse for gunshots or explosions, pounding music takes over. These are films you often see described as a "nonstop roller-coaster ride." Real roller coasters don't work that way. What makes the amusement park ride exciting isn't just the long fast plunge; it's also the anticipation while the cars are being slowly dragged to the top. The best roller coasters even have a couple of breaks in the middle of the ride: cars go up a stub of track, slow down as they near the top, and then reverse and come screaming down again.

Give viewers a break. Let different kinds of elements take turns dominating the track. You've got a lot to choose from:

- Characters are usually on-camera, talking to each other. But for a more intimate sound, consider treating parts of some scenes as voice-over. You'll be able to record these with much closer mics and more acoustic treatment.

- Don't keep on-camera voices in the same acoustic surrounding for too long. Let your actors move around the room or walk into a hallway or next to an open window, so the reflections and ambience change. Do similar processing to on-camera dialog you've replaced in postproduction studio sessions.

- Additional voices can be added in post to make a scene busier and give it a richer texture. Crowds can be from a stock library but work better if you also record specific phrases appropriate to the scene.

- Voice-overs are almost always intimate and close up. It sounds like the announcer is talking directly to us. But that's a fairly modern conceit. Until the mid-50s, announcers usually projected as if they were trying to reach a crowd and sometimes artificial reverb was added to simulate a theater. In the earliest films, voice-overs were treated as oratory and declaimed like a political speech. In the future, voice-overs may be yelled or whispered. Feel free to experiment.

- Some sound effects, such as doorbells or car crashes, may be called for in the script. You'll add these in post. But don't stop there. Exteriors and busy interiors almost always need additional background sounds. Quiet interiors do also, unless you'll be using a limited medium like broadcast TV.

- In real life, standing in one place usually means hearing a continuous background. Movies don't have to work this way. If characters are on a sidewalk, vary the traffic noises. Plan to make them quieter as the audience gets more involved with the dialog. Or add occasional things we can't see but could exist off-camera, such as children playing or a distant siren.

- Sound effects don't have to be realistic. Consider designing sounds from the characters' point of view, emphasizing things that would be important to them.

- Vary the music as well. Few films benefit from a constant underscore. It won't hurt to let some scenes rely on dialog and effects. Or consider having some scenes use only music, with no dialog or effects.

- Music doesn't have to sound like it was added in post, even though it almost always is. Let some of it be *diegetic* (also known as *source music*), taking place naturally in the scene. This could be dictated by the situation—you'd expect a nightclub or party to have music, even if we don't see the band or stereo system. But source music can also be used to help set up a location: stores and restaurants usually have canned background music playing. Choose an appropriate style—rock, country, classical, ethnic, or elevator—to help the viewer identify what kind of place it is.

Preproduction for Postproduction

Sounds like an oxymoron, doesn't it? Actually, you should start planning for post in the earliest stages of filmmaking. It definitely saves time and can also save a lot of money.

Before You Shoot

Know what you'll need from the shoot. This includes technical considerations, such as what sound formats you or a post facility will require, and what kind of mic technique will work best for the way you'll be mixing. Getting this wrong almost always means extra steps converting, processing, or rerecording.

Don't assume a scene doesn't need sound. Even if it will be covered by voice-over and music, or you're going to replace all the sound effects, plan for recording natural sound. Because you're shooting DV, it's free. (Film requires a separate recorder and operator and extra editorial steps.) Point a good mic at the shot, and you'll have additional elements for the mix or a guide track to use when syncing new effects. Even a built-in camera mic can be useful for this kind of sound.

Do some research before assuming you'll be able to replace dialog. *Automatic Dialog Replacement* (ADR), Chapter 8) is complicated and time-consuming. For many DV productions, it's just not practical. Unless you've got large budgets and very patient actors, rethink the sequence to eliminate most of the lines that would need to be replaced or choose a different location.

Make note of *nonsync* (*wild*) sound effects and voice-over dialog that can be gathered easily at the location, such as extra character lines or prop noises. These can be recorded in your video camera, or you can assign an assistant to capture them with MiniDisc, DAT, or even a good cassette recorder. A few minutes of extra recording while actors and props are in place can save you hours in post. (Make this commitment before you start shooting; nobody ever seems willing to do anything non-visual once they arrive on the set.)

Before You Post

It's tempting to just load in the footage and start editing, but this can be a mistake unless you've done other films in the same format. Spend a few minutes making some basic decisions about sound to avoid problems later.

Analyzing the budget

There's a tendency among hobby filmmakers to buy new toys before starting a project. Audio software, an effects library, a voice-over mic, or high-quality speakers for mixing may seem like a good idea. But first, ask yourself if you'll be able to amortize their cost over other projects. You may find that it's cheaper to rent equipment just for this use, or hire a studio for specific functions like ADR and mix. Business-oriented filmmakers should be making this kind of decision already.

Consider the cost of your time as well. Even if you're doing this as a labor of love and not paying yourself professional rates, your time is a limited commodity. You can spend time debugging and then learning how to use new software or special sound techniques; or you can concentrate on things you do best, possibly storytelling or visual composition, that will make a bigger contribution to the film.

Budgeting outside audio services

In large cities, a good audio-post or narration studio with experienced engineer will cost $125–250 per hour plus stock. A lot of the price variation isn't related to quality, but glitziness: ad agency clients are willing to pay extra for services like a dedicated traffic department, or amenities like a kitchen staff and well-appointed lobby. You can save some money, if you don't need to see picture while doing a narration, by hiring a studio that specializes in radio. Many narrators have their own studios and throw that service in for free.

A narration session can take about an hour for each twenty minutes of finished audio, but a lot depends on the script, the narrator's experience, and your own directing style. Mixing properly prepared tracks takes about the same time, plus whatever is necessary for transfers to and from the studio's system. Add at least an hour if the client is in the studio for narration or mix. But this may be more efficient than having to come back for changes.

Full audio post takes a lot longer. If you want the studio to start with your tracks and clean up voice edits as necessary, then add well-timed music and appropriate sound effects, process everything for proper impact, and mix, figure between four hours and a day for a 20-minute video. A lot depends on what shape your tracks are in to start with, how much prep you've done, and how experienced the engineer is. It also depends on what kind of equipment the studio has. Typical mouse-driven computer systems are much slower than audio workstations with dedicated control surfaces and built-in mixers designed for media production.

Even if the studio is providing music from their library, you can often save time and expense by booking a separate session to select the music. Library music costs between $15–$125 per selection, or about $100–$500 for unlimited music in a 20-minute video, for basic corporate or educational use. The lower end covers basic buyout music, often performed by a single musician on keyboards. The higher end covers the same sources Hollywood features often rely on, with hot session players, top composers, and vocals or symphony orchestras when appropriate. Costs rise when more people are likely to see a video, so they'll be slightly higher for local broadcast, much higher for national broadcast, and up to $1,500 per selection for a low-budget movie that's going to be in theaters, possibly broadcast, and sold as home video.[6]

Original music is negotiable. Composers who specialize in video scoring will charge between $100–1,000 per screen minute, depending on their talent and experience, what kind of instrumentation is necessary, and how soon you want it. But you may be able to find a band or young composer who's willing to do it for free, in exchange for the exposure. Follow the tips in Chapter 10 about rights, licenses, and written agreements.

Sound effects are free if you gather them yourself. Commercial ones, with full rights to use them in your film, are fairly cheap: you can download them from reputable suppliers for a few dollars per minute. Most audio post facilities have immense sound effects libraries already on-hand. Costs may be negotiable even if it shows up on the studio's rate card (a standard is $15 per effect); the studio needs to cover the cost of buying the libraries but doesn't have any incremental expense when using them.

Technical decisions

Before you start editing, you also have to make some basic operational choices:

- How are you planning to use the tracks in your NLE? If you use a consistent layout, with specific tracks dedicated to on-camera dialog, voice-over, sound effects, and music, you'll

---

6. Fortunately, you can create your opus with a film festival license for a few hundred dollars per song and then upgrade to full theatrical when a Hollywood distributor discovers you.

make subsequent processing and mixing go a lot faster. Complex music or sound effects sequences will require multiple tracks.

- What sample rate should you work at? If all your footage is being imported via FireWire, 48 kHz is probably the most efficient. It's the primary standard for DV cameras, and the alternate standard—32 kHz—is easily converted to match. But music and sound effects CDs are 44.1 kHz, and many NLEs don't handle the conversion between 44.1 kHz and 48 kHz well (see Chapter 7). If you're redigitizing source footage through an analog connection, it makes sense to set everything at 44.1 kHz.

- Do you need timecode? If so, what format? This may be dictated by how the video will be used—TV stations often insist on dropframe

> ⚠ **Gotcha** _____
>
> **They call it "temp love."** In Hollywood, editors will frequently grab a song from another project—or even a commercial CD—to suggest a rhythm and mood for a sequence. The intent is to use this *temp track* while the piece is being worked on, and then replace it when the final score is available.
>
> But music has a way of getting under your skin. Producers or advertising clients can get used to the temp track and decide that no other song will do. Sometimes there's an unexpected scramble to secure rights—usually for more money than was originally budget.
>
> This may be okay for features and national ads, but I've seen it happen on corporate films and local spots. If your music budget is limited, it can be a good idea to choose—and have the client approve—the actual piece before you start cutting picture.

for long programs—or by the production contract. In many NLEs and most audio software, it's difficult to change the timecode format after you start.

Creative decisions

There are some things you should know about the entire track before you start editing. How detailed should the soundtrack be? It's silly to waste time and tracks on things that won't be heard when a video is broadcast or put on the Web. Think about music as well. Know where important cues will be before your start editing, so you can leave time for them in the sequence. If a montage is going to be driven by musical rhythms, you need the actual song or a close substitute. This means you have to think about music sources and rights before you start editing (Chapter 10)—but that's a good idea anyway, considering how significant music can be in a post-production budget.

Choosing an Outside Studio

It's not enough to decide to take some audio operations to a professional studio. You'll have to do a little research to find one that can do a good job for you. While your town might have a lot of music studios, the techniques and philosophy of audio post are different—so is a lot of the equipment, software, and backup facilities. Even a simple voice-over requires a different kind of mic, room acoustics, and processing than a pop vocal. ADR is a completely different process from anything done in a music studio and can even be beyond a studio that specializes in radio and TV voice-overs.

This isn't to say that a music studio can't do the job or can't have an engineer experienced in the proper techniques. But I've found the crossover to be rare, except in very large facilities that can devote separate operations to each kind of recording. In Hollywood, the situation is completely opposite: sound is so specialized that separate companies will be devoted to recording a feature's music, editing it, recording ADR, creating and editing sound effects, and mixing the final track.

A good way to find an appropriate studio is to ask local ad agency producers. A video post facility can tell you where their clients get tracks done. If you have to rely on a Web search or the Yellow Pages, look for a studio that specifies this kind of work as a specialty and can show you past projects.

You should also check the facility itself. If you're going to be recording voice-overs, a large studio isn't critical, but you should be able to clap your hands in it and not hear any echo. (A fairly large and echo-free room is a must for ADR.) The control room should be businesslike, with plenty of room for a producer to spread out scripts and other notes, and have a prominent high-quality video monitor centered between the speakers. Look for a large, licensable music and sound effects library, even if you'll be supplying your own elements—this is usually a sign that the studio does a lot of this kind of work. Look at what's hanging on the wall as well: Emmys, Clios, and other media awards are usually given for creative reasons rather than technical expertise, but having them around suggests the studio's got a good amount of experience.

Many composers specializing in film and media scores are also competent at voice-over recording and mixing, though they might not have the equipment to do it as efficiently as a specialized studio. If you're hiring someone to write and produce music for your film, ask if they want to be considered for mix.

Make your final judgement based on actual final soundtracks the studio, engineer, or composer has worked on. Any professional will have a demo reel available, and most also post segments of representative projects on their Web sites. When you're watching a reel, forget the picture: close your eyes and see if the sound makes sense.

The Postproduction Sequence

There's a definite order to putting a track together. The sequence below should work for any small project, from a local spot to an independent feature. If you've got lots of money and people available, and speed is more important than efficiency, you can do many of these steps simultaneously; that's how mainstream features are done.

1. Capture dialog along with the original footage. Or capture dialog from a double-system recorder such as DAT or MiniDisc, and sync it to the footage. It's usually best to capture at high quality even if you're editing low-resolution video; audio doesn't take very much hard disk space. If the film will have an original score, get a copy of the script to the composer.

2. Gather any other voice material you'll need. If this is a narrated documentary, it makes sense to use a scratch track while editing—possibly your own voice recorded in your camera or computer. Don't invest in a final narration recording until you've put the actual elements together, because you might have to change the script to accommodate editorial changes in the interviews.

3. Gather anything else where the timing is essential to the video, such as music for montages. If an audio element has to be approved separately by the client, such as a main title theme or logo effect, get that process started now.

4. Edit the on-camera dialog.

5. Edit any voice-over material.

6. Add any nonvoice sounds that are critical for timing.

At this point, you're probably getting client approvals and starting to think of the picture as being in its final form (*locked*). Subsequent audio steps can rely on accurate timings, and may have to be redone—at additional cost—if you change the picture. If the film will have an original score, get a copy of the locked video to the composer.

7. Choose and edit the score.

8. Add any backgrounds or ambiences that seem missing once the music is in place.

9. Add other sound effects that seem missing when you can hear the music and backgrounds.

10. Process and clean up the voices. If necessary, record and edit narration and ADR.

11. Add any special audio effects that are necessary for the plot, including processing to enhance sound effects.

Stop for a while. Give your ears a chance to recover and your creative judgement a chance to have the proper perspective before going on to the next step. If you've been working on this project for most of the day, do something else for half an hour. If you've been working on it for two weeks, take the rest of the day off.

12. Mix, using processing as necessary to make tracks work smoothly together.

13. Review the mix and check it on appropriate speakers and in mono.

14. Marry the mix to the final video. Postprocess as necessary for Web or other media.

Six months later, take it off the shelf and listen to the mix again—ideally with an audience. Figure out what you could do better next time.

Chapter 7

Getting Audio into the Computer

Remember this:

- Digital audio transfers are usually flawless. Any problems can often be resolved by changing a few settings.

- Analog transfers require a little more care with levels. Unfortunately, you can't automatically trust the meters. Some calibration is almost always necessary.

- Lipsync problems may seem intractable, particularly when lipsync involves film as well as digital media. Understanding the principles will help you resolve them.

Commercial television is often accused of a lack of originality. Critics complain that almost everything is a copy of something else.

That's certainly how most shows used to be edited: by copying. You'd put a blank piece of video-tape into a recorder. This would become the *master*. You'd put the original footage into a player. Then, scene by scene, you'd find the desired takes on the original and copy them to the master. If you were going to add music or sound effects, you'd copy the assembled master's dialog onto a multitrack tape. You'd copy the other elements to other tracks and then mix them. Then you'd copy the completed mix back to the master. This was the only way to edit video for decades, and many shows are still done this way.

This means that TV audio may have been copied four or more times before there was a tape that could be sent to the stations. Back in analog days, each copy operation was a chance for noise or distortion to creep in. Once it did, the junk could never be removed.

Today, sound is digital and you can copy or edit with no loss of quality at all. But first you have to copy it *into* the computer. If you do this through an analog connection, all the old bugaboos are back. If you do it digitally, traditional noise and distortion isn't a problem—but you can introduce other problems. Because this is the easiest place for gremlins to sneak in, getting a signal onto a hard drive can be the most important technical step in postproduction.

Transfer Technology

Apple's FireWire,[1] a high-speed serial protocol, is now the most common way of capturing audio and video from the original footage. With a properly equipped camera or deck, Firewire can also control tape movement. FireWire comes standard as a 6-pin jack on all Macs and some Windows machines, and can be added to other computers with third-party cards. Most DV cameras also have FireWire jacks, with only four pins (Figure 7.1). A simple adapter cable is all that's needed to connect between 6-pin and 4-pin fireWire.

Analog video decks, such as VHS or BetaSP, don't have FireWire connections. But you can capture footage from these by using a powered converter box, also known as a FireWire interface or media converter; it has conventional

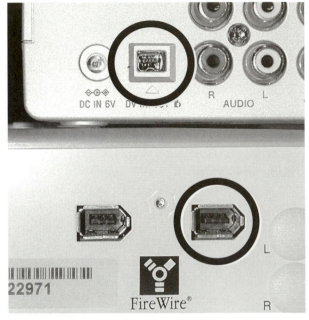

7.1 FireWire connectors on video *(above)* and computer gear *(below)* are different, but a simple cable will connect them.

audio and video inputs and outputs on the analog side, and a FireWire jack on the other. The computer sees it as a digital camera.

Some very high-end NLEs accept AES/EBU audio directly. Not surprisingly, the issues with AES/EBU are very similar to those when transferring with FireWire.

⚠️ *Gotcha*

One-way street. While FireWire is bidirectional—data flows in both directions simultaneously—most FireWire analog interfaces aren't. You have to flip a switch to determine whether the box will turn analog signals into digital for capturing in your computer, or convert the computer output back to analog for your deck or video monitor.

---

1. Apple invented it, trademarked it, and opened the standard up to other manufacturers. But until the middle of 2002, Apple charged a license fee to use the name, so companies often called it IEEE 1394 to save money. Sony gave the standard its own handle, i.Link. It's all the same thing.

Digital Audio Transfers

When a DV signal is carried from camera to computer digitally, there is no audio loss. Unless there's a setup problem, the computer file will be a clone of the DV tape. There's no need to adjust levels—in most cases, there's no *way* to adjust levels.

The most critical part of the setup is making the sample rates match. DV audio runs at nominal 32 kHz or 48 kHz s/r. Your capture setup controls must be set to the same rate as the camera or converter, or else the audio is likely to be damaged. Problems range from sound at the wrong pitch, to periodic clickings, to silence.

If most of your project's audio is coming from the camera, the project or sequence should be set to 48 kHz. That's also the rate you're most likely to use when printing the final project to video. But if most of the sound is coming from 44.1 kHz sources, and you'll be outputting for the Web or CD-ROM, you should use 44.1 kHz for the project as well. The goal is to have as few places as possible where the clip's rate doesn't match the project. Each mismatch requires on-the-fly conversion for previews—which can sound bad—or a separate rendering at the new rate. Most video software is not very good at this kind of conversion. If a clip's rate doesn't match the project, it's usually a good idea to open the file in an audio program and covert it to the project's sample rate.

Even when sample rates match, there can be problems. Some NLEs require precise sync between the digital audio words and the video frame rate, and a few cameras don't have this precision. When this problem occurs, you may hear momentary dropouts in the track. The only cure is to transfer the audio as analog. (This isn't the same kind of sync problem as having sound and picture drift apart, which is covered later in this chapter.)

Audio should always be set to 16-bits, even if your final output will be in an 8-bit format. Crossfades, volume adjustments, and other processing can get very noisy in an 8-bit environment. Edit and do your final mix at full resolution, and then make an 8-bit copy of the final output.

A lot of dialog is recorded in mono with a single mic. There's no advantage to capturing this kind of footage in stereo. Stereo material, of course, should be captured in stereo. If the footage has a boom and lav on separate tracks, capture one as stereo left and and the other as stereo right—you don't want to combine the mics yet and possibly never will. Edit as stereo, and sort it out in the mix.

Many cameras give you the option of adding extra audio tracks by setting a 32 kHz sample rate and 12-bit format. NLEs convert this to 16-bits as the file is being transferred. If footage has four tracks, some NLEs will give you the option of capturing either the 1-2 pair or the 3-4 pair (look in the advanced audio settings). If you need all four tracks, you'll have to capture twice. But since these extra tracks are intended for adding narration or music in the camera—something you're better off doing in a computer—it usually makes more sense not to use the option in the first place.

<table>
<tr><td>

⚠️ **Gotcha** _____

MiniDisc quality loss. Many filmmakers use pocket consumer MiniDisc recorders in the field, as an alternative to wireless or the poor audio circuits in some cameras. While the format itself can provide acceptable audio,[1] the players' analog outputs are designed for casual listening and aren't high quality. A few portables have digital outputs, which should be used instead. Or get a separate AC-powered player designed for home stereo systems; almost all of them have digital outputs.

_____

1. While there's no guarantee a particular $300 recorder will sound better than a $3,000 camera, most do.

</td><td>

If you're bringing a signal in from DAT or MiniDisc, you can also capture digitally to preserve quality. You'll need a player with a digital output and one of the input devices discussed in Chapter 4. Or use HHB's portable MiniDisc recorder, which connects directly to the computer as a USB input device.

The same sample rate issues apply to DAT or MiniDisc transfers as to camera transfers. MiniDiscs run at 44.1 kHz. DATs may be at that rate, or at 32 kHz or 48 kHz. If the transferred audio doesn't agree with your NLE's project settings, it's best to use an audio program to convert.

</td></tr>
</table>

Direct File Transfers

You can save time by transferring audio data as a file, rather than a stream. A few field recorders don't use tape or disc; instead, these recorders write standard audio files to CompactFlash cards or miniature hard drives. A computer with a matching card slot can copy CompactFlash files directly, much faster than real time. Sample rate and bit depth are specified in the file header, so there's no chance for setup error. Most of these recorders use MPEG-2

⚠️ **Gotcha** _____

Too hot to handle! Many pop CDs are recorded at extreme levels, sometimes louder than your computer's audio output can play without distortion.[1] In my experience, it's a good idea to soften these files by a decibel or two in an audio program before importing them to the NLE.

_____

1. There's probably a lot of distortion built into the recording as well, if levels are that hot. But that's a creative decision on the part of the producer and mastering engineer.

compression to pack more sound onto its expensive media. Depending on the recorder and settings, the compression algorithm may be mp3—which some NLEs can open directly—or MPEG-2 Layer 2, which has to be converted first. But even if your NLE can handle the compressed file, it's a good idea to use audio software to change it to 16-bits at the project's sample rate.

A similar process happens when you capture (*rip*) a file from an audio CD in your computer's CD-ROM drive. It's a perfect digital transfer, as fast as your CD-ROM can spin. Ripping functions are available in most audio programs and shareware utilities. Mac-based NLEs can also do this, since it's part of the underlying QuickTime system. CDs are always at 44.1 kHz, so sample rate conversion might be necessary before you use the file.

Analog Audio Recording

It's called *digitizing* in the NLE world—audio is usually captured at the same time as video through different connections. It's just called *recording* in audio-only programs. The process is the same. You connect an analog audio signal to a jack on the internal sound card or NLE's connection pod, or you connect an analog audio signal to an external FireWire or USB input device. Because it's analog, you have to set levels properly and avoid noise.

Despite the need for extra care, there can be advantages to using analog. Nonstandard or badly synchronized sample rates are easily handled. You can also adjust audio levels as you digitize.

These advantages come at a cost. Each time the signal goes from digital to analog and back to digital again, the signal picks up a little more distortion. One such pass, with good equipment, is seldom a problem if everything is adjusted perfectly. But the transfer can pick up a lot of problems if the levels are wrong.

Headroom and Noise

Analog circuits have a limited range between their own internal noise and the loudest signal they can carry accurately. Unfortunately, accuracy is a slippery concept. Unlike digital audio, which has negligible distortion below full scale and then fails utterly, analog begins to add distortion as the signal approaches 0 VU, and it then increases the distortion for signals above 0 VU—a volume range often known as *headroom*—until the equipment reaches its maximum volume. But how much distortion is added and how many VU of headroom are available varies depending on the equipment. Think of the rectangle in Figure 7.2 as representing the full range a circuit can carry and the upper gray area as increasing distortion. It's up to the manufacturer to decide how much distortion is acceptable.[2] The volume that produces that amount of distortion becomes the nominal level and will read as 0 VU if the product has a meter.

---

2. It also depends on the type of equipment. Analog amplifiers and processors typically have a few hundredths of a percent distortion at 0 VU. Pro audio tape recorders would be around 0.3 percent at 0 VU, and 3 percent around +6 VU above. Pro video tape recorders would be somewhat worse because the tape moves at a slower speed and the track width is smaller.

You can reduce the possibility of distortion by lowering the volume, but system noise is always present. If the signal gets too soft, a lot of it will be obscured by the noise. The noise mixes with the signal, and this kind of noise can't be eliminated by equalizers or noise-reduction software. (It *can* be made less annoying, though. See Chapter 16.).

You have to compromise, making things loud enough that noise isn't a problem but not so loud that distortion is noticeable. These problems are cumulative: each time you pass through any analog circuit, more noise and distortion are added.

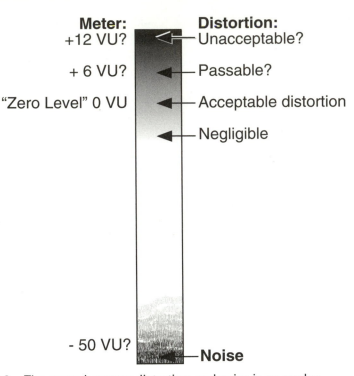

7.2 The range between distortion and noise in an analog circuit. The question marks are because actual values vary, depending on the quality and type of equipment.

Crest factor

Professionals typically line up their equipment using a tone at the nominal or average level. But this gives no indication of how much higher the peaks will be. The volume range between average and peak—known as the *crest factor*—depends a lot on what you're recording.

- Original dialog can have peaks 12–18 dB above average, if the acting is dynamic. But an on-camera spokesperson with a well-controlled voice might not have peaks more than 6 dB above average.

⚠️ **Gotcha**

You can't trust things at the top. Some forms of pop music tolerate a lot of distortion. A lot of today's prosumer analog audio mixers and processors are sold for this kind of music, so the peak-reading meters on this equipment may extend to +10 VU or higher before turning red. Dialog is more sensitive—even a little distortion can affect intelligibility—so filmmakers should check anything above +6 VU. Of course, all of this depends on the quality of the equipment itself.

- Many background ambiences are fairly even. But sound effects can be unpredictable, and a gunshot may be 30 dB louder than the background.

- Pop music is usually processed to stay within a 6 dB crest factor. Older recordings may have higher dynamic range. Some newer dance music can be 2 dB. Classical music can have an extreme range.

Production sound recordists and studio engineers rely on their experience and try to guess a recording level that'll have the least amount of noise but never go into distortion. Fortunately, you don't have to guess when you're digitizing existing material. You can scan the entire take and set levels according to the loudest part, or redigitize if a file is distorted.

Level Setting and Meters

Back in analog days, the VU meter made level setting easy. You'd adjust so the occasional peaks were just above zero, and you could trust that everything was as good as it could be. The device would output a reliable average −10 dBV or +4 dBu at 0 VU, just right for the next piece of equipment the device was connected to.

Things aren't as simple at the interface between analog and digital. There's no precise way to say how many bits should be triggered by the nominal level. It can't be 0 dBFS because analog signals frequently exceed the nominal on short peaks, and digital has absolutely no headroom.

Circuit designers are in a bind. If they set things so a good analog level results in a high digital value, peaks might overload the analog-to-digital converter chip (ADC) and push it into distortion. Once this happens, a software volume control is of no help. But if circuit designers make the digital level too low, it'll be close to *two* sources of noise: low-level digital noise which increases with processing, and noise from the analog circuits that feed the ADC, which can be relatively high in low-cost equipment. Basically, all the designers can do is compromise and hope for the best.

Professional broadcast equipment is considered good enough that the standard can be more conservative. Networks specify −20 dBFS as the nominal level, and high-end equipment is usually set so the nominal level produces +4 dBu on the analog connectors. It leaves 20 dB for the crest factor but still puts the average signal some 60 dB above the equipment's analog noise. Digital processing noise is also less of a problem in pro equipment, which often uses 24- or 32-bit math internally.

But −20 dBFS may not be appropriate on the desktop, where cheap analog circuits and 16-bit effects processing raise the noise level. Besides, a −20 dBFS waveform looks wimpy in a waveform display (Figure 7.3); users expect something bigger.

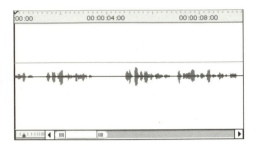

7.3 This typical dialog recording averages –20 dBFS and peaks around –14 dBFS. The waveform is possibly too small for visual editing.

Many desktop NLEs specify –12 dBFS for a nominal level, not only so the waveform looks better (Figure 7.4) but also to avoid processing noise. But if a sound source has a wide dynamic range, this might not provide enough room for peaks.

There's a danger in digitizing at too high a volume. Figure 7.5 shows original dialog with an average level of –6 dBFS and peaks at –0.2 dBFS. While it's acceptable for a processed or mixed file to become this loud, if original footage looks like this, there's a good chance peaks have been distorted.

So what level should you digitize at? In a desktop environment, I recommend –12 dBFS for average signals. But you have to be flexible and lower the digitizing level if the meter is coming close to 0 dBFS, or if the waveform comes close to filling the clip display. That's the approach used in music production as well, where standards range between –20 and –12 dBFS, based on the program material.

If you're preparing material for broadcast, you can still work at this elevated level. Just turn the final mix down to –20 dBFS nominal before making digital tapes for the stations.

Calibrating Analog Transfers

You can't automatically trust the meters. Presumably, meters on a mixer or analog video deck equal 0 VU when the device is putting out its nominal line level. But there's no standard for how a NLE's input device will translate that nominal level to bits. Until you've calibrated your system, the meters on an analog source device are useless for setting digitizing levels.

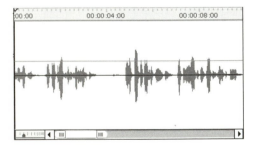

7.4 This one averages –12 dBFS and peaks around –6 dBFS, probably about as high as an original capture should go.

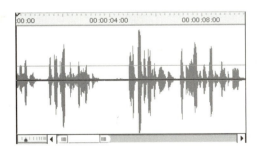

7.5 Dialog with average level around –6 dBFS, peak at –0.2 dBFS; living *very* dangerously.

7.6 These meters appear to be calibrated in decibels relative to full scale (dBFS) and are logarithmic. You can tell by looking at the top number and by the decibels decreasing linearly below it.

Calibration step 1: Meter versus file

These days, you generally can trust software meters, if they're calibrated in dBFS. The meters in Figure 7.6 are; you can tell by the fact that zero is at the absolute top. These meters are also somewhat logarithmic: –6 dBFS or 50 percent of the maximum signal voltage, is fairly high in the scale. A meter calibrated this way will encourage you to digitize at safe levels.

The meter in Figure 7.7 is also calibrated in dBFS. But note how –6 dBFS is at the middle of the scale. This meter is calibrated in linear volts and will tempt you to digitize at too high a level. If your software has meters like this, avoid letting unprocessed dialog get above the midpoint.

7.7 This dBFS meter isn't logarithmic. Although it's reading –12 dBFS, a good level for digitizing dialog, it's only lit up about a quarter of the way. A meter like this will tempt you to record at too high a level.

If your system's input meters are calibrated in dBFS, you can skip down to the next section. But some meters are arbitrary. One may seem to indicate VU and extend to +6. Or it may have no markings at all (Figure 7.8).

If your system has meters like Figure 7.8, you'll have to do your own calibration:

⚠ *Gotcha* _____

The mysterious overload. Note how the two horizontal meters in Figure 7.6, and the one in Figure 7.7 have an overload warning light to the right of 0 dBFS. But digital audio values can't exceed zero; there are no bits left to express a higher voltage. If these meters were absolutely, precisely calibrated to 0 dBFS, the light would never turn on!

Instead, many systems count consecutive samples that reach 0 dBFS. When three or more samples in a row hit the 0 dBFS level, the software considers it an overload and lights the warning. Other meters are simply calibrated to show an overload at some level slightly below 0 dBFS, such as –0.5 dBFS. But there is no absolute standard—I've seen some meters that light a warning at –6 dBFS.

1. Play and digitize—don't just rip—Track 19 of the book's CD, which has a steady tone for five seconds at –20, –12, and –6 dBFS. On some computers, you may be able to play it from the CD-ROM drive and see the levels on your NLE's digitizing meters. If your system's meters don't work when transferring from CD, you'll need to play the disc on a separate player, plugged into your input device. Note how the meter looks at each of the three levels. You may want to sketch them or grab a screenshot.

2. Open the file you just created in a NLE or audio program that has an output meter. Set any volume sliders to 0 dB and read the levels you just recorded. There's a good chance your levels won't match the nominal values I recorded. Adjust the input volume control to compensate and repeat step 1.

3. Eventually, you'll record a file where the levels are reasonably close to the ones I recorded. Keep the notes you made about meter readings for that pass: those are what it should look like when digitizing at the correct levels.

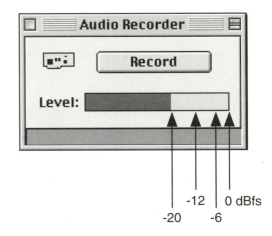

7.8 Meters like this aren't much help until you calibrate them.

7.9 Calibration marks for Macintosh Premiere.

Hear for yourself

Track 19 consists of steady test tones for checking a record-level meter. It has a 1 kHz sine wave, with five seconds at –20 dBFS, –12 dBFS, and –6 dBFS.

Figure 7.9 shows the input meter in Premiere for the Mac, with calibration marks that I've added after doing similar tests.

Meter calibration workarounds   If your NLE doesn't have an input volume control, you can use the one in your computer's control panels (Figure 7.10). This isn't a good idea for setting levels during actual digitizing, for reasons discussed in the next section, but is okay for this calibration step.

If you don't have a program with a playback meter, go to www.dplay.com/postfiles. Download levltest.zip (about 34 KB[3]), unzip it, and import it in your NLE. This is a properly calibrated file made from Track 19. Open it in a clip window and note how big the waveforms are. Use this as a reference when measuring your own digitized files.

Calibration step 2: Analog signal versus computer

The previous procedure only deals with the relationship between a program's meter and the file it creates. To get the cleanest sound, we also have to be sure the meter is properly indicating what the ADC is seeing. Those volume or gain sliders in Figure 7.10 are between the ADC and meter and prevent you from accurately setting the level.

- If the input is receiving too much signal and the ADC is starting to distort, your turning the slider down will make the meter look better. But the chip will still be distorting.

- If the input isn't getting enough signal, you'll have problems with noise from the analog circuits as well as the ADC. You can turn the slider up until the meter reads a good level. But this will amplify all the noise you've picked up.

Note

Set these system-level input controls to their midpoints—that's probably the default—and never touch them again. Some input devices let you disable them completely, which is a good idea.

A lot of NLE and audio programs have their own recording volume controls. Because these programs are software-based, they can cause just as much trouble as the system-level ones. Set software recording volumes to their midpoints and leave the levels there.

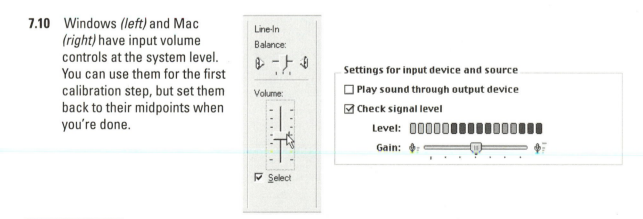

7.10 Windows *(left)* and Mac *(right)* have input volume controls at the system level. You can use them for the first calibration step, but set them back to their midpoints when you're done.

---

3. The actual file is 1.3 MB when you unzip it. Test tones are one of the few audio signals that algorithms like PKZip can compress effectively because the wave is so repetitive. An ordinary music or speech file of the same length is too random to zip well and often doesn't compress smaller than 80 percent of the original.

Calibration step 3: External mixer versus computer

The best place to adjust volume levels for digitizing is on the analog side. A small mixer, connected between the sound source and your computer's input, will give you more noise-free control than most software-based adjustments. It can also serve as a preselector for multiple digitizing sources, a preamp and phantom power supply for a microphone, and a monitor controller.

Connect all of your analog sources to a mixer, and mixer to computer input, by using the tips in Chapter 4.

Mixers often have LED output meters. But there's no guarantee the meters match your computer's input. To check, first do the calibration steps above. Then play a steady signal through the mixer—CD Track 12 is good for this—and adjust the mixer's output until the software's input meters indicate –12 dBFS.

If you're very lucky, the mixer's meter will come exactly to 0 VU. You can trust this setup to accurately indicate digitizing levels. Otherwise, note what level the mixer displays—you can mark it with tape—and use that as your nominal level.

If the mixer is indicating a very low level when the software meters indicate –12 dBFS, you may have plugged into your input device's mic jack. Check the connections and try again. Or you may have a conflict between a –10 dBV computer input and a +4 dBu mixer output. If the mixer is indicating a very high level, considerably above 0 VU, you may have a prosumer mixer connected to a professional input device. See Chapter 4 and check the cables and input device settings.

Mixer tips   While low-cost mixers can be helpful in a digitizing setup, they don't have the noise and distortion performance of a studio recording console. A few extra steps will help you get the best sound out of them.

- Many mixers have small, *trim* controls near each channel's input jack. Follow the adjustment procedure recommended in the mixer's manual to reduce distortion and noise. If your mixer has these controls, but you don't have the manual any more, set the channel and master faders to its nominal position (sometimes marked 0 or U). Play a normal signal through the channel and adjust the trim until the meter reads 0 VU.

- Inputs generate a small amount of their own noise. You can reduce this by turning all the faders down except for the input you're digitizing and the master. If the mixer has effects return controls (usually small knobs above the master), turn those down as well.

- Avoid using the mixer's equalizers. You can do a more controllable (and undoable) job in software. Leave equalizers at their midpoint or neutral position.

Digitizing from Analog Tape Decks

Analog tape is a simpler technology than DAT or computer backup tapes, and in many ways, the information is not as robust. Couple that with the likely age of any playback deck you're likely to be using, and it's reasonable to assume that some adjustment will be necessary to get the best results when grabbing sound from archived open-reel or cassette tapes.

The heart of these decks are the *tape heads*, small coils wound around a magnetic core and mounted in plastic or metal cubes. Tape is pulled past the heads by a capstan, a spinning metal or ceramic rod with a free-turning rubber idler that presses the tape against it. The tape's track can be thought of as a row of tiny magnets whose strength and polarity varies with the sound wave. When the tape track is pulled past the playback head, the magnets generate a tiny voltage which is amplified to re-create the sound. Depending on design, a deck may have two, three, or four heads, but the one closest to the capstan usually does the playback. Check the rubber idler next to the capstan. It should be slightly resilient and a matte color. If it's glazed or cracked, it should be replaced; take the deck to a technician.

Cleaning

These heads have to be intimately close to the moving tape. Dirt, grease, or worn-off magnetic oxide from previous playings can get in the way, which makes the audio sound dull. So before you transfer, clean the tape path. Most good decks have a head cover or cassette door that can be pulled off to give you access. (Low-cost cassette decks have nonremovable doors and you have to reach in to clean things. It's harder, but not impossible.) The heads and rubber rollers that you need to clean are usually retracted in cassette decks, but they pop up when you press the Play button.

You can get a kit of tape head cleaning solution and lint-free swabs for a few dollars at electronics stores. Moisten a swab with the solution and rub it firmly across the heads and any nonrotating tape guides. Then examine the swab, if you see any dirt, throw the swab away and start again with a clean one. Eventually, the swabs won't find any more dirt to pick up, so rub the heads with a dry swab to wipe up any leftover fluid. Cleaning solutions can damage the bearings of rotating parts, so make sure solution doesn't flow down into them. You also should clean the capstan rod and rubber idler—the procedure is the same—but be extra careful not to let fluid get into the motor bearings.

Demagnetizing

Now the fun begins. *Demagnetizing* is an arm-waving ritual that seems so arcane you'd expect incense and a pentagram to accompany it. But there are good reasons for all of the steps. Tape recorders have a lot of metal, and as the magnetic tape moves through the recorder, the tape can magnetize the heads and guides enough to interfere with playback and cause extra hiss. You'll need a large electromagnet plugged into a standard AC socket, so the magnet is constantly changing polarity. You can get a pro-quality demagnetizer for about $75 from broadcast suppliers, or you can do the same job with a small, handheld tape eraser (such as Radio Shack's #44-233, $37) or even a transformer-equipped soldering gun.[4] What ever you use has to generates a strong alternating field and have a switch that can be kept on. The switch is important because you don't want the magnet turning on or off anywhere near the tape heads; the rapidly building or decaying field of the magnet switch near the heads will do more harm than good.

Hence, the arm-waving dance. Move any tapes, floppy discs, or other sensitive material at least five feet away for safety and hold the demagger at least three feet from the tape deck. Then turn it on. Now, very slowly, move the demagger toward the tape head. It should take at least fifteen seconds to travel the three feet. Get as close to the tape head as possible—a quarter inch or so is good—but don't rub against it because you might scratch the tape head surface. Now start pulling the demagger away, just as slowly. This action randomizes any magnetic alignments that might have built up in the tape deck. When the demagnetizer is at least three feet away, you can safely turn it off.

Alignment

The tiny magnets in the tape track were created when the powdered iron surface of the tape was pulled past a vertical gap in the recording head's core, and are parallel to that gap. The playback gap has to be exactly in line with the magnets or it'll miss subtle variations. Precision is important; an error of one degree can seriously hurt the high frequencies and the stereo image. Professionals use lab-generated tapes to set the gap angle—called *azimuth*—to be exactly perpendicular to the tape movement. (The test tapes are necessary if you're preparing analog tapes for other people. You can get these tapes for $80–175, depending on format, from broadcast suppliers.) Because there's no guarantee your older tapes were recorded on well-calibrated machines, forget the standard and adjust the playback deck directly to the tapes.

Every tape deck has a way to set the azimuth of each of its heads; it's usually a small screw just to the side or rear corner of each head. (If you see a lot of adjustment screws, check the deck's manual or leave the job for a pro.) I've drawn circles around the proper screws on two decks, in Figure 7.11. Even cheaper cassette decks with nonremovable doors have an azimuth screw; look on the lower part of the door, or just beneath it, for a small hole. The hole lines up with the screw when the heads are engaged.

Once you've found the screw, the rest is easy. Grab a matching, nonmagnetic screwdriver (you can demagnetize it with the same procedure you used for the heads). Start playing the tape you'll want to transfer, using the widest-range speakers you own. Turn the screw a little bit and listen for the high frequencies to get brighter. If they don't, try turning the screw in the other direction.

---

4. Radio Shack also sells demagnetizers built into cassette shells. These aren't as effective.

7.11 Alignment screws on an open-reel and cassette deck.

These adjustments are sensitive—once you're in the ballpark, a degree or two can be critical—but you can do them by ear.

These three steps—cleaning, demagnetizing, and aligning—are critical before analog audio tape transfers. There is no way to simulate their effects in software without seriously raising the noise level.

Analog video decks need similar cleaning and demagging if you're playing from these decks' linear audio tracks. But the inside of a VTR is complicated, and the job should be left to a pro. Use a head-cleaning tape when you notice minor problems, and have the deck serviced regularly.

Not Digitizing At All

If most of your work uses FireWire transfers of camera audio or audio transfers from the NLE's CD-ROM drive, occasional digitizing might not be worth the effort to set up properly. Contact local sound studios instead. These days, most music and voice production is handled in computers, and studios are apt to have high-quality digitizing equipment already installed and calibrated. These studios can copy your analog sources directly to CD-ROM in file formats and sample rates you specify.

Synchronization

If you're capturing sound and picture simultaneously from a videotape, the resulting file should be in lipsync. But if you're using *double system* sound, where audio comes from a different playback deck than video, you'll have to synchronize manually. Double system is the standard when shooting film instead of video and is also preferred by some videographers. Videographers use it as a way to avoid wireless mics—hiding MiniDisc recorders on talent or the groom in a wedding video—and they use it as a workaround for the sometimes awful internal sound on low-end camcorders.

Speed Issues

Fortunately, speed control is much easier in the DV world than it ever was for conventional filmmakers. Both DV cameras and digital audio media (MiniDisc, DAT, computer file, or audio CD) are inherently speed stable. The crystals in all but the cheapest digital recorders should hold sync within a frame for at least fifteen minutes. Most will go longer. But crystal stability is influenced by temperature, and there is some variation between units. If in doubt, transfer to your computer using the same recorder at about the same temperature you used in the field. Once a double system track is transferred into your NLE, the computer's common system clock should keep audio and video rolling at the same speed.

Gotcha _____

Sync woes. I've used the qualifier "should" twice in the adjacent paragraph. Here's one more:

NLEs should stay in sync when everything is done exactly as the programmer assumed it would. But with all the variation in system-level drivers, third-party cards, and recording systems, a lot of things can get in the way. If transfers don't look like they're in lipsync, or things seem to drift as you play or output a file, check the troubleshooting tips at the end of this chapter.

If you're shooting operas or other long events and require perfect double system stability, you'll need a common reference between audio and video. This has to happen both at the shoot and during the transfer. Check Chapter 4 for advice about blackburst and audio word clock.

Establishing Sync

For most of the past century, double system sound was synchronized by lining up a sudden sound with a one-frame event on the film. That's how Hollywood's familiar slate worked: two pieces of wood would be slapped together in front of camera and microphone. Diagonal stripes on the wood made it easy to see the precise frame where the wood met. An editorial assistant would match this film frame with the *crack* sound on perforated magnetic (mag) stock,[5] and sprockets or code numbers would be used to keep film and audio together for the rest of the take.

_____

5. Professional 35 mm film and magnetic stock has four sets of perforations per frame. Skilled editors learned to guess, based on the amount of visual blurring in the frame where the sticks came together, how late in that frame the slap actually occurred. Then they'd slide the sound to match, achieving quarter-frame accuracy.

You can use a similar scheme to sync video with double system digital sound because it's easy to slide sound and picture in a NLE until it matches. Slates are available at video suppliers. Or have an assistant clap hands on-camera or tap the end of a mic in close-up.

For very long takes, put a slate at the tail as well as the head. Sync the front slate manually in your editor. Then jump to the end. If things aren't in sync, count how many frames picture and audio have drifted. Then divide by the number of frames in the shot and apply a correction using the clip speed setting. This may require some rendering time. If your NLE distorts the sound on tiny speed changes like this, try tweaking the video speed instead.

Slateless sync

Because DV tape records a soundtrack, you can use this track for a sync reference even if it won't be part of the final track. Using a wire or a cheap wireless rig, send the same audio to the double system recorder and the camera. Slip the double system track in a NLE until it matches the DV track. If there's subsequent drift, you'll hear it immediately as an echo between the two tracks. Once you're satisfied things are in sync, delete the reference and lock the remaining audio and video tracks together.

It's possible to use a camera mic to record the reference track, but stay aware of the speed of sound; if you're shooting from the back of an auditorium, the camera will see on-stage lips move immediately but won't hear them until more than a frame has gone by. Be prepared to slide tracks to compensate. Also, a camera mic will hear a lot more echo than a properly placed dialog mic. This can confuse your efforts to get things into sync.

Timecode

Most films and high-end video projects use SMPTE timecode for sync. Crystal-controlled code generators are provided on the camera and sound recorder. A few times a day these generators are *jammed* to synchronize their clocks; the rest of the time, internal crystals are adequate to keep things together. Traditional slates have been replaced by ones with internal timecode generators and large counting displays. The numbers are shot on film and read visually during post-production, or encoded as a digital pattern along the edge of the film, or recorded on a high-definition videotape timecode track. These numbers become the master. Professional DAT and multitrack digital decks with matching timecode, speed up or slow down automatically to get things in sync. Of course, this disturbs the sample rate and can distort or mute the audio. But as soon as audio and video are in sync, the decks switch over to blackburst or word clock for sample-accurate speed control.

If film is being transferred to videotape for broadcast editing and release, new continuous timecode is added to the video master. At the same time, the production DAT is played in sync with the film timecode and dubbed to a second DAT with timecode matching the videotape. This *simulDat* becomes the audio master for postproduction. Because simulDat is a digital clone of the original, there's no quality loss.

SMPTE timecode is also the standard for keeping things in sync as tapes are exchanged between large postproduction facilities and as tracks are passed to composers and sound designers. MiniDV uses similar code to cue up scenes during batch digitizing, but file exchange has largely replaced timecode on tapes in desktop post.

Timecode types: LTC and VITC

Timecode was developed by the Society of Motion Picture and Television Engineers (SMPTE) as a way to put a unique number on every frame in a videotape. At first, it was an audio stream around 2.4 kHz[6] modulated with biphase serial data, sounding very similar to a fax transmission. This audio stream was designed to be recorded on a conventional audio channel, though low-quality *address tracks* were added to tape formats so channels wouldn't be wasted. Conventional audio wiring carried the signal to timecode readers and other equipment.

Videotapes are edited by copying scenes. Timecode was the natural way to identify where a desired scene started and stopped on the original, and where it should be dubbed on the master tape. *Edit controllers* would read the code from both tapes, synchronize the tapes so the right scenes lined up, and start recording on the appropriate frame. The system worked just as well on multitrack audio tapes. Timecode was used to sync audio with video, and in many cases, to control multiple analog decks for programmed editing.

The audio channels of early videotape were parallel to the edge of the tape—unlike the perpendicular video track—so timecode was also called *LTC* or *longitudinal timecode*. (The name was also used to refer to timecode as an analog audio signal.) LTC doesn't work when jogging or paused, but early video decks didn't have those functions. Helical-scan video recorders could jog and still-frame, so a second method of recording timecode was developed. Flashing lights were placed in the black band between the bottom and top of the picture. This *VITC* or *Vertical Interval Timecode* could be read whenever there was a picture. Modern analog BetaSP video decks support both code types internally, switching between them as appropriate, and outputting the data both as LTC on an audio jack and as data in response to RS-422 control signals. Professional digital video decks use a dedicated data channel on the tape but output the data as LTC or VITC for compatibility.

Timecode types: Dropframe and non-dropframe

Timecode identifies each video frame with integers for hour, minute, second, and frame number. This works perfectly when there's an integral number of frames per second—24 fps for film, 25 fps for PAL video, and an arbitrary 30 fps in audio-only applications. The math is simple. For

---

6. The precise frequency depends on the frame rate.

example, PAL timecode counts 00:00 (seconds:frames) through 00:24. Then it adds one second and resets the frame counter for 01:00.

But NTSC video, used in most of the Americas and the Pacific Rim, runs at (approximately) 29.97 frames per second. This tiny difference—for all practical purposes, 1/10 of a percent slower than 30 fps—causes problems. You can't simply count 0 through 28.97 frames and then increment one second because the system doesn't understand what a hundredth of a frame is. It only knows when a frame edge goes by.

You could count NTSC timecode as 0 through 29 frames, then add one second and reset the frames. But this would mean that each of our timecode seconds is a tiny bit slower than one second on a clock. Over an hour, that error adds up to 3.6 seconds, a serious issue for broadcasters.

Or you could fudge the numbers. If things were exactly 30 fps, there'd be 1,800 frames in a minute. One-tenth percent of that is just about two frames. So you count 30 fps for most of the time, but once per minute, you *skip* two frame numbers. The frame after 1:29 (seconds:frames) is 2:00. But the one after 59:29 is 1:00:02. In that first second of the new minute, frames start counting with 2 instead of 0. Figure 7.12 shows how it all fits together.

The scheme almost works. But 1/10 percent of a minute is really 1.8 frames, not the 2.0 frames we're skipping. That's 0.2 frame error per minute, or 2 frames in ten minutes. The error is in the other direction, making our skipped timecode a little early. So to make things come out even, once every ten minutes we *don't* skip any frame numbers. Got it?

That's *dropframe* (also *drop* or *df*) timecode, used by broadcasters for program production. *Non-dropframe* (*ndf*) code is easier to deal with in commercial production. Standard practice is to begin each :30 spot at the start of a minute, so the editor can see that when seconds and frames read 29:29, the commercial is over. But in dropframe, most minutes begin two frames in; a :30 spot starting there would end at an unintuitive 30:01. So postproduction facilities—particularly those dealing with advertising—usually prefer non-dropframe.

If you're doing nonbroadcast pieces where it isn't critical to know the exact length, it doesn't matter which format you use.

- It's important to remember that dropframe doesn't actually drop any frames. Every image of your precious picture is put on the screen. It's just that some of them are numbered strangely.

- Dropframe and non-dropframe are indistinguishable for most of the minute. You can start syncing audio in one format to video in the other. But as soon as a nonzero minute starts, sync will appear to be off by two frames. The best audio equipment and software lets you ignore this apparent error and keep playing—sometimes things really are still in sync—or choose to slew the speed until the numbers match. Some NLEs will not let you import a clip if its timecode format doesn't match the project.

Time	Wall Clock	30 FPS	29.97 NDF	29.97 DF
	1 min, 1 sec	1:01:00	1:01:00	1:01:00
		1:01:01	1:01:01	1:01:01
		1:01:02	1:01:02	1:01:02
		...	...	...
		1:01:28		
		1:01:29	1:01:28	1:01:28
	1 min, 2 sec	1:02:00	1:01:29	1:01:29
		1:02:01	1:02:00	1:02:00
		...	1:02:01	1:02:01
		...	...	...
		1:59:28		
		1:59:29	...	...
	2 min, 0 sec	2:00:00	1:59:28	1:59:28
		2:00:01	1:59:29	1:59:29
		2:00:02	2:00:00	* 2:00:02

7.12   Dropframe de-mystified. If there were exactly 30 frames to a second, timecode would always agree with the clock on the wall (first two columns at 1 minute, 2 seconds and at 2 minutes). But NTSC frames (3rd and 4th columns) are slightly slower. When nondrop (3rd column) thinks it's two minutes, the clock says two minutes, two frames. Dropframe (4th column) catches up by skipping two numbers.

- Most NLEs and audio programs start clips based on timecode numbers. If you change a project's timecode format after you've started editing, long clips starting before a minute boundary may not line up properly with those starting later. There is no cure for this other than manually resyncing. The best audio workstations use an internal, sample-based time-code and translate it to the specified SMPTE format on the fly. This completely eliminates the problem.

- LTC and VITC carry a one-bit flag to indicate whether timecode is dropframe or non-drop-frame, so a device can tell immediately which it's dealing with. Most programs and decks substitute a period or semicolon for the final colon when displaying dropframe time data.

Timecode summary

Table 7.1 shows the common video timecode formats. There are others, which are used outside the film and video industries.

Table 7.1   Timecode formats.

Type	Frame Rate	Counting Format (seconds:frames)	Used For
24 fps	24 fps	00:00, 00:01, 00:02, 00:23, 01:00, 01:01	Nonlinear editing of film
25 fps	25 fps	00:00, 00:01, 00:02, 00:23, 00:24, 01:00, 01:01	PAL video
29.97 non-dropframe	29.97 fps	00:00, 00:01, 00:02, 00:28, 00:29, 01:00, 01:01	NTSC video, shortform and nonbroadcast
29.97 dropframe	29.97 fps	00:00, 00:01, 00:02, 00:28, 00:29, 01:02, 01:03 (minutes ending in 0 count like non-dropframe)	NTSC video, longform broadcast
30 fps non-dropframe	30 fps	00:00, 00:01, 00:02, 00:28, 00:29, 01:00, 01:01	Some film and PAL double system audio; music production
30 fps dropframe	This rate and format combination is very rarely used; it's found only in some film-for-video applications.		

All of these formats count hours (0–23) and minutes (0–59) as well as seconds and frames. Common practice is to start each video and audio tape with a new hour number. Be careful during that 23rd hour; most timecode equipment can't deal with tapes that go past 23:59:59:29.

Timecode transmission and deck control

LTC over an audio cable used to be the standard in analog video editing suites. But it's largely abandoned now, outside of some audio applications. Its high frequencies can jump into nearby unbalanced audio circuits, causing a chirping noise. Besides, other methods of transmitting time information are more reliable and convenient.

RS-422   While the name refers to a standard computer interface, most video people use RS-422 to identify the high-speed Sony control protocol found in almost every professional device including switchers, special effects generators, and digital audio multitracks as well as video decks. Commands include obvious transport instructions like play or rewind, but there are also "go to frame xx" or "play at 1/32nd speed" commands. Responses from the RS-422 device are usually a simple acknowledgement or status report. The actual transactions are strings of Hex bytes, rather than a language humans can read. This protocol is also sometimes called *P2*[7] or simply *Sony 9-pin*.

There is no continuous timecode on P2, but the controller can ask, "Where are you?" and the deck will answer with a timecode address. Split-second timing is necessary for this to be reliable, so both the controller and the deck need a common video reference or blackburst. If an LTC track isn't precisely aligned to the video frame rate—that is, if timecode frames don't change at exactly the same time as the video—synchronization can be a frame off in either direction.

Sony P2 is the common control language in high-end video and audio post suites. High-end digital audio workstations (DAWs) use it to slave video decks to its timeline, something that can't be done with the simpler LTC. While most desktop computers don't have RS-422 ports, USB and RS-232 adapters are available, and some NLEs can speak to P2 over USB or RS-232.

P2's commands include frame accurate video and audio inserts. If your equipment supports P2, this can be a good way to dub small corrections from NLE or DAW into an existing master tape. While the P2 command set is fairly universal, some of the commands—such as audio track enables or switcher wipes—are machine specific. Most controllers use downloadable drivers to fine-tune the commands to a particular device.

RS-422 data is also used by the *ES Bus* protocol, an open standard developed by the European Broadcast Union and SMPTE. Unfortunately, it appeared about the same time as Sony's P2 and market forces buried ES Bus.

RS-232   The RS-232 electrical standard is unbalanced but otherwise similar to RS-422; the data protocol is almost identical. Because the circuits are cheaper to build, RS-232 found on semipro analog video equipment. The command structure is similar to P2, though it's more limited.

FireWire   The FireWire high-speed data standard, described earlier in this chapter for digital audio and video transfers, can handle simultaneous timecode and transport instructions as well. It's become the most common control protocol in DV setups. Additional LTC, sync, or serial wiring isn't necessary. There are two standards with different levels of control; good NLEs let you choose the one that matches your deck or camera.

LTC via an audio channel   Some NLEs can interpret LTC that comes in over one of the sound-card inputs. This can be handy for syncing double system audio tapes with matching timecode on a DV tape.

V-Lan   V-Lan is an English language system designed by Videomedia to simplify P2 control. RS-232 or RS-422 can be used at almost any speed from the computer. V-Lan communications

---

7. Early Sony decks had two jacks on the back to plug in both a conventional remote and the new-fangled RS-422 controllers. A front-panel switch let you choose plugs, and the *P2* jack was the RS-422 port.

resemble chat rooms and timing isn't critical, so NLE programmers can incorporate V-Lan easily for batch capture and timecode logging. Or you can use any terminal software or simple BASIC language commands to control a professional video deck or switcher. The key to the system is Videomedia's microprocessor equipped adapters, which convert the language to P2. An additional advantage to V-Lan is addressability; a single V-Lan port can control multiple adapters which simplifies workstation wiring. The disadvantage is the cost of Videomedia's adapters.

VISCA, LANC, and others   These are proprietary communication and control schemes mostly seen on analog prosumer equipment and largely replaced by FireWire in DV.

MIDI   The Musical Instrument Digital Interface serial format, used to control synthesizers, can also handle limited timecode and machine control. Wiring is more complicated because the data flows in one direction only, and it often is augmented with LTC. But the technology is familiar to music studios, and most studios already have the interfaces, so MIDI control may appear in smaller audio post suites.

Using Film with Digital Audio

Despite miniDV's incursions into documentary and storytelling, some filmmakers want to shoot, well, *film*. Good equipment—including excellent lenses—may be easier to find for film, it can perform better in low-light situations, some people prefer the look of film, and there can be a visceral satisfaction to holding up a couple of feet of images instead of a tiny, plastic box of tape. The media is more expensive and requires special handling, but film is definitely not dead.

Outside of film schools, however, the audio medium that traditionally accompanied film—1/4-inch analog tape run through portable Nagra recorders—is considered obsolete. In feature film production, timecode DAT is the norm, and 24-bit, 4-channel hard disk recorders are the gold standard. Matching timecode slates or edge code is used on the film, and synchronization is largely automatic.

For low-budget filmmakers, timecode may be out of the question. However, professional non-timecode DAT, MiniDisc, and CD recorders are cheaper, easier to sync, and in most cases, better sounding than analog location tape recording.

Location tracks used to be transferred to 16 mm or 35 mm magnetic stock and cut on desk-sized mechanical editors that kept the stock in step with picture. This technology is also relegated to film schools now. Feature films and filmed TV shows are transferred to video, and both sound and picture are edited in computers. Then, if necessary, the original film negative is matched to the computer version. So the marriage of film and digital audio is inevitable. Some of film's peculiarities make it a marriage of inconvenience.

Compensating for camera speed

Double system digital audio works beautifully with DV cameras because both are speed-stable. Older film cameras weren't that accurate. Instead, these sent a *pilot* signal, based on the film speed, to the audio recorder during shooting. In post, the pilot signal compensated both for deck speed errors and tape slippage.

So the first step is to figure out how things were shot. If the film was run through a modern, crystal-controlled camera or one that has an AC-sync motor, things are fine. Dub the digital audio to mag stock if you're editing that way, or digitize it into your computer. But if you're editing in the computer and using NTSC video, read about speed changes on the next page.

If the film was shot with a noncrystal, double system camera with a pilot generator, a single system sound camera,[8] or a camera designed for silent film, you may be in for a painful experience.

Pilot track   If a 60 Hz pilot signal from the camera was recorded on one channel of the audio, you'll need an audio deck with continuous vari-speed to resolve it. Many timecode DAT decks have continuous vari-speed, or you can digitally dub to an audio CD and use a vari-speed CD player. You'll also need a way to measure frequency. This can be a lab-quality frequency counter or an oscilloscope.

1. Connect the pilot signal to the counter. If you're using a scope, connect it to the vertical input and connect a reference signal (usually stepped down from a wall outlet) to the horizontal. This lets the scope display the ratio of the two frequencies in a *lissajous*: when the frequencies are perfectly matched, you see a circle; but if they're slightly different, you see complex cat's cradle patterns.

2. Play the track on the vari-speed machine and dub it to a speed-stable medium, such as another DAT or a computer. Digital vari-speed decks change the sample rate according to the speed, so unless you've got equipment that can handle nonstandard s/r while recording, you'll have to use an analog connection.

3. While you're dubbing, constantly adjust the speed so the pilot stays at 60 Hz on the counter. If you're using a scope, try to keep it showing a circle. If the circle starts to wobble, correct the speed immediately. If the scope shows a cat's cradle for more than a frame, the speed has drifted too far and you'll have to start over.

It may be possible to do all this in a computer by transferring the audio from a speed-stable deck and then using an audio program's pitch-bend function to gently manipulate small sections of the audio and pilot track together. You'd have to keep visually comparing the pilot track with a computer generated 60 Hz file to make sure things are in sync. Hooking up a scope is a lot faster.

---

8. Some cameras record sound to a magnetic track on the photographic film. This kind of film is virtually impossible to find now, but the cameras still exist.

If the camera's pilot signal is 50 Hz, make the obvious adjustments in the steps above. If the pilot track didn't come from the camera—if it was generated from a crystal or derived from wall current—this exercise has no point. That kind of pilot is helpful for analog sound recordings but useless for digital.

No pilot track   If the film camera didn't have an internal crystal or wall current regulating its speed, and you don't have a pilot signal generated by the camera, there is no way to mechanically recover sync. You have to do it by eye.

This is not an exercise for the faint-of-heart. You'll need to digitize the film and use a computer with a large video monitor, or put the track on mag stock and use a flatbed editor with a large screen. Then follow the sync-spotting tips in Chapter 9.

If you're in a situation like this and have control over the project, it may be a good idea to rethink the footage, editing it as mostly voice-over.

Speed changes when editing film as video

Many projects are now shot on film, using modern crystal-controlled cameras, and transferred to video for editing and final release. Since film and video are usually at different frame rates, the audio is manipulated to compensate.

Normal film speed is 24 frames per second. In PAL countries, video runs at 25 fps, so motion will be sped up 4 percent when film is transferred to video. Audio is sped up to match. Traditionally, this resulted in a noticeable pitch change, but now the pitch can be shifted back digitally. A better solution is to run the camera at 25 fps instead of 24 fps. This raises stock and processing costs 4 percent, and may require special equipment for flicker-free lighting, but assures perfect sound and video with no speed change necessary.

If you think that's complicated, consider the situation in NTSC countries. Converting 24 fps film to 30 fps is easy because those two speeds are a perfect 4:5 ratio. NTSC uses two interlaced fields per frame,[9] and transfer equipment simply alternates between copying one film frame to three video fields and one film frame to two video fields (see Figure 7.13). The process is known as a *3/2 pulldown* and is standard in all film transfer equipment. Overall speed isn't affected, though very fast motion can appear uneven.

But NTSC video runs slightly slower than 30 fps. That's the reason for the whole dropframe weirdness discussed earlier. To make 3/2 pulldown work at 29.97 fps, the transfer equipment has to slow the film down an additional 1/10 percent—too small a difference to be noticed visually. Sound has to be slowed to stay in sync because that tiny change is almost two frames per minute. The cleanest method is to lower the sample rate slightly, and all digital timecode decks have a

---

9. They carry alternating scan lines.

–0.1% switch. If your equipment doesn't have this option, transfer the audio into your computer at its normal speed and then apply a speed change in software. Don't worry about pitch correction.

Cameras can also be adjusted to shoot at 23.97 fps, making the 0.1 percent correction unnecessary, or cameras can shoot at 29.97 fps so no pull-down is needed. If you have to deal with any nonstandard settings for film or digital audio, you need a copy of Wolf Seeberg's self-published *Sync Sound and the New Media* ($35). Seeberg is a Hollywood recordist and equipment consultant, and his 150-page manual is constantly being updated to cover the latest techniques.[10]

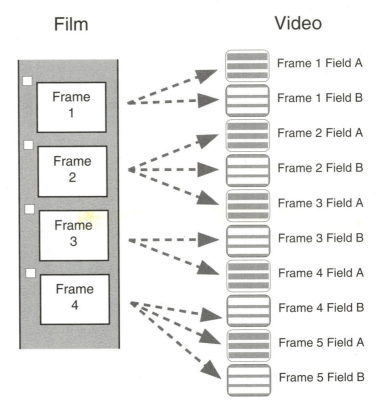

7.13 A 3/2 pulldown to turn four film frames into five video ones.

Music videos on film Many music videos, and other films that are lip-synced or danced to sync to a playback, take a different approach. Rather than slow down the song in post to compensate for the 0.1 percent difference, music is played 0.1% *faster* at the shoot. Portable timecode DAT decks often have a setting for this function. If that's not available, a special DAT or CD is prepared at 44.056 kHz s/r; when played in a normal machine, the music speeds up.

Of course, there's always the possibility of one of those off-speed DATs being played with a sped-up setting, throwing all calculations off. And some videos are shot to normal speed playback, with the intent that music will be slowed –0.1 percent at the film transfer. In other words, audio post on these projects can be a nightmare without adequate communication.

Fortunately, none of this affects music videos shot on video. And even in film, the format usually has so many fast cuts that sync can be fudged during editing.

---

10. Call 310-822-4973 for details.

If any part of a project involves film, every aspect of camera speed, sample rate, and sync technique should have been written down on both the camera report and the sound log. This is the standard in all professional production. Trying to work any other way wastes money.

Troubleshooting the Transfer

In a well-designed digital editing suite with a knowledgeable operator and good tapes, audio transfers are clean and sync is perfect. Believe it or not, that's how things work in professional situations. Pro systems often run years before tweaking or troubleshooting is necessary. Or you could say we're *always* troubleshooting, since clients expect us to hear and fix problems before they notice them.

But desktop systems—particularly ones with cards and software from multiple manufacturers, and ones built on a budget and run by someone who's more interested in storytelling than soldering—are more apt to develop trouble. There are three ways to deal with this: you can develop a hacker's mindset and diagnose problems technically; you can look for solutions in a book like this or online; or you can hire a tech. All three methods are appropriate, and a little of each can get you through most problems smoothly.

The first step is to figure out exactly what's wrong.

- Noise and distortion are usually a question of improper levels. If the tape sounds good but the transferred version doesn't, follow the advice in the first section of this chapter. If the tape sounds bad, try it on another deck or camera. If that fixes it, get your deck checked.

- Changes in timbre—sound that's too thin, bright, or dull—can be a configuration issue.

- Ticks, pops, and *splats* (very loud signals lasting slightly longer than a frame) can have multiple causes, so can thin or dull sound. Follow the steps in the next section.

- Loss of sync can be hardware or software incompatibilities, operator error, or in some cases, a mystery you can correct but never understand. See "Loss of Lipsync" on page 146.

Other than for loss of sync, the terms used to describe these problems can be subjective. So I've put samples of most of these problems on Track 20. Listen to them to see which sound matches your troubles.

Hear for yourself ___

Track 20 includes samples of most of the gremlins that can sneak into a transfer.[11] It's not great party listening but can help you diagnose a problem.

> ⚠️ *Gotcha* _____
>
> *Where's my problem?* Noisy locations, mumbling actors, hum in the microphone, and other gremlins can sneak into a track. So can effects that sound great when you're mixing and fall apart on a client's dub or broadcast. But these aren't transfer problems and don't belong here.
>
> You'll find a quick troubleshooting guide in Chapter 1 and advice on cleaning tracks starting with Chapter 12.

Thin, Overly Bright, Spitty, or Dull Sound

These are usually problems with wiring or improper digital audio settings, and most can be fixed easily. But these problems may be inherent in the medium or a particular track and have to be worked around rather than fixed.

- Transformer-balanced circuits, found in some high-end studio equipment and field XLR adapters, can be sensitive about proper termination. Highs may be boosted when a transformer is feeding a typical computer input; this shows up as too much treble or as extra hiss. Put a 680Ω or 820Ω resistor across the output.

- Some transformers show an extreme loss of low end if they're not receiving a properly balanced signal. This can happen with field XLR adapters when the mini-jack input is used for a conventional unbalanced line input. If you come across a track like this, there's not much that can be done; the damage is usually so great that attempting to fix it with an equalizer merely adds noise. Next time, use a balanced cable or the XLR jacks for line level.

- Sample rate directly affects high-frequency limits. If a transfer sounds significantly duller than the original, make sure it's set to 44.1 kHz or 48 kHz s/r, rather than 32 kHz or lower.

- Inadequate filters in a digitizing circuit (Chapter 2) can cause aliasing distortion, which can seem like spittiness or jangling extra notes on high-frequency sounds. This can happen in some soundcards when digitizing at a low sample rate because the cards don't switch filters properly. Digitize at the highest rate the card will support. If you need a low s/r file for the output, convert it in software.

- Inexperienced sound recordists may apply equalization at the shoot by using the very broad controls on a music mixer. They think they're solving problems but are actually creating bigger ones. Don't try to compensate while you're transferring. Do what you can to fix the file later, when it's possible to experiment and undo—and tell the recordist to be more hands-off in the future.

- Early digital audio equipment included a pre-emphasis equalizer that added highs to compensate for inaccurate filters. A matching de-emphasis equalizer had to be used during

---

11. I had to simulate some of them because I couldn't get my equipment to cooperate by breaking on cue.

playback, or else the sound could be too bright or too dull. While modern filters make this technology obsolete, you may come across it on old tapes or DAT recorders. Try different de-emphasis switch settings.

- Band-limited analog media such as the linear track on a VHS or audio cassette tape, or FM broadcasting, use pre-emphasis also. Matching de-emphasis is built into all players and FM radios. But the media are so boosted that loud, high-frequency sounds can be pushed into distortion. Spitty /s/ sounds can result. A multiband limiter or de-essing processor can help a lot during recording or before broadcast. If a track already has the problem, an equalizer dipping the offending frequency (usually somewhere between 3–6 kHz) can make it a little less annoying. See Chapter 12 for tuning tips.

Ticks, Pops, and Splats

Is it periodic?

If ticking is relatively rhythmic and repeats at once per second or slower, it's probably a digital audio sync issue. Periodic ticking can be masked by loud sounds, so it may seem intermittent in places.

- Make sure the sample rate you're recording or saving to a file is the same as the source sample rate. If the pitch seems wrong, a sample rate error is the most likely cause. But some systems can hide these problems, having them appear only as lipsync drift.

- Make sure the digital input card or recorder is set to lock to its input, or that both source and input are locked to the same word clock.

- If nothing else works, transfer through an analog connection. If the analog output of the source device is ticking, suspect a problem with the source material.

Is it repeatable?

The ticking doesn't have a rhythm, but it always appears at the same place in the source material.

- You could have level problems. These can be in your NLE's output even when the file is okay; try lowering the playback level. It could be that parts of the original tape are too hot for the playback deck's analog output; a FireWire or AES/EBU transfer may be more successful. Or it could be the levels were recorded too loud at the shoot and can never be fixed.

- Some tape damage can also cause clicking. If switching between digital and analog outputs doesn't help, try the tape on a different deck.

Many of these problems are intractable, and the best you can do is edit from alternate takes.

Is it absolutely random?

You're plagued by ticks, but can't predict when they'll happen.

- There could be equipment damage. Try a different deck or soundcard.

- Your computer could have fragmented memory or cumulative errors. Try rebooting.

- Make sure you're not running any other processes, and the computer isn't being accessed over a network.

- Defragment your hard drives.

- Make sure SCSI chains aren't being hobbled by slow devices or improper termination.

- Record to a different hard disk.

Loss of Lipsync

Long-term drift

Individual clips are in sync when they start. But as you get into a long clip or play from the time-line, sync gets progressively worse. This can happen during previews, or it might not appear until you're printing the final project to tape.

- Is there a dropframe/non-dropframe conflict? Some NLEs insist that NTSC projects be dropframe, even if you want to work in non-dropframe.

- Is there a break in timecode? This can happen if the camera tape was improperly wound between takes, if you're doing a long transfer to the NLE, or have transferred in batches.

- Are your FireWire drivers the latest version? Surprising things can happen to sync if not. Check your card manufacturer and system software vendor's Web sites.

- NLEs expect precise 32 kHz or 48 kHz sample rates. Some cameras are slightly off because of sloppy or price-conscious design. Check NLE settings to see if there's an automatic sample rate adjustment when capturing longer clips. Or transfer the sound as analog.

- If drift appears only when printing to tape, and you can't find any other cure, try printing in small sections. Some machine-to-machine video editing might be necessary afterwards. Or try exporting as shorter AVI or QuickTime movies and assembling those in other software.

- If an AVI or QuickTime is out of sync, try rendering it again at a different frame rate.

- Some third-party capture cards have known issues. Check with the manufacturer.

- If nothing else works, measure the amount of drift over the length of the show and apply a speed correction to compensate.

Erratic sync problems

A clip may appear out of sync from the start. Or it may be in sync and then suddenly jump out. Some clips might be affected more than others.

Before you try any of the other cures, ask yourself if this particular setup—source, system software, system hardware, and NLE software—has ever given you reliable sync. If not, you'll have to trace things down through the manufacturers involved. Some FireWire cards might not be supported by system or NLE software. Some memory or hard disk configuration problems might not appear until the system is stressed by the demands of full-size, full frame rate video with lipsync.

Be prepared for a lot of finger-pointing, particularly if you've assembled your own system from multiple manufacturers. It's easy for a company to blame the other suppliers involved. It may even be appropriate; if a company can make the system work using its recommended components, the fact that you've used other components could be the problem. Dealing with a single manufacturer or system integrator can save a lot of grief.

- Have you tried the suggestions listed in the section "Long-term drift"?

- Are you sending audio and video to the same output device? Some NLEs have a problem directing picture to FireWire and audio to a soundcard or USB device.

- Dropped or stuttered video frames can appear to be an audio sync error because it's easy for the eye to ignore occasional missing frames. Make sure no other programs or processes are running, and DMA is enabled on your hard drives. Adding RAM can help, too.

- Are you using the presets suggested by your video card manufacturer?

- Are you stressing your system with too deep a color setting? 32-bit color is overkill for digital video—cameras don't record that much color detail—and 32-bit color can steal resources while capturing.

When All Else Fails...

- Check the manufacturers' Web sites.

- Check the DV.com Forums under the Community section, where users share experience and professionals often answer questions.

- Look for answers in the rec.video newsgroups (searchable at groups.google.com).

- Call the manufacturers' tech support lines.

- Ask a local audio or video facility to recommend someone who fixes equipment.

- Walk the dog. I've said it before, but this is one of the most helpful pieces of debugging advice I've even gotten. When a problem seems intractable, turn everything off and get away from it for half an hour. Do something else entirely. When you come back, you might have a fresh insight. Or at least you'll have calmed down enough to call tech support without screaming.

Chapter 8

Voice-over Recording and Dialog Replacement

> **Remember this:**
> - Voice-overs should usually sound different from dialog. That's why they're recorded using different techniques.
> - The acoustics of your recording space are as important as the mic you use.
> - Microphone pickup patterns depend on frequency. The more directional a mic, the stranger things will sound coming from off-axis.
> - Low-budget ADR is possible, but it requires thought and preparation.

Surprisingly few films are made using nothing but dialog recorded at the shoot. Most documentaries and sales or training pieces have voice-over narrations, of course. But many people don't realize that most feature films and TV movies replace at least some of the production dialog with voices recorded in post. It's common practice on big-budget projects to *loop* or *ADR* scenes where location problems or noisy effects machines make good recording impossible. When looping is done properly, the studio tracks fit the actors' lips perfectly and sound completely convincing.

On the other hand, some projects don't need studio voice recordings at all. Event videos, short or low-budget narratives, sketch comedies, and some commercials use nothing but production dialog. If that's what you're working on, feel free to skip this chapter.

Voice-over Perspective

The goal of production sound is to get dialog that sounds like it belongs to the picture. Boom operators learn to position their mics to pick up some of the location's acoustics and background noise. This becomes part of the dialog track. One of the reasons Hollywood frowns on using lavs in feature films is because they're *too* clean; instead of hearing the actor in a proper visual perspective, it sounds like we're leaning our ears on his chest. When lavs have to be used, extra time is spent in post to make them sound like booms.

But there's no such thing as a voice-over that's too clean. A good voice studio doesn't contribute its own sound. The narrator should sound like she's right inside the speakers, talking directly to us, not performing in some other room. This immediacy and intimacy makes us part of the conversation, something that doesn't happen when one actor is talking to another. Cleanliness refers to technical quality as well as acoustics. A track with no noise, echo, or distortion can be processed more. That's one of the secrets behind those rich-sounding Hollywood trailer voices—though the narrator's talent is arguably the most important factor.

> ⚠️ **Gotcha**
>
> **What about character voice-overs?** Frequently, on-camera characters will have off-camera lines. This may be part of dialog while the camera is aimed at someone else. Obviously, off-camera characters should be recorded on the set using the same mic as the rest of the dialog.
>
> But occasionally a character will deliver voice-over lines directly to the viewer. The voice-over tradition that started with film noir was based on radio, and should have the same acoustic intimacy as a good narration.

What's Needed for Voice-over Recording

Sure, you need a mic and an announcer. But the most important factor can be the room. And some little accessories may be very important.

Acoustics

My favorite announce booths are designed to have no noticeable reverb. The back and sides are soft, and the front has only a moderate reflection. This reflection is important; it lets an announcer hear himself in the real world as well as in his headphones, which helps him modulate his voice. If the room were completely dead, there'd be a tendency to speak too loudly. But because the reflection is coming from the front of the announcer, it hits the back of the mic and almost none of the sound gets into the recording.

The booth in my studio was designed as a compromise between perfect sound and real estate costs (see Figure 8.1). Walls and the true ceiling are sheetrock on RC-1 channels for soundproofing. Three walls are covered with foam and fiberglass absorbers, shown in Figure 8.2. Both these construction features are described in Chapter 3. The front is a thermal glass sliding door; it's more reflective than ideal, but comparatively far from the mic so the inverse square law keeps echoes at a low level. Good glass doors provide about the same isolation as solid wooden ones, and you can't glass door sight lines. Even though the front of the room is reflective, it isn't parallel to the back wall, so resonances don't build up.

The finish ceiling is fiberglass tiles, rather than the more common wood fiber, to absorb reflections from the floor. With a ceiling height of 8 feet, the room has about 336 cubic feet of space—comfortable for one or two performers but just barely large enough in acoustic terms. As rooms get larger, critical resonant frequencies drop, and these can support deep voices at greater distances. Tests at the BBC have determined that a radio studio should be at least 1,500 cubic feet to sound ideal,[1] though that includes drama studios where mics are typically used at greater than voice-over distances.

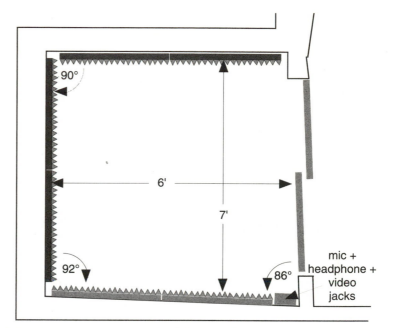

8.1 A typical voice-over booth (mine). There's a lot of absorption, and no two walls are parallel.

8.2 The absorbers in my booth are low-cost foam tiles over fiberglass, as described in Chapter 3.

---

1. Indeed, my mix room is about 1,560 cubic feet and sounds great.

Guerrila acoustics

Most filmmakers have to live with even smaller booths or none at all. This isn't necessarily a problem. If you've followed some of the suggestions in Chapter 3 for your editing room, it's probably adequate for recording. Turn off computer towers and other noisy equipment, and use a directional mic as described in the next section.

Soundproofing is important for voice-overs. Audiences can forgive some noise in a location shoot because they can see the noise source; it makes the location seem authentic. But the same noises are distracting in a voice-over. Before you record, close all the windows and doors and turn off HVAC systems. (If air systems can't be shut off, remove the grill. Getting those metal vanes out of the air path can cut the noise down significantly.) Warn neighbors to be quiet and post signs or production assistants in nearby hallways. You may have the best luck recording late at night or very early in the morning.

Echo control is just as important. Unless a room has been specifically treated, it has lots of echo. Even if it's too fast to be heard as reverberation, it colors the voice by reinforcing random frequencies. If you can't mount permanent absorbers, put up sound blankets, furniture pads, or slabs of Owens-Corning 703 fiberglass (Chapter 3) wrapped in bedsheets.

Consider that echoes are influenced by surface treatment, angle, and distance. Once the absorbers are up, walk around the room. Stand in different positions and face different directions, while speaking in a moderately loud voice. Listen to what the room does to your voice. The best positions are usually a couple of feet from a corner and face diagonally into the room. Some corners sound better than others. Once you find the best place for your voice, you'll know where the announcer should stand.

Some filmmakers record narrations in clothes closets. They reason that those hanging coats *have* to absorb sound. This is true at mid and high frequencies. Lower frequencies punch right through the clothing, and the tiny dimensions of most closets can make for a boxy sound on the low end. But if you're using a light voice with a moderately soft delivery and close micing, a closet will provide adequate sound.

Microphones

I used to shill for AKG, an internationally-respected microphone company[2]. I'd say nice things about AKG products, and in return I'd be sent to trade shows in Geneva, Amsterdam, and other nifty cities. One time, I lost the ID badge that let me onto the show floor. The product manager told me not to worry; he always ordered a spare with a fictitious name. For the rest of that show I was *Mike Rafone*. It was sort of an honor to wear that badge since few gadgets are as essential

---

2. That's an AKG C-414 mic in Figure 8.2, one of my favorites for voice-overs in good acoustic surroundings. Despite having worked for the company, I paid real money for that mic.

to audio work. But mics that may be ideal for production dialog are seldom the best for voice-over. To choose the right mic, you have to understand how it creates a signal and how its pickup pattern works.

Microphone elements

There are three basic kinds of mics suitable for voice-over work: dynamic, condenser, and ribbon. Each has its advantages.

Dynamic   The simplest voice mics used regularly are really tiny electric generators. Just like a power plant's dynamo, *dynamic* mics use a coil of wire suspended in a magnetic field. Dynamic mics can't be as sensitive as condensers used in production, and don't create enough voltage to be plugged directly into most camcorders. On the other hand, since dynamics convert sound directly into electricity, they can have very low distortion and don't contribute any electronic noise. Many announcers prefer their sound.

Condenser   A *condenser* mic doesn't turn sound into volts; instead, it modulates a voltage coming from some other source. A metalized plastic diaphragm with an electric charge on it is mounted close to a rigid plate. As sounds vibrate the diaphragm near the plate, varying amounts of electrons can jump across. This tiny current is much too weak to send to a recorder—even a few feet of extra cable would destroy it—so a low-noise preamp is mounted in the mic itself. Since condenser mics don't use a magnet, they can be smaller and lighter than dynamics. That's why most location mics are of this type.

Traditional condenser mics are *externally polarized*. The diaphragm is charged up to a couple of hundred volts at a tiny current. This means the mic can be highly sensitive—or create very little electrical noise of their own, which amounts to the same thing—so this design is preferred for the highest-quality mics. You can also charge small items chemically instead of electrically, with a process similar to that used in making static-charged dust mops. The result is the ubiquitous *electret* condenser, found everywhere from cell phones to lavs to most studio or boom mics under $500.

All condenser mics require power for the preamp, but there are different and incompatible ways of getting power to it.

- Cameras and consumer recorders with mini-jack inputs put a low DC voltage on the audio line. You can buy compatible mics, but they're seldom good for voice-over use. The voltage can cause trouble with standard mics.

- Studio condenser mics are usually *phantom powered*, a system that puts a low DC voltage on both wires of a balanced audio cable and returns it through the cable shield. Most mixers and preamps supply this voltage, nominally 48 V, though some mics will operate with much less. Battery-equipped phantom adapters are also available from broadcast suppliers.

Because the DC is applied equally to both signal wires, balanced circuits don't see a voltage difference and it doesn't affect the audio.

When power is first applied to a condenser mic, it can produce a loud *thunk*. As a general rule, leave the mic's volume turned down when you change the battery or plug it into a phantom supply.

Ribbon Ever notice the large jellybean-shaped mic on David Letterman's desk? It's a classic RCA 77DX, one of the all-time greats for making a voice-over sound both warm and natural. It's a shame that Letterman's is only a prop—his voice is really picked up by a wireless electret lav.

> ⚠ **Gotcha** _____
>
> ***Beware the phantom!*** Theoretically, phantom voltage should be invisible to a balanced mic that isn't designed to use it. But a damaged cable or connector, or the wrong kind of adapter, can short the voltage or put it across the mic element. Either can result in equipment damage.
>
> Most devices that provide phantom power have a way to turn it off. Leave it off unless you're sure a mic requires it.

The 77DX and other *ribbon* mics use the same basic principle as dynamics, but without a diaphragm. Instead, sound waves vibrate a delicate foil strip while suspended in a very strong magnetic field. This produces a tiny electric current. Because the foil has so little mass, the ribbon can be extremely accurate—particularly on relatively loud sounds that lack extreme highs, like the human voice.

The low output of a ribbon mic requires a sensitive, impedance-controlled preamplifier with an input transformer. Prosumer mixers usually aren't good enough; if you've got one of these classic mics, treat it to a good preamp. A few contemporary versions of the mic include an internal preamplifier; its output is similar to that of a condenser mic and will work with any mixer. These modern ribbons also require phantom power for their preamps. But be sure of a ribbon mic's requirements before applying power: some of the early ones may be wired in a way that phantom power could harm the ribbon.

Those tiny ribbons are also physically fragile. A strong wind or other shock can knock it out of position, requiring an expensive repair.

Microphone directionality

Few things are as misunderstood as mic pickup pattern. In fact, the very term is misleading: a mic's pattern isn't a template, where sounds falling inside a boundary are picked up and others are rejected. Despite what they're called, all mics are somewhat *omnidirectional* and hear sounds from every direction.

A mic is not like a lens.

* You can't point a mic at one person in a crowd and exclude someone nearby.

- You can't narrow the focus of a mic to pick up a distant object.

- Even the best mics are far less directional than your own ears.[3]

However, some mics are more sensitive in particular directions than in others. This can make objects directly in front of them seem slightly louder, or closer, than those to the side. Consider the analogy of Figure 8.3 as what an omnidirectional mic—one that picks up equally from all directions—would hear.

If we wanted to concentrate on the happy bride, we could use a shotgun mic from the same distance. The result would be similar to Figure 8.4. Notice how she's a bit bigger than she used to be—that's analogous to the mic picking her up a little louder—and the folks to the side are a lit-

8.3 A nondirectional mic would pick up all the members of this wedding party evenly.

8.4 A shotgun mic would make the bride seem louder, but it doesn't exclude the rest of the group.

3. Based on tiny timing variations at different frequencies, people learn to locate and discriminate between sound sources. Having two ears is part of the process, but it's more than simple stereo. The frequency-dependent effects are based on the convolutions of your outer ear and the shape of your head, and are slightly different for each person. There's no way a microphone can match that.

tle softer. But notice also that the groom and the woman to the bride's left are also bigger. And other members of the party are still in the picture; they're just slightly smaller. No microphone made could pick up just the bride and ignore everybody else, from this distance.

There's another consideration; mic directionality varies with frequency. Most mics aren't very directional at the low end. Even good shotgun mics can be relatively sensitive to specific frequencies from the sides or rear. Wide-range sounds coming from the

> ⚠️ **Gotcha** _____
>
> **Spherical world, flat page.** These wedding photos are only a partial analogy. Mics pick up sound from all three dimensions—above, below, and behind—as well as from the front. But since my budget doesn't include holograms, you'll have to imagine the pictures wrap around you.

wrong direction get equalized by the mic, and their timbre can sound wrong. Figure 8.5 updates our analogy to include this. The groom is only partly affected because he's near the center. Other members of the party seem like cardboard cutouts. It's an interesting effect—and may even be how the bride saw things that day—but doesn't lend itself to accurate or natural sound.

Polar patterns Microphones are categorized by their directionality. *Cardioid* mics are named for a theoretical heart-shaped pickup pattern, which lowers sounds from the rear but not from the front and sides. Since they're directional, there's a little coloration from the rear, but because they're not too directional, it rarely causes problems. *Short shotgun* mics, used frequently on DV shoots, can also be useful for voice-

8.5 Unfortunately, directional mics color sounds that aren't coming from the front.

overs. But because they're very directional, voices or room reverb from the sides can sound strange. That's why professional recordists often boom with *hypercardioid* mics, a cross between a cardioid and a very short shotgun.

💿 **Hear for yourself** _____

Track 21 is a short piece of orchestral music,[4] played as it would sound from the front of a good mic, then from the rear of a cardioid, from the side of a short shotgun, and from the rear of that shotgun. Pay particular attention to the sound of the sustained string choir, and how it balances with the other instruments.

Choosing a voice-over mic

- If your recording space has good acoustics, use a cardioid. This will give you a smooth sound, while rejecting reflections from a studio window, even if the talent moves around a little.

- If your space has a larger reflective area, use a hypercardioid to reject it.

- If the acoustics aren't very good, treat the walls with extra absorption. Then use a short shotgun, close to the mouth and aimed to avoid reflections from the sides. Be aware that the rear of this kind of mic doesn't reject as well as the sides.

Omnis are not on this list unless you have absolutely perfect acoustics. Lavs are almost always omnis and should be rejected for the same reason. (Cardioid lavs are sometimes used as hidden mics on a set, but they're hard to mount for a voice-over.)

If you can't afford a really good mic, choose condenser instead of dynamic. Modern electret cardioids in the $150 range are quite respectable. Low-cost dynamic mics are generally designed as handheld mics for singers, have a restricted frequency range, and may lack sensitivity. More expensive condenser and dynamic mics—starting in the $300 range—often have larger diaphragms, which can be flattering to voices and sound warmer. But the difference usually isn't significant for broadcast or Web projects.

A voice-over mic should not create any noticeable hiss or other noise. Dynamics and ribbons don't produce the kind of hiss that comes from a condenser's preamp, but these unpowered mics have a lower output voltage than condensers. This can reveal mixer or camera preamp noise when you turn the level up to compensate. Mics with internal transformers—all dynamics and ribbons, and some of the better condensers—can pick up hum from power panels, large transformers, or nearby video monitors. Moving the mic or rotating it 90 degrees can help.

Unless you're specifying a top-notch studio mic with a good reputation, it's not a good idea to buy a mic without listening to it. When auditioning the mic, listen through good monitors and value a smooth, natural sound. Some mics add high-frequency boost and distortion which can make them sound brighter at first listen, but this becomes fatiguing over time. Despite large signs in discount music stores, I have never heard of a health regulation that prevents customers from returning a shoddy mic or headphone. It may just be the stores' way to keep customers from evaluating products in a real setting.[5] Professional dealers are usually willing to lend you mics for a short evaluation period, or you can rent a mic you're considering buying. If you have no other way to evaluate a mic, ask in the Forums at DV.com.

---

4. "Fingal's Cave" (Mendelssohn, DWCD70/11). From the DeWolfe Music Library. Protected by copyright and used by permission.

5. Or it may be protection from being ripped off by bands that buy six mics for a one-night gig and try to return them all the next day.

Mic placement

There is no magic place to put a mic that will always assure a good recording. The exact spot varies with the talent's working style. Over the years, I've found some basic positions that give a clean, intimate sound with a minimum of problems. I start there and then adjust to fit the talent.

You'll need a flexible way to position the mic. The most common is a floorstand with a 2.5-foot boom; these usually sell for about $50 at broadcast suppliers and music stores. You don't need a shockmount or heavy windscreen; the mounting clamp and foam windscreen supplied with the mic should be sufficient. While some engineers prefer pop screens—4-inch diameter frames filled with nylon mesh that clamp in front of the mic—I've never found them useful for voice-over work. They don't stop pops any better than using a good mic position, and are one more large item in the talent's face to break his or her concentration. (Pop screens can be helpful for singers who prefer to belt a performance directly into the mic.)

Ask the talent to start reading, so you can see how he or she holds their head when working with a script. Then try one of the positions below. Listen through speakers and adjust as necessary. Closer will be more intimate but can pick up more vocal problems. As you move off-axis from the mouth, sibilance and pops decrease but so can warmth. The best compromise is often to be off-axis but close, with the working end of the mic about 9 inches from the talent's mouth. Don't get so close that quality changes when the announcer's head turns slightly to read the bottom of a page.

For a small diameter cardioid or hypercardioid, start with the mic angled down toward the mouth from just below eye level. The mic comes from the side, so it doesn't get in the way of reading the script. This position seems very good for getting an intimate sound

8.6   A good starting position for a small mic.

without pops or sibilance. Figure 8.6 shows this from three angles.

This position also works with large diaphragm cardioids. Or as an alternative, try at mouth level and slightly toward the side. The front of the mic, of course, should be angled toward the mouth. Figure 8.7 shows this placement for a large cardioid that accepts sound from the side. If the mic is a type that accepts sound from the top, rotate it 90 degrees.

You can use a short shotgun in the same position as a small cardioid, though a couple of inches farther away (Figure 8.8). Angle things so the nearest reflective surfaces are about 90 degrees from the mic's axis (direction A), though as far from the mic as practical. For best results, the talent should be facing the largest dimension of the room (direction B). The dashed lines indicate

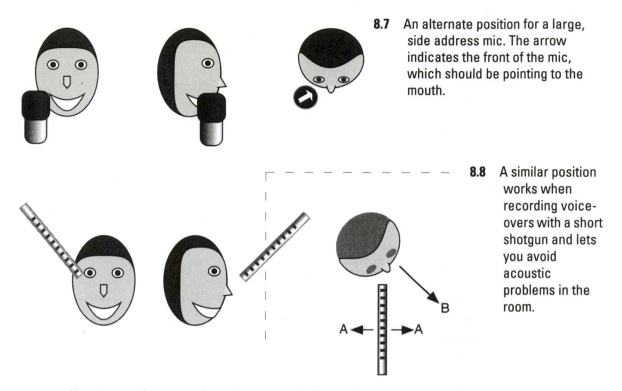

8.7 An alternate position for a large, side address mic. The arrow indicates the front of the mic, which should be pointing to the mouth.

8.8 A similar position works when recording voice-overs with a short shotgun and lets you avoid acoustic problems in the room.

walls at least 3 feet away from the mic and talent and show how the best position might be diagonal.

These drawings are intended as starting positions. Take time to learn how your mic works best with the announcers you use. As you're experimenting, there are a couple of positions to avoid:

- Don't put a large diaphragm mic directly in front of the talent's mouth (Figure 8.9A). Some announcers assume this is the only way to work—it's popular in radio—but it's sure to pick up pops and clicks.

- Don't put any mic at chin level or slightly below, pointing up (8.9B). As the talent breathes, you'll hear blasts of air.

- Don't point a mic directly toward the mouth from in front, unless you're at least 16 inches away (8.9C).

Other Necessities

Obviously, you need to record onto something. This can be your NLE, but for most narrations it makes sense to use a separate recorder. Tape, MiniDiscs, and CD blanks are cheaper than hard disk and often more reliable. Dedicated recorders can be started, stopped, and paused at the touch of a button, so the session isn't interrupted by file-saving routines. Having all the outtakes

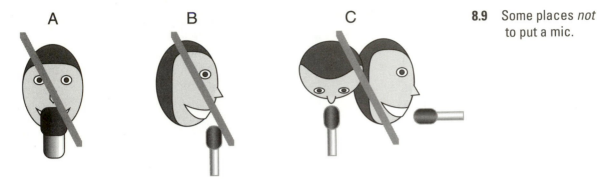

A   B   C

8.9 Some places *not* to put a mic.

on a shelf can be handy if you spot a problem while editing, or a client requests a change after the project is done. If you don't have a separate recorder, use your camera with its Automatic Gain Control turned off.

A couple of other items (Figure 8.10) can make a voice-over session go smoothly and help talent give you a good performance.

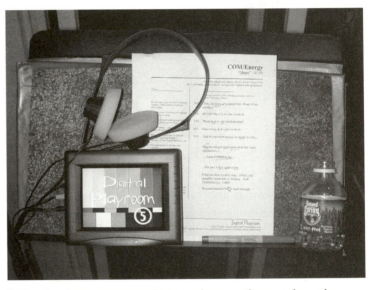

8.10 A voice-over recording needs more than a mic and recorder.

- Headphones are a must for professional talent. Voice-over actors should be able to hear their own voice accurately and comfortably, and slightly louder than they hear their voice acoustically in the room, with no delay through digital processors. Walkman-style phones are usually too small to do this well. Some amateurs find headphones distracting; others work well with them.

- You need a tall script stand that talent can read from without having to hunch over. Solid metal orchestral stands—about $40 in music stores—are convenient and provide good support for a multipage script. But these also reflect sound back to the mic, which can add a hollowness to the track. That's why I've gaffer-taped a piece of fiberglass ceiling tile to the stand in the photo. Other echo-free alternatives include a wire-frame portable music stand, a lighting flag in a C-stand, or just putting a small clamp on a gooseneck mic stand and hanging the script from it (Figure 8.11). But none of these provide a surface where talent can make notes on the script.

- If talent is working to picture, they'll need a monitor. I use a small LCD on the copy stand itself. This way they can glance between video and script quickly, without having to refocus.

- Water is essential. As the narrator's mouth dries out, saliva thickens and can cause a snapping sound. The water shouldn't be ice-cold; that can tighten the throat.

Some narrators prefer to sit for long scripts, but sitting in a regular chair compresses the diaphragm, making it harder to take a full breath. A bar stool is usually the right height to let them sit while still leaving room to breathe.

You also need a talk-back system, if you're not right in the room with the talent. Sessions flow more smoothly when there's immediate communication and feedback about a performance. Recording and broadcast consoles have this function built-in, but small mixers rarely do. You can assemble your own with a push-to-talk microphone and a small amplifier and speaker, but the

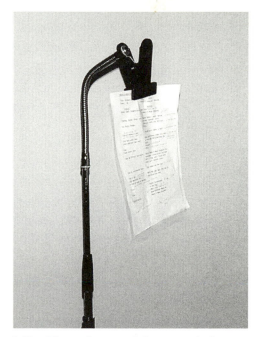

8.11 The script stand that wasn't there. A gooseneck mic stand with a stationery store clip can hold a script without the echo that plagues music stands.

easiest solution is to use an FM wireless intercom, which costs about $60 at electronics chains. Most of them have fairly good squelch; this keeps the unit in the announce booth from making noise until you press the talk button on your station.

The Human Factors

Video directors will often concentrate on the look of a scene—dressing, lighting, and blocking—and trust the actors to interpret the script based on some broad guidelines. This can lead directors to a hands-off attitude when directing voice-overs. Professional narrators are used to this, and many can give a credible performance without much direction at all.

But a narrator can't know as much about your project as you do, and even the best can't interpret every sentence of a complex script properly without some help. Narators are trained to read *cold*—not really interpreting the script at all but relying on standard conversational patterns and simple rules to give each paragraph a reading that sounds plausible. Often a couple of sentences miss the mark, and the talent might never understand the overall logical flow of the script. The result is a track that sounds polished and says every word, but doesn't communicate exactly what the writer or director wanted.

It's easy to direct a voice-over session properly, by giving the talent just enough guidance to do the best job without getting in their way or slowing things down. Good narrators welcome this kind of direction because it makes them sound better. (They also hate bad direction, which just wastes everybody's time). So it's worth mastering the technique.

Script Preparation

The first step in good direction is often overlooked: a few days before the session—when there's still time to fix problems—read the script *aloud*. Make sure the wording sounds conversational and that sentences aren't too long or try to express too many concepts. It should be obvious from the context which words are important in every sentence.

Feel free to ignore the formal rules of written punctuation. If a sentence is too long, and it's not obvious where the pauses should be… break it up. Like this. If a paragraph is trying to express a lot of thoughts, split it in half. Or turn it into a bulleted list. Use ellipses, hyphens, and italics liberally. The worst that may happen is the talent sees all these marks and reads with over-emphasized expression. But you'll spot that in the first couple of sentences and can tell them to pull back.

While you're reading through the script, mark it into sections. Be aware of subject breaks and changes of emotion. Put double paragraph breaks where these changes occur, so the talent can see a new thought is starting. Don't be afraid to tell them, during the session, where each section is trying to go.

Note any difficult-to-pronounce words, and make sure you know how to say these properly. If there are just a few, add phonetic spellings in the script: "As diakinesis (DIE-uh-kuh-NEE-sis) sets in…". If there are a lot, warn the talent ahead of time. They'll probably ask for either a separate list of the words with pronunciation hints, or a tape of an expert saying the words.

As you're formatting the final script, pay attention to readability. Use a large font and short line length, with at least a half line of space between the lines and double spacing between paragraphs. Use upper- and lowercase. And number the pages—they're sure to get out of order sometime during the session.

Session Flow

Master shots of narrative films are usually done in full takes, repeating the entire scene until it's right. This also makes sense for very short narrations, like commercial voice-overs. But if a script is long, it's most efficient to record straight through, stopping only when there's a problem.

Start by giving the talent some direction about the tone you're looking for. Descriptions like *proud, conversational,* or *formal* are helpful here. If the style is particularly demanding, ask them to read a few sentences for you to evaluate. Otherwise, slate the first take and start recording.

During the first paragraph or so, pay particular attention to the pacing, energy level, and intimacy. If it's right for the project, keep going. If not, stop and give notes. It's not unusual for even a good narrator to do the first paragraph four or five times before the style is right.

⚠️ **Gotcha** _____

Why slate? The Hollywood slate started as a way to identify scenes in silent movies. At first the scene and take number was just written in chalk, but when sound was added, someone would also speak that data. This technique is just as useful for identifying pieces of a session. Even if you're using timecode or DAT index numbers, a verbal slate—something as simple as, "Take two"—can save time when you're editing.[1] If you don't have a slate mic, say it into the talk back so it's picked up on the talent's mic. Hearing that slate also lets the talent know that you're recording and ready for him or her to read.

_____

1. Much longer slates—"This is the third paragraph of page twelve, starting with the announcer"—just waste time. Jotting the take number next to that paragraph on the script accomplishes the same thing.

But once the narrator starts going the way you like, *let them keep going.* Don't interrupt with directions like, "That's good. Please continue." A nod or smile should be sufficient.

On the other hand, if you hear something wrong or if the style is starting to drift, stop as soon as the sentence is finished. Explain what you need, back up to the paragraph or line before the error, reslate, and continue recording. Keep notes on your copy of the script of where each new take starts. Recording continuously like this, interrupting only when there's a problem, keeps the style consistent and makes editing easier.

If you don't know exactly what you want for one or two paragraphs, it's okay to stop and ask for an alternative reading. If you think something was read properly but aren't sure, it's usually best to keep going.

Put a question mark in the margin. After the script is finished, play back that paragraph and check it. If necessary, record a replacement to drop in during editing.

How to Talk to a Narrator

Directing is not a zero-sum game or an adversarial process. A good narrator will take direction happily, knowing that you're going to make their contribution to the project more effective. The key is giving meaningful directions.

Strike a balance between insufficient feedback and too much direction. "I don't like it, do it again," isn't very helpful. Ask for something once, make sure they get it, and continue recording. If you don't get what you want on the next take, *don't repeat the direction.* It didn't work. Try different words, or better yet, a completely different method of directing. There are at least three:

- Actors generally give a better performance if you tell them what they should be thinking and let them translate it into a performance. ("I need more awe when you say, 'The moment had arrived.'")

- Some actors need a little help solving the problem. ("Please slow down and deepen your voice on, 'The moment had arrived.'")

- Try a line read: say it exactly the way you want to hear it, and let the talent mimic you. This often works best with announcers as opposed to actors. It can also be helpful when directing novices. But use line reads only when you hear a problem. Reading the whole script to an announcer wastes time and accomplishes little.

To err is human. Admitting your errors can be a powerful directing technique, putting you and the narrator on the same side and enlisting their help to solve problems. If there's a technical problem, admit it and go on to the next take. If you ask for a particular kind of reading and get it but it's not having the effect you hoped for, let the announcer know it's not his or her fault you need a different approach.

How to Talk *Like* a Narrator

If you're going to give line reads or narrate your own film, take some time to improve your reading chops.

The *vocal folds* are two flaps of skin in your throat. As you push air past them, they vibrate like a reed. This creates the buzzing that is the basis of your voice. It takes a lot of air to make these folds vibrate properly and to sustain that vibration for the length of a scripted line. The only way to get enough air into your lungs is to expand the chest cavity and create a partial vacuum. Children usually learn to take big breaths by forcing their ribcage out and their shoulders up. But that's not efficient because chest muscles are puny compared to the diaphragm, a thick domed wall just above the stomach and intestines. You need to move that diaphragm to get a decent lung's worth of air.

Here's how: Stand up and put the palm of your hand on your stomach. Open your mouth and inhale in a very quick gasp. You should feel the stomach press out as the diaphragm pushes down on it to create a vacuum above. Do this a few times to get used to the feeling, then slow the movement down until it's smooth. Practice breathing this way. Your diaphragm will get stronger, and you'll be able to take in more air at a time.

Avoiding stress

Involuntary muscles around the vocal folds clench when someone is nervous, changing the way the vocal folds vibrate. As the folds get tighter, the natural reaction is to force more air past them, stressing the musles even more. As humans, we learn to recognize this sound as fear—probably not the ideal emotion for a narration. Yawning is a great cure; the physical act stretches the muscles in question and you get a nice slow breath of air. Professional announcers learn what a yawn feels like from inside and consciously repeat the motion to open their throats.

There's also good advice in the western movie cliché, "Smile while you say that, pardner." Vowel sounds are made by filtering the buzz of vibrating vocal folds through resonators in the mouth and sinuses. Smiling changes the way these resonators work, making a brighter sound that comes across as friendlier. Unless the copy is totally somber, it's worth forcing a smile while you read. (Besides, psychiatrists have learned that putting your body into a position associated with happiness can fool the mind into being happier.)

Creating stress

Part of the announcer's skill is adding emphasis to appropriate words. Unfortunately, most people stress words by making them louder, which isn't a good idea in a narration. It wastes breath, makes the words harder to record, and gets defeated by postproduction compression. Instead, add emphasis by slowing words down, putting a slight pause before the important word, or raising its pitch slightly. Or use combinations of these techniques simultaneously. Try them as you read aloud the examples in the next three paragraphs.

There's a simple logic to deciding what words to stress. Information theory says the most intelligence is contained in the least predictable part of a message. So in general, the most important words in a sentence are the ones that don't repeat what came before. "Take some *shallots*, chop the *shallots*, and then sauté the *shallots* in butter," sounds like you're producing Cooking for Idiots. But read as, "Take some *shallots*, *chop* the shallots, and then *sauté* the shallots in *butter*," makes sense. Better yet, replace the second and third "shallots" with "them." We already know what's cooking.

When you stress a word, you're also reinforcing that its opposite isn't true. "I was *hoping* you'd call," means you're really glad to hear from a person. But "*I* was hoping you'd call," suggests nobody else cared, and "I was hoping *you'd* call," sounds like other calls have been from telemarketers. "I was hoping you'd *call*," means you're unhappy they showed up in person.

It's almost never appropriate to stress prepositions or conjunctions. There's a famous outtakes tape where Orson Welles is asked to give more emphasis to the first word of, "In July, peas grow there." He reacts with scathing anger.[6] And to say, "our employees are smart *and* loyal" implies the two characteristics aren't usually found in the same person; anyone with brains would be long gone.

---

6. As of this writing, you can hear it as streaming audio at my Web site, www.dplay.com/humor. But if anybody ever figures out the copyright—I had it passed to me 30 years ago by another engineer—I might have to take it down.

ADR

Hollywood cheats. When you hear beautifully clean dialog in a horribly noisy setting, like the middle of a windstorm or a busy public building, it's not because magic microphones were used. It's because the track was actually recorded in a quiet studio, sometimes months after the picture was shot. Dialog replacement is so common that its name is usually abbreviated to ADR—the A stands for "automatic," though it's a labor-intensive process. ADR is also still called *looping*, after the original method used to create it. The film was cut into individual loops for each line of dialog. The loop would run continuously while an actor tried to match the lip movements.

While ADR is an accepted practice, it's frowned upon by feature directors and sound supervisors because the acting is seldom as good as during the original performance. Producers don't like ADR either, because it's expensive. Many actors hate the process. They have to read the scene line by line without other performers to work against. It's difficult to recall the original emotions or motivations for a reading and to keep an appropriate projection level. It can also be intimidating to have to perform while listening to cues in a headphone and watching yourself on a screen.

> ## ⚠ Gotcha
>
> **ADR avoidance**. If looping is difficult in Hollywood, where there are experienced technicians with the right equipment, it's even harder when you have to do it ad hoc. The best strategy is to do as little as possible. Some of this has to take place long before post.
>
> - Strive for the best production sound. Renting better equipment or hiring a good boom operator is usually cheaper than rerecording later. Ten minutes of extra setup time at the shoot can save a day of ADR. If you must replace dialog, the session will go smoother if you have decent guide tracks. If the original was recorded indoors with a camera mic, ADR can be long and painful because the guide track will be blurred by echoes.
>
> - If you think ADR will be necessary because of a noisy setting, block the scene so lip movement isn't too obvious. Have extras mime their conversations. If you can, rewrite the scene with a lot of back-and-forth dialog; short lines are easier to replace.
>
> - While you're shooting, pay attention to intermittent noises like car horns or airplane flyovers. It's cheaper to retake a scene immediately than to try to record it later. Even if the second performance isn't as good, you may be able to lift just enough dialog to save the first one. Or forget about picture. Have the actors record problem lines wild, right after the bought take. They'll still be in the right mood, and the acoustics will match.

ADR Equipment

You'll need an A/V playback device: a NLE is ideal because it can cue quickly. If you can't isolate its fan noise, use a camera or a VCR instead and prepare a tape with each line repeated multiple times. You'll also need a separate audio recorder with at least two tracks, so you can record the original audio on one channel as a sync reference. Timecode helps but isn't necessary, so a consumer MiniDisc may be adequate for this. You'll need the same kind of mics that were used at the shoot. For the actor, you'll need headphones, ideally isolating ones so that cue tracks aren't picked up by the mic.

Hook everything up as in Figure 8.12. Studios that specialize in ADR have more complicated setups and specialized software to drive it, but this will do the job for casual sessions.

You'll also need a quiet room with little or no reverberation. Even though the production dialog has natural room reverb, every room sounds different, and you don't want replaced lines to stand out. If the new audio is echo free, you'll be able to simulate reverb that matches the shoot when you mix. If the new audio has its own echo, you probably won't.

The room should be larger than a typical announce booth, unless the production

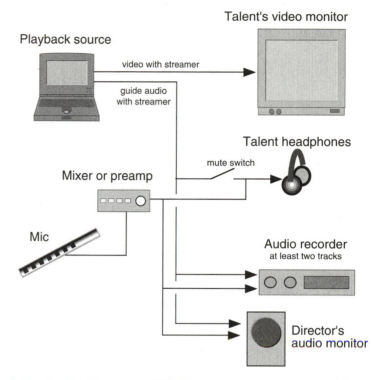

8.12   A setup for casual ADR. (Streamers are described in the next section.)

track used lav sound and was low-key. New dialog has to be recorded at the same mic distance and with the same energy as the original, and most booths aren't big enough to support this. So plan on a lot of sound blankets or other absorbers. If you have to simulate exteriors, the room must be absolutely dead. Outdoor echoes are nothing like the ones you get indoors.

The mic should be mounted on a boom, at about the same distance and position as it would be used at the shoot. Some ADR recordists prefer two boom mics, one slightly closer and one slightly farther. Each is recorded to a separate track, and the most appropriate one is chosen in post. If the shot originally used a lav, of course use a lav for the ADR.

ADR Technique

The first step is to do your homework. Watch the edited project with a script handy and mark which lines need replacing. Jot the line's timecode on the script, along with why you're replacing it and anything else that might be useful. Knowing whether a shot was interior or exterior and how it was miked will save time at the session.

Then check for alternate takes. You may be able to lift a few words from a cleaner track and slip them under the existing video.

If you must loop, turn each line into a separate A/V clip. If characters overlap, make two clips. Record each separately and mix them later. Besides, it's better to book each character for a separate session: ADR skills vary, and there's no sense making one actor wait while another blows takes.

Video-dominant ADR

There are two principal ways to record ADR. The traditional method is to make picture dominant. Each clip should start a few words before the desired line and end a few words after.

You'll need to add visual *streamers* to each clip, lead-ins that stop on the fram before the target line. Originally, this was done by scribing a diagonal line across a few dozen frames of the film itself; when the film was projected, the streamer would appear as a white line moving across the screen from left to right. These days, streamers are usually generated in video by the ADR equipment, which may be part of a specialized audio workstation. If you're trying ADR on a desktop NLE system, it's easiest to superimpose the streamers from another video track. Also add an audio streamer to the track: three short beeps about 20 frames apart, forming a rhythm that ends as the new line starts.

The actor watches a playback of the clip on a large monitor, with production audio in headphones, to get comfortable both with the delivery and with the way the streamer leads into the line. Then the guide track is muted. The actor records a new version while watching the screen but without hearing the original. (The director may want to listen to both tracks, with production audio at a slightly lower volume, as a guide for sync.) Multiple takes will probably be needed, and it's important that the takes form a predictable rhythm. Start-and-stop ADR, when it takes a random time to cue each pass, puts extra stress on the actor. Eventually, the new performance will start to match the guide track. You don't have to achieve perfect lipsync: small errors can be fixed by editing.

The advantage of this method is that actors can feel freer to experiment with delivery because the original version isn't being played in their headphones during the actual ADR take[7].

---

7. It's said the reason Brando liked to mumble on-camera was to force producers to let him polish the performance later in a looping session.

Audio-dominant ADR

Traditional ADR can be intimidating to an actor. A modern alternative is to make sound dominant. Set the playback device to play the clip and streamer in a continuous loop. Let the actor hear the rhythmic beeps and line over and over, and then record him or her speaking along with the original until the new and old voices match. The advantages to this method are that it can be faster with performers who aren't used to looping, it often produces a tighter match, and since it isn't necessary to concentrate on picture—you don't even need the video monitors—the actor can be looking at a script instead.

Whichever method you use, make sure your actors' energy and pitch match the original. It can help to give actors a little small-room reverb in their headphones, so their voices sound similar to what they heard at the shoot. But don't record with echo. This will make editing more difficult and rarely matches the original without a lot of fine-tuning.

ADR Editing

Capture both the new audio and its guide track to your NLE. Slide them together on the timeline until the guide track matches production audio. Then delete the production audio and the guide track. Lock the new audio to picture. It's a good idea to keep ADR on a separate track from production audio, since you'll be processing it differently during the mix.

To fine-tune ADR, you can use software like VocALign (Figure 8.13); it analyzes the guide track at critical frequencies, then makes tiny edits in the new track to make it match. Or do it yourself using the techniques in Chapter 9. Either will be less painful than demanding perfection from an actor.

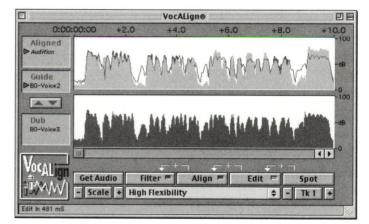

8.13 VocALign software can automatically tweak an ADR take to match the guide track—within reasonable limits.

Editing Dialog

Remember this:

- Blobs on a screen aren't sound. You can use waveforms as a guide, but it's best to cut by ear.

- Thinking phonetically will make you a faster and better editor.

- You need a strategy to restore lost sync. You also need luck.

There's an approach to cutting dialog that appears in most NLE manuals. It's even taught in some film schools: look at the waveform, find a pause where it drops to zero, and edit during the silence. This kind of editing is simple, easy to describe, and somewhat appealing to visually oriented filmmakers.

But frequently it's the only method taught, and that's a shame. There's nothing wrong with using waveforms and cutting in silence, for some material. But it's not the best way to edit location audio with background noises, it limits your creativity when cutting ad-lib dialog, and it can lead you to discard an otherwise perfect scripted take that has minor sound problems.

The issue with this method is you're not editing sound, you're editing incomplete *pictures* of sound. Lots of things you can hear don't show up on waveforms. That's why professional sound editors use waveforms as a guide but mark their edits while scrubbing and listening. It's faster, more flexible, and can be more precise.

It's also easy to learn how to edit the right way. All you need is a little ear training and an understanding of how sounds fit together. Then you'll be able to replace individual syllables of on-camera dialog, piece together the most difficult interview, and have finished voice-overs that are inhumanly perfect. So while we'll start with basic waveform-based editing, we'll quickly move on to a better way.

Waveform-based Techniques

Track 22 of the CD contains audio from a typical narration and a talking-head sequence. Let's start with the narration, recorded in a quiet studio. The woman is saying three sentences; we'll take out the middle one. You can load the first part of Track 22 into your NLE and follow along—though this example is so trivial, you'll understand it easily from the pictures.

 *Hear for yourself* _____

Track 22 contains source audio for this example and the next.

1. Put the clip on a timeline, set so you can see its waveform.
2. Visually locate the two pauses between the three sentences.
3. Put the cursor in the middle of the first pause and plant a marker. Repeat for the second pause.
4. Using the razor tool, cut at the two markers. It should now look like Figure 9.1.[1]
5. Delete the middle section and slide the other two together. Or do a ripple edit, dragging the second razor cut over the first.

This edit works fine if the background is quiet. But the method starts to fall apart when there are constantly changing background noises, such as traffic or machines. That's because there's a good chance the noise will change abruptly at the edit point.

Coping with location noise

Unlike the previous exercise, which can be understood from the figure, this one is worth actually doing. Load the second part of Track 22 (a location interview in a moderately noisy medical lab) into your editor. Cut out the middle sentence using the steps above. The razor cuts should look similar to Figure 9.2.

After you do the deletion or ripple edit, look closely at the cut (Figure 9.3). That tiny change in the background noise exactly at the edit point can sound significant. Listen to it in your version or play the first part of Track 23.

You could apply a long cross-fade, but that takes time to render and still might not sound natural. In fact, as a general rule:

 Rule _____

Cross-fades longer than a half frame have very little place in dialog editing.[2]

---

1. This picture is from Final Cut Pro. But it should look about the same in most NLEs and many multitrack audio programs.
2. You'll learn about 1/4-frame cross-fades later in this chapter.

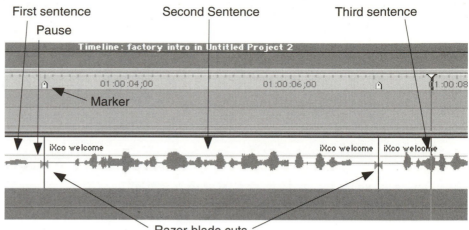

9.1 A basic, almost brainless edit of a narrator recorded in a quiet studio.

9.2 Razor cuts in an interview shot on location. The background noise will cause problems.

For a better, faster fix:

1. Grab the cut with a rolling-edit tool.
2. Drag the clip right up to the start of the next sentence (Figure 9.4).

That tiny shift, eight frames in this example, hides the jump in the background sound. Hear the difference in the second part of Track 23.

👉 *Rule* _____

Edits in the middle of a sustained sound are often obvious. Moving them to the beginning of the next loud sound almost always helps because the new sound distracts the ear.

9.3 You'll hear that jump in background level at the edit point.

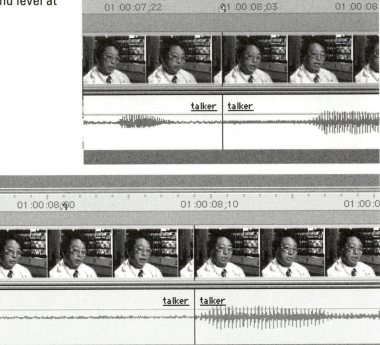

9.4 Rolling the edit to the start of the next loud sound will hide the problem.

Audio-based Editing

Spotting where that next loud sound started was easy in the example above: the first sound in the "And" starting the third sentence makes a large blob on the waveform display. But if the sentence started with "So" or "For"—with softer initial consonants—spotting would be harder. And if the sentence started with "However," it would be almost impossible to mark the edit visually. That's because /h/ is the softest consonant and could easily start softer than the noise.

 **Hear for yourself** _____

The first part of Track 23 lets you hear how the background noise jumps, as in the edit from Figure 9.2. The second part of Track 23 fixes it with a rolled edit.

Professional sound editors rely on programs that let them hear where they're going to edit. There are a couple of ways a program can do this:

- The easiest way is to let you drop markers as you play the audio in real time; every program can do this. Then you edit from marker to marker. This is fine for crating a dialog rough cut, though speech moves too quickly to fine-tune edits this way. It's also a very useful technique for editing music, as you'll learn in Chapter 10.

Quotes? Italics? Slash marks? Bars? I've tried to stay consistent, using italics to introduce technical terms and quotes to set off dialog that might be spoken in a track.

But if you're going to be a good editor, you also have to pay attention to *phonemes*—the smallest units of sound the mouth can make, which combine to make words. Standard convention is to indicate phonemes with slash marks, as in the /h/ used previously.

Phonemes have a written alphabet as well, *IPA* (*International Phonetic Alphabet*). It's got some strange looking characters because phonemes don't necessarily match letters in the alphabet. Some letters don't have a sound of their own: "c", for example, is always sounded either as a /k/ or an /s/. Other letters, such as "a", have different sounds in different contexts.

IPA is an obscure alphabet. You don't have to bother learning it (I'm not even sure CMP Books has it on its computers). I'll use dictionary-style equivalents instead, like /ay/ for the "a" in "play." I'll also use double vertical bars ‖ to indicate where an audio edit takes place.

- Most NLEs let you jog forward and play one frame at a time, as you press a control (often the → key) or move a jog slider. It's the best way to find the /s/ or /f/ in the examples that started this section.

- Also handy are the scrub algorithms in many audio programs and the similar shuttle function in many NLEs. They let you cruise forwards or backwards through the audio at a controlled speed. You can slow down to find an exact edit point.

Oddly enough, some mainstream two-track editors don't support scrubbing or jogging directly in the waveform. But there's a workaround:

1. Play at normal speed to find an approximate location for the edit mark.

2. Select the waveform, starting from a quarter-second or so *before* where you think the mark will be, to a few seconds after.

3. Convert the region you've selected into a loop (this command may be in your program's Special menu).

4. Start the loop playing. As it plays, grab the front border of the loop (this

may require grabbing the loop marker) and slowly slide it to the right.

5. As you move the border, the loop will begin playing later into the sound. (You may need to let go of the border to hear it change.) You can move the border quickly to get close to the exact sound you need, then slow down and nudge the border backwards and forwards until you've located the sound exactly.

6. Stop playing. The front border of the loop will be located precisely at the target sound.

Figure 9.5 shows the process of locating a phoneme within a word in Sound-Forge. I chose an example that would be visually obvious for the figure, moving from the /l/ to the /k/ in the first word of the woman's voice from Track 22. But the process works as well on noisy or mumbled speech, or with consonants that don't start as cleanly. Try it a few seconds later where she says, "It takes a lot of…". You should be able to mark the start of, "a lot of…" quickly, even though the /uh/ looks almost the same as the end of the /s/.

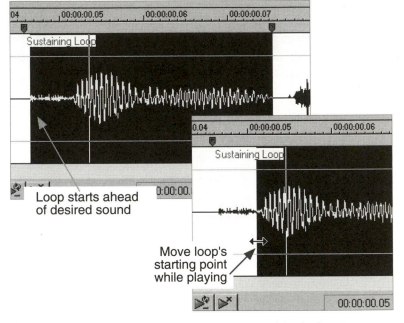

9.5 You can move a loop's starting point while it's playing, to precisely locate phonemes within a word.

SoundForge also lets you loop around a sound by holding the mouse down when the cursor is in the overview. But you'll find you've got finer control when zoomed into the waveform and using the loop method.

Hear for yourself

Track 24 lets you hear how easy it is to find either of those two edit points using the loop-moving technique.

Breaking the Frame Barrier

Editing in an NLE with jog or shuttle is certainly easier than using a loop technique in an audio editor. Unfortunately, most NLEs force you to edit on frame boundaries. Those that don't, still require clips to be a whole number of frames. But a few tenths of a frame can make the difference between a perfect edit and a poor one.

9.6 The same dialog, edited on the left in an NLE and on the right in an audio program. The circled spike in the NLE version is a very noticeable click.

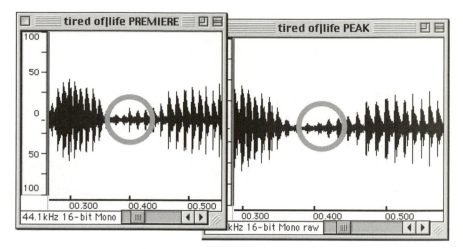

Track 25 consists of three short audio clips. In the first, an announcer says, "Tired of living life in the slow lane?" In the other two, the third word has been deleted: "Tired of ‖ life in the slow lane?"

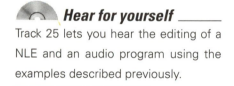

Hear for yourself

Track 25 lets you hear the editing of a NLE and an audio program using the examples described previously.

But the first edit was done in a NLE. You can hear a click at the edit point because it was impossible to mark the precise start of the /l/. I did the second version in an audio program. It was easy to mark exactly where the /l/ starts, so this one sounds like the announcer actually read it that way.

While the difference is immediately apparent to the ear, you can hardly see it on the waveform. Figure 9.6 shows the two edited examples, zoomed in fairly close. If you look closely, you'll see a tiny spike at 0.400 second in the NLE example on the left. That spike doesn't exist in the audio program's smooth-sounding version on the right.

Spikes, clicks, zero crosses, and cross-fades

The click in the above example is caused by a sudden jump in the waveform, visible when you zoom in (Figure 9.7). In just a couple of samples, the wave goes from almost perfect silence to around –18 dBfs. It's because the waveforms didn't match at the edit: the out-point of the first clip was very low, and the in-point of the second was much higher. The sudden voltage jump creates a click.[3]

---

3. Clicks can also happen on edits if DC voltage is getting into your signal chain because of a hardware problem. The best cure is to fix the hardware, but you can diagnose the problem by rendering a suspect clip through a low-cut (also known as *high pass*) filter and then re-editing. If DC was present, the filter will remove it and there'll be a lot fewer pops. Some audio software includes a Remove DC Offset function to compensate.

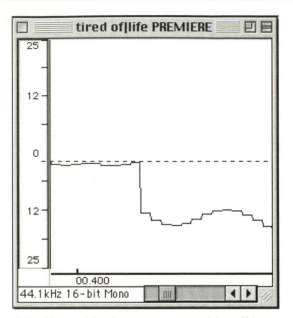

9.7 The sudden jump was caused by editing together two waves that were at different voltage levels. The result is a click.

If you're cutting from silence to silence, there won't be much of a voltage jump. But if you have to cut within a word, voltage levels at the edit point are a matter of luck. A lot of NLE edits have clicks like this. They go unnoticed on desktop speakers in noisy editing rooms but can be atrocious in a theater. There are two ways to avoid them, and good audio software does it automatically.

Most waves pass through zero—the center line in our screenshots—once per cycle at the fundamental frequency. If you mark all your edit points at *zero crossings*, the voltages will match and there won't be a jump. Some audio software automatically snaps to the closest zero crossing when you make a selection. Depending on the fundamental frequency of the sound, this can be as much as a half frame away; but it's usually much less. If the software doesn't snap to zero, you can zoom in and see a zero crossing, then nudge the edit to it.

⚠ **Gotcha**

My NLE won't let me do any of this! No, it probably won't. Frame-based NLEs can't nudge edits to zero points because they seldom occur on a frame line. The shortest audio cross-fade in a NLE would be two frames, or 60 ms—long enough to eliminate clicks, but much too long for precise dialog editing.

If you want to avoid clicks in tightly edited sound, you have to cut in an audio program.

Or you can make the jump smoother by applying an audio cross-fade. It works like a video crossfade, gradually moving from the first piece, to a blend of both pieces, to the second piece. This eliminates the possibility of a sudden jump. The fade doesn't have to be very long; a few milliseconds—less than a quarter frame—is enough. Good audio software lets you apply *automatic cross-fades* or *blending* at each edit.

Figure 9.8 shows both of these click-reducing methods applied to an extreme edit, from silence to a fairly loud 40 Hz wave. The version on the left is the untreated original; it clicks because of the sudden jump from silence to the wave's peak. The version in the middle used automatic snapping to a zero crossing; the edit was moved the edit 1/80 second from where I put it, eliminating the click by cutting at the start of a whole wave. The version on the right used an automatic crossfade. A 2-millisecond blend was enough to ramp the voltage up, so there was no click.

You can also eliminate clicks manually by using an audio program's pencil tool to smooth them out—essentially making a cross-fade by hand. But this is so labor-intensive, it's hardly worth the effort.

👉 *Rule*

If an existing NLE track clicks at an edit, move it to an audio program, select a couple of milliseconds around the click with snap-to-zero or blending turned on, and erase. Or use the program's pencil tool to manually smooth over the click.

Moving between NLE and audio program

Unless you deliberately do something wrong, there's no loss of quality or sync when you move audio clips between NLE and audio program. It makes sense to use whichever program lets you work quickly and accurately. But it's up to you to make sure audio and video start on the right frame when you put the edited version back into a NLE. In the professional world, we use time-code for this. A few NLEs have a menu command to pass clips directly into a companion audio editor. When you're finished editing, the new version shows up on the timeline. This only works with a couple of specific programs and doesn't let you edit multiple clips on a track as one element. With most other software, you'll need to rely on simple reference points to keep things in sync.

Pop reference   You can put a one-frame sound, lined up against an easily identifiable frame in the picture, on the audio track. The most common example is the 2-pop, a beep that matches the number 2 in a countdown leader (see Figure 5.8, page 97). But any short, sudden sound and eas-

9.8 Three different edits. The first one clicks; the other two use program features to sound cleaner.

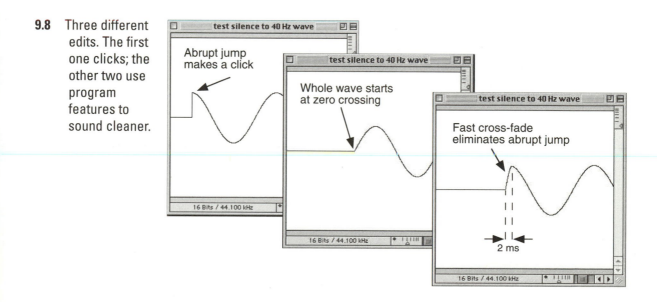

ily identifiable video frame will do. Many editors cut a single, all-white frame into a black leader before picture starts, to match with an audio pop. This is the same principle as the traditional Hollywood film slate; it's easy to match the slapping sound with the first film frame where the striped sticks stop moving.

Select what you want to edit along with the reference sound. Export it from the NLE as an uncompressed AIFF or wav, at the same sample rate as the project. Open that file in an audio program, edit as desired, and save. Then import this new version back to the NLE and slide the reference to match the picture. If you've done things that don't affect timing, such as erasing clicks or replacing sounds with equal-length alternatives, sync should be fine.

If your audio program has a video display window, you may want to export as QuickTime or AVI with picture. The file will be much larger, but you'll be able to check sync while you're working.

Self-reference   Pops and reference video frames are unambiguous, easy to match, and require only a single audio track on the timeline. They're the standard for matching entire tracks to video, particularly in cases where video and audio may get separated and processed differently. But you can skip this step when you're exporting audio to deal with just a small section of track. It's also not much good when you're doing an audio operation that will change the timing. Instead, use two audio tracks—one with the original and one with the imported edited version—and use one as a sync reference for the other.

Select just the area you want to work on, plus about ten seconds of existing dialog from either side, and export. Edit as desired, changing the length if necessary; save it and import the edited version back to a different track on the timeline. Then slide it into sync:

1. Grab the edited clip and move it until the front syncs up with existing audio. You may be able to do this visually (left circle in Figure 9.9), or you can play both tracks and adjust until you don't hear an echo.

2. If your edit changed the timing, you'll have to adjust the end as well. Make a cut in both the original audio track and its picture at a point where the new audio will cover the edit. Slide the original audio with picture until it matches the end of the edited clip (right circle in Figure 9.9).

Once you've done this, you may want to use the razor tool to cut through both audio tracks near the start and end of the edited audio, and move the edited version onto the same track as the original. This will simplify things when you mix (Figure 9.10). If you've done step 2, you'll probably also have to add a visual cutaway to cover jumps in the picture.

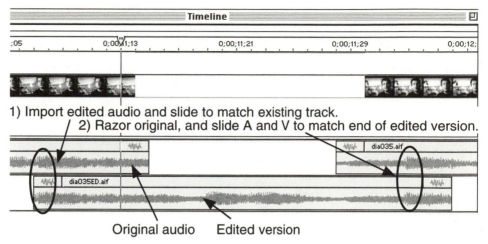

1) Import edited audio and slide to match existing track.
2) Razor original, and slide A and V to match end of edited version.

Original audio   Edited version

9.9 You can use existing audio as a sync reference, matching new to old at the head of an edited segment, and old to new at the tail.

Learning How to Listen Quickly

Film and video work because your eyes blur still frames into an illusion of motion, when they're flashed quickly enough. But you can easily hear individual sounds that are shorter than a single frame. The click in Figure 9.7, only a couple of samples, takes about 1/1000 of a frame. Meaningful sounds don't have to be much longer.

Consider two phrases, "the small pot" and "the small tot." I recorded them both and lined them up on two channels of the stereo file in Figure 9.11. The /p/ from "pot" is called out on the top track, and the /t/ from "tot" on the bottom. The two vertical dashed lines are exactly one frame apart. You can see the critical difference, changing the meaning of the phrase, takes only about half a frame.

9.10 A couple of additional steps may be necessary to clean up the operation.

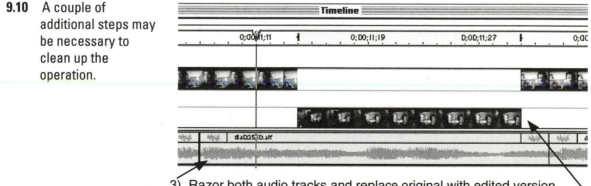

3) Razor both audio tracks and replace original with edited version.
4) Add video cutaway as necessary to cover edits.

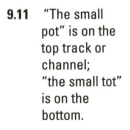

⚠️ **Gotcha**

I should mumble at my desk? This chapter uses spoken-word exercises to improve your short-term audio memory. The goal is to help you learn to analyze what you're hearing. Say the words out loud, not just in your head. If this upsets your colleagues, tell them you'll be a better editor because of it.

Most of us are born with this ability to hear and understand fast sounds. If you want to edit, you just have to learn to recognize what you're hearing. It takes a little bit of acoustic memory. Musicians and actors usually have this talent. But even if you can't carry a tune, you can still improve your listening skills.

1. Say, "the small pot" aloud, and listen very closely to your own voice while you do.

2. Immediately afterwards, try to remember exactly what your voice sounded like. If you can, hear those three syllables again in your head.

3. Repeat this a few times, and you'll find that you can recall the actual sound of your voice more and more accurately.

Try saying the phrase with different intonations and timings, and hear those versions in your head as well. Try saying slightly longer phrases until you can recall those also. Then try listening to playbacks of very short dialog clips and practice until you can recall them as well. Now do one more thing.

4. Slow down what you're hearing in your head so you can hear the tiny changes inside each word. In "the small pot," you should be able to hear definite transitions between /th/, /uh/, /s/, /maw/, /l/, /p/, /ah/, and /t/. Those are the phonemes.

9.11 "The small pot" is on the top track or channel; "the small tot" is on the bottom.

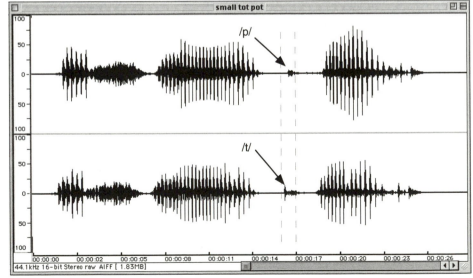

Don't give up if you aren't hearing individual sounds immediately—this is a skill that can be difficult at first, particularly for someone who's visually oriented. But I've found that most video editors catch on in fewer than a dozen tries. After that, it's easy.

Eight sounds for only three words?

Most meaningful syllables contain at least one vowel and one consonant sound. But some syllables have more than that. Take my name, "Jay." It's a single syllable, but has four distinct phonemes: /d zh ay ih/. Track 26 is me saying "My name Jay." First you hear it at normal speed, then slowed down to 1/6 speed. You should hear 11 phonemes in those three syllables: /m ah ih n ay ih m d zh ay ih/. Almost all of them can be used as edit points.

Common combinations of phonemes are called *diphthongs* and my name has two of them. The *j* sound is always a /d/ followed by a /zh/ (as in the middle of "leisure"). The vowel in my name always includes an /ih/ at the end. If you try to say just the /ay/ sound, my name sounds clipped.

Hear for yourself _____

Track 26 contains the previous example. The second part might sound like I'm on drugs, but it's actually the first part slowed down in software, so you can hear individual phonemes.

Phonetic-based Editing

We could predict exactly which tiny sounds made up, "the small pot" or "my name Jay" because there aren't very many ways humans move their mouths during speech. Standard American English uses only about three dozen of them.

Tables 9.1 and 9.2 show them organized into groups based on their usefulness to editors. Note how there's no phoneme for *c*, because it's sometimes /s/ and sometimes /k/. But there are 15 phonemes and diphthongs for the five vowels. That's why, when you're scanning a script or transcript to find replacement sounds or likely edits, it helps to say the words aloud. The two columns—*unvoiced* and *voiced*—have to do with how the sound is generated. You'll see why this is important later in this chapter.

Table 9.1   The consonants of standard English. The groupings are based on how you edit them.

	Unvoiced	Voiced
Stop Consonants	/p/ (punt)	/b/ (bunt)
	/k/ (cut)	/g/ (gut)
	/t/ (tot)	/d/ (dot)

Table 9.1   The consonants of standard English. The groupings are based on how you edit them. (Continued)

	Unvoiced	Voiced
Friction Consonants	/f/ (food)	/v/ (very)
	/s/ (silly)	/z/ (zebra)
	/sh/ (shoe)	/zh/ (leisure)
	/th/ (thin)	/TH/ (then)
	/h/ (horse)	–
Nasal Consonants	–	/m/ (mighty)
	–	/n/ (nap)
	–	/ng/ (lung)
Glide Consonants	–	/w/ (willing)
	–	/y/ (yes)
	–	/l/ (locate)
	–	/r/ (rub)
Diphthong Consonants	/t-sh/ (church)	/d-zh/ (judge)

Using Phonemes

People slide words together when they're speaking, so you can't always tell where one word ends and the next begins. But you can almost always hear when one phoneme ends and another starts. Consider Track 27—two takes of, "This is a special occasion." While the first is usable, the second has more emotion. But the second has a noise under the first few words. The only way to get a performance that starts cleanly and ends enthusiastically is to use a few words from each: "This is a," from one and "special occasion," from the other.

Hear for yourself

Track 27 is the audio for this exercise. It will look like Figure 9.12 when you capture it.

The line was delivered at normal speed and there's no pause between "a" and "special," so you can't cut in silence between those words. But the /p/ in "special" is a stop consonant; it creates a pause *inside* the word. You can scrub through the two takes, easily hear and mark that pause in each take, and edit from one to the other. The whole process shouldn't take more than ten seconds and should sound perfect.

Table 9.2   The vowels of standard English.

Single Vowels		
/ee/ (eat)	/ae/ (hat)	/eh/ (lend)
/ih/ (sit)	/aw/ (all)	/ah/ (father)
/o/ (note)	/u/ (bull)	/oo/ (tool)
/uh/ (about)	/UH/ (up)	/er/ (worker)

Diphthong Vowels		
/ay-ih/ (play)	/i-ih/ (high)	/aw-ih/ (toy)

This principle also works when the words aren't strictly identical. If you had the right words from elsewhere in the clip, you could join them to the first phrase to say, "This is a spectacular show," or "This is a specious argument."

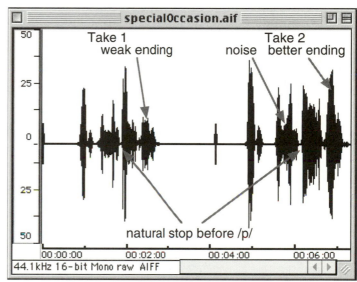

9.12   Two takes of, "This is a special occasion." The first is clean; the second is noisy but has more emotion.

Phoneme-based Editing Rules[4]

Cutting the way we just did is fast, precise, and usually seamless. First, hear the phrase you want to edit, slowly, in your head. Identify any phonemes that might be useful for the cut you want to make, using the rules below. Then scrub through the clip to find those points.

---

4. It really *does*, man. But what I meant was, "Here are some rules that use phonemes to improve how you edit."

All the **stop consonants** are created by storing air pressure in your mouth and then releasing it in a burst. There's a moment of silence in the middle of each stop consonant, right before the pressure is released. It can be as short as a third of a frame.

 Rule _____

Stop consonants will always give you a moment of silence.

- If a stop consonant is followed by a pause, it usually has two distinct sounds: one when the pressure is cut off, and another when it's released. But the second part isn't important and can be deleted to shorten the pause or edited to some other word.

- If two stop consonants are next to each other (as in, "fat cat"), they're usually *elided*; the closure comes from the first consonant, and the release from the second. But when people are self-conscious, they often pronounce each stop separately, making four distinct sounds. Editing out the middle two stops will make a nervous speaker sound more relaxed.

With the exception of /h/, **friction consonants** are created by forcing air through a narrow opening: between the lips for /f/ and /v/, between the tip of the tongue and back of the teeth for /th/ and /TH/, and so on. This always makes a high-pitched sound that's easy to spot while scrubbing.

 Rule _____

Friction consonants give you a high-pitched cue.

Air pressure also creates /h/, but air is flowing through an open mouth. There's very little friction, so this phoneme can be very quiet and not even show up on a waveform display. Be careful you don't accidentally delete it.

- You can usually edit from the start of one friction consonant to the start of a completely different one.

- Friction consonants are frequently stretched when a speaker is talking slowly. You can usually speed things up by making a small deletion in the middle.

For the three **nasal consonants**, air comes out of the nose instead of the mouth: try saying a long, "nnn" as you pinch your nostrils together—it'll feel as if your head's about to explode. If your performer has a head cold, nasals may sound wrong

 Rule _____

Nasal consonants might be mispronounced.

and need to be replaced from elsewhere in the dialog. But be aware that nasals are always voiced (see the following section, "Cognate Pairs"); the replacement sound will have to be at the right pitch.

- The /ng/ phoneme is written that way because it's heard at the end of words like "ring." But it's a phoneme on its own, not a diphthong made up of /n/ and /g/. Many people add a

/g/ anyway, as in the New York regionalism, "Long Guyland." Feel free to delete the /g/ to make your performer sound more polished.

The **glides** make the transition between sounds on either side. This means glides are influenced by adjacent sounds, and their own sound changes while they're being pronounced. This can make them very difficult to mark or match.

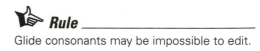

Rule _____

Glide consonants may be impossible to edit.

- In general, the only successful glide edits occur when both the consonant itself and the leading or trailing sound are identical.

- The /l/ glide involves lifting your tongue from the ridge behind your upper front teeth. If the speaker's mouth is dry, saliva can stick and cause a tiny click in the middle of this sound. You can delete the click easily.

Even though we hear **consonant diphthongs** as a single sound, they're actually two separate and predictable phonemes. If you scrub through them slowly, you can hear the transition and mark them separately.

Rule _____

Diphthongs can be cut in half.

The /d zh/ at the front of my name (Track 26) can be cut into two phonemes. Go ahead and try it. Delete just the /d/, and my name sounds French. Delete just the /zh/, and my name turns into the opposite of night. Similarly, you could borrow a /t/ from the front of "chicken" if you needed one to use elsewhere.

Cognate Pairs

There are two columns of consonants in Table 9.1 for a reason. The paired sounds in each row use exactly the same tongue and lip movement. The only difference is that the first in a pair relies on air pressure alone (unvoiced), while the second adds a buzzing from the vocal cords (voiced). The pairs are called *cognates*. Not all consonants have them.

Try saying "gut" and "cut" aloud, with your hand loosely on your throat. The tongue movement is the same for each. But you'll feel the buzzing in your throat start before the /g/, and not end until after the /k/.

Every aspect of a voice that we interpret as *pitch*—from what note is being sung, to the vocal difference between me and James Earl Jones—is based on the fundamental frequency of the buzzing vocal cords.[5] Unvoiced consonants simply don't have that buzz.

Rule _____

You don't have to worry about pitch with the unvoiced consonants.

- Unvoiced phonemes tend to stay consistent even if the speaker has a lot of tonal variety. This gives you more choices when editing.

- Unvoiced phonemes don't carry much that's identifiable as a specific voice. You can often substitute one person's voice for another's.

Hear for yourself ⎯⎯⎯

Track 28 is the two voices from the above example; first in the original readings and then edited together.

You can even substitute a male voice for a female one. Grab the first part of Track 28. It consists of my wife asking, "Have you read Jay's book?" and me responding, "I've written a couple of books." Merge the sexes to correct her question. Because both /k/ and /s/ are unvoiced, the edit, "Have you read Jay's boo ‖ ks?" works almost perfectly.

Unless you listen very closely, you're not aware that the sources have completely different voices.[6] In fact, because /k/ is a stop consonant, there's a convenient silence for you to edit in (Figure 9.13).

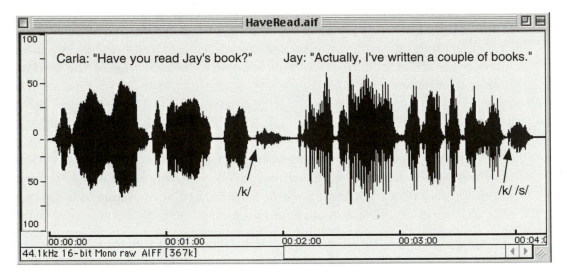

9.13   Amaze your friends! Learn to make this sex-changing edit.

5. While the differences we hear as pitch are based on the fundamental frequency, the differences we hear as voice character or specific sounds on a single pitch are based on *formants*—harmonics of that fundamental. You'll learn more about formants in Chapter 12 and some ways to manipulate them in Chapter 15.

6. And you could make the edit absolutely perfect by applying about a semitone's worth of pitch shift up (Chapter 15).

Because the mouth movements are identical, you can occasionally substitute one cognate for its brother. This may be the only way to save an edit, or create a new word.

 Rule _____

You can sometimes substitute one cognate for another.

- Depending on the context, this may add a slight accent to the voice. That's because we're used to hearing foreigners confuse cognate pairs when they first learn English.

- When the voiced stop consonant /b/ begins a word, some people start their vocal cords humming a fraction of a second or so before the release. This turns a word like "baby" into "mmmbaby." Deleting the hum, or replacing it with room tone, makes it sound better.

When *s* is added at the end to pluralize a word, its pronunciation is influenced by whether the vocal cords were buzzing on the phoneme that came before. There are two different *s* sounds in, "cat's

Rule _____

A final /s/ might actually be a /z/.

toys." The unvoiced /t/ leads to an unvoiced /s/, but the voiced /aw ih/ forces a voiced /z/. Be aware of this when looking for replacement sounds; the presence of an *s* in the written script doesn't guarantee a /s/ on the track.

The Vowels

Learn to recognize individual vowel phonemes in dialog. You can't substitute one for another. In Table 9.2, the unstressed /uh/ in "about" and the stressed /UH/ in "up" are separate entries. Even though they're made the same way, the difference in volume is critical.

- Vowel diphthongs can sometimes be separated into their component phonemes and used elsewhere. This is a lot harder than separating a consonant diphthong.

- Vowels and voiced consonants carry the pitch of a voice, which varies a lot during normal speech. After you edit, make sure the pitch doesn't jump unnaturally. If it does, try moving the edit to a nearby unvoiced consonant instead.

- Vowels carry most of the pacing of a voice. If a word is said too slowly, you can often make a small cut in the middle of a vowel to pick up speed—but this works only if the pitch is constant.

- When nervous performers pause before a word that starts with a vowel, they often build up pressure in the back of their throats. When they release it to say the word, the result is a *glottal shock*—a tiny click, almost like a stop consonant. It sounds tense. Calm things down by deleting the click.

Some More Tips for Great Edits

Speech is continuous, and the end of one word is influenced by the word that follows. If you say, "Mary grabbed the knob," the end of "the" will be slightly different than if she grabbed "the doorknob." The stop consonant /d/ changes the /uh/ in ways the nasal /n/ doesn't. A lot of interview edits feel subtly wrong because a producer put the words together while reading a transcript, without paying attention to how the edits sound in context.

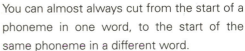 *Rule* _____

You can almost always cut from the start of a phoneme in one word, to the start of the same phoneme in a different word.

On the other hand, you could easily take a /n/ word and replace the "knob" with it. So she could grab "the ‖ knocker," "the ‖ needle," or "the ‖ neighborhood cat."

Because the stop consonants cut off sound entirely, there's more flexibility when editing between them. If Mary originally grabbed "the doorknob," it wouldn't be hard to have her grab "the ‖ bagel," "the ‖ gavel," or "the ‖ cat" instead.

 *Rule* _____

You can often cut from the beginning of one stop consonant to the beginning of a different one.

It's almost always best to hide a voice edit in the middle of a visual cutaway rather than right at the cut back to the speaker's face because the visual discontinuity calls attention to the aural one. Similarly, it's almost always better to edit *inside* a word rather than at its start. The mind tries to complete partial words based on their context and beginning, and that helps you hide the edit.[7]

Say you wanted to combine, "Mary grabbed the neighborhood cat," and "She liked her neighbor's car," to suggest she's also a car thief. The best place to make that cut is inside "neighbor." "Mary grabbed the neigh‖bor's car." This also works when combining identical words, as we did in the "This is a special occasion" example of Figure 9.12.

 *Rule* _____

Try not to edit where it's expected.

People change pitch while they're speaking, so two syllables you're trying to join may be at different places in the musical scale. Sometimes this shift makes sense in the edited version. If it doesn't, try

Rule _____

Make sure the sound quality matches.

a small amount of vari-speed or clip speed adjustment. But any more than a 3 percent speed change will make the voice sound artificial. If extreme adjustments are necessary, look for a different place to edit.

---

7. This is one of the reasons the she/he cut in Figure 9.13 works so well.

Sound quality can also change across an edit because the two halves had differences in mic placement or inconsistent digitizing. That's a lot easier to fix; instead of cutting the two clips together, put them on separate audio tracks. When you get to the mix, add equalization or reverb to make them match.

Sometimes you have to cut from a word to silence, even though the narrator had kept on speaking in the original cut. This happens frequently when pulling interview bites or when deleting a /s/ to turn a plural noun into a singular one. Cutting to room tone instead of silence can fool the ear into thinking the subject paused naturally. The same trick works when a bite starts abruptly; add a little room tone in front.

 Rule _____

Use room tone to extend abrupt cuts.

Room Tone or Presence

Every shooting location has a unique sound. It consists of the obvious background noises such as distant traffic, clocks ticking, and HVAC systems. But it also includes the room itself—its size, shape, and surfaces—and how those factors affect the noise. A recording of that room sound can be very useful.

When I started in film sound, it was customary to capture a minute or so of a location's background before striking. I'd yell, "Room tone!" and the crew would stand still while I taped. We did this right after the film takes because a room's sound can change during the day. We did it while the crew was still there because their breathing and subtle movements were recorded on the dialog takes as well. The procedure remains common in feature production today—though now it's referred to as *presence* because it can include outdoor ambiences.

More casual shoots often skip this step, but there's still plenty of presence available. You can often grab a few usable seconds between, "Action!" and the start of dialog, before the camera stops after a take, or while an interview subject is thinking about an answer. A loop of that sound may be all you need. If you're planning to collect room tone this way, here are a few tips.

- Be sure you're hearing only presence. Voices will echo for a second or more after dialog stops, depending on the room. Wait until the echo has died out before grabbing the presence.

- If you're taking presence from pauses in an interview, make sure you're not hearing the subject inhale, which can be fairly loud if picked up by a lav. A looped breath sounds like Darth Vader.

- If the presence includes constantly changing elements, like ocean waves, there can be a noticeable jump when you transition from the end of one pass to the start of the next. Use a *C-loop*, described in Chapter 11.

This presence can be used to fill pauses during cutaways or to cover noises during a take. If a character has a long voice-over, tighten things up by replacing breaths with somewhat shorter clips of presence—usually, about 2/3 the length of the breath sounds about right. Presence is also necessary for matching studio ADR to location dialog.

But there are also times when room tone isn't needed. A well-designed narration studio is so quiet that presence disappears on TV or computer media and is barely perceptible in theaters. You can edit faster if you use silence instead of room tone.

Restoring Lipsync by Eye

You've got a clip with picture and no sound and a different clip with sound only, and you need to sync them up. If both clips are exactly the same length, chances are they were originally recorded together and all the job needs is to place their starting points together in the timeline.

But if the clips are from separate media, or if they were digitized separately, it will be much harder to match the track with the right mouth movements.

- It helps if you're sure both audio and video are speed stable. This usually happens when both are digital. But if you're matching film shot with a noncrystal camera, or audio was recorded on analog tape without pilot or timecode, restoring sync can be impossible.

- It helps if both audio and video start on the same word. If the audio track has a few extra syllables that don't appear on the picture, you'll find it difficult to link mouth movements to their sounds.

- Check the clip's statistics to make sure there are no dropped frames. If there's a problem that slows down the software when digitizing or capturing, most NLEs will skip a video frame or two to catch up. NLEs are more likely to do this to the picture than to the sound because video jumps are less perceptable than audio ones. But each dropped frame knocks subsequent audio out of sync and has to be treated as a separate resyncing operation. There are tips for avoiding dropped frames in Chapters 1 and 7.

- It's essential that audio and video are of the same event. I was once asked to resync a scene, only to find out later that the client had inadvertently used picture from one take and sound from another. It was an expensive learning experience for the client.

It also helps to make your editing setup as sync-friendly as possible. Use a large picture monitor and play at full frame rate. The best environment for sync matching is an audio workstation with *bump controls*. These let you slip sound against picture in controlled increments of a frame or less, while both are playing, by tapping a button.

There's a general procedure to make sync matching a little easier.

1. Play the track and find the first stop consonant. Place a marker where the sound returns after going silent.

2. Note approximately how far that marker is from the start of speech.

3. Find the frame at the start of the video where the subject's mouth first opens.

4. Move the picture about the same distance as you noted in step 2, less a few dozen frames. Shuttle forward slowly until you see the mouth close.

5. Jog forward until you see the lips start to open again. Place a marker on that frame.

6. Line up the markers and check sync.

If things aren't quite right when you check, move the sound a frame forward. Check again. If that looks worse, go back the other way. If moving helps but doesn't fix things, add another frame in the same direction. If things don't look right at all when you first check, you found the wrong stop consonant in step 5.

You may be able to skip steps 2 and 4, and just match the first sound with the first picture where the mouth is open. Sometimes this works, but often it doesn't. I've found it faster to always go for the stop consonant.

Psychological Sync?

Years ago I was cutting TV sound in a facility originally designed for radio. The front of the room, where the monitor speakers were, was taken up by a window into the studio. So the client's picture monitor had to be put on the left side of the room. To watch, clients would turn sideways. But the sound still came from the front of the room, on their right sides. (TV was mono in those days, so this wasn't a problem.)

One day we were syncing some field audio to picture. It hadn't been recorded properly, so the job took a long time, but I finally nudged the voice to match the lips. Still, the client wasn't satisfied. I knew it was right; they thought it was wrong. I told them to take a lunch break and I'd have it fixed by the time they got back.

While they were out, I rigged up a speaker on top of the video monitor. When they came back, sound was coming from the same direction as picture. Now they were able to accept the track as being in sync—even though I hadn't changed the timing at all.

Chapter 10

Finding and Editing Music

Remember this:

- There's no reason a film can't have a fully professional-sounding score, even on a limited budget. But doing it the wrong way can get you into serious legal and financial trouble.

- Today's music libraries have an incredible range of good music. If you take some time, you'll find exactly what you need.

- Music editing isn't difficult once you apply a little ear (and finger) training.

Even before they learned to talk, movies had music. Every theater had at least a piano player; bigger houses had elaborate organs that could also make sound effects and some even had small orchestras. While the choice of music was often at the whim of theater management, the more important feature films came with original scores on sheet music. You could even say silent films sparked the singing commercial: As new technologies like the Victrola and radio became popular, movie producers commissioned ballads that incidentally included the film's title. (The old standard, "Janine, I Dream of Lilac Time" was actually written to promote the movie *Janine*.)

But film music didn't take off until the synchronized soundtrack was possible. Many early talkies followed the musical tradition of silent films, with somewhat random instrumentals playing under dialog. Then Hollywood began importing European composers with a tradition of orchestral *program music*—music designed to tell a story. Movie scoring became an art form. Some of the greatest classical composers of the twentieth century, including Prokofiev, Copland, and Bernstein, also wrote for films.[1]

If you're making a narrative film, you're probably already thinking in terms of music. But even if you're producing documentary, corporate, or event video, music can be used the same ways: to

---

1. A suite from Prokofiev's *Lieutenant Kijé* score is now part of standard symphonic repertoire, as is Copland's *Our Town*. Copland even won a best-scoring Oscar for *The Heiress*. Leonard Bernstein wrote one film, then vowed never to repeat the experience (see chapter 6). Prolific film composer Elmer Bernstein was no relation.

set the mood, underscore emotions, provide a rhythm for visual sequences, and comment on what we're seeing. The techniques for spotting, obtaining, and applying music are the same for any film, whether it's a drama or a factory tour.

Spotting Notes

You don't need to be a musician to figure out what kind of music your project needs. It does help to be familiar with a wide variety of musical styles, but even that isn't essential. What's critical is that you know your project and its goals.

The music selection process should start before you hire a composer or gather library discs. Read the script or watch a rough cut and see where music is needed. Most likely, you'll want a main title and ending, even if it's just for a few seconds while we see "Installing Your New Disposal" in front and "Acme Gearworks" at the end. But there are probably other places where music can help.

Find places for music by making spotting notes, even for something as simple as a 10-minute sales film. For each scene or segment, write down what the music could be doing. It doesn't need to be in musical terms. Terms like *music swells with inspiration*, or *exciting sports music* are useful. If music is just there to tie testimonials together or support a narrator, it should still reflect the mood of the piece. Be aware of any emotional or subject shifts because that's where the music should change. Of course, if something suggests a particular style or tempo—perhaps a period piece under historic footage or a fast rhythm for a montage—write that down as well.

Break your list into *cues*—segments of music between a few seconds and a few minutes long—linked to specific on-screen sequences. This lets you deal with music pieces efficiently when searching libraries, talking to a composer, and putting the music in place. If there are only a few cues, give them descriptive names. If there are many, numbering them helps.

If a scene doesn't suggest music, perhaps silence is more appropriate. Hold back from time to time, and alternate scored sequences with dialog only or with sound-effects driven sequences. One common approach for documentaries is to score narrative sections but let the interviews stand on their own without music. Some short films work best with continuous music; longer films often benefit by dropping the music for a while, so we're aware of its return. Also consider if you'll need *source* (also known as *diegetic*) *music*, which is music presumably coming from something on the screen. Any scene that involves a working radio or TV, or is set in a restaurant or a party, probably needs source music.

Spotting notes are important even if you're the only one who'll be seeing them because they provide a structure for music selection. If the music is coming from a library, it's a lot easier to search the library when you know what you're looking for. ("I'll know it when I hear it," is a great philosophy for wasting time.) If you're using original music, the spotting notes can help narrow your search for a composer or band, and be essential when you start discussing the project with the musicians.

Getting the Music

Music is subject to the Golden Triangle of Production: You can have it excellent, fast, or cheap—pick any two. If you're on a limited budget, it's worth taking time to find great music that doesn't cost much. One place you *won't* find great inexpensive music is at a record store. Law and common sense both get in the way.

Copyright Considerations

Students and other low-budget filmmakers sometimes ask why they can't use songs from their personal CD collections; after all, they paid for the music (if they didn't download it from a sharing service). Copyright law takes a different view. When you buy a CD, you get the right to play it for yourself and close friends, or to record a backup copy for your own personal listening. Syncing it with images or playing it outside your immediate circle is almost always specifically forbidden. Copyright violation might not bother you—and a low-profile infringement might never get noticed—but if the lawyers come after you, they'll win.[1] If you're not sure about any of this or think it doesn't apply in your case, talk to an attorney *before* you use the music.

- You can't defend yourself by claiming Fair Use. That doctrine allows criticism, parody, and commentary on the music itself—not the use of the music as a video underscore. (Fair Use is a set of principles you may use to defend yourself in court if you've been accused of infringement; it's not a free ticket for certain kinds of copying.)

- You can't defend yourself by claiming that you couldn't afford to pay for a song, so its creator isn't losing anything when you use it for free. Economic loss is only one of the things courts look at. Paupers and nonprofits are subject to the same laws as professionals.

- You can't argue you're actually promoting the music by giving it more exposure, unless the owner of the music has agreed to this exposure in advance. A band has the right to decide what vehicles it will be associated with.

A couple of copyright myths are based on misunderstandings of real situations where usage is legal. TV stations pay fees to ASCAP and BMI to broadcast songs as entertainment, but those fees are legally defined as compensation to the composers and lyricists for the public performance of their creation. The fees have nothing to do with using a specific recording or syncing the music with video. Also, at one time courts accepted that copying fewer than eight bars of a

---

1. It's possible your lawyers could build a convincing case that a wedding video or nonprofit fundraiser *is* Fair Use. I've never heard of this being done. Even if your lawyers manage to pull this off, you'll probably end up paying more for them than a proper license would have cost in the first place.

song was not plagiarism. But the 8-bar rule applied only to the notes on paper, not the performance, and was specifically eliminated many years ago.

> ### ⚠ Gotcha _____
> **But it's the client's CD...** Some wedding videographers believe they can avoid copyright issues by using music from the client's personal collection. Wedding videographers may even give the client a particular music CD as a wedding present, just so they can use its music in the video.
>
> While it's unlikely a record company will pursue an amateur who sets his or her own wedding video to music (even though it's clearly an infringement), professional wedding videographers are considered fair game.
>
> I've heard of producers being put out of business because they claimed innocent use of a copyrighted song in a wedding video. The happy couple just happened to show their wedding album to the wrong neighbor, an employee of the giant corporation that owned the song. Some companies even reward their employees for spotting these infringements.

I personally believe the large record companies tend to exploit their artists shamelessly. A band can have two or three hit albums before it sees a penny. Unfortunately, some of the money record companies don't give to artists goes to staff attorneys, who protect copyrights vigorously. So as a professional, I follow the rules.

But there are more practical production reasons for not stealing music. Well-known songs get tied up with viewers' personal memories. Unless the music is incredibly appropriate, it may draw the viewer away from your message. You also don't have as much editing flexibility. If viewers know the original well, they'll be distracted by cuts. Even if you stick to obscure tracks and are never spotted by the record companies, using unlicensed music limits your options for the film. Exhibitors, festivals, and networks won't touch a film unless the producer guarantees it's fully cleared.

Using music legally, for free   You can avoid paying for music if you enlist local musicians to perform their own songs or public domain standards, in exchange for a screen credit and a copy of the film. Some very fine scores have been done this way. You can occasionally find musicians eager for scoring experience, popping up on the Internet and advertising in the `rec.video` newsgroups. Just be sure you're happy with their musicianship, you understand the production costs that might be involved, and you have a written agreement that covers the rights listed below. If there's nothing in writing and either the film or the band strikes it rich, someone is going to want to sue somebody.

If your cause is noble enough, you may be able to get well-known musicians to let you use their recordings for free or for a nominal amount. Check with the record company first because it probably owns the master recording. You may have to then negotiate separately with the composers for performance rights. But it's worth the legwork: I've done PBS promos using Beatles songs, and a recruiting piece for a music school featuring the New York Philharmonic, and the rights didn't cost a thing.

Or check the Web. Musicians' collaboratives and some stock libraries sometimes offer legitimate producers the first license for free, as enticement to buy more. Some let you use their recordings in broadcast projects with no fee and only require that you report the public performance properly (discussed further in this chapter) so the composers get paid under the stations' ASCAP and BMI licenses. But don't assume that just because a song is legally downloadable, it's in the public domain. Many bands give away their music to build a fan base, but they still keep the copyright.

Temp tracks   While not quite legal, it's very common for editors to drop a commercial recording onto a timeline as temporary music. It can serve the same emotional purposes as a score while the sequence is being developed, and then it can also be an example for the composer or library search. The music is deleted before the film is ever seen by anyone outside the production team.

The real danger of this is temp love: A director or client gets so used to the temp track that nothing else will do. If this happens in a big-budget production, there's a possibility of licensing the original recording. On lesser projects it usually leads to frustration. Use temp tracks sparingly and make sure everyone understands the score's status.

Rights and Licenses

Most music, no matter how old or obscure, is protected. While songs fall into the public domain after a while, old standards may be in copyrighted arrangements, and classical music often gets new copyrights by contemporary scholars who edit it. Besides, this concept of public domain applies only to your right to perform the notes and lyrics. There's almost always a separate copyright on the recording—even of public domain songs—which belongs to the musicians or the record company.

But a copyright owner can let you use their music for a specified purpose. There are at least two different kinds of licenses you'll have to consider.

Synchronization and Master License   A *synchronization license* lets you match your images or other audio to a recording of a copyrighted work. It's controlled by the composer or publisher and has to be issued by them.[1] Oddly enough, sync rights don't include the right to use the recording itself; that's a separate *master license,* usually controlled by the record company. Music libraries always combine these licenses, but if you're negotiating for nonlibrary recorded music, you'll have to get the licenses separately. If you're having music exclusively recorded for your film, be sure to specify all the rights the musicians are giving you in your letter of agreement.

---

1. You used to be able to get sync licenses from the Harry Fox Agency in New York, but it dropped that service in the middle of 2002.

Cue Sheet

Film or series:	Inside Boston	Episode:	The New Berry #IB-2-09
Production #:	4902	Air Date:	TBD
Production Co:	Digital Playroom	Show length:	26:30
	see bottom for contact info	Music length:	14:12

BI: Background Instrumental	BV: Background Vocal	TO: Theme Open	VI: Visual Instrumental
W: Visual Vocal		TC: Theme Close	EE: Logo

Cue #	Title	Composer	Publisher	Society	Usage	Timing
01	Audiocom	Eric Fauret	Franklin-Douglas	ASCAP	BI	1:45
02	Give Me One Chance	Colin Kiddy	DeWolfe Limited	ASCAP	BI	2:08
03	Tranceporter	Chris Slack / Steve Johnson	DeWolfe Ltd	ASCAP	BI	3:21
04	No Good Man	Paul Lenart	Three Under Music	ASCAP	BV	1:01
05	Ocean Hopes	Eric Fauret	Franklin-Douglas	ASCAP	BI	2:15
06	Cookin Blues	David Grimes	DG Music	BMI	BV	:45

10.1   A TV show's cue sheet. It goes to the station, so the station can report the performance.

Public performance license   The public performance license gets tricky, but can be important. Any time you play a song for anyone other than family and friends, the law says you're performing it in public and the composers must be paid. Obviously, this applies to very public performances like TV broadcasts and theatrical releases. But it also covers the Internet, trade show booths, factory tour videos, and point-of-sale demos. It isn't covered by any form of sync or mechanical license.

The performing rights societies—ASCAP, BMI, and SESAC in the United States—grew up to track these performances. Different composers and publishers belong to different organizations, but ASCAP is by far the largest. Broadcasters and trade show promoters often purchase annual licenses from the societies to cover all the music the societies control. If you're creating a TV show, the station usually requires that you prepare a cue sheet (Figure 10.1). The station reports the information to the societies, who then pay the composers a tiny share of the annual fee. The societies' formulas are heavily weighted in favor of pop music, but scoring and library composers are starting to have an impact on the societies.

Commercials don't use cue sheets because they're not under the stations' control. But spots are sometimes tracked by the first line of copy, and a composer or music library may ask for that text so the composer or library can report the use themselves.

Strictly speaking, any nonbroadcast public performance also requires a license; even a point-of-purchase video or attract loop that runs continually at a kiosk requires a license. These two applications may be covered by a store's or venue's blanket license. If these are not covered, skip the giant societies who charge high fees. Instead, negotiate performance rights directly with the composer or publisher.

Most music libraries can also supply a performance license when you buy a sync license from them. Depending on the use and your relationship with the library, the cost can range from zero to a few hundred dollars. Nonbroadcast library performance licensing has historically been ignored: Libraries haven't insisted on it, and many producers have never heard of it.

Original Music

Working with a composer on a full score is an artistic collaboration, so there are as many ways of working as there are composers and filmmakers. But some things are essential for a successful relationship. David Grimes (www.davidgrimesmusic.com), a busy Boston-based scoring composer, stresses the importance of communication.

> "I expect to go over the project with the producer as soon as I'm hired. Usually I prefer that they be pretty specific… then, if I have an idea, I'll suggest it. If they want me to spot the project, it's going to be a lot more difficult. I don't have their vision.
>
> The best producers use a musical or emotional language when they talk about individual cues. Temp music can be a problem if they get too used to it, but bringing commercial recordings to use as examples can be a good idea. Unless a producer has a good musical background, what they ask for and what you hear in your head can be different things.
>
> What I don't like is people who only know what they don't like. I'll suggest something; they say 'no' but not much else. I'll respond by asking for negatives: 'You don't want a rock drum kit?', 'You don't want hand percussion?'. This is often the quickest way to narrow stuff down."

Grimes and other composers are often willing to produce multiple demos of some cues, once they've agreed with the producer on basics about the sound and musical approach. But unless you're working with big budgets and long lead times, the better composers insist on picture being *locked*—no more changes that will affect timing—before they actually start writing.

You and the composer will have to agree on contract terms, including not only licensing but who owns the basic themes and how extensive the production will be. Many composers aren't willing to write a score as *work-for-hire*, assigning all ownership to you. They'd prefer to keep the musical ideas, give you nonexclusive licenses, and then sell rearranged versions to music libraries. Agreeing to this can save you money.

You and the composer will also have to agree on delivery media. Traditionally, composers got VHS or 3/4 inch tapes with linear timecode and a burn-in window, and delivered on DAT with timecode or 2-pop. But recent trends are to give composers individual videos for each cue as QuickTime or AVI files and get back audio files or CDs. Keep markers on your timeline, showing where each of the reference files started. Ask the composer to deliver files that start in sync with the reference ones, even if the music enters later. Then you can drop their files against your markers for perfect sync.

Communication is also important if you're commissioning songs, rather than a score, and the process is much simpler. Generally there'll only be a couple of pieces of music, often created before the final edit. You'll end up trimming the video to fit.

Loop-based original music   Many filmmakers with moderate musical skills have been turning to programs like Sonic Foundry's Acid. The program uses CD-ROM libraries of loops—short snippets designed to repeat endlessly. These can be as simple as a bass or drum pattern, include melodic or harmony parts, or even be pieces of a hot solo. You drag the loops onto tracks in a timeline, where they automatically snap into musical sync and can play together. By combining loops, switching to alternative versions, and adding on-board studio effects, you can create a score of any length.

Working with Acid takes creativity, but you don't need composing or performing skills. The program helps you by tweaking each loop's tempo and key in realtime so it'll sound good with your combination of other loops. It even has a brush to randomly paint families of loops across the score. If you do have musical chops, you can record your own solos or vocals and add them to the mix. There's so much possibility for variation that it's unlikely your loop-based score will sound like any other, a definite advantage over other forms of canned music.

On the downside, arranging a loop-based score and fine-tuning the mix can be very time-consuming if you don't have musical and production skills, and it's hard to keep long cues from becoming boring. While the program advertises loops in styles varying from classic country to orchestral, it only works well on highly rhythmic or repetitive genres such as contemporary dance and pop, techno, and trance.

Acid discs cost about $50 each, are well produced, and may contain hundreds of loops within a particular style. The program itself costs about $400 with a collection of loops to get you started, and requires a very fast PC. Mac users can get in on the fun with BitHeadz' Phrazer, which offers similar features for the same price. Other loop-based alternatives are starting to appear in the market.

Library Music

A mix of original and library music may be the best solution for a modest-budget project, hiring a composer for exposed pieces and scoring the rest from existing pieces. A low-budget project can rely on library music exclusively; with a little luck and careful editing, library music can be just as effective. But you need the right music.

Library music has been around almost as long as movies. During the silent film era, a British composer named Meyer de Wolfe started publishing generic sheet music for the staff orchestras common in large European silent cinemas. When the talkies came, De Wolfe Music and a few competitors started recording these pieces for films that couldn't afford original scores. The music was first supplied as optical tracks, then on 78 rpm disc, then on 10 inch LPs. By the late 1940s, newsreels and other low-budget films were using DeWolfe extensively.

If you've ever listened to a corporate or classroom film from that era, the nicest thing you could say about this music was that it sounded canned. Libraries didn't have much money for production. A handful of composers cranked out songs that were mostly predictable and boring. Songs were produced so cheaply that horn sections were often out of tune. Film editors frequently had to remove *clams*—wrong or badly played notes that shouldn't have been on the disc in the first place. When I started producing tracks in the early 1970s, there were still only a few libraries to choose from, and those clams were still swimming. It was unusual to find more than a couple of really good cuts on a new disc.

But by the 1990s, cheap, bad studio sessions had been replaced by cheap, good digital instruments. Computers and sampling keyboards made it possible for composers to create well-produced music on their own, without a studio. Some sold cues to the established libraries, but many others started libraries of their own. Today, a Web search for "production music" yields close to one hundred publishers. Competition has raised the standards and widened the variety. Some stock music still sounds canned. But if you pay attention while choosing and fitting library music to your film, you can create an exciting, custom-sounding score for very little money.

Library pros and cons   The main reason for using stock music is economic. You can buy decent-sounding cues for as little as $8 each, comparable to what a synthesizer-based composer might give you for $100/minute. If your tastes are a little richer, you can get top-quality productions with real orchestras, vocals, or hot session players starting at $75 per use—music that, if written for your film, would cost thousands.

Time is also money. An original score can take weeks, but any well-equipped audio post house or music service has hundreds of hours of music waiting on their shelves. Or use your browser: Many publishers let you search and audition over the Web. They'll burn a custom CD of only the songs you like and get it in your hands the next day. Downloading at true CD quality is still too data-intensive for most users (a three minute song takes more than an hour at 56 kbps), but a few libraries are experimenting with online delivery. As broadband gets more common and people get used to working with technologies like mp3 properly[1], this mode of delivery will probably dominate the industry.

On some projects, flexibility is an important consideration. A well-stocked library lets you switch from boogie to Broadway to baroque at the change of a client's mind—something that may not be possible if you've committed to a specific composer.

A minor problem with stock music is that to sound right, it should be edited to picture. This isn't at all hard, even for musical klutzes; instructions are further on in the chapter. A bigger problem

---

1. mp3 can sound darned good. See Chapter 19.

is the total lack of exclusivity. Library publishers make their profit by selling the same songs over and over. Some years ago, I scored an insurance company film using one of the bigger libraries. A week later, I heard one of the themes from my score as background music at a supermarket (fortunately, my client didn't). Today, there's so much music available that it's less likely you'll have a conflict—but it's still possible.

Costs and licensing   There are two ways of paying for stock music, *needle-drop* and *buyout* (sometimes called royalty free, though you're really paying for the usage up-front). Despite the fact that a couple of libraries are willing to work both ways, the two are very different philosophies. It affects the music they supply.

Needle-drop was the original payment scheme. Newsreel editors would report a usage and pay a fee each time they dropped the phonograph needle on a record to copy its music for editing.[1] Discs are cheap—between $12 and 15—and may even be free to good customers. But having the disc just gives you the right to listen to it. If you actually use a song in a production, you send or e-mail a form (Figure 10.2) and the library bills you. After you pay, the library sends you a written license. Fees per drop are based on the size of the potential audience. They range from about $70 for a local commercial or corporate video, or $300 for films headed to a festival, to up to $1000 for a license that covers TV, Internet, home video, and new media invented in the future.

Blankets are offered by almost every needle-drop library. *Production blankets* are discounted licenses to cover all the music in a project. The cost depends on the library and the kind of use, but its often equivalent to the library's rate if you were to use four individual drops per ten minutes of total running time. If you like to match different cues to the changing moods in a scene (in my opinion, the best way to use library music), blankets can be a significant bargain compared to individual licenses.

Many of the libraries also offer *annual blankets*, you pay a set amount per year, depending on the kind of media you produce. In return, the library licenses every cue you use, for every project destined for your media. It'll also lend you its full library for the life of the blanket, including new CDs as they're released, plus it'll give you a discount on licenses for other media and let you consult with their librarians if you get stuck in a search. Libraries often prefer this arrangement because it lets them predict income. Annual rates vary with the library publisher (and size of its library) as well as the media involved, but for a busy producer it can be a bargain.

If you're buying a blanket, you still report each use and the library issues individual licenses.

---

1. Today some libraries call it *laser drop* instead, though that's not how a CD works.

Needle-drop libraries don't make money until you use the music, so it's in the needle-drop's interest to get as much good music in your hands as possible. Needle-drop libraries tend to put a lot of good cues on each disc—usually 20 or more, plus variations—with very little filler or repetition. They also understand they're competing with other libraries each time you search for a cue, so standards tend to be very high. As a general rule, needle-drop music sounds much better than buyout. (I'm basing this on overall experience. Please don't send me e-mail to point out the many exceptions.) The downside of needle-drop is that, in the long run, it costs more.

Buyout libraries have been around a long time, but these exploded with the development of good-sounding MIDI, digital desktop recording, and cheap CD replication. The discs cost $70–175 each, with discounts for multiple purchases, and include permanent licenses for anything you do. You can use a song over and over, for a price equivalent to a single needle-drop, and not even tell the library when you do. The disadvantage is there may be only one song on a CD you want to use.

Buyout libraries make their money selling CDs, so it's to their advantage to put just enough good music on each disc to keep you

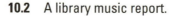

10.2 A library music report.

coming back. Really great tracks often get spread over as many discs as possible; other tracks may be as filler, like a keyboard player ad-libbing over a computer-generated rhythm. Buyout CDs usually include 8–12 themes with a lot of repetitious material.

Choosing a library

Some buyout libraries are a waste of money. Others are incredible bargains. That's also true of needle-drop libraries but to a lesser extent—needle-drop publishers who don't sell a lot of licenses usually don't survive. I keep library reviews on my Web site, www.dplay.com/tutorial/lib-cards.html. I've tried to be as unbiased as possible. But your tastes might not agree with mine, and it's your money. Here are some pointers for making a good decision:

- Don't judge a library by its pretty Web site, brochure, or list of satisfied clients. Anyone can hire a designer, and the lists just show who bought (or were given) the discs—not whether the purchasers are using them. Network and feature-film credits may simply mean that a rushed producer grabbed something to put under an unimportant sequence.

- Don't judge a library by its listings. Some publishers describe every track with meaningless labels like, "A winner! Great for corporate, extreme sports, and romantic drama!" But cherish the libraries with descriptions like, "Rock anthem with slow, inspirational start; builds to high-energy finish." These can make searching much easier.

- Don't judge a library by its online samples. Many publishers have databases on their Web sites that let you search for a particular style and stream a short excerpt. These databases are great for finding a specific track once you've chosen a library, but the data compression can make it hard to check production quality, and the excerpt won't tell you if a song continues to develop or just repeats the same figure for three boring minutes.

- Don't even judge a library just by its demo CD. These narrated montages can tell you a lot about how many different musical styles the library supports and give you a good idea of its production quality. But CDs can't tell you how good the writing and arranging is. For that, you have to hear complete tracks.

- *Do* judge a library by auditioning some of the discs along with the demo. Good libraries will send discs on approval or give you an evaluation period. Listen carefully. Is the music interesting? Even a narration underscore should have some development and changes, so you can move parts of it around to fit the mood of each paragraph. What about production values? Does the music sound rich and full? Does it fill the area between the speakers? Pay attention to musical values as well. Unless you're dealing with obvious techno styles, the music should sound like it's being played by live musicians, not computers. Orchestras are particularly hard to synthesize well, but some composers manage. Don't be swayed by claims of live orchestras or choirs if the sound is bogus—some publishers stretch the truth.

10.3 A library search engine with audio previews. This one's from DeWolfe.

- Give extra points to a library that has a CD-ROM or online search engine with meaningful categories and audio previews, such as the one in Figure 10.3. You might not need the search utility with only a few discs, but libraries grow and these programs can be a great time-saver.

Choosing the music

Grab your spotting notes and start to search. If you don't have a searchable database, flip through your collection and collect appropriate discs based on the track descriptions. If you do have a database, use it to make a short list—not the final decision. To pick music properly, you want to be able to scan through the whole song.

Play each candidate. If it's a reject, turn it off immediately. One key to a successful search is keeping your musical memory free from distractions. If it's not an absolute klunker, listen to different parts of the track. The melody often starts some ten seconds after the beginning, but a well-written piece will have variations or texture changes farther in. Check the ending as well, to make sure it's appropriate.

When you find something that you think will work, play it against the video or narration. Still like it? Then let the video or narration continue but turn the music off! If a piece is just right, you should feel a loss when it goes away. This kind of love-at-first-listen happens surprisingly often. But if it doesn't, don't despair; mark the track as a possible and move on. If a piece is almost right but you think it could be better, look for other tracks with similar descriptions by the same composer.

No matter what you do, don't forget music is an artistic element. No book, catalog description, or software can replace directorial judgement. Don't be afraid to go against type (I once scored a network sports documentary with Bach fugues), and don't be afraid to make a statement.

Choosing source or diegetic music

By and large, any library cue that's in an appropriate style should sound fine coming from an on-screen jukebox or television.[1]   A good library will even include pop-sounding vocals designed specifically for source use.

Presumably live music—the off-screen band at a dance or club—is harder to match. Performing bands seldom have the polish or production techniques of a recording. If you can't find something that sounds right in a stock library, see if you can license a recording by a local band.

Music Editing

One of my clients calls it *retrofitting*; after he cuts a documentary, he chooses music from my library. Then he has me move sections of the music around changing melodic treatments when the scene changes, hitting musical peaks against the more dramatic shots, building in sync with the narrator, and ending perfectly with the final fade-out to complement the picture. This editing doesn't take very long, and the result is a score that sounds original—on a much friendlier budget.

Surprisingly, the basic skill is not difficult to learn and doesn't require musical training. It's one of the handiest things you can pick up. Even if you use original music exclusively, the ability to edit gives you the flexibility to make last-minute timing changes or cut an end-credit montage without having to go back to the composer.

Basic Editing

The basic editing technique is shared by music editors throughout the industry. It doesn't require special equipment or software and can be adapted to virtually any program—or even a tradi-

---

1. It'll need some technical mangling as discussed in Chapter 18.

10.4   Each dot represents a tap when you sing the song.

tional online editor. It's faster and more accurate than looking for waveforms or using the "guess, stab, and trim" method of marking cuts some picture editors use.

If you can count to four while tapping your finger, you've already got most of the skill required. It helps if you're also sensitive to chord changes and melody, but counting is the most important part. That's because almost all the music used in film and video has a structure based on groups of four beats.[1] Learn to hear those beats and mark the groups, and the chords and melody will often follow. Ignore the beats, and even the most elegant harmonic flow sounds wrong.

Teach yourself to count along

If you've ever studied an instrument, this section should be a piece of cake. If you haven't, don't despair, it's not hard. You just have to do a few exercises. Start by singing the "Marine Hymn" ("From the halls of Montezuma, to the shores of Tripoli..."). As you do, tap your index finger for each beat. In Figure 10.4, I've indicated each tap with a dot.

There's a tap for almost every syllable. "From the" is sung twice as fast as most of the other syllables, so those two words share a tap (I made them narrower to indicate this). The third syllable in Montezuma lasts twice as long as the others, so it gets two taps. (If you're a musician, please note I'm thinking in terms of a square performance where every note falls on a beat.)

Now sing it again, noting which syllables get the most stress. "Halls," "zum," and the final sound in Tripoli are emphasized.

Track 29 is an instrumental performance of the "Marine Hymn." Play it once or twice until you're used to tapping its tempo. Then play it while tapping and counting aloud, once for each tap, and restarting from 1 whenever you hit a stressed syllable. It all fits together like Figure 10.5. If you get totally lost, use Track 30 as a reality check.

10.5   Counting with a 1 on the loudest syllables.

---

1. Some use groups of two or three beats. We'll deal with those later in this chapter.

Hear for yourself

Track 29 is the "Marine Hymn" for you to tap and count with.[1] This track and the other examples in this chapter are excerpts of much longer pieces from the immense DeWolfe Music Library. They're protected by copyright, but DeWolfe has graciously let me copy this and other musical selections to the book's CD for tutorial purposes. They've also given permission for readers to load the tracks into a computer, where appropriate, but only to practice techniques. You cannot legally use the music in a project without a specific license from DeWolfe, but its needle-drop rates are reasonable. To learn more about this versatile library, call 800-221-6713 or 212-382-0220, or visit www.dewolfemusic.com.

Track 30 is the same piece with me counting. My voice is on the left channel only, so you can mute it to hear only the music.

Note how there are always four beats before a 1. Those groups of four are *measures* or *bars*, with 1 being the *barline*. Four beats to a bar happens in so many songs that musicians call it *common time*.[2] Note also how each 3 count is slightly louder than the 2 or 4 count next to it. Almost every song with four beats to the bar has this pattern. Try tapping and counting along with songs on the radio. Once you can count and spot the barlines, you're ready for easy and accurate music editing.

Tapping and marking

Track 31 is a library cue that might be used in a high-tech documentary or corporate video. This kind of straight-ahead music is the easiest kind to edit. Load it into your NLE.

Start playing the music and tapping while you play. Once you get a sense of where the barline is, count along, but don't stop tapping.

Hear for yourself

Track 31 is a typical documentary or corporate cue from DeWolfe. ("City Power" (D. Molyneux/R. Hudgson), DeWolfe CD 190/1. © DeWolfe Music)

---

1. "Marine Hymn" (arranged by J. Howe), DeWolfe CD 248/12. © DeWolfe Music.

2. Also known as *4/4 time*. The first number means there are four beats to the bar; the second number means that each beat is a quarter note, which is important if you're performing the piece but not important if you're editing it.

Open the piece in a clip window. Your software has a keyboard command that drops unnumbered markers on a clip. Start playing the clip, and tap that key gently in time with each beat. Touch it lightly on most beats, so it doesn't drop a marker. But on each 1, tap hard enough to place a mark. When you're finished, the markers should be regularly placed. Figure 10.6 shows how it should look for the piece we've been using.

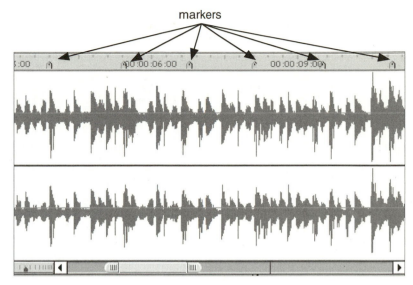

10.6 Markers placed on each barline.

Why not hold your finger still for most beats and just press the key on 1? It's usually not as accurate, because the finger tenses up and can't react as quickly. Tapping on every beat keeps your finger loose.

Using markers to shorten music

Having regular markers on a clip, once at each barline, makes the rest easy. For example, here's what you can do if you want to trim a piece of music by deleting some of the middle.

⚠️ **Gotcha** _____

I can't drop markers while playing. A few NLEs won't let you place markers while playing and mark clips only while they're stopped.[1] You can still edit in these programs, but it takes much longer. Music editing depends on marking barlines precisely, and that's easiest when you let your fingers dance to the tune.

If you can't mark while playing, you'll have to use a two-step approach; listen to the music at full speed until you have a good idea what note sounds on the barline. Go back to the approximate location, and shuttle and jog until you find that note. Then stop and mark. Planting multiple markers will take quite a while; so you might consider moving to an audio program for the music edits.

_____

1. The method described in some Premiere 6 documentation—pressing the * (asterisk) key while playing—doesn't work in the clip window. But it does if you drag the music clip from the bin to a dual-view monitor window.

10.7   The first cut at the start of the deleted section.

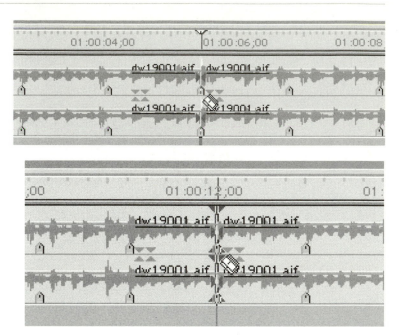

10.8   The second cut at the marker five bars later.

1.   Put the marked clip on one track, starting where you first want the music to begin. For these tutorials, we'll start music at exactly one hour and refer to edit locations in seconds:frames past that point.

2.   Count how many marked measures extend past the desired length. This is how much you'll have to delete. In this example, we'll cut five bars or just under seven seconds.

3.   Play through the clip and find a likely starting place for the deleted section. This doesn't have to be the start of a verse, but it helps if it's the start of a musical figure within the melody. Make a razor cut at the closest marker there, as in Figure 10.7. Here, we're cutting at the marker near 5:14.

4.   Move forward the desired number of bars and make another cut there. This will be the end of the deletion. In our example, that's at the marker around 12:16 (Figure 10.8).

5.   Do a ripple delete, cutting out the middle segment and pulling anything that follows up to fill the gap. If you're using an audio editing program, select cut—it's the same as a ripple delete in a NLE. Play back the edit. If things sounds right, you're done.

Debugging 1: Syncopation

If you followed our example and marked the bars accurately, things should sound *almost* right. But you'll hear a tiny hiccup at the edit point. You can also hear the hiccup in the edit I did, at about five seconds into Track 32. It's not our fault; it's the composer's!

Track 32 has a double note at our edit point, even though we did everything right. It's the composer's fault, but it's easy to fix.

What happened is the composer placed a melody note slightly ahead of the bar line. Play the marked clip and count along, and you'll hear the note start before 1 or the marker. When we made the first cut exactly on the bar line, that note was already playing. *Syncopations* like this—and also, delaying a note slightly—are common in music. In fact, even when the composer hasn't specified it, a soloist will often come in slightly ahead of or behind the beat as a matter of style.

At the second razor cut in our sample, the melody note started exactly on the bar line. So when we did the ripple, we picked up both the early start at 5:14 and the normal one at 12:16. You can't fix this by merely moving one of the razor cuts: That would distort the basic rhythm and make it sound wrong. Instead, use your NLE's roll tool to move *both* razor cuts by the same amount. In this case, rolling 21 frames earlier catches a place where the notes are more accurately timed. This is one of a few occasions you can rely on waveforms (Figure 10.9) because you already know the edit will be on the beat.

Audio editing programs don't have an equivalent to a rolling edit (I wish they did), but there's a workaround. Select an appropriate region between bar lines, open the Set Selection dialog, and copy or jot down the region's length. Cancel out

10.9   Rolling the edit to catch a properly timed note. Since we already know the edit is accurate to the beat, we can use the waveform display for fine-tuning.

of the dialog box. Then find the note towards the end of the region where you'd like to have the edit start and park the cursor there. Reopen Set Selection, tell it to modify the start of the section, and paste or reenter the region length.[1]

This fixed the edit, moving it a little earlier to pick up a shaker sound. Your version should sound like Track 33.

_____

1.   That's a lot of steps for what should be a simple operation. As you get better at counting along, you'll find you can mark on beats other than 1—or even divide beats in half (counting, "1 and 2 and 3 and 4 and...")—to mark accurately off the bar line. Just make sure you mark both sides of the edit at the same point in their respective measures.

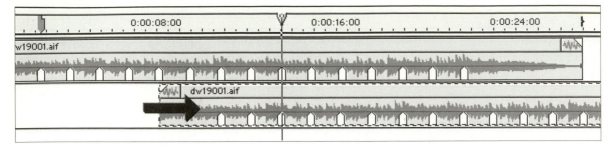

10.10 Slide the second clip so some of its markers line up with some of the first's.

10.11 I'm about to press delete to get rid of the first clip on Track 2.

Hear for yourself

Track 33 is essentially the same as Track 32, but it's fixed by rolling the edit point a few frames earlier.

Using markers to lengthen music

Sometimes you need to extend a piece of music. This is also easy, but you'll need two audio tracks.

1. Put the marked clip on one track, starting where you first want the piece to begin.

2. Put a second copy of the marked clip on another track, and offset the clip by the amount you want to lengthen it. In this example, I wanted to extend the music about seven and a half seconds. Since the first clip started at 0:00, I started the second one at 7:15.

   If you prefer, you can simply slide the second clip until the song's ending is where you want it. The effect is exactly the same.

3. Now you have to fine-tune the two clips' relationship so they share the same beats. Slide the second clip until one of its markers is in line with a marker from the first clip. In this example, it means moving the second clip to start at 8:00 (Figure 10.10).

4. Play the timeline with both tracks audible. When the second clip comes in, its rhythm should be in perfect sync with the first. (If not, try lining up a different pair of markers. If that doesn't work, check that you marked the clip accurately.) The melody and chords probably

won't be in sync most of the time, and may even clash in places, but both clips should have the same beat.

5. Listen again and find a place where both melodies are similar or create a pleasing chord. Make a razor cut thorough both tracks at the nearest marker. Or, if there's a syncopated note on the second track at that marker, where the note starts. In this example, we used the marker near 13:15.

6. Delete the part of the first clip that falls after the cut (Figure 10.11) and the part of the second clip that falls before it. You can move the second clip up to the first track if you want.

7. In step 3, matching the markers extended the piece 15 frames more than we actually needed. But the fade at the end of this music is almost two seconds long. Use the rubber band to fade it half a second sooner, and the piece will end perfectly.

If you can't get exactly the length you need by fading the ending, use some of the fine-tuning techniques in the next section.

Making internal hits

The above technique—with a slight modification—lets you fit a drum hit, key change, or any other musical detail in the song to a specific video frame.

1. Put the marked clip on one track at the point where you first want the piece to begin.

2. Put another copy of the marked clip on another track. Slide the second so the drum hit lines up with the desired video frame.

3. Follow steps 3 through 7 above to make a good transition between the tracks. It often works best to make your cut in the bar right before the hit. If this doesn't get you close enough, use the fine-tuning techniques in the next section.

You can do this as many times as you want in a song. It's probably the most powerful technique in music editing, letting you customize an existing cue to fit your video perfectly. Of course, you can use the same technique to make the music swell in sync with emotional peaks in the dialog, complement action sequences, or calm down under narration.

Debugging 2: Too loose/too tight

If you edit in the middle of a note or from one key to an unrelated one, you'll know it immediately and you can try moving the cut. But sometimes an edit just doesn't sound *right*, even though there's no obvious error. This is almost always because the edit changed the rhythm. It happens when the bar lines aren't accurately marked.

This kind of problem will have different characteristic sounds, depending on where the mistake was made. Learn to identify them, and you'll know what needs adjusting. As you get more experienced with counting and tapping, you'll find these errors disappear for all but the most complex music.

Load Track 34 and mark its downbeats.

 Hear for yourself _____

Track 34 is taken from a mellower cue from the DeWolfe Library[1].

Using your marks, delete the two bars that fall roughly between 15:10 and 19:07. If it sounds right, congratulations. If not, see which of the next examples match your version: I deliberately did the edit wrong four different ways in Track 35.

 Hear for yourself _____

Track 35 shows some of the ways that missing the beat can hurt an edit.

1. The first time, the marker at 15:10 was a little late, falling behind the actual bar line. This causes a double note. It also causes a slight delay in the rhythm, which is why this kind of double note can't be fixed with a rolling edit.

2. The second time, the marker at 19:07 was late. This clips the front of a note.

3. The third time, the 15:10 marker was too early. It makes the next measure jump in a hair too soon; something you may have to listen to a few times to recognize.

4. The fourth time, the 19:07 marker was early. It makes the rhythm hesitate a little at the edit point.

5. The fifth time, I marked the edit properly.

When you hear one of these problems, undo and move the incorrect edit point slightly off the marker to compensate. Or go back and re-mark the clip.

Chord and key changes

The chords in a song keep changing, often on bar lines but sometimes in other places, to add interest under the melody. That's why long cross fades between sections of a song can sometimes sound awful, when two sets of chords don't work together. Cutting on bar lines—even if the chords aren't usually related—often works better because the changes sound intentional.

But some songs also change key, which creates a totally different harmonic structure. Cutting from one key to another may work, but it often sounds jarring. Before a song changes key, it usually has a bar or more of transition chords. They're important. If you have to edit together two

_____

1. "The Main Chance" (D. Molyneux/R. Hudgson), DeWolfe CD 190/8. © DeWolfe Music.

sections of a song that are in different keys, look for the bar where the key changes and be sure to include a couple of bars *before* that change in the final version.

The Rock 'n Roll Problem

There's a classic Chuck Berry song, covered by the Beatles and countless other artists, "Rock and Roll Music." If you remember it, you probably recall the line about having, "a backbeat, you can't lose it." A *backbeat* is used in almost all rock, pop, modern country, and dance music today. The drummer plays softly on beats 1 and 3, but hits hard on 2 and 4.

Don't let that backbeat throw off your count. Even though the drummer doesn't stress 1, the melody does. Load Track 36, a contemporary rock piece.

  Hear for yourself _____

Track 36 is taken from a DeWolfe Library cue. It's somewhat reminiscent of a Sheryl Crow song about having fun.[1] Okay, *very* reminiscent.

_____

During the four second intro, you'll hear hand claps on 2 and 4. The drum plays a one-second riff, then a bass and melody part start. The bass enters strongly on 1. The slide guitar comes in around 7:15 on a 2 beat, but it's just leading up to a strong note on the next 1. And that bass keeps repeating its 1-based pattern.

Actually, the slide guitar is a tiny bit behind the bar line for emphasis, when it hits the 1 near 9:00. But the note clearly belongs to that beat. Syncopated melody lines are also characteristic of pop music.

Count and mark this tune, paying attention to the bar line. It should look like Figure 10.12.

Even though backbeats might be the largest things on a waveform display, counting and marking bar lines is the most reliable way to edit pop music because melodies and chord changes are

10.12 Track 36, properly marked. Note how bar lines aren't at the loudest drum beats.

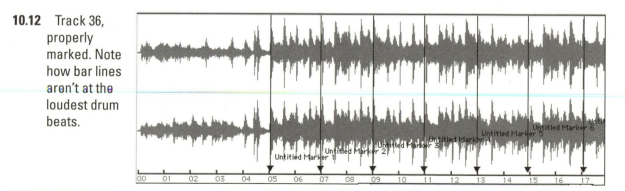

_____

1. "Toot, Root, Shoot" (A. Hamilton/B. Lang), DeWolfe CD 225/11. © DeWolfe Music.

based around 1. However, pop melodies seldom start exactly on the bar line, so you'll probably find it necessary to roll the edit to catch the lead instrument.

The Orchestral Problem

The bar lines in orchestral music aren't always obvious, and the percussion section is usually doing something other than beating time. But you can still hear the beat. Load Track 37, a piece appropriate for an adventure film score.

Hear for yourself _____

Track 37 is from a John Williams–style march in the DeWolfe library. It may remind you of the theme to *Raiders of the Lost Ark.*[1]

As you listen to the track, pay attention to the first three notes of the repeating figure. It's two unstressed short notes, followed by a longer stressed one. Mark that third note as beat 1, and everything else will count properly.

Fast marches like this are usually written with two beats to the bar instead of four. There's no reason you can't count them in fours, subdividing the beat. But you might find it easier to count "1, 2, 1, 2," still making a mark at each 1. (Each bar in this piece is a tiny bit longer than one second. Your marks should be that far apart.)

> ⚠ **Gotcha** _____
> **What about John Williams' copyright?** Or Sheryl Crow's, for that matter? Composers can get away with these seeming rip-offs because they borrow only a few actual notes from the original. They're called *stylealikes*—drawing on the same common pool of musical styles as the originals, along with similar arrangement and production.

Try a few cuts on this music. Edits in large orchestral string sections like this sometimes sound abrupt even if you mark them properly. That's because a little bit of one note continues to echo while the next note is played, and the part you're cutting to doesn't have the right echo. A two-frame cross-fade can help smooth things out; so can applying some reverb (Chapter 14). Sometimes the best solution is a much longer cross-fade on two tracks, holding the first theme, bringing the second in over the course of one or two beats, then fading the first.

Other patterns

Not all music moves in four or two beats. Waltzes move in threes and have to be counted that way. Load Track 38, a charming folk waltz.

_____

1.   "Epic Movie Adventure" (F. Talgon), DeWolfe CD 272/11. © DeWolfe Music.

Track 38 is an excerpt from a longer piece in the DeWolfe Library.[1] It sounds French, but is actually a traditional Scottish tune.

By now you've probably gotten the idea that DeWolfe covers lots of different musical genres. I haven't scratched the surface. Go to www.dewolfemusic.com and check its dozens of demos in different styles.

The first time you hear it, listen for the oom-pah-pah pattern in the accordion. The *oom* is always on 1. Then you can pay attention to the melody, which obviously stresses 1 as well.

Occasionally, you'll come across music in five, six, or even more beats to the bar. These are usually divided into repeating patterns of fewer beats. For example, a piece in six will usually break down to either two waltz-like sections per bar, or three march-like ones. In either case, the first beat of the first section—at the bar line—will always have a stronger stress than the first beat of the others.

Fine-tuning the Length

Basing your edits on bars is almost always the fastest way to achieve smooth, musical edits. But depending on the music's tempo, a single bar can last a long time. Whole bars might not be small enough to fit a piece of music to the length you want.

There are some effective ways for dealing with this. First, rough out the music using whole bars so the tracks is about the right length. Then do one of the following:

- Make a half-bar edit. Open the second clip you've laid on the timeline and count with it again, but drop the markers on 3. Then line a 3-beat marker on this clip with a 1-beat on the clip above it. You'll end up with a pattern of 4-4-2-4. It might be hard to dance to, but the melody often hides the edit—particularly if the music is under dialog.

- Make a *fermata*—a musical pause that stretches a single beat longer than usual, but then continues counting. You'll need a part of the music where a one note or chord is held over a couple of beats, without any other instruments playing shorter notes. Make a copy of the clip lined up with the first, but slid a little later on another track. When you get to the held note, do a cross-fade between the clips. This can be particularly effective on cues with a high emotional content.

- Export your edited music to a single file, and move it to a program that lets you change duration without affecting pitch. Or use a clip speed setting with a pitch shifting plug-in to compensate. Both of these are covered in Chapter 15.

_____

1. "Ranza Waltz" (arranged by C. Jack/D. Aran), DeWolfe CD 288/26. © DeWolfe Music.

- Use a clip speed setting on the entire piece, without a pitch-correcting plug-in. This will change the key as well as the tempo, and affect the timbre of the music. Acoustic instruments and voices can rarely be shifted more than 3 percent faster or slower before they start to sound strange. Electronic music including a lot of keyboard pop, can shift as much as ±12 percent. Unless you're very careful, changing the speed will make the music fall into a nonstandard key. This can sound offensive if the piece is near another cue.

Automatic Music Editing

Trimming library music to a desired length is easy, but it does take time if you're new to the process. Sonic Desktop's SonicFire Pro gives you an instant alternative: Select a song, tell the program how long it should be, let it percolate for a couple of seconds, and play back a perfectly timed version.

This seeming miracle is possible because music editors at Sonic Desktop have already broken each song in its library into short phrases, using the bar line–marking technique above. The editors then write templates for how the phrases should link together. This editing information is saved along with the audio on CD-ROM. When you run the program, it collects enough phrases to reach the length you want. Because the computer's editing is based on human judgments, the result doesn't sound mechanical. But if you're not happy, you can also juggle phrases manually before exporting the final version to your NLE.

SonicFire does exactly what it promises—quickly spitting out songs of a specified length—though it can't match hits within a cue to specific timings. The big limitation is that it only works with factory-encoded music.[1] This means you can use only a few dozen CD-ROMs, mostly containing custom versions of buyout music from a few mainstream libraries. These discs cost $70 in a bandwidth-limited version, or $120 with a key to unlock full quality. The program itself is $350.

The system also includes a search engine to simplify selecting tracks, and is linked to online previews of the songs. But, again, it can only be used with Sonic Desktop's library of discs; you can't add your own music to the database.

SonicFire makes sense if you do a lot of very similar programs for different audiences, so you can amortize the cost over numerous productions, and you need to turn out odd lengths of music in a hurry. If you're not in that situation, it's probably better to edit the cues yourself (and use the money you save to buy a much bigger library).

---

1. You can import a standard audio file into the program, cut it into pieces yourself, and juggle them manually. But I can't think of any reason why you'd want to.

Embellishing the Music

After you've edited music to fit, you can customize it even more by layering other musical sounds on top.

Find a drum hit or cymbal crash elsewhere in the cue and put it on a second track, in sync with an important visual frame (Figure 10.13). Don't worry about the song's rhythmic structure. Even though you'll be placing this sound off the beat, it'll seem like the drummer was watching and played along with picture.

If you can't find an isolated drum hit in the cue, look for an appropriate sound in an effects library. Most drum sounds aren't pitched, so you don't have to worry about tuning it to the song's key. If you're using orchestral music, the only appropriate drum sound might be timpani, which does have a pitch. However, libraries with timpani hits often have variations on different notes. Play the cue from your NLE while trying different versions to see which sounds best.

A harp glissando or cymbal ride mixed with the music can be a good accompaniment for title wipes or other transitions.

If you have musical chops, feel free to add your own synth pads, piano chords, or whatever else you think might complement the video. Don't worry too much about playing in sync: Just digitize a few different versions and slide them on the timeline until one works.

When it's time to mix, you'll be able to blend the new sounds to match the cue.

10.13 The song from Figure 10.12 is on audio Track 1, with an extra drum hit—taken from the song's intro—in sync with the spotlight frame.

Chapter 11

Working with Sound Effects

Remember this:

- A kiss is still a kiss, but a sigh can be turned into a roaring monster[1].

- There are limitless sources for sounds: camera tracks, commercial libraries, foley, even mouth noises.

- Sound selection and placement is easiest if you follow some simple rules.

- When designing new sounds, it's best to start with well-defined palettes.

---

1.   Sorry. I couldn't resist.

Sound effects have been part of the movie process almost as long as music. In the silent movie days, theater organs had effects on their keyboards. Bells, birds, and even breaking crockery were available at the touch of a finger. By the mid-1920s, Wurlitzer was building one of these magnificent machines a day.[1] Companies sold hand- or mouth-operated boat whistles, dog barkers, fog horns, and rain machines on the premise that increased realism would help a theater's box office. In Japan, *benshi* stood next to the screen and provided running commentary, dialog, and vocal sound effects; these versatile live performers often became more popular than the film stars they accompanied.

We have better ways to make sounds now, but the reasons for using sound effects haven't changed. Sound effects are another way to direct the viewer's attention:

- Sound effects involve us with on-screen actions. The giant crashes and explosions of action features literally shake us in our seats. But an actor's footsteps in an empty corridor, or a single cry from a baby can be just as engaging.

---

1. Today, samplers are an important part of feature film sound design. Samplers assign digital recordings to notes on a keyboard, making the sounds easier to manipulate. The technology is different, but in one hundred years, the user interface hasn't changed very much.

- Sound effects put us in the film's reality. The average living room or theater can be a noisy place, with lots of real-world sounds competing for our attention. Surf, jungle, or other backgrounds on the track help us forget the room we're in and concentrate on the location we're seeing.

- Sound effects complete the illusion. Closing a door on a plywood set, hitting a burglar's head with a rubber candlestick, or firing a quarter-load blank just doesn't seem right until you add *slam*, *bonk*, and *bang*.

- Sound effects provide continuity. An establishing shot of a busy mall with lots of extras can be followed by close-ups done days later on a stage; but if we keep hearing the crowd, we'll know we're still at the mall.

- Sound effects tell the off-screen story cheaply and quickly. An approaching siren, car door slam, running footsteps, and shouted "Police!" speaks volumes, even if all we're seeing is the murderer's eyes.

- Sound effects help the on-screen story. The same scene—say, a character lying in bed—will have different meanings depending on whether we're hearing children playing, a watchdog barking, or somebody hammering on the door.

- Even in nonnarrative films, various wooshes and zaps call attention to animations, title wipes, and other screen features.

Sound effect terminology

Background, BGs, ambience, and *presence* all mean the same thing: birds, traffic, machinery, crowd noises, computer fans, and the other sounds that surround just about everything we do. *Walla* is the spoken equivalent—background voices where only a few words may be distinguishable.

Hard effects are individual sounds in sync with on-screen (or scripted off-screen) actions. In feature work, they're separated into *editorial effects* such as telephone bells, which can be added by the sound editorial crew, and *principal effects* like explosions and crashes, which are done by a sound designer. *Stingers* are short individual sounds added to an ambience to make it more specific, like an ATM's beeps and whirrs in an otherwise generic bank lobby.

Sound on tape, SOT, and *nat sound* are sound recorded along with picture. Sound on tape is often not usable for hard effects because of noise and mic distance, but it can serve as a guide and sync reference when adding new effects. It may be sufficient for backgrounds.

Wild sounds are recorded without picture.

Sound Effect Sources

An audio post house will have thousands of sound effects on hand, often delivered to individual editor's workstations instantly from a central server.[2] But you don't have to amass that kind of collection to use sounds effectively. It's easy to find exactly the ones you need for a project.

Sound on Tape

The camera's natural sound (often called nat sound) can include room tone, which is useful for editing dialog (Chapter 9). But in documentary and location work, nat sound can also provide active backgrounds. Crowds, machinery, or traffic can be gathered from places where there's no dialog—don't forget to check the outtakes—and then looped to bridge scenes or link close-ups to the master shot. This kind of sound can also be mixed with library backgrounds to make the canned backgrounds sound more authentic.

Unlike traditional film sound, which needs a crew and separate recorder, DV sound is free. Take advantage of this. Even if you don't think a scene will generate usable sound, it's a good idea to mic it. If you can't get a boom mic over the shot, use a camera-mounted shotgun—the echo and room-noise pickup that make camera mics useless for dialog can be appropriate for backgrounds. If you're shooting inserts of small activities—handling a prop, dialing a phone, grabbing a doorknob—record the sound and keep it in your edit.

Dialog and sound effects frequently get different treatment in the mix. If you've got the time and tracks, isolate any prop sounds that were picked with dialog. Move them to a different track where they can be cleaned and treated as a sound effect. Fill the hole in the dialog track with room tone.

Commercial Libraries

In the 30s, radio started using live sound effects to tell their stories. Realistic sounds were used to enhance dramas, and some comedies had humorous sounds that were almost as well-known as the stars. Fibber McGee had his closet, and Jack Benny had his Maxwell. These sounds were performed live for the visual amusement of the studio audience; viewers at home heard both the effect and the studio laughter. Film started using similar techniques—the Three Stooges had an incredible collection of bonks, plunks, and whistles—and would often have sounds created specifically for the scene. But editors realized they could save time by reusing effects from previous films. At about the same time, radio started using custom recordings of the larger, live effects to simplify production. These private collections became organized by a few companies, and the sound effects library was born.

---

2. My more modest one-person facility has (so far) 21,000 indexed effects on CD and DAT.

Today, you can buy complete libraries of beautifully recorded sounds to use in productions. Or you can purchase sounds as needed over the Internet and have them delivered electronically in a few minutes. Sound effects are almost always sold as buyouts: You pay for them once and can use them forever in any of your films, with no additional licensing.

Full libraries

These are collections of sounds on one or more CDs, usually sold together, though some publishers will let you buy individual discs. *General libraries* attempt to cover all the sounds commonly used in production and are

11.1   Some of the specialized libraries in my studio's collection.

usually organized with a disc for exterior backgrounds, another for interiors, one for cars, one for animals, and so on. *Specialized libraries* have multiple CDs of sounds in a single category. For example, I have two commercial libraries—about 10 discs each—just for human movements, two for classic and modern cartoon sounds, one of nothing but mechanical clicks and ticks, and a 12-CD set of wind and other air sounds. General libraries usually sell for about $50 per disc, and specialized collections can be as much as $100 per disc.

A few small general libraries are also available on CD-ROM. There's no quality difference between a standard audio CD (*Redbook*[3]) and 16-bit, 44.1 kHz computer files, but the CD-ROMs may be more convenient. CD-ROMs are easier to transfer and can include search engines with preview and automatic file copying. They can also hold more than an audio CD because mono effects can be only one channel—something impossible in Redbook format—and there's no time wasted on silence between sounds. Some CD-ROMs are compressed using MP3 or proprietary formats, or limited to 22.050 kHz sample rates. That does cause a loss of quality but lets the publisher fit as many as one thousand effects on a single disc. CD-ROM libraries range in price from $30 per disc for small, low-fidelity collections licensed for Web and presentation use only, to $100 per disc for high-quality, full-usage libraries. But CD-ROMs never caught on in the production community, so the selection of discs in this medium is limited.

---

3.   The original specification for audio CDs had a red cover. Other formats, such as CD-ROM, had different color covers.

👉 *Go Get It*

A great freebie! Hollywood Edge's demo CD has 99 sound effects you can use in your own productions. These are well-recorded effects, ranging from audience reactions and airplane flybys to gunshots and explosions, in both CD-ROM and Redbook format. The disc also includes Flash demos of its full libraries and a Mac/Windows search program for the almost 34,000 effects it sells. More about that database farther in this chapter.

The disc of free effects is a marketing gimmick, and it works; it's convinced me to buy quite a few Hollywood Edge libraries. Legitimate producers and potential customers can get a copy by calling its number, below. If you're in a hurry, or don't think you'd qualify for the free disc, go to their web site and pick from 90 free effects of well-encoded mp3 files. The database is also there for download.

The best place to buy a sound effects library is directly from the companies listed below. Some video equipment dealers also sell effects libraries, but the specialty companies have wider selections, knowledgeable staff, Web-based previews and demos, and frequent Web or mail-order specials.

- Hollywood Edge, 800-292-3755, 323-603-3252, www.hollywoodedge.com. A corporate sibling of a giant audio post facility, Hollywood Edge publishes its own effects and represents other libraries—about two dozen total. Hollywood Edge was kind enough to let me reproduce some of its effects for this chapter's tutorials.

- Sound Ideas, 800-387-3030 (U.S.), 800-665-3000 (Canada), 905-886-5000, www.sound-ideas.com. This Toronto-based company created the first, large, modern effects library, and now sells about sixty collections of its own and other publishers'.

- Gefen Systems, 800-545-6900, 818-884-6294, www.gefen.com. Gefen Systems makes the networked sound effects system used in large post facilities, and it stocks just about every sound library in existence.

The worst place to buy sound effects is at a record store. While some CDs are available at normal retail prices, the quality is variable. A few seem to be sloppy copies of vinyl records sold in the 60s and early 70s—before copyright law protected sound effects—and include turntable rumble and groove noise. Others are more modern but still of limited quality. While some advertise as being royalty free, the fine print specifies for home use only. On the other hand, you may be able to find a few bargains with decent recordings and clear licensing.

Individual effects

Despite my fairly extensive collection, there are times when it doesn't have a sound I need. These times are usually late at night, when I'm working on projects due the next day, and the sounds are often impossible to create in the studio. At times like those, my production goes to the dogs.

SoundDogs.com is probably the largest online effects library, with close to 100,000 high-quality sounds available for virtually instant download. Sounds can be searched or browsed by category, then previewed in low resolution. You fill a shopping cart with winners—usually only a couple of dollars per effect. The price depends on data size. After you've selected effects, you check the specifications you want: MP3 or 16-bit linear, mono or stereo, a variety of sample rates, and how many seconds you want each to run. The Web site computes the file size and tells you how much the effect costs in the chosen format. Then you complete the order.

A minute or two later, SoundDogs.com e-mails you an FTP address. Go there, and the sounds are waiting for download. Since effects are sold on a buyout basis, you can add them to your personal library for future projects as well. If you have a slow Internet connection and need full quality, SoundDogs.com will burn a custom CD and ship it instead.

There are other professional effects libraries on the Web, but in my opinion none are as comprehensive or reliable. Some make you wait hours for a human to transfer and upload the sound; one even announces, "If we fail to deliver, you get your money back," suggesting these failures have happened in the past.

There are also sites that offer free sound effects. These come and go, but a Web search will usually turn up half a dozen or so. You won't find many free pro-level effects like the ones Hollywood Edge offers. In fact, many of these sites don't have any sounds at all: They're merely

11.2   Finding a downloadable effect at SoundDogs.com.

banner-ad cluttered indexes to hobbyist pages of sounds from movies and TV shows. Copyright and quality are not guaranteed.

Recording Your Own

Sound effects are also free if you make them yourself. Techniques include foley, capturing hard effects and backgrounds in the field, using electronic sounds, and even manipulating mouth sounds. Unless an effect is very large, like an explosion or car crash, it's usually recorded in mono and panned as necessary during the mix. Backgrounds are usually recorded in stereo.

Foley

Jack Foley was a Hollywood second-unit director and editor. In the late 1940s, he became known for performing sound effects live while watching a projection. He'd mimic actors' movements to create footsteps, clothing rustles, and prop movements in time with picture. This was not a brand-new idea, but Foley popularized it among producers, and his name—reduced to lower case—became attached to the technique.

Foley is still the standard for big productions, and it's a lot of fun to watch (or be part of). But it needs a specially built studio with large video playback and a separate room for monitoring and control. A computer-age adaptation, *digital foley*, may be more appropriate for the low-budget or solo filmmaker. Instead of worrying about performing in sync with playback, just make a list of movements you'll need and record them wild. Then, with a NLE or multitrack sound program, trim the sounds to fit the picture.

While foley is fun, it's also time consuming. Before you decide how much is needed, build the rest of the track. Scenes with music may need very little foley. Ambiences may have random movements that, with a little editing, can match what's on the screen.

Foley is often recorded in multiple takes—once or twice for footsteps, once for clothing rustles, and once for prop movements or fights. Both the room and the recording chain should be quiet, so hiss and noise don't build up when all these tracks are mixed together. Foley for theatrical films should be miked at boom distances, two to three feet from the action, so the perspective matches dialog when played through large speakers. This means the room shouldn't have any echo. If you're aiming for the small screen, you can get by with a less-than-perfect room and very close, directional mics. I usually record clothing rustles and prop movements at about 10-inches with a short shotgun, in a reasonably echo-free space.

Foley doesn't start to sound realistic until you process it in the mix. The level, equalization, and amount of reverb have to be very carefully tuned to match dialog. Other processing, such as compression and gating, can help change the character of some sounds—even turning male footsteps into female ones. There are specific suggestions in later chapters.

Foley footsteps Practice walking in place, keeping a constant distance from the mic. Practice different walking styles as well. Have a variety of shoes available to match the types of shoes the actors wore. There's not much difference between men's and women's steps, other than high heels. It mostly depends on how heavily you put your feet down. For best results, wear shorts and empty your pockets. If the character is supposed to have keys or coins jingling in a pocket, record these sounds separately.

Professional foley studios have sections of floor with different surface treatments and pits full of gravel, sand, or water to walk through for exteriors. But some old-time radio tricks work almost as well:

- To simulate a hardwood floor in a carpeted studio, use a piece of half-inch or thicker plywood, about 2-foot by 3-foot. Tack strips of carpet on the bottom of the plywood to stop it from sliding around and to keep it from bouncing as you walk.

- To simulate concrete, sprinkle some sand on the plywood.

- For marble, walk on clean plywood and add gating and echo in the mix. Or get a large piece of slate or marble at a lumber yard if you don't mind lugging it around.

- If your studio has a hard floor and you need carpeting, get scraps of carpet from a flooring dealer. Get some padding as well and glue it to the underside of the carpet scraps. It'll improve the sound and keep the carpet from sliding as you walk.

- To simulate grass, walk on carpet and mic it from a couple of inches away. The crunching fibers are fairly convincing.

- You can use a child's wading pool as an adhoc foley pit for water. You can also use it for sand or gravel, but it's cleaner to put dry materials in a large burlap bag. Fill the bag half way, seal it, and spread it flat for walking.

- If you don't need a lot of pit sounds, it may be most efficient to work in miniature. Fill a large plastic dishpan with cornflakes, rice, or dry or semisoft pet food and walk with your hands.

- For snow, squeeze a cardboard box of cornstarch rhythmically. After a half dozen "steps," you'll probably have to shake the box a little to loosen the starch.

- For wooden stairs, use a double layer of half-inch plywood or very wide shelving, about 2-feet long. Prop one edge up with a couple of books or scrap lumber, so it's about 5-inches higher than the other; this adds hollowness. To walk upstairs on this board, scrape your foot slightly against the top edge as you step with your full weight. To walk downstairs, skip the scraping and land on your heels first, then your soles.

Foley clothing noises   You'll need an item made of the right material—cotton, silk, synthetics, and wool all sound different. For most clothing rustles, don't wear the item and mimic the actor's movement; this moves the action too far from the mic. Instead, hold cloth close to the mic and rub or crumple it with your hands. Be careful not to actually touch the mic. If the character is putting on a jacket, you'll have to do the same action. That sound is too identifiable.

Foley prop movements   These small sounds are best when you mimic the movement as closely as possible. It helps to work at a table, both to keep props handy and to have a hard surface when needed. You'll have to reposition the mic depending on whether the action is in the air (keychains or cigarette lighters) or on the table.

Experiment with different ways to hold each prop. Where you grab an object and how tightly you hold it can make a difference in how it resonates.

Make sure you've got the right props:

- Rustling papers need the right stiffness and surface. Newsprint, glossy magazine pages, and copier paper sound different.

- If the character is writing something, use the proper instrument and the right paper. A pencil doesn't sound the same as a felt-tip pen, and both change depending on how smooth the paper's surface is.

- If a character is working at a computer, type on a keyboard. It doesn't matter what you write—or even if the keyboard is connected—but remember that larger keys like the spacebar or delete have a different sound than the letters, so be sure to hit those occasionally. The microswitch in a mouse or trackball has a distinctive sound when you press its button. Resist the temptation to fill the scene with beeps; most programs don't sound like that.

- Modern residential telephones are lightweight plastic with a flimsy sound. I've found that heavier, multiline office phones make better noises. Old-fashioned dial and early Touch-Tone phones were very solid and had a mechanical bell that vibrated slightly with each movement. You can't fake these with a modern phone.

⚠ **Gotcha** _____

Look, ma, no feet! Often you can't see the actor's feet in a shot. It's still important to capture the right rhythm for footsteps. You usually can do this by watching the actor's shoulders.

If the characters are walking at a normal pace or faster, one shoulder will rise slightly just after a step lands, as they push off for the next step. Put the sound one or two frames ahead of the shoulder rise.

If the character is walking slowly and pausing between steps, there may be a dip as each step lands. Put the sound on the first frame of the dip. There'll be a rise when they push into the next step, but it doesn't make noise unless they're wearing squeaky shoes.

- An old briefcase can give you a bunch of suitcase and pocketbook sounds. The leather creaks as you flex it, the hinge squeaks, and the snaps, uh, snap.

- Heavy cookie sheets can be flexed or struck. Depending on how you hold them and whether they're in the air or resting on the table, they can stand in for almost any metal object.

Foley fights   Your body can be good for realistic sounds; just cup your hand slightly while you hit yourself on the trunk. Add a tiny echo in the mix. Many filmmakers prefer bigger—and sometimes wetter—sounds, particularly in fights. Useful techniques for this include wrapping two phonebooks in wet towels and slamming them together, or crashing a head of cabbage on a table. Twisting a bunch of celery works for broken bones. Body falls can be done by slamming both arms against a table, slightly out of sync with each other, or by taping a large phonebook closed and throwing it on the floor.

Field recording

Some sounds can be captured only in their natural habitat. You can't bring a car or a horse into an adhoc foley studio, and background ambiences are impossible to fake.

You'll need a good recorder. Your camera may be adequate for this, but it's probably too bulky for convenient use. A consumer MiniDisc recorder can be okay for many sounds, but make sure you can turn off its automatic level control for anything other than calm backgrounds. As the circuit constantly adjusts the volume, it increases apparent noise. Slightly larger, professional MiniDisc or DAT portables give you the best control and recordings.

You'll also need a good microphone—the camera's mic is useful only for loud ambiences—but what kind of mic to use depends on what you're recording.

Hard effects   Background noise is a problem when recording individual effects in the field. The time of day is important—most places are quietest after midnight or very early on a Sunday morning. Relatively still air is also important. Wind noise can ruin exterior recordings; the more directional a mic is, the more likely it is to suffer this kind of noise. But don't throw away your directional mics: these can be ideal at very close range to a sound source, when you can't get the location quiet enough. If the sound is very loud, you might need a dynamic mic to avoid distortion.

For maximum versatility the best effect recordings have very little echo. You can take a clean recording of a car door slam recorded in an open field with no wind, and add reverb to make it sound like it's in a parking garage. But you can't take a garage recording and make it sound outdoors. Be careful of this when recording animals as well: Indoor dog barks don't sound like outdoor ones.

Backgrounds   Noise is the point of an ambience recording, but it takes a little planning to capture it well. If your track is going to be broadcast or released on home video, mono compatibility is important. Use a single stereo mic to prevent flanging when the two channels are combined. For best results, this should be an *m/s* (*mid/side*) mic, but a standard *x/y* stereo mic can work

> ⚠️ **Gotcha** _____
>
> ***Mono ambiences, stereo mix.*** Don't worry if you don't have a proper mic for mono-compatible stereo. There are ways to simulate stereo with a mono recording (Chapter 17). Or you can take sections of a mono ambience track, recorded a few minutes apart, and put them on different tracks. When you mix, pan one mostly left and the other mostly right and add a little reverb.

if its capsules are very close together. A stereo mic is also good for tracks that will only be heard in stereo, of course, but you can also get a realistic—though not mono compatible—sound with a pair of spaced omnidirectional mics. (I've even gotten decent results wearing a pair of lavs, one clipped to each shoulder.) If the project is mono, use a single omni to pick up the true ambience of an interior. You can use a very directional mic for exteriors, if you have to avoid a specific noise source.

Choose interior locations based on the size and shape of the room, and its floor treatment, as well as on the level of its activity. Don't worry about matching the actual purpose of the room. If the scene shows an old-fashioned bank lobby, a modern shopping mall branch won't work. But a post office lobby—with some added bank-related walla or stingers—may be perfect. Watch out for background music. Even if it's appropriate for the location, it'll restrict your ability to edit, and you may find it impossible to license.

Often, if you and your equipment aren't conspicuous, you can record public environments without worrying about permission. If voices aren't identifiable you won't need a release. Recording audience reactions in a theater or club usually requires permission from the venue, and the act may need a guarantee that you're not going to record its performance. Prior authorization is always needed in a casino, where guards are trained to spot electronic equipment.

You can customize any ambience by recording some specialized walla appropriate for the activity or reacting to a situation. You'll need a quiet and echo-free room, and the mic should be a few feet away from the sound source. Gather half a dozen friends, pair them off, and give each pair a specific topic to ad-lib about. Record at least one minute of all three pairs talking simultaneously. Then assign new topics and have them ad-lib in slightly different voices.

Record at least twice as much background as you think you'll need, because you'll probably find some noisy parts that have to be edited out. Backgrounds can be looped, particularly if they're under dialog, but most shouldn't repeat more than once every minute or two.

Electronic sounds

Sirens and bells used to be mechanical; now they're electronic. Microwave ovens and other household devices beep when you press their buttons. These sounds can be captured in the field, but it's faster to make them on the spot.

It takes a little playing around to make convincing electronic sounds, but you don't need a synthesizer or other special equipment. Many audio editing programs have an FM signal generator in their menus; this may be all that's necessary for anything from a siren to a spaceship. As an example, we'll make a telephone ringer. I'll list specific steps from SoundForge, but the technique is about the same in any other program.

1. Create a new mono document .

2. Open the Tools>Synthesis>FM panel.

3. Set the configuration (lower right in the panel) for a simple circuit with one operator feeding another. In other programs, the first operator might be called frequency and the second modulation.

4. Set the first operator *shape* or waveform to a sawtooth, and its frequency to 3 kHz.

5. Draw an envelope that's full on for about half a second, and off for the other half. Figure 11.3 shows how the panel will look for the first operator. This operator, by itself, can work for an alarm clock or microwave beep.

6. Now we'll add the warble of a telephone ringer. Set the second operator to a square wave around 10 Hz. Turn its amplitude down to about 1 percent. On another program, this might be called the *modulation depth*.

7. Preview the sound and adjust it to your liking. Then click OK to put the sound in the document.

8. This will give you a single ring followed by an equal-length silence. Select the entire sound, copy, and paste it for as many rings as needed.

By making subtle variations in the settings, you can create a variety of small beepers or a room full of phones. With

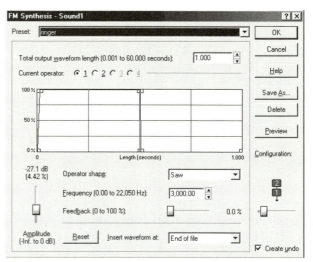

11.3 Creating an electronic telephone ringer in SoundForge. This is one of two operators; the other provides the warble.

larger variations and more operators, you can make science-fiction sounds, police sirens, and virtually any other kind of electronic sound. If you're using SoundForge, play with its presets. If you're on a Mac, try SFX Machine (www.sfxmachine.com), a versatile plug-in for sound mangling and synthesis. Here are some points as you're learning the technique:

- Start simple. Know what a single operator or oscillator sounds like with different frequencies and wave shapes.

- Sawtooth and square waves can sound richer than sines and triangles for the basic sound; triangles and sine waves can be useful for the operators that modulate the sound.

- When you're trying to tune a basic tone for operator 1, turn the amplitude of other operators all the way down. Create a preset with the other operators off, and use this preset as a starting point.

- If an envelope has to turn on or off, give it a slight ramp to avoid clicks (as in Figure 11.3).

Vocal sounds

Wes Harrison is a genius at mouth noises. With no more than a standard microphone, he can create convincing explosions with debris falling; footsteps on just about any surface; and train rides complete with engines, passing warning bells, and the klacking of wheels as you cross between cars. He's mouthed off for Disney and MGM, and works his sounds into a very funny nightclub act as Mr. Sound Effects.[4] I'm never going to be in his league, so I get my explosions and train rides from library CDs. But you can create monsters and other organic sounds vocally, and vocal sounds are a great trick for spicing up fanciful machines.

Close-miking vocal sounds is essential. This means you'll need an omnidirectional mic, which can resist pops. If you're making subtle sounds, hold the mic right against your mouth. Growls are best an inch or two away. If the sound is going to be loud, you might need a dynamic mic to avoid distortion.

Once you've recorded the sound, remove anything that reveals it was made by a human. Delete breaths, mouth clicks, and glottal shocks. Equalization can also help; there are some settings for this in Chapter 12.

Further dehumanize a sound by radically slowing it down in a program that doesn't try to preserve pitch. Once you get beyond 50 percent of the original speed—an octave deeper than normal—resonances change enough that it's not identifiable as a voice. Try the speed variation in a couple of different programs; some add aliasing that would be horrible in music but can enhance a deep effect. At around 10 percent of the original speed, friction consonants like /s/ become scrapes. Pitch bend can also help (Chapter 15), and so can playing the sound backwards.

---

4. For a CD recorded live at some of his performances, send $10 to Box 901, Park Ridge, IL 60068.

For machine noises, start with short, unvoiced consonants and mouth clicks. Cut into them slightly so they start more abruptly, and then edit a bunch of these sounds closely together. Copy the entire set and paste it multiple times to form a mechanical rhythm, then use a pitch bend to vary the machine's speed.

Selecting Effects

Once you've got more than a few dozen sound effects in your personal library, you'll need a way to find the right one quickly. The most efficient method is a computerized database. If you've purchased libraries from Hollywood Edge, you can use the database that's on their demo disc and downloadable from their Web site (Figure 11.4). It contains entries for every sound they sell.

11.4 A searchable sound effects database. This one's available free from Hollywood Edge.

The database is actually a FileMaker Pro file, with included run-only client software for Windows and Mac. Sound Ideas puts a similar database, using the same format, on its demo disc. The files are password protected against modification, and the client software has limited capability. So you can't customize these files to add effects you've recorded or bought from other sources, nor can you delete libraries you don't own. But you can search by library or disc, export the selected data as tab-delimited text (universal database format), and pour it into a database or spreadsheet program of your own.

If you're serious about sound effects, I'd recommend buying FileMaker Pro or some other fast database.[5] Build your own searching system using the Hollywood Edge or Sound Ideas files as a model, and import data for the libraries you own. If you buy a library that isn't included in those files, ask the publisher for data—most will provide it at no charge—or scan and OCR the catalog pages. When you collect your own sounds, enter them as well. This housekeeping pays off quickly in time saved during postproduction.

---

5. You can also use the program to handle your invoices, track music licenses, estimate production budgets, etc.

Searching

For the most efficient searches, you have to get used to how libraries describe their sounds. The Hollywood Edge or Sound Ideas databases will give you a good idea.

- Search using the shortest possible terms. "Jet plane" will also find "jet airplane," but not the reverse.

- Libraries can be inconsistent about the words they use. Some Hollywood Edge libraries use "car," others use "automobile." Try both.

- Limit your searches by including additional terms on the same line. "Dog bark angry" will get you closer than only "dog."

- If you can't find a particular sound, search for something that makes a similar movement. The small motor in a car's electric window can work well for any kind of servo; a fight bell, looped and repeated, can be an alarm.

Once you've performed the search, read each description carefully. Pay attention to words that might disqualify an entry: A "dive, swimming pool (interior)" description sounds nothing like jumping into the old swimmin' hole. Don't close the database just because you've found likely entries; descriptions aren't sounds. Pull the CD and audition the effect before deciding it's the one to use.

Placing and Editing Sound Effects

The rule in Hollywood is if you can see it, you must hear it. Sound editors will spend a week fine-tuning the effects in each 10-minute reel of a feature, by syncing noises to every movement on the screen. Often, the director throws many of these effects away at the mixing stage, but as one sound editor told me, "You have to give them more than they could possibly want."

Hollywood works this way because music, dialog, and effects are prepared by different teams, and there's often no way to decide what's needed until everything comes together at the mix. More modest projects can avoid this wasted effort. It just means applying a little judgement as you work.

1. Lay the music in before you start editing effects. Listen to music and dialog or play them for the director. You might decide that plot-critical hard effects are all that's missing. This is often true for dialog-driven TV projects.

2. After those critical effects are in place, play all the tracks again. If scenes seem sparse or the hard effects seem to come out of nowhere, add an ambience track.

3. Listen again. The ambience may cover smaller sounds, saving you from having to put in editorial effects or foley. Hits and other random noises in the ambience can be moved to sync with on-screen actions.

⚠️ *Gotcha*_____

Backgrounds, interiors, and TV comedy. Sitcoms made in the United States generally avoid using presence tracks for interiors and often ignore presence in studio-shot exteriors. Restaurants, offices, and even subway stations are remarkably noise free. It's a cost-saving measure, and nobody seems to mind.

British sitcoms sometimes do add backgrounds to indoor shots, which makes those restaurants and offices more realistic. They also add natural ambience to quiet residences. Unfortunately, in the real world that's often distant traffic coming through a window. It's jarring—at least to this American viewer—to see a couple having a quiet conversation at home and hear cars and trucks in the background.

4. Finally, add whatever small effects seemed to be missing.

It's a good idea to separate plot-critical effects, small editorials and foley, and backgrounds onto different tracks or groups of tracks. This will make life easier when you mix.

Hard Effects

Hard effects need to be placed exactly on the right frame. It's frustrating to do this on the timeline, since you have to keep bouncing between single-frame and wider resolutions, and it may be difficult to find a visual cue on a thumbnail-sized image. Instead, watch the scene in a preview window. When you get near an effect, jog to find the proper frame and drop a marker. Repeat for every effect in the scene. Then go to the timeline set for a wide resolution and drag sounds to their markers.

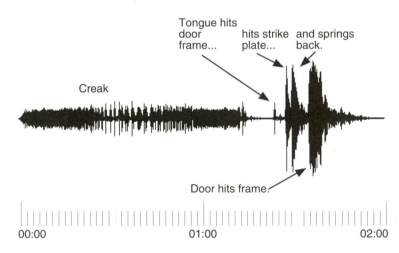

11.5 A lot of smaller sounds go into this 2-second door close. Line up the first hit (at 1:11) with the frame where the door stops moving, and everything else should fall into place.

In most cases, hard effects should start at the first frame where the action occurs and be trimmed to the length of the action. But there are plenty of exceptions:

- Percussive sounds like door closes and body hits should be placed where the action *stops*. Watch for the first frame where the door or fist is still, after it's been moving, and put a marker there. Many percussive effects are preceded by a lead-in sound, such as a hinge squeak before a door close (Figure 11.5). Mark the actual hit, not the start of the sound, and line that up with the video's marker. Then play the sequence to make sure the earlier sound doesn't start before the action does, and trim the front of the sound if necessary.

Hear for yourself

Track 39 is the sound from Figure 11.5 [6].

- Explosions usually aren't on-screen long enough to support their sound. Let them continue to decay after the camera is on something else. It's even acceptable in many cases to have an explosion extend half a second or so into the next scene. By the way, it's a film convention that most explosions are followed by falling debris.

- If a gun is shot on-camera, there's almost always a barrel flash (Figure 11.6). That's where the sound should be.

11.6 Look for the flash (3rd frame), and start the *bang!* there.

- Sometimes there's no specific frame for an action. Figure 11.7 shows six frames of a golf ball bouncing off a tree and moving so quickly that it's a blur. Even though we never see the ball hit, it changes direction between frames 3 and 4. The clunk should start with the fourth frame.

- Sometimes the frame for an action doesn't exist. It's fairly common to cut from one shot of the hero's fist flying in the air, to another where the punch has just landed and the villain's head is snapping back. The best place for the sound depends on the editing rhythm: Usually, the hit should start on the last frame of the flying clip; sometimes it wants to be right on the cut.

---

6. This and other sounds in this chapter are copyright Hollywood Edge and reproduced by permission.

Golfball heading towards tree...

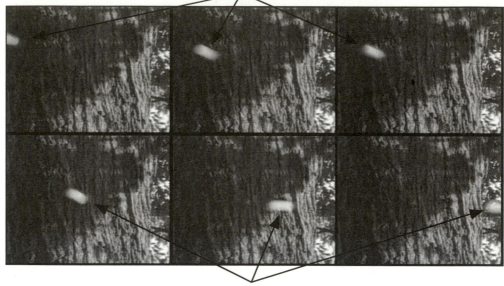

...and away.

11.7 That blur is a golfball bouncing off a tree. It's moving too fast for us to see it actually hit.

In narrative films, the speed of sound is often equivalent to the speed of light. We expect to hear things on the same frame that we see them. Things don't work that way in the real world, but they do in the movies. Even TV documentaries, supposedly based in truth, usually follow this rule when sound effects are edited.

Some sound editors working on theatrical features used to compensate for the speed of sound in an auditorium. They'd place sounds as much as a frame early, putting sound and picture in sync for people sitting 33-feet back from the screen, which made sense in the days of giant screens and orchestra pits. But with miniature multiplex theaters and home viewing so common, this isn't a good idea any more.

⚠️ **Gotcha**

Give them time to think? If the script calls for an off-camera sound, consider characters' reaction times before placing the sound. You can use this method to reveal more of the characters mood.

For example, Mary might be working at her desk when the phone rings. If she picks it up on the first ring, we know she was easily distracted or eager for the call. If she lets it ring a few times before reacting, she was concentrating on the task at hand.

Think it through, trim the sound to the right length to tell the story, and place its out-point right in front of the reaction.

Backgrounds

Ambience tracks should run the length of the dramatic scene, even if the scene includes close-ups and other angles that don't show what's making the noise. If you're dissolving in or out of the scene, extend the ambience a few seconds past the dissolve. Audio cross-fades are seldom as quick as video dissolves.

Many filmmakers like to extend ambiences a few seconds on both sides of a scene, even if the video cuts instead of dissolves. An early cross-fade can set up the scene and make a smoother transition. This can be very helpful if you're cutting to a scene that has dialog within the first few frames.

If an ambience isn't long enough, you'll have to loop it, repeating the effect over and over. Sometimes just putting multiple copies on the timeline, with a short cross-fade between each pair, is enough. But some backgrounds need a little help before they can loop successfully.

> ⚠ *Gotcha*
>
> ***Bag the fades.*** Many commercial effect recordings fade in at the start and fade out at the end. Looping the entire track would give you unexplained level dips at each loop as they fade. Instead, move the in- and out-points to where the track is playing at full volume.

Looping by rhythm

Track 40 is a machine hum sequence. We hear it cycling for about three seconds, then the cycles slow down and stop. Looping the entire effect, starting and stopping all over again, would be silly. Instead, we'll loop just one of the cycles.

Open the sound in an audio editor and select a cycle. Set the program to play that selection as a loop. If it sounds smooth, copy the selection and paste it as many times as you need.

 Hear for yourself

Track 40 is a mechanical, cyclic hum from Hollywood Edge. First you hear it as it was published on the demo CD; then you hear it properly looped.

It may be impossible to select an individual cycle by eye (Figure 11.8). The best way is to use the program's scrub feature to mark what you think is the beginning and end of a cycle, turn it into a loop, and then fine-tune. Play the loop while moving its boundaries, until things sound right. If you hear a click at each repeat of the loop, make sure the boundary is at a zero crossing. I selected about 17 frames starting around 1:06; the result is the smoothly looped machine sound in the second part of Track 40.

A stereo effect may have zero crossings at different times on each channel, so finding a click-free loop can be difficult. A 10- or 15-millisecond cross-fade at each splice can help. Or convert the sound to mono, loop as needed, and apply a stereo simulation process (Chapter 17) before you mix.

C-loop

Some sounds don't loop well because they change over time. The first part of Track 41 is a short, city traffic background. Its timbre changes slightly during the length of the effect, so the end doesn't sound quite like the beginning. Looping it gives you the abrupt shifts in part 2 of Track 41.

When you've got this kind of situation, a *flip loop* or *C-loop* can work wonders.

1. Select the entire sound and copy it.

2. Move the cursor to the end of the sound, and paste. In many programs this will leave the newly

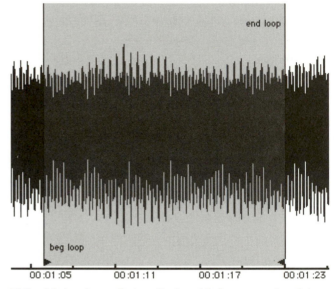

11.8 It's hard to tell visually, but this is one cycle of the machine hum.

pasted section selected; don't deselect it. In other programs you might need to select the second half manually. Since this needs to be precise, drop a marker at the end of the file before pasting and use the marker to select the pasted half.

3. Apply a *backwards,* or *reverse,* or *–100 percent speed* effect to the selection. This will turn it head for tail. Now the newly pasted version starts with the same timbre the first section ended with and should sound perfectly smooth at the splice. If it doesn't, look for zero crossings or use a short cross-fade.

4. Select the entire sound with both the forward and backwards version. Copy and paste as many times as needed.

If you're doing this in a NLE, it will want to render each backwards copy separately, wasting time. Instead, skip step 4. Export the single forwards/backwards pair from step 3 as an audio file. Use the new file for conventional, straight-ahead looping.

Hear for yourself

The first sound in Track 41 is a traffic background from Hollywood Edge. Because its timbre changes, conventional looping can be obvious (second sound). But the C-loop works fine (third sound).

Sounds with foreground voices or percussive hits don't C-loop well because you can spot individual sounds going backwards. But a surprising number of sounds work fine in reverse. Consider the echoey truck horn about size seconds into our traffic track. When flipped, the echo comes before the horn, but it still sounds like it's realistically bouncing off buildings.

Sound Effects Design

The most creative use of sound effects may be when the track divorces itself from reality. Monsters, laser swords, and magic machines should have equally strange sounds. Using manipulated sounds, or slightly wrong ones, in sync with the action can help us appreciate a character's point of view. Manipulated or manufactured ambiences can make unusual settings more convincing.

Creating New Sounds

Computer-generated imagery has gotten so sophisticated that an artist can sit at a workstation and create a monster or machine from scratch. While music synthesizers have come a long way, they still sound electronic. If you need a monster's voice instead of a robot's, you have to start with something nonelectronic and manipulate it.

Sound palettes

Sound effects fall into three broad (and sometimes overlapping) categories. In most cases, it makes sense to think of these as different artist's palettes. Sounds within a single palette can often be substituted or combined successfully. Sounds from multiple palettes contrast and tend to be heard separately, even if you mix them. Of course, like all things artistic, these rules aren't absolute. The real key is how creatively you apply the sounds.

Organic sounds   These include human and animal noises, and naturally occurring sounds like wind and water. Since our monster is organic, it helps to start on his voice here. Library recordings of animal roars can be slowed down, layered, or pitch shifted to be scary and inhuman. But the recording has to be clean, close-up, and echo free. Otherwise, you won't be able to apply realistic effects to it in the mix.

Wind can be made otherworldly by changing resonances with an equalizer or by layering multiple sounds. Wind-driven musical instruments, including the brass family and the organ, can be slowed down and pitch-bent (Chapter 15). Water works nicely at drastically changed speeds, with some reverb.

Mechanical sounds   Machines are obvious noisemakers, but so are other objects that vibrate when they move. Nonwind musical instruments, random pieces of metal, scissors closing, and rocks rubbed together are all useful in a sound effects studio. As with the mouth-made machines described earlier, the key is to change the sound so its source isn't immediately recognizable, and then layer and loop pieces to form a rhythm.

Mechanical sounds tend to occupy wider frequency ranges than organic sounds. Unless you're dealing with very small machines, use a mix of bass-heavy sources as well as bright and tinny ones. You might want to leave the midrange fairly sparse if the sound will accompany dialog. The octave from 700 Hz to 1.4 kHz isn't important for intelligibility; you can put mechanical sounds there and these won't compete.

Electronic sounds   The electronic palette is the least versatile. While layering multiple organic or mechanical sounds thickens them and adds interest, synthesized sounds tend to blend into a single (and often bland) pudding when played simultaneously. Because synthesizers have such a wide range of frequencies, manipulation tools such as drastic pitch changes merely turn one synth note into another.

There are some uses for electronic sound, of course. A synthesizer or FM generator can create punctuations and science-fiction sounds as well as the telephone ringer described earlier. White noise, creatively filtered with multiple resonant peaks, can serve as a mechanical drone. Low square waves, with proper filtering to simulate vowel formants, can be an inhuman vocal drone. But both these sounds will be richer if they start with real ingredients.

Don't confuse synthesizers with the *samplers* mentioned in the first footnote of this chapter. Samplers play digital recordings of real sounds from an electronic keyboard. These tools are tremendously useful in sound effects design, but they don't create the sounds they're manipulating.

Chapter 12

Equalization

Remember this:

- Equalizers are incredibly handy tools, both for fixing problems and for getting elements to come together nicely during the mix.

- If you want to use an equalizer effectively, you have to understand where different parts of a sound fit in the audio band.

- Then, knowing approximately what frequency you want to control, tune the equalizer by ear.

Equalizers are precise tone controls, changing the timbre of a sound by making one part of the spectrum louder or another softer. But they didn't start out that way.

It began, as do so many other things in this book, with the phone company. In the 1920s, broadcasters would lease cables from the phone company, first for remote broadcasts within the same city, and later for intercity hookups and networks. But the wires that were okay for phone calls had too much high-frequency loss for radio. So a telco engineer would send test tones at various frequencies from a remote location. A colleague would sit at the other end of the line with a voltmeter, and he would clip capacitors and inductors to the line until the voltage was equal for each tone. When the tones were equalled, they declared the line *equalized*.

A few years later, when movies started talking, producers discovered that very few of the newly equipped theaters sounded the same. A track could sound fine on the rerecording stage,[1] but be muffled in one auditorium and brittle in another. So engineers borrowed the phone company technique to tune theater sound systems. Instead of using jury-rigged collections of components, however, they put the capacitors and inductors in a box with switches and called the unit an *equalizer*. Someone tried one of the boxes on a rerecording stage to spiff up dialog and sound

---

1. Hollywood's term for the mix-down room.

effects, and the idea caught on. By the mid 1930s, a couple of companies were building equalizers specifically for film mixing.

Today, equalizers are indispensable in audio post. But they're rarely used to make voltage at different frequencies equal. Instead, equalizer uses include:

- Equalizers can improve intelligibility in a dialog track.

- Equalizers remove some specific kinds of noise.

- Equalizers help a mix by keeping elements from competing with other sounds and each other.

- Equalizers subtly change the character of a sound.

- Equalizers emphasize bass rhythms in a piece of music.

- Equalizers simulate telephones, intercoms, and other real-world speakers.

- Equalizers compensate for minor deficiencies in the playback system.

Despite all this usefulness, there are certain things an equalizer can't do. It can't eliminate most kinds of noise. Chapter 16 covers ways to hide noise, and equalization plays a part, but the noise is still there (it's just not as noticeable). You can't use an equalizer to fix a distorted track either, even though you can use an equalizer to make the track easier to understand.

Equalizers can't create sounds that weren't there in the first place. They won't put back highs that were lost to a low sample rate nor add bass to a telephone recording. They can't change a voice: No amount of bass boost will turn me into James Earl Jones.

And they can't be used as a kind of spotlight either, to pick out a voice in a crowd or to eliminate a soloist or most groups of instruments in an orchestra. The only way to accomplish picking a voice out of a crowd is to use a very close, directional mic in the original production. There's a technique for eliminating soloists in some recordings (Chapter 17), but it doesn't use equalization.

Frequency Bands

The point of an equalizer is to raise or lower the volume in a specific frequency band, without affecting other frequencies. So before you can use an equalizer—or even think about what kind of equalizer is appropriate—you need to understand what's going on at different parts of the audio spectrum. That's easiest to do by ear.

Tracks 42–50 are eight versions of the same voice-and-music montage. Each includes male and female narration, pop and orchestral instrumentals, a middle-of-the road pop song sung by a woman, and a hard rock piece sung by a man. These songs are from the DeWolfe Music Library and used by permission.[2]

Track 42 is the montage in full fidelity. The other tracks are have been processed through a lab-quality digital filter to remove everything other than the specified band. If you try to replicate this on your desktop, you may be disappointed. That's because the filter I used had 24 dB reduction, an octave away from the cutoff frequency. The filters in many programs aren't nearly as precise (Figure 12.1). But you may be able to make the tracks sharper, using a technique in the next section.

⚠ Gotcha _____

That's not what I read in Hi-Fi Weekly... If you're a stereo enthusiast or have spent time in music studios, some of the following descriptions of various audio bands may seem wrong. That's because they're based on film and TV sound, not music recording (or advertising hype). You can verify everything I've described by listening to the book's CD.

🔘 *Hear for yourself* _____

Tracks 42 through 50 are the examples for this section. You may be able to understand audio bands using just the text, but you'll get a much better feel for them if you actually listen to the tracks.

Play Track 42 first, as a reference on the best speakers you've got. Then work your way through the others. Remember all that's changing is the filter frequency, not the volume or any other settings. If a track seems softer than others, it's because there's less going on in that band. Don't turn up your speakers to compensate.

Deep bass

Track 43 is the band between 10 and 100 Hz. Most of this band is often deliberately filtered out during dialog recording, to avoid noise. A lot of this band can also be thrown away in post. The first four seconds of silence are the woman's voice—it's quiet because she has almost no vocal energy in this band. But there's also very little of the man's voice in the next four seconds. Even the corporate and orchestral music are sparse, with only occasional notes that deep.

_____

2. The montage includes two pieces we worked with in Chapter 10, plus "You Are My Fantasy" and "Hell Child," DeWolfe CD 77, Tracks 9 and 13. Both are by C. Kiddy and © DeWolfe Music.

12.1 A tale of two filters. These are *spectragraphs*, graphs of signal strength at various frequencies. They're both of the same section of orchestral music, run through a high-pass filter at 1.2 kHz and a low-pass one at 2.4 kHz. The top was done using filters in Premiere, with barely 6 dB per octave rejection. The bottom one is track 47 from the CD; it obviously used a much sharper filter.

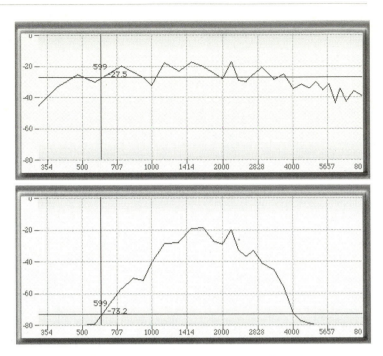

Figure 12.2 is a spectral analysis of the track, shown in a *spectragram*: a kind of three-dimensional spectragraph that plots time as well as volume and frequency. The horizontal axis is time and is roughly the length of the montage. Frequencies are plotted along the vertical, and volume is reflected in the amount of color. You can see how quiet things are during the voices. Note how there's virtually nothing below 60 Hz for even the orchestral music.

Midbass

Track 44 is the band 100–300 Hz. These are the fundamental frequencies for most spoken voices. Note how both male and female voices have about the same amount of energy here. But you can't make out which vowels are which—that depends on higher harmonics, created by resonances in the mouth. The music uses these frequencies primarily for accompaniment, rather than rhythm or melody. The singers also have fundamentals in this range, but these are masked by instruments, and you can hardly hear these fundamentals.

12.2 A spectral analysis of Track 43 shows how little deep bass there is in most audio.

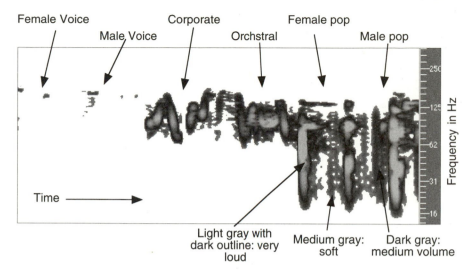

Female Voice

Male Voice

Corporate

Orchstral

Female pop

Male pop

Frequency in Hz

Time ———————→

Light gray with dark outline: very loud

Medium gray: soft

Dark gray: medium volume

Low Midrange

Track 45 is 300–600 Hz. These are the lower harmonics of the basic voice frequency. As you speak, your tongue forms various cavities in the back of your mouth. The cavities act as filters, emphasizing different harmonics in each position. We hear the combinations of harmonics as vowels. These are remarkably robust. While this is the first band where you

12.3 Track 44 shows how much busier things are between 100 and 300 Hz, both for voice and music.

can distinguish vowels, it's not a critical one for intelligibility. The harmonic combinations extend upward, and vowels can be recognized even if the entire midrange is lost.

However, this band and the next contain most of the energy of the human voice. These bands also contain the fundamental and most powerful harmonics of most melody instruments. So there's a potential for voice and melody to compete when mixed together. You can hear how the melody instruments in the two pop songs hold back when the sing-

12.4 Track 45 has about the same amount of activity for both voice and instrumental music between 300 and 600 Hz. But things calm down during the vocals, so we can hear the lyric.

ers are belting. Most jingles and other songs where lyrics are important are arranged this way.

Mids

Track 46 covers the 600 Hz to 1.2 kHz range. Now we're entering harmonic country, where much of the energy is generated by harmonics (Chapter 2) of lower fundamentals. Notice how the female voice, naturally brighter, is stronger in this range. But neither voice is fully intelligible because unvoiced consonants don't start until the next

12.5 Track 46, 600 Hz – 1.2 kHz, is where you can start to tell instruments apart. Things don't look very different from the octave below it, but the ear is very sensitive to subtlety in this range.

octave. This band is critical for instruments: While the lower midrange lets you hear the melody, these first and second harmonics help you tell instruments apart. Most instruments have significant energy here.

High Midrange

Track 47 (Figure 12.6) is the octave 1.2 – 2.4 kHz. This is an important range for dialog: There's enough harmonic energy to tell most vowels apart, and all of the consonants are covered. It's also important for brass instruments, which have loud upper harmonics. The singers are particularly strong in this range because they're trained to sing *in the mask*, opening resonators in the front of their face to emphasize harmonics.[3] But despite all the activity in this octave, volumes aren't as high. Only the orchestral material has about the same energy as it did an octave below.

12.6 Track 47 shows the rand 1.2 – 2.4 kHz. This is also a critical range, even though volumes generally aren't as high.

12.7 Track 48 shows that when you get to the octave starting at 2.4 kHz, things start to calm down—except for the rock music at the end.

---

3. The same thing starts to happen if you force a smile while you're speaking.

Lower High Frequencies

Track 48 (Figure 12.7) is the octave 2.4–4.8 kHz. You might not think of these numbers as being high frequency, but take a listen. While most vowels have appreciable harmonics up here, they're not important for intelligibility and only establish presence. (Telephones cut off halfway through this band at 3.5 kHz, yet retain enough of the voice for you to not only understand the words but identify who's speaking.) There's also very little of the synthesized industrial theme. The orchestral brass is strong here. Most brass is very rich in upper harmonics, and that's what helps us differentiate one brass instrument from another. The laid-back female song is mostly calm strings in this range. On the other hand, the rock number has a lot going on: That's typical of dance and rock music production.

Middle High Frequencies

Track 49 (Figure 12.8) is the 4.8–9.6 kHz range. Even though we haven't yet hit 10 kHz—what some software marks as the middle of the audio range[4]—this is definitely high. You can hear just a little of the female voice, and only friction consonants are left for the male voice. The synthesizer is almost completely gone. But the brass is still going strong up here. About the only thing left with any strength in the two pop songs are the upper harmonics of the strings, the guitar wail, and the percussion.

12.8 Track 49, between 4.8 and 9.6 kHz, shows there's still activity, but the very bright, loud sounds are much farther apart than in lower octaves.

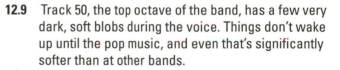

12.9 Track 50, the top octave of the band, has a few very dark, soft blobs during the voice. Things don't wake up until the pop music, and even that's significantly softer than at other bands.

High Frequencies

Track 50 (Figure 12.9) is the top of what's generally considered the top of the audio band, 9.6 kHz to 20 kHz, and it's the highest octave on a CD. For most of the track, you might not hear much at all. There's still some orchestral brass at these frequencies, but what's left of the pop music is mostly unidentifiable sizzle.

---

4. That's flat-out wrong, as we discussed in chapter 1.

⚠️ *Gotcha* _____

Magic ranges? Most of these examples are an octave wide. Since we hear logarithmically, this width makes the most sense—each band contains the same number of musical notes. The two lowest bands are significantly wider, not because our hearing is less acute there,[1] but because there's less going on of interest to a chapter about soundtrack equalization.

The actual frequencies involved are fairly arbitrary. I chose them to reveal interesting things about voice and music, not because you should be using them to set an equalizer.

_____

1. Though it is.

Equalizer Characteristics and Types

Just about every equalizer has a frequency knob. But a good program or audio post suite will give you a choice of equalizer types: cutoff filter, shelving equalizer, peaking equalizer, parametric, or various forms of graphic. You can't choose the best one for a specific purpose until you understand the differences. But that's fairly easy when you look at some of the characteristics beyond frequency.

Slope and filters

A filter is an equalizer that passes part of the band perfectly, while rejecting frequencies beyond a cutoff point. How it makes the transition between pass and reject is a matter of design and can vary greatly. Glance back at Figure 12.1 on page 248. It showed how much orchestral music was left at various frequencies, when run through the filter in Premiere (top), and one used for lab research (bottom).

The average level of that music was –20 dBfs. The crosshairs in the figure show how loud the audio was an octave below the filter's low-frequency limit of 1.2 kHz. In the top screenshot, the signal was –27 dBfs, just about half the strength of the original signal. In the bottom one, it was –73 dBfs, less than 1/200 of the original. It's an impressive difference, but it can be misleading. Part of what we're seeing depends on what the music was doing at the precise moment when I grabbed each screenshot. If the second one was slightly softer in the low midrange, the filter would look better.

There's a better way to visualize filter performance. Instead of showing the volume of an arbitrary signal at different frequencies, we'll draw a graph of how much *any* signal would be rejected. We can plot signal loss in dB along the vertical, and frequency along the horizontal. The result looks like Figure 12.10.

A theoretically perfect filter would have a vertical line at 1 kHz; 999 Hz falls to the left of the line and gets infinite attenuation; 1001 Hz is on the right and not affected at all. But you can't build a working filter that way. Real-world filters start working gradually, with a gentle transition between where they're not affecting the signal, and where they're reducing it. Because of this, a filter's cutoff frequency is defined as where the signal is reduced –3 dB.

Even with that gradual transition, there's a big difference between the two filters in Figure 12.10. You can see it in the angle of the line below the cutoff. The top filter, with roughly a 45 degree angle, loses 6 dB per octave. At 1 kHz, the loss is –3 dB. At 500 Hz, it's –9 dB. At 250 Hz, its –15 dB. This

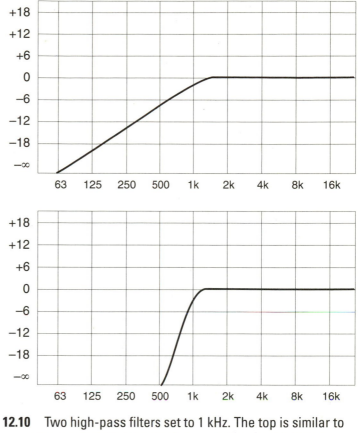

12.10 Two high-pass filters set to 1 kHz. The top is similar to the one in Premiere; the bottom is like the lab filter I used.

is a *first order* filter, like the one in Premiere. The filter on the bottom has a steeper line, losing 24 dB per octave; it's a *fourth order* filter.

More is not necessarily better. Filters with a steeper slope have more *phase shift*, a form of distortion, around the nominal frequency. This is a subtle effect. It's harder to pick out than the more common overload distortion, but it does change the timbre. The shift is inherent in filter design, so generally speaking, very sharp filters are reserved for special effects or eliminating noises. More gentle filters are used to preserve sound quality.

These drawings show high-pass filters, rejecting sound below a cutoff frequency. But the same rules apply to low-pass filters, which reject sounds above their frequency setting.

- High-pass filters are often used at a fairly low frequency, for example to remove room rumble below 80 Hz. Since high-pass filters appear on the low end of the spectrum, it may be simpler to think of them as *low cut* rather than high pass.

- Similarly, a low-pass filter at 12 kHz may be used to remove hiss from dialog. You could also call it a *high cut* filter.

- To create Tracks 43–50, I used a high-pass filter followed by a low pass. This left a clearly defined band between two filter frequencies, and rejected everything else.

Most high- and low-pass filters have only one control, to adjust frequency. While a few studio and lab filters also have a slope control, this characteristic is properly determined by the circuit or software design and usually not variable. However, you can create a higher-order filter by stacking multiple first-order filters in series, all set to the same frequency. Each additional filter adds 6 dB per octave (and more phase shift). Figure 12.11 shows how you'd use Premiere to accomplish the sharp filters for the previous section.

12.11   It may look redundant, but stacking multiple filters at the same frequency has the same effect as choosing filters with a steeper slope.

A *comb filter* is a particularly sharp collection of notches, handy for noise reduction. But it's actually created with a small delay, and is discussed in Chapter 14.

Boost or attenuation, and shelving equalizers

Sometimes you don't want to completely reject sounds beyond a specific frequency; you only want to adjust their volume.

A *shelving equalizer* has a slope like a filter, but the slope stops at a preset amount of boost or cut. The volume adjustment is applied from the nominal frequency all the way to the end of the spectrum. A low-frequency shelf will boost or reduce sounds below its nominal frequency; sounds above it aren't affected at all. A high-frequency shelf works on signals above the nominal.

Shelving equalizers can be set to any boost or cut value within their range. The ability to lower levels beyond a preset frequency is helpful for reducing noise at either end of the spectrum without totally losing the signal.

The slope of a shelving equalizer is fairly shallow and can extend more than four octaves. This gentle, low-distortion action, coupled with the lack of an obvious peak, makes shelving filters very useful for subtly brightening, warming, or filling out a sound. But be careful: when a shelf is boosting, it will also emphasize noises at the extremes of the band.

Shelving equalizers have two controls: frequency and amount of boost or cut.

Bandwidth or Q, and peaking equalizers

The most common use for an equalizer in audio post is to fix something, such as reducing camera whine or boosting intelligibility. This kind of fix requires lowering or raising just a specific group of frequencies within the band, while leaving others alone. *Peaking[5] equalizers* let you select frequency and amount of boost or cut, like a shelving equalizer, but peaking equalizers work on a narrow range of

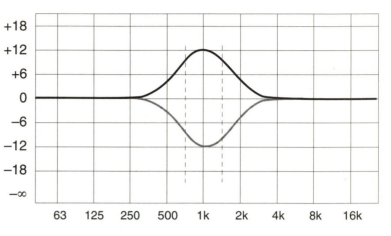

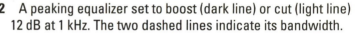

12.12 A peaking equalizer set to boost (dark line) or cut (light line) 12 dB at 1 kHz. The two dashed lines indicate its bandwidth.

frequencies, like the combination high-pass/low-pass we used for the frequency band examples. Figure 12.12 shows how peaking equalizers affect a sound.

You can see that the equalizer in Figure 12.12 has a slope of roughly 6 dB per octave, appropriate for gentle timbre correction. But if we tried to remove a 1 kHz whistle with this gentle slope, we'd muffle dialog between 500 Hz and 2 kHz. A more precise equalizer is needed. This concept is so important that there are multiple ways to specify it.

⚠️ *Gotcha* _____

Plus 18, minus infinity? You'll notice the graph is not symmetrical. It's reasonable to want an equalizer to reduce parts of a signal below audibility, so many designs offer 24 dB or more of cut. But boosting a signal that much can cause problems with noise or oscillation, so practical equalizers are often limited to ﹣12 dB or +18 dB.

There's also an existential reason for this asymmetry. I have no problem making a signal infinitely soft; that just means turning it off. But how do you make a signal infinitely loud, without involving all the energy in the known universe?

---

5. Peaking Equalizers also dip, though it's not reflected in their name.

An equalizer's *bandwidth* is defined as the range where its action is within 3 dB of maximum. In Figure 12.12, that's shown by the two dashed lines at roughly 700 and 1400 Hz. So the bandwidth of this equalizer is 700 Hz. But that's a clumsy measurement. Because frequency is logarithmic, an equalizer with the same slope would have different bandwidths depending on where it's set. If we dialed in 250 Hz, the 3 dB points would be roughly 175 and 350 Hz—a bandwidth of 175 Hz. If we dialed in 4 kHz, those points would be around 2.8 and 5.6 kHz, and the bandwidth would be 2.8 kHz.

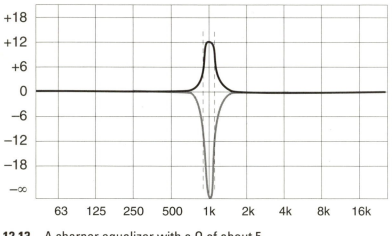

12.13 A sharper equalizer with a Q of about 5.

Instead, we use the concept of *Q*: the center frequency divided by the bandwidth. In each case above, the Q is roughly 1.4. This is a gentle-sounding equalizer. Contrast it with the one in Figure 12.13. This one has 3 dB points at roughly 900 and 1100 Hz, for a Q of 5. Practical equalizers can have Qs many times that. A Q of 15 or higher lets you surgically remove a constant-frequency sine wave without noticeably affecting anything around it. Some of the special-effects equalizers in my studio go up to 100 Q; at that high a Q, an equalizer can start oscillating as it boosts its own internal noise. The Q is sometimes expressed as a fraction of an octave centered around the nominal frequency.

Graphic equalizers An equalizer doesn't need user-settable Q, or even user-settable frequencies, though this seriously limits a equalizer's usefulness in audio post. The *graphic equalizer*, found on most boom boxes and in simple software, is actually a bank of low Q, fixed-frequency peaking equalizers with their outputs combined. Figure 12.14

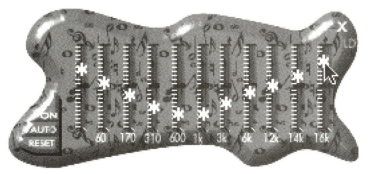

12.14 A not-very-serious graphic equalizer.

shows a typical graphic equalizer. The choice of one that looks like a toy was intentional.

⚠️ **Gotcha**

Be afraid of Mr. Smiley. It's just too easy to misuse a graphic. Most boom-box owners know that if you slide the knobs so they look like a grin, as in Figure 12.14, music has more impact. The bass seems stronger, and there's more sparkle to the highs. So some producers ask for *smiley* equalization on their entire track. It really does make a mix more exciting on good monitor speakers, if the original track is clean to begin with. But that's where the good part ends.

While boosted bass and treble may sound great on professional monitors, they can turn to distortion on other kinds of speakers. The track will still seem loud, but with a muddiness that gets in the way of the message—something hard to spot in a production environment but damaging on the air. The cheap, narrow-range speakers in most TV sets won't carry the hyped frequencies, but the distortion still comes through. Besides, unless you monitor a smiley track on very good speakers, you're apt to miss noise at the extremes of the band.

Even though the boost isn't heard on small speakers, it shows up on station's meters. An engineer or transmitter processor may turn down the overall volume to compensate, making a smiley track seem softer than others on the same station.

The problem with graphic equalizers is their lack of precision. Not only do the sections have a low Q, but the frequencies are arbitrary and not chosen for usefulness. Sometimes the frequencies an octave apart, centered around 1 kHz; sometimes they're two or more octaves wide. Sometimes graphic equalizer logic is a complete mystery.

Graphic equalizers do have a place in professional sound. Serious hardware units, with bands a third of an octave wide, are often used to fix minor problems in otherwise acceptable monitoring systems. But this has to be done subtly, with accurate measuring equipment. More than a few dB adjustment at any frequency can introduce more problems than it's worth.

Analog graphic equalizers got their name because a bank of volume sliders looks something like the graphs we're using. But there's a newer form found in some software. It lets you draw the graph directly, and then equalizes the sound to match. Figure 12.15 shows one of them, from SoundForge. There's a similar one in the otherwise very useful, Mac-based shareware Amadeus.

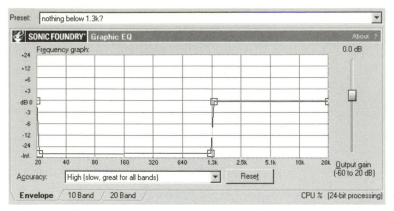

12.15 A different kind of graphic equalizer lets you draw an ideal curve, but probably won't actually sound like it looks.

The problem with these graphics is that nothing stops you from drawing an impossible equalizers. You can be fooled into thinking what you've drawn is actually being applied to the sound. Figure 12.15 shows a graphic equalizer set up as a filter, with a slope of greater than 96 dB per octave. When I measured the result, it was actually 12 dB per octave.

Parametric equalizers If you want to repair a sound, the best peaking equalizer is one that lets you specify all three parameters: frequency, Q, and boost/cut. That's why it's called a *parametric equalizer*. The first parametrics appeared around 1972, and revolutionized production. Figure 12.16 shows a particularly nice implementation, Waves's Renaissance plug-in. Like many parametrics, it combines multiple peaking sections in the middle of the band with switchable cutoff/shelf/peaking at the ends. Here, section 1 is set as a highpass

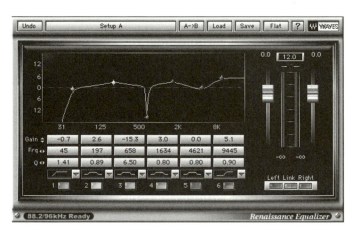

12.16 A parametric equalizer. This one includes a graph. But unlike the one in Figure 12.15, it won't let you ask for something impossible.

and section 6 is a shelf. There are simpler parametrics in most NLEs and audio software, but you can combine multiple instances to get the same effect (as I did with the filters in Figure 12.11).

Parametric equalizers sound exactly the same as any other kind of peaking equalizer, assuming the same circuit or software quality. A parametric's value is the ability to precisely tune multiple sections in real-time, to catch specific sounds and fix problems. You'll learn how to do this later in this chapter.

Dynamically-controlled equalizers

It's common practice to control low- or high-frequency noise with equalizers that constantly change either frequency or level depending on how much energy there is at the extremes of the band. This noise reduction technique is discussed in Chapter 16.

Equalizer quality

There's alot more to an equalizer than knobs or sliders, and you can't assume that two equalizers with identical settings will perform the same. Depending on its design, an equalizer may contribute noise or distortion, or be hard to tune.

Analog equalizers   While music producers revere the sound of some classic analog equalizers, these are expensive and are arguably overkill in the post suite. Cheaper, standalone ones, along with the equalizers in analog mixers, can be noisy at their extremes. Their frequencies are usually chosen for music, not media. If you use FireWire and your signal normally stays in the digital domain, there's nothing to be gained—and a lot to be lost—by running through an analog equalizer. If you use analog connections when digitizing footage or sounds, resist the temptation to pre-equalize. It's better to leave the serious equalization to software that lets you save the good settings and undo the bad ones.

It may be appropriate to add a little tweaking—no more than a couple of dB—when outputting from NLE to analog tape. Otherwise, set a mixer's equalizers to the neutral position (or bypass these equalizers, if at all possible).

Digital equalizers   Software-based equalizers can be of varying quality, depending on how well the algorithm was designed and how much they're allowed to load down the CPU. Two critical design choices are the internal gain structure, and how many bits are used in the internal bussing and floating-point math. Both can influence noise, and bad gain staging can also lead to clipping. Third-party plug-ins, available in DirectX, Premiere, or VST format, usually have much better noise and distortion performance than the equalizers supplied with NLEs.

Standalone digital equalizers with AES/EBU connection are often found in sophisticated audio post suites. These are usually DSP-driven boxes with additional processing functions.

Tuning an Equalizer

Forget about specific frequencies. There are no magic numbers that will always improve a sound. It's okay to use your knowledge of different bands to get you in the ballpark, but you can't fine-tune an equalizer mathematically. You have to use your ear.

This means you must hear the sound while you're adjusting. A few software equalizers don't let you do this; these are virtually worthless. Better equalizers work in realtime, by changing their

---

⚠ *Gotcha* _____

Dude, where's my frequency? One problem with some digital equalizers is the trade-off between resolution and responsiveness. In many designs, the frequency knobs rely on an internal lookup table to speed up operation. Instead of smoothly varying from one frequency to the next, these digital equalizers click over in small fractions of an octave. If the fractions are small enough, you can tune them precisely. Otherwise, there's a chance you'll miss a sound that you're trying to remove with a high Q dip.

Equalizers that let you enter a numeric frequency don't have this problem. However, knobs or sliders make tuning much easier.

---

sound as soon as you move a knob. Others require a few seconds to render a preview after you've let go of a control. Obviously, the realtime equalizers are more efficient, but the equalizers that need to render are still workable if you make small changes and have some patience.

Highpass, lowpass   Tuning a cutoff filter is intuitive: Turn the knob until what you want to lose goes away, without doing too much damage to what you want to keep. If the slope is too gentle for this to happen, apply a parametric instead and find the offending frequency using the steps under parametricbelow. Then turn off the parametric and enter the frequency you found into multiple, stacked filters.

Shelving Equalizer   Tuning a shelving equalizer takes a little more care since the controls can seem interactive. Because of its gentle slope, a large amount of boost at a high frequency might sound like it's doing the same thing as less boost at a lower frequency. But it's really adding more noise. The same happens on the low end. If you want to use more than 3 dB of boost or so with a shelf, check on very good monitors. In fact, if you think you need that much boost, consider using a low Q peak instead.

This problem of extra noise pickup doesn't exist when lowering levels with a shelf.

Parametric   When using a parametric for subtle, low Q effects, start with a fairly large amount of boost and a medium Q. Find the right frequency. Then lower the Q and adjust the level.

Tuning a parametric to eliminate a noise isn't intuitive. The trick is to forget about removing the noise at first; instead, make the noise jump out by boosting.

1.   Set both the Q and boost as high as they'll go (Figure 12.17A)

2.   With the clip playing, slowly sweep the frequency until you hear the noise suddenly jump up (Figure 12.17B). Then fine-tune by sweeping even slower in that area: When you've got exactly the right frequency, you'll hear the noise resonate and possibly even distort. Don't worry about the distortion.

3. Don't touch the Q or frequency but turn the gain or boost/cut as low as it'll go Figure 12.17C). On a really good parametric, this may be marked -∞. The noise should be gone.

If the noise doesn't go completely away, try lowering the Q slightly. If that doesn't help, raise it again. Then apply another section, set to the same parameters as the first to it. This doubles the amount of rejection.

If you now notice another noise, related but at a higher pitch, you're hearing a harmonic. Add another section and start sweeping around a frequency that's twice what you found in the first.

 ### *Hear for yourself*

Track 51 lets you hear what these steps can sound like. It consists of a 9-second piece of exterior dialog, repeated five times. The first pass is the original, with a nasty whistle in it. The second pass is step 2: You can hear the equalizer sweep and then find the right frequency, emphasizing the whistle. The third pass is step 3, and the whistle is gone. But now you're aware of a boomy resonance in the space. In the fourth pass, we're sweeping a second section of the parametric to find the boomy resonance. The fifth pass is the result of both sections. It starts with the equalizer turned off, then it turns on, then off and on another time.

Track 52 is an even more extreme example. It's a short clip from an interview recorded on a motorboat, with the mic too far from the subject. An equalizer alone can't save this track—nothing can make it perfect—but it can make the voice more intelligible, as you can hear in the second part of this track.

There's more that can be done to both these clips, but that's for other chapters.

Equalizer Cookbook

A good chef starts with an idea of how to prepare a dish but will always taste and adjust to the ingredients at hand. Think of these recipes the same way: They're good starting places for most source material, but they're not exact and won't apply to some clips. *Always adjust by ear.*

Most of recipes assume a parametric equalizer. Values are expressed as frequency/boost or cut/Q; for example, 1 kHz/–3 dB/Q = 0.5 means set the frequency to 1 kHz and the level to –3 dB, with a Q of 0.5. Vary the frequency around there, until it works best with your material. Then fine-tune the level for the sound you want.

The high- and low-pass filters should be at least 12 dB per octave, and work even better at 18 dB per octave. If yours aren't that sharp, consider stacking a couple of sections.

12.17 The steps to eliminate a noise with a parametric aren't intuitive. But they work.

Working with Voices

- Because the area around 1.75 kHz is the fundamental of most consonants, a 1.75 kHz/+3 dB/Q = 1 boost can subtly improve intelligibility, 1.75 kHz/+6 dB/Q = 0.5 can add strength to some voices.

- An octave above that is the first harmonic of most consonants; 3.5 kHz/+3 dB/Q = 1 can add clarity, but don't do this if you're using the boosts at 1.75 kHz.

- Male voices can gain a little extra power with 160 Hz/+2 dB/Q = 1.

- Sibilance (spitty /s/ sounds) often happen between 4 and 5 kHz. Sweep around there with +12/Q = 5 until you find them, and then dip as much as possible. This can reduce the sibilance, but if you want to really eliminate it, skip the equalizer and use a *de-esser*, described in Chapter 13.

- Many interior locations are boomy somewhere around 200–400 Hz, depending on the room size. A 3 dB/Q = 2 dip can help, but use maximum boost first to find the exact frequency.

- If dialog sounds dull because of bad mic technique, try 4 kHz/+6 dB/Q = 0.25. This can be better than using a shelf, since it doesn't emphasize high-frequency hiss.

- Popped /p/ and /b/ sounds can sometimes be fixed by selecting just the pop and applying a sharp highpass around 160 Hz.

Working with Music

- If a melody is interfering with dialog or voice-over, but you don't want the rhythmic elements of the music to get lost, cut a hole in the melody for the consonants. Start around 1.75 kHz/−3 dB/Q = 1 and vary for the most effectiveness.

- Modern pop-style recordings are often very bright, with a lot going on above 10 kHz. If you have to mix them with older recordings, try a shelf 10 kHz/−3 dB. Then add 5 kHz/+3 dB/Q = 0.5 to the older material.

General Fixes

- For low-frequency noise reduction in dialog, try a sharp highpass around 130 Hz (male) to 200 Hz (female).

- For high-frequency noise reduction in dialog or music, try a sharp, lowpass around 8 kHz.

- What we call 60 cycle hum, can have harmonics all over the band. Start with a sharp, highpass at 130 Hz, and then add at least four or five parametric sections tuned to harmonics by ear. Or use a comb filter, described in Chapter 14.

- If these fixes leave the track sounding too dull, add +3 dB/Q = 1 around 1.5 times the highpass frequency.

Special Effects

- For telephone use sharp, highpass at 400 Hz, followed by a sharp, lowpass at 3.5 kHz. Then add some compression (Chapter 13).

- For a radio speaker depending on quality, use a highpass at 300–500 Hz, and then a lowpass at 5–6 kHz.

- A thin voice reminiscent of old-time radio's *The Shadow*, but used in a lot of current radio station promos, can be done by using a highpass at 800 Hz and a lowpass at 10 kHz.

- Put voices in the next room with a low shelf around 500 Hz/−24 dB, a resonant peak around 1.3 kHz/+12 dB/Q = 5, and a high shelf at 2 kHz/−24 dB. Make sure the peak isn't clipping in your equalizer. Then add reverb (Chapter 15).

- Make outdoor sounds more distant by reducing the highs and emphasizing the lows: low shelf 500 Hz/+12 dB, high shelf 1.5 kHz/–12 dB. Then lower the volume.

- To dehumanize a voice for sound effects, start notching out vowel formants with a sharp parametric. Depending on the vowel, you'll find them around 400 Hz, 800 Hz, 1.2 kHz, 1.6 kHz, 2 kHz, 2.4 kHz, 2.8 kHz, 3.2 kHz, 3.6 kHz, and 4 kHz.

Chapter 13

Dynamics Control

Remember this:

- Automatic level processors can be a lot more subtle and sophisticated than the AGC in a camera, and they can be a powerful tool for adding punch and controlling some kinds of noise.

- While there are a variety of dynamics processors with different purposes, they all have similar controls. Understand how these controls work in one device, and you'll be able to use them in others.

- You can also use these devices to make elements fit together better in a mix, or even change the character of sound effects and musical instruments.

A *compressor* works like an automatic volume control. It uses the envelope of a signal to control the signal's level, keeping the output volume relatively constant even when the input volume changes.

For most of the history of film and TV sound, compressors—and their close cousins, *limiters*—were used sparingly. Distortion-free compressors were hard to build, so their use was restricted to technical necessities like avoiding high-frequency problems.[1] But in the late 1960s, relatively clean units started to appear on the market, and soon they were considered essential tools—first in music production, then to increase loudness at radio and TV transmitters, and finally in postproduction.

The most obvious use for a compressor is smoothing out unwanted jumps in volume. But compressors are also useful for creatively shaping a soundtrack:

- They can add punch and power to a voice.
- They can keep elements from competing during a mix.

---

1. To overcome noise, optical soundtracks and broadcast TV boost high frequencies as much as 17 dB at the film lab or transmitter. The projector or receiver has a matching loss, cutting the noise while restoring the original timbre. Unfortunately, all that boosting means that loud, high-frequency sounds are apt to distort.

- They can change the character of sound effects (or destroy the character of music).

- They can compensate for predictable problems in the playback system.

With a slight circuit or software change, a compressor becomes an *expander*, emphasizing volume changes by turning down parts of the original signal that were already soft and turning up the ones that were already loud. Expanders (and their cousins, *gates*) can reduce or eliminate some kinds of noise, change the character of sound effects and musical instruments, and add impact to percussive sound effects.

Characteristics and Controls

Figure 13.1 shows what goes on inside a very simple compressor.

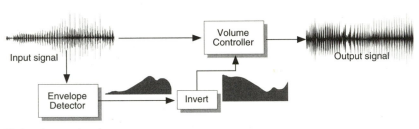

13.1   A very basic compressor.

The input, on the left of the drawing, is about one syllable's worth of dialog. The tiny waves are the frequencies of the voice itself. The overall volume, small at first and then louder, is the envelope—what a meter would show when you play this sound.

The envelope detector generates a voltage which tracks the volume. The voltage is then inverted: Where the signal was loud, the voltage is low; where the signal was soft, the voltage is high.[2]

This inverted voltage is fed to a volume-control circuit. Where the original signal was soft, the control voltage keeps the volume control fully on. Where the signal was loud, the control voltage is low and the volume is reduced. The result is the constant-level signal at the output.

This is a brain-dead compressor, appropriate for a telephone or two-way radio but not a soundtrack. A lot of the emotional impact of a film depends on the dynamics of each sound, and how it relates to other sounds. This compressor would destroy those dynamics. But by adding just a few additional functions to the inverter and detector, we can create smarter compressors that do useful things for a track.

---

2. There's another compressor design that looks at the envelope of the output instead of the input. But for our purposes, the effect is the same.

⚠️ **Gotcha** _____

Classic Compre;ssors It was a real challenge to control the volume of a signal in early analog compressors. Tube-based circuits had to be constantly tweaked as the tubes aged, or else they'd add a thunking noise. Solid-state offered more options, but each had its own form of distortion and a characteristic sound.

Music engineers took advantage of the differences between compressor designs, preferring specific ones for various instruments and musical styles. Some classic 60s- and 70s-era compressors still sell for thousands of dollars. So do newly manufactured analog clones. A few companies attempt to emulate these classics in software.

There's no advantage to using analog (or analog sounding) compressors in audio post. Digital algorithms can have a lot less distortion. If you want to spend a few dollars to improve your sound, skip the classic compressors and just get modern software that has all the control functions listed here. With the money you save, you can buy better monitor speakers.

Compressor Controls

Ratio

The inverter in Figure 13.1 multiplied the envelope by −1, turning every decibel of additional loudness into one of more softness. But there's nothing magic about this number. If we multiplied by −0.5, for example, less of the envelope would be reflected so more of the original dynamics could be retained. The compression would be more subtle. On the other hand, if we multiplied by −4, small volume changes in the input would result in big changes in the control. A very loud signal might be turned down so much that it becomes the softest part of the track.

Real-world compressors have to consider the response of a particular envelope detector, volume controller, and other factors, so you can't predict how a compressor will perform based only on the multiplier. Instead, compressors have a *ratio control*. It's calibrated in how many decibels the output will change for each decibel of change in the input. A ratio of 2:1 means that if the input gets 10 dB louder, the output goes up 5 dB. A ratio of 10:1 means that a 10 dB change in the input results in only 1 dB change in the output. Some compressors have ratios as high as 100:1, and a few click to ∞:1—though these ultra-high ratios are useful only for special effects. Ratios can go the other way as well. A 1:2 ratio means that a 10 dB change at the input produces a 20 dB change at the output, and then the compressor is really acting like an expander (discussed later in this chapter).

Figure 13.2 shows another way to think about this. Assume that bar graphs *A*, *B*, *C*, and *D* are tones of different volumes. A 2:1 ratio cuts each in half—reducing the volume difference. A 4:1 ratio makes the difference even less. At 8:1, the four tones are almost the same volume.

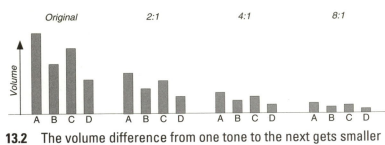

13.2 The volume difference from one tone to the next gets smaller and smaller as the ratio goes up.

Peak versus RMS The envelope detector in Figure 13.1 is responding to the loudest waves, and you can see that the envelope follows their *peak level*. But you can also see that only a few waves reach that level; even at the loudest parts of the signal, most of the waves are much softer. This signal doesn't seem as loud to our ears as a peak-reading meter or detector would indicate. An *RMS* detector averages levels over the short term, creating an envelope that's closer to how the signal actually sounds.

⚠ **Gotcha** _____

An irrational ratio If you set the ratio to 1:1, a 10 dB change in the input results in a 10 dB change in the output. There's no compression going on at all!

A ratio of 1:1 means you've turned the compressor off. Despite this, most software compressors have 1:1 as their default. If a compressor doesn't seem to be doing anything, make sure the ratio control is set to a more useful number.

In general, peak level detectors give a compressor better control over the signal, at the risk of having a more audible compression effect. RMS detectors may let some of the loudest waves get past a compressor, but the overall sound will be smoother and more natural. A few compressors let you choose which mode the detector will use. It's common practice to use an RMS-detecting compressor followed by a peak-detecting limiter (described later in this chapter).

Stereo link If you compress each channel of a stereo signal separately, voices and instruments can appear to dance around between left and right. Consider the case of a loud gunshot on the extreme left of an exterior scene. It would cause the left-channel compressor to lower the level. But the background ambience—birds and traffic—should be evenly distributed between both channels. When the compressor lowers everything on the left, this leaves comparatively more ambience coming from the right. Suddenly all the birds and traffic will swing toward the right side. Then, when the left-channel compressor recovers, they go back to their proper places. It can sound very strange.

The best way to deal with this is to use a single-level detector fed with a mix of both input channels, feeding separate level controllers for each output channel. Or use two detectors, one for each channel, but feed an average of both envelopes to the two level controllers. Both schemes work equally well because both channels are always reduced the same amount. The stereo image stays stable.

Hardware-based stereo compressors usually have a *link* or *stereo switch* on their front panels, to let you choose whether the channels should work independently as two mono compressors or in tandem as a single stereo one.

Software-based compressors usually have two detector algorithms, one mono and one stereo. The software chooses which one based on whether the file is mono or stereo. This works fine for normal stereo or mono clips. But if you're compressing split dialog, where a boom is on one channel of a stereo file and a radio lav on the other, a sudden noise burst in the lav or hitting a prop with the boom will cause both channels to be lowered. Similarly, if you're using a NLE that lets you edit each channel of a stereo track separately, a stereo compressor can give unpredictable results. If your tracks are likely to be affected this way, split them into two mono files before processing.

Makeup gain

You probably noticed a problem in Figure 13.2: High ratios made the graphs so small that they're almost useless. That happens in the real world, as well. As a compressor applies more volume reduction because of high ratios, the output can get very low.

So all compressors have a way to add amplification to make up for this loss. Technically, it's usually an offset added to the control signal. But it works like an extra amplifier after the volume

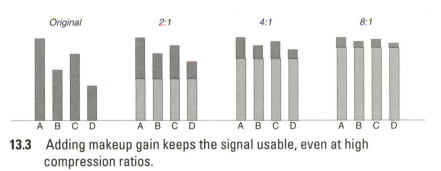

13.3 Adding makeup gain keeps the signal usable, even at high compression ratios.

controller. Figure 13.3 shows it graphically. The dark gray bars are the signals from Figure 13.3. The light gray bars are the *makeup gain*, which stays the same for each ratio no matter how loud the input was. As the ratio goes up, we apply more gain to keep the output up.

Some compressors call this function *Output Gain* or simply *Gain*. Others don't even let the user control it; these vary the gain automatically as you change the other settings.

Threshold

Often, you want to compress only part of a signal. Louder sounds need to be controlled so they don't distort or overwhelm a mix. But softer ones may be fine as they are; compressing them could bring them closer to background noise and room echo. We need a way to tell the compressor when to kick in—what input volume is loud enough to worry about—so it can ignore anything softer.

The dashed line in Figure 13.4 represents the *threshold control*, part of the envelope detector. It's designed so that signals below its level don't produce an envelope at all. Volumes A and C are louder than the threshold, so they get compressed. You can see that A and C's levels are fairly close together after compression. Volumes B and D are below the threshold and don't generate an envelope. They're still affected by makeup gain, so they get amplified a little, but their relative volumes aren't changed. B and D are both much softer than A and C, and D is still softer than B.

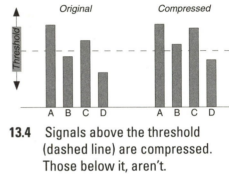

13.4 Signals above the threshold (dashed line) are compressed. Those below it, aren't.

Threshold controls are usually calibrated from 0 dBFS down to –40 dBFS or more. But there are no right settings—even if you know exactly how much compression you want, the proper threshold depends on how loud the original signal is. Good compressors give you a way to tell how much compression is going on, so you can set them properly.

> ⚠️ **Gotcha**
>
> **Threshold madness** If you set the threshold at the top of its range, nothing will be compressed—just as if you'd set the ratio at 1:1. Some programs make this the default.
>
> Again, if a compressor doesn't seem to be doing anything, make sure you've set an appropriate threshold.

Gain Reduction Meter

If we monitor the control voltage, we can actually see the compressor doing its thing. Adding a meter there lets us know how much the volume will be reduced. When the meter is fully up, the control voltage is high, and there's very little compression. As louder sounds go over the threshold, the voltage goes down and so does the volume control circuit. If there's a high ratio, the meter will swing a lot between loud and soft sounds. If there's a low ratio, the meter may hardly move. Figure 13.5 shows where a meter would be applied.

Good compressors have a *gain reduction meter*, calibrated to show how many decibels will be lost in the volume controller.[3] It's an important function, particularly when you're first learning to use a compressor. Subtle amounts of compression, which might cause only –3 dB or –4 dB loss on peaks, can be extremely effective. Yet their very subtlety makes them hard to hear—you can't tell whether the sound is being technically manipulated or whether the original performance had a little more control.

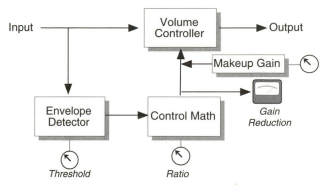

13.5 A compressor with some additional controls and a gain reduction meter. The block called Control Math can be a circuit as well as software. It can be as simple as the inverter in Figure 13.1, or it can be very complex and mimick human hearing in a sophisticated unit.

Even experienced mixers keep one eye on the gain reduction meter while they're adjusting a compressor's controls, and will often glance at it during the mix. Since compression is so dependent on the nature of the incoming sound, engineers often prefer to describe a compressor's settings in terms of how many decibels of gain reduction is occurring and the approximate ratio, rather than a specific threshold setting.

Knee

Below the threshold, there's no compression—a ratio of 1:1. Above the threshold, the compressor uses the ratio you've set. But what happens exactly at the threshold? A sudden switch from zero compression to full ratio can be helpful for certain effects, or with a high ratio can absolutely hold the level to a maximum setting. A gentle transition is more subtle and can add strength to a sound without calling attention to itself.

Some compressors have a *knee* switch or control to adjust the transition. There is no standard calibration, but generally a *soft* knee will let compression start gradually, going from a ratio of 1:1 to whatever you've set, over a range that can be as wide as 10 dB around the threshold. A *hard* knee will make the transition at exactly the threshold.

Compressor Graph

Engineers have another way of looking at what a compressor's doing, and it can be handy for visually oriented filmmakers. If we draw a graph with volume going into the compressor along

---

3. Curiously, SoundForge has gain reduction meters in its multiband compressor but not in its wideband one.

the horizontal and volume coming out along the vertical, we can then plot the action of the compressor as a line. Figure 13.6 shows how it would look.

The two edges are calibrated in dBFS, from –96 dBFS (softest possible sound in a 16 bit system) to 0 dBFS (loudest sound in any digital system). The solid gray line represents a ratio of 1:1. If you track along the bottom to an input level of –40 dBFS, follow up to that line and then across to the left side; you'll see the output is also –40 dBFS. The dashed line represents a 2:1 compressor. An input of –40 dB crosses this line at –68 dBFS[4] ouput. If you don't want to mess with numbers on a graph, just look at the angle of the dashed line. It's 22 degrees, indicating fairly gentle compression.

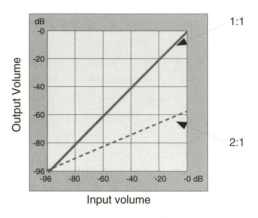

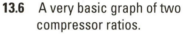

13.6 A very basic graph of two compressor ratios.

The beauty of this kind of graph is that you can also add the other compressor characteristics we've discussed. When you do, you can understand a lot about what a particular bunch of settings will do to a sound. Figure 13.7 shows a practical compressor. Point A is the threshold, where compression first kicks in. For inputs above this level, the ratio is about 10:1 (Figure 13.7B). Below this level, it's 1:1 (Figure 13.7C). But compression starts gradually, with a fairly soft knee at Figure 13.7D. A signal of any level is affected by the makeup gain (Figure 13.7E).

So at a glance, you can see that signals above –40 dBFS will be heavily compressed, and the entire clip will be boosted so its levels hover around –20 dBFS.

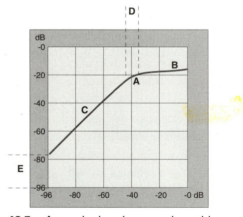

13.7 A graph showing a real-world compressor in use. The text explains what those letters mean.

4. –40 dB input is 56 dB louder than the threshold of –96 dB. That volume change is cut by the 2:1 ratio, becoming 28 dB (half of 56 dB). At 28 dB above the threshold, you have –68 dB. But this footnote is just for the curious reader. You don't need math to interpret a compressor's graph. You can tell just as much by looking at the angle and position of the line.

Compressor reaction time

It's possible to build a compressor which would respond virtually instantly. Such a device would lower the output volume as soon as the input exceeded the threshold, and restore it the moment that the input went below the threshold. It would sound awful.

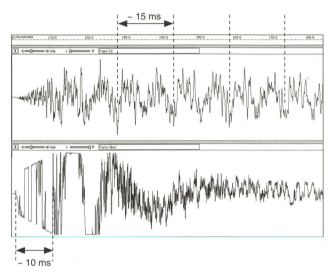

13.8 The repeating fundamental wave of a moderately low piano note (top) is slower than the initial envelope of a pistol shot (bottom).

The problem—as discussed in Chapter 2—is that the only difference between the voltage changes that make up an audio wave and those that we hear as an envelope, is timing. Changes that are faster than 1/20 second are usually considered waves. Slower ones are usually envelopes. But in the range between roughly 1/20 and 1/100 second, there's no way to be sure precisely which a particular voltage change is.[5] The envelope of a pistol shot takes about 10 milliseconds to go from zero to full volume. But even a moderately low note (C2 on a piano, two octaves below middle C) has a fundamental frequency of 65 Hz, meaning each cycle is about 15 ms (see Figure 13.8).

A compressor fast enough to control the pistol would attempt to adjust the piano's volume in time with its fundamental, distorting the sound. A few deep-voiced announcers have serious vocal energy at 100 Hz or below, so these timing issues aren't just for the music-recording crowd.

One solution is to set the threshold carefully, so the piano or voice doesn't get compressed and the pistol does. But this isn't always possible. For more flexibility, a good compressor lets you adjust how quickly it responds to a new loud sound and how long it keeps the volume reduced after the sound subsides. Both settings are important. Using them creatively can even change the nature of a sound.

Attack time   Attack time affects how long it takes the compressor to respond when a sound first exceeds the threshold. A fast attack—some compressors let you set a fraction of a millisecond—can control sharp transient sounds. But it may also cause distortion. A slow attack is less apt to distort, but of course will prevent the compressor from reacting to fast sounds. This can be

---

5. If there are a lot of repeating changes with that kind of timing, you can be sure it's a low-frequency tone.

a useful effect when you want hear the initial part of a sound without having it compete too much in a mix. (The last section of this chapter includes some examples.)

Figure 13.9 demonstrates various attack times. The first envelope is the original signal, a 1 kHz sine wave at –6 dBFS, lasting half a second. The other three envelopes are through a

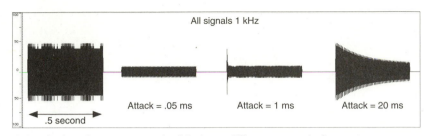

13.9   A signal, compressed with three different attack times.

compressor set with a threshold of –20 dBFS and a ratio of 10:1. For the second envelope, the compressor had an attack time of 0.05 ms. You can see that the compressor completely controlled this signal. But if you listen to the first part of Track 53, you can hear how the short attack time—1/20 of an individual cycle of the test signal—caused significant distortion. The third envelope used an attack time of 1 ms. You can see how one cycle of the signal passed through without compression. But listen to it on the CD: Because 1 ms is too fast for human ears to perceive as a volume change, it has the same volume as the second envelope, only without the distortion. The fourth envelope used an attack time of 20 ms. You can see the volume gradually get lowered. On the CD, this envelope has a pinging quality.

Hear for yourself

The first part of track 53 lets you hear the envelopes in Figure 13.9 and the attack time's effect on the signal. It's more than you'd guess from the picture.

None of the numbers in the preceding paragraph are golden; they're just intended to help you understand how an attack control affects the envelope. Depending on the compressor, attack times can range between a fraction of a second to about one second. Choosing the right timing depends on the signal involved and how other controls are set. You should always tune a compressor by ear.

Release time   All things eventually come to an end, and that includes loud parts of a signal. How a compressor responds after the input drops below the threshold is also critical. You don't want it to return to normal levels too quickly because dynamics can be destroyed and noise may seem to go up.

A moderately slow release can fight the distortion effects of too fast an attack, by keeping the envelope detector from tracking individual waves. In the previous example, we used a release time shorter than a single cycle. If we had raised the release time to about 10 ms—a few cycles of the 1 kHz test signal—there wouldn't have been distortion.

On the other hand, you don't want too slow a response, or else loud sounds can *punch a hole* in the track. Imagine an exterior scene. We hear traffic and birds, but they're not compressed because they're lower than the threshold. Then there's a loud gunshot, followed by a softer scream. If the release time is too slow, the volume controller will stay down after the shot is over, and then slowly recover. The scream will also be turned down—more than is justified by its own volume. And we wouldn't hear the traffic and birds for a moment until the volume control-

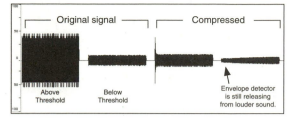

13.10 The first two envelopes are the input signal. The second two envelopes are the result of compression with too slow a release time. You can see how the softer sound, which shouldn't be compressed at all, is affected.

ler returned to its normal level. Figure 13.10 shows this graphically. The first two envelopes are a 1 kHz tone at –6 dBFS, then at –20 dBFS. The second two are identical but run through the compressor used in the previous example. The release time is 500 ms. The compressor successfully controls the –6 dBFS tone, but it doesn't recover in time to properly handle the softer one. It adds a rising envelope that wasn't there originally. Part 2 of Track 53 lets you hear this effect with real-world signals.

Hear for yourself

Part 2 of Track 53 consists of the gunshot, scream, and outdoor tone described above, first compressed with a slow release time, and then with a faster one.

Most compressors let you choose a release time between a few milliseconds and a couple of seconds. Some vary the release time, depending on how much gain reduction was applied, and are calibrated in decibels per second.

Gated compression   If you're applying a lot of compression to location audio, noise can be a problem during pauses. While characters are speaking, their voices rise above the threshold and—depending on the ratio you've chosen—can be reduced 10 dB or more. Naturally, you'd apply makeup gain. After the compressor releases and there's no more gain reduction, the background noise is boosted 10 dB compared to the dialog level.

One solution is to use a *gated compressor*. It has a second threshold control. As soon as the input level falls below the gate's threshold, gain reduction is frozen at its current level. If you're using a moderately slow release time, there'll still be significant reduction, and noise will be controlled. A few gated compressors add a gate release time and *target setting* in negative decibels. If the signal stays below the gate's threshold, gain reduction slowly settles toward the target value.

Don't confuse a compressor's gate with a *noise gate*, described later in this chapter. A compressor's gate is a sophisticated control on high-end processors. A noise gate is a level-triggered switch, used for noise reduction and special effects.

Types of Dynamics Processors

Dynamics processors have evolved to solve different problems. Most NLEs let you choose among a few; a good audio program or collection of plug-ins will have many more. This kind of processing is so useful that a mix theater or audio post suite specializing in broadcast will often have hardware-based units as well as software ones.

But despite the variety, dynamics processors fall into a half-dozen or so specific categories based on their design.

Compressor

A compressor is the basic device described previously. It's generally used to smooth out levels in voice-overs and the overall mix, with an attack time of a few dozen milliseconds, a release between a half-second and a second, a ratio under 10:1, and a threshold that makes the gain reduction bounce around –6 dB—though more aggressive settings may be appropriate for broadcast.

Current pop music styles use a lot of compression on individual tracks and then on the overall mix, but that's a subject for another book (and for considerable discussion at engineering conferences).

Limiter

A limiter's architecture is similar to a compressor's, but it's intended to protect the signal from exceeding a preset maximum. It's used in production to prevent digital clipping or analog overloads, and in broadcast to keep the transmitter within legal limits. For this reason, attack times are typically extremely fast and ratios are high. Release timing is chosen as the best compromise between distortion and avoiding holes in the audio after a loud signal. Sophisticated limiters vary their release time based on the material.

Since digital limiters are often used with thresholds close to 0 dBFS, good ones are designed with internal protection from overloads: The input is reduced by a fixed amount, processing actually occurs at a lower level than you've set but at a higher bit depth to avoid noise, then the output is boosted and dithered to match the input spec. This is transparent to the user, but indicates why limiting may use a different algorithm, and more processing power, than compression.

Limiters are usually the last stage in a processing chain. It's common practice to use a compressor to make a track seem louder and follow it with a limiter for protection.

De-esser

Voice tracks sometimes have problems with excessive sibilance because of bad mic technique, unusual vocal conditions, or being passed through some analog media. The effect is that /s/ sounds, which have the most high frequencies of any phoneme, become emphasized or distorted. Other friction consonants can also present these problems, but it's more rare and usually the result of faulty equipment. An equalizer could be used to reduce those troublesome highs, but this would affect the entire track and make it sound dull. The best solution would be an intelligent equalizer that turns itself on whenever it hears an /s/ and stays out of the circuit at other times.

One way to provide this intelligence is to combine a compressor with a high-pass and low-pass filter, set to a frequency just below the sibilance. Figure 13.11 shows how. High frequency signals, including /s/ sounds, are split off and sent to a compressor with a high threshold, fast attack, and no makeup gain.

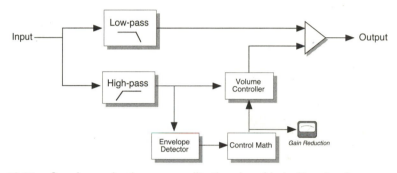

13.11   One form of a de-esser splits the signal in half and only compresses the highs. It works like an intelligent equalizer.

Low frequency signals, including most of a voice's energy, are combined with the compressor's output. A high but average-volume sound doesn't reach the threshold, so it passes through unchanged; when it's combined with the lows, the full spectrum is restored. But loud high-frequency sounds get reduced by the compressor. For just those moments that sibilance is present, the spectrum is tilted away from the highs. Since the /s/ sound had too much high-frequency energy in the first place, the spectrum still sounds normal.

That split-band processing works for dialog-only signals because /s/ sounds are the highest pitches in a voice. But if the voice is mixed with music or broadband sound effects, its timbres will be affected as high frequencies get muted. Fortunately, with a simple circuit or algorithm change, we can turn the intelligent equalizer into an intelligent compressor. It lowers the entire signal when /s/ sounds are present, reducing sibilance but preserving timbre.

In Figure 13.12, the high-pass filter is moved to the input of the envelope detector. As in the split de-esser, only loud, high-frequency sounds will reach the threshold. But the input to the volume controller *isn't* filtered. Once a /s/ triggers the action, the entire spectrum has its volume lowered.

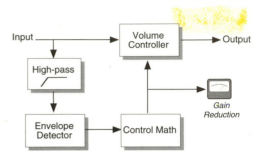

A dynamics processor's envelope detector and control circuit or software is considered its *side chain*, and Figure 13.12 works by filtering the side chain so that only specific frequencies cause an effect. Side chain processing can be very helpful in noise

13.12   A different kind of de-esser compresses the entire signal, but only when there's sibilance.

reduction. (Even though noise reduction is mostly a combination of dynamics processing and equalization, the subject is so important it gets Chapter 16 to itself).

Look-ahead or feed-forward compression

There's a limit to how fast a compressor's attack time can be. A certain number of processor cycles are required to detect loudness, perform the necessary math, and trigger the volume controller. But by treating the side chain differently from the main signal path, we can create a compressor with instantaneous response. In fact, we can even make a compressor that can read the future and start fading *before* a loud sound occurs.

Figure 13.13 shows a compressor with a *delay* in the main signal path, but not in the side chain. Delays are discussed fully in Chapter 15; for now, just consider a delay as a device whose output is exactly the same as the input—but a preset number of milliseconds later. Loud sounds are detected by the side chain in realtime, telling the volume controller to apply gain

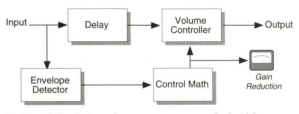

13.13   A lookahead compressor can fade things down before a loud sound occurs.

reduction. But since the main path is delayed, this reduction occurs before the loud sound gets to the controller. If you use a short delay and fast attack time, the level will be turned down just in time to catch the front of a loud sound. If you use longer delay and attack times, the volume can be turned down slowly and subtly before a sudden, loud sound occurs, making a gunshot or thunder clap seem louder because it stands out more from the background.

A delay of a millisecond or two can be sufficient for some look-ahead processing, and this tiny fraction of a frame won't affect perceived lipsync.[6] If you're using a longer delay, of course, you'll want to slide the source clip to compensate: Make it one frame earlier for each 33 milliseconds of delay.

While there are a few hardware-based lookahead compressors available, for some reason they haven't caught on with the plug-in manufacturers. You can simulate the effect for mono signals by duplicating your clip onto two tracks of a stereo file. Slide one track later and call it the delayed main signal. Then run it through a stereo compressor (if there's a stereo link, make sure it's turned on). The nondelayed track gets to the envelope detector first and causes the detector to lower the volume for the delayed track. After processing, discard the nondelayed channel. The ratio and release time have to be chosen carefully because the delayed track is also fed to the envelope detector and can cause two compression actions: one for the original signal and one for the delayed one.

Multiband compressor

Remember disco? That music of the mid-70s was the first style to include a constant, thumping bass. It was great for dancing, but hard to transmit at a radio station. The bass notes were often the loudest thing in the song. They'd trigger the station's compressors, lowering the overall volume. This wasn't a problem at the studio, where there were good monitors to hear the bass. But listeners with portable or desktop radios wouldn't hear the bass, only how it affected the overall volume. The result was a song that rhythmically changed volume for no apparent reason.

The solution was to split the signal into multiple bands, compress each separately, and combine the results—a kind of jumbo extension of the de-esser in Figure 13.11. Bass notes could be controlled without interfering with the midrange, and a loud midrange wouldn't stop the highs from sparkling. This multiband compression changed the spectral balance of the music, letting radio stations create and jealously guard recipes for their own special sound.

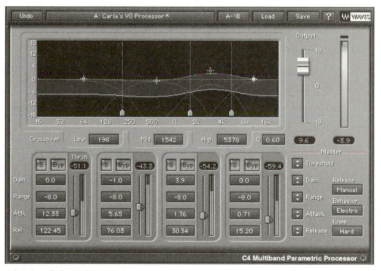

13.14 A four-band dynamics processor—Waves' C4.

The radio station multibands were complex, expensive boxes that also included other processes to maximize a station's volume. But about a decade ago, smaller hardware-based units started

---

6. Each millisecond of delay is approximately equivalent to moving your viewing position 1 foot farther from the TV set. If you customarily sit 8 feet from the set, that's an 8 ms delay.

appearing in production studios. There are now a few available for the desktop producer. Figure 13.14 shows the Waves's C4 plug-in. There are four bands, in this case chosen to separately compress bass, vowel harmonics, consonants, and presence. Most of the controls are what you'd expect on a normal compressor, multiplied by five: one set for each band and a master that scales all four bands. The Range control is roughly equivalent to the ratio, but lets you specify an amount of gain reduction around the threshold.

The parabolic curves in the graphic display of Figure 13.14 show the filter action; as you can see, these are gentle, first-order filters. Anything sharper could introduce swishing sounds as the spectral balance drastically changes.

Multiband processing is used by just about every radio, TV, and major Web broadcaster now. It's also part of the secret behind those in-your-face movie trailer and commercial voices. (The other part is talented announcers.) When combined with a low-distortion signal chain, multiband can be the most important tool for creating consistent, strong mixes that don't sound overly processed.

Noise gate

A compressor works by inverting the envelope and then using it to control volume. But if you replace the inverter with a simple switch that turns on when the input exceeds the threshold, it becomes a *gate*. Loud signals pass through unchanged, but quieter ones are cut off—the audio equivalent of a luminance key. If the threshold is just slightly louder than background noise, the gate opens for dialog and other useful parts of a track, but it closes during pauses and turns off the noise. That's why this device is called a noise gate. Gates are also useful for other things, including controlling multiple mics in a quiet environment[7] and processing sound effects. Some poorly designed digital devices even include a noise gate to hide their own circuit noises.

A few extra functions can make a gate's action more subtle:

⚠ *Gotcha* _____

A gate isn't an eraser. Noise gates don't remove noise. Instead, they count on listeners being distracted by the louder sound that opened the gate. If that sound is loud enough and in the same frequency band as the noise, *masking* takes place, and the noise is hidden. (Masking is used by other forms of noise reduction, and is one of the principles behind mp3.) Unfortunately, most signal-and-noise combinations don't provide this masking. Instead, we're likely to hear the background switching on and off. This can be more distracting than leaving the noise alone.

---

7. Automated mixers, typically used when miking panel discussions, include a noise gate on each input. When somebody isn't speaking, his or her mic shuts off, and overall system noise is lowered.

- A gate's attack and release controls work like the ones on a compressor. You can adjust them to smoothly fade background noise in and out.

- Some gates have adjustable bypass controls, often labeled *floor* or *range* and calibrated in decibels. When the gate closes, it lowers the sound by the range amount. Reducing background noise –10 dB or so can sound more natural than absolute silence.

- Some gates put an equalizer in the side chain. You can tune it so the gate opens only for important sound, like dialog, and stays closed for loud wind noise or camera whine.

- Most hardware gates, and a few software versions, provide external access to the side chain. This *external key* input lets you trigger one sound with another—useful in music production and special effects—or delay the main signal, creating a look-ahead gate that doesn't cut off soft initial sounds like /h/.

A few gates include other functions, including a hold control to keep them from reopening until a preset time has elapsed or separate open and close thresholds. These are rarely needed in audio post.

Expander

An even more subtle cousin of the noise gate is the *expander*. As the name implies, it does the opposite of a compressor. In most units, sounds below the threshold have their dynamic range increased, so that very soft noises are lowered but moderate background ambiences are raised in comparison. Above the threshold, the unit functions like a gate and the sound isn't changed.

Expanders can be better at reducing noise than gates because their action is smoother They let desirable soft sounds mask even softer noise, and—unless you set them to extremes—they never cut the sound off entirely.

This device is also known as a *downward expander*, since its action takes place below the threshold. *Upward expanders* are useful for special effects because they increase dynamic range above the threshold, making loud sounds even louder but not affecting moderate sounds. In theory, an upward expander could be used to cancel out the effects of too much compression or automatic level control in a track, but getting the ratio, threshold, and timing just right would be tricky. Removing any distortion the compressor introduced would be virtually impossible.

Companding

On the other hand, if you design them together, a compressor and upward expander can have absolutely complementary actions. A signal could be compressed, stored or transmitted, and then be effectively uncompressed in the expander. The result would sound the same as the original.

This *companding* is the basis for analog system noise reduction schemes such as Dolby and dbx. Companding lets you send a signal with wide dynamic range, like a digital master, through an inherently noisy channel like cassette tape or optical film sound. Betacam SP video—the professional standard for analog video—also uses companding on its main audio tracks. But there's no reason to use these schemes with digital media.

A form of companding is also used in the popular mp3 and AAC digital file compression algorithms. Audio is broken into short chunks,[8] and the volume of each chunk is boosted to work in the algorithm's best range. The amount of boost is noted for each chunk, and on playback the volume is set back to the original level. But there's a lot more to these algorithms, described in Chapter 19.

Dynamics Cookbook

The best settings for a compressor or expander depend on how loudly the source material was recorded, how dynamic the performance was, and even some design choices within the software. So take these recipes with a grain of salt. Use them more as suggestions for how a process could work, and listen to how they worked in the before-and-after examples on the CD.

💿 *Hear for yourself*

Tracks 54 through 61 are before-and-after examples for this section. They're described with the individual recipes.

---

8. They're called *frames*, but they're not 1/30 of a second. The actual timing varies with the bitrate.

Working with Voices

Production audio

Track 54, part 1, is a well-recorded lav track from a documentary. The male speaker has uneven dynamics which could make him difficult to mix with music, or cause problems with limited-range media like TV and Web audio.

- Part 2 of that track shows the result of moderate compression. The ratio was 4:1, and the threshold was set for about –6 dB gain reduction on peaks; in this example, its about –13 dBFS. The attack was about 1 millisecond, but a 300 ms release prevented the fast attack from causing distortion. There is reasonably low background noise in the original, but the compression makes the background comparatively louder.

- Part 3 of that track uses downward expansion to control the background noise. Compression is turned off for this example. The threshold is chosen to be just below his softest words, in this case around –40 dBFS. Attack is about 1.5 ms, release 50 ms, and a –10 dB floor prevents noise from totally disappearing, which would sound unnatural.

- Part 4 uses the compression followed by the expansion. This version makes our subject seem stronger, makes the location cleaner, and will be easier to mix. But the differences are subtle. After you listen, go back to part 1 and compare.

Track 55, part 1, is a poorly recorded documentary track. The shooter used a camera mic (almost always a bad idea). Since the subject is far from the mic, noise is relatively louder. The similar distances from mic to subject and mic to reflective surfaces emphasizes the room's echo. The first step in cleaning it should be to use an equalizer to dip the room's resonant frequencies and notch out the noise, and to add some low-frequency energy back to the voice. But we'll skip that step for this chapter and concentrate on dynamics.

- Part 2 of Track 55 shows how a downward expander can partially hide room echoes as well as reduce apparent noise. Again, the threshold should be just below the softest words; in this case its about –33 dBFS. The floor is increased to –25 dBFS from the previous settings. Since that makes the expander work over a wider range, there's a chance the background noises will click if they turn on or off quickly. So the attack and release time are doubled, to about 3 ms and 100 ms respectively.

Listen carefully to part 2. The room problems are reduced during pauses, but they're still present when the subject is speaking. If a track has moderate echoes, this technique can make the echoes less annoying. But if there are extreme echoes, they'll still interfere with intelligibility during the words, even if you cut the echoes off entirely during the pauses.

While these examples use documentary audio, the voice work is similar in narrative films and dialog for broadcast can be treated the same way. Dialog for theatrical use is often processed a lot less. It's usually shown in a quiet auditorium using a wide-range monitor system, with an audience that's concentrating on the film, so there's less worry about softer words being lost. Frequently, only a little limiting is used for protection: Set a threshold around –2 dBFS, a ratio of at least 20:1, an attack in the single-millisecond range, a release of a few dozen milliseconds, and a hard knee. If the processor has a looka-head feature, use it.

Voice-over

Announcers and narrators are usually recorded in quiet, low-echo environments. They also frequently have better control over their dynamics than interview subjects do, but compression can still smooth things out and add strength to their voices.

Track 56, part 1, is a newscast-style documentary voice-over. While the announcer has a fairly even level, she tends to stress words with volume as well as pitch.

- Part 2 fixes the stressing tendency with a compressor. The threshold is set around –12 dBFS, enough for 4 or 5 dB reduction on peaks. Ratio is 10:1, attack is about a millisecond, and—since her voice isn't particularly deep—release is around 10 ms. A male voice would require a release time double that.

- Part 3 shows extreme compression. It destroys most of the dynamics of her voice, but can be useful for special effects (add appropriate filters and it can be a radio or telephone for diegetic sounds) or to help intelligibility in poor playback situations. The ratio is 20:1, and the threshold moved to –35 dB—low enough that there's about –24 dB reduction for most of the words in this example. Attack is 2 ms, release is 35 ms. Although we want a fast response, these longer times are necessary because there's so much more gain reduction than in the previous settings.

- Part 4 shows the effect of a de-esser on her voice. The signal was split at about 4.5 kHz, with a Q around 0.5. Low frequencies were passed unchanged, so there's very little apparent compression on her voice. High frequencies were processed with a ratio of 8:1 and about –6 dB reduction on sibilants—in this case, a threshold of –28 dB. Attack was 1 ms, release was 5 ms; since we're dealing with highs only, there's no worry of distortion because of too fast a response time.

Multiband

If you've got a multiband processor available, you can get more subtle control that results in stronger tracks without obvious compression. Start with crossover frequencies at 200 Hz and 2 kHz for a male voice, 300 Hz and 2 kHz for a female. Attack and release times should be around 1.5 ms and 1.4 seconds respectively, on the low band, 0.7 ms and 1 second on the midband, and 0.7 ms and 750 ms on the high band. Use a ratio of 2:1, but a threshold that results in as much as –10 dB reduction on peaks.

If the multiband also includes expansion, you can clean up soft room noises and echoes at the same time. Use a 1:4 ratio, a −18 dB floor, 0.3 ms attack and 300 ms release, and set the threshold sufficient for the expander to act only between words. Even with the fast attack time, look ahead helps avoid clipped words and makes threshold setting less critical.

Music

Generally, compressing preproduced music isn't the most successful way to keep it from fighting a voice. The piece was compressed when it was mixed, and further processing will hurt the dynamics that make it interesting.[9]

If music and voice are competing to the point that you can't mix the music as loud as you'd like, compress the voice. Then use some of the equalization techniques in the previous chapter. If it still competes, chances are the rhythms are conflicting. Sometimes, sliding voice or music half a dozen frames is all that's necessary to fix it. Otherwise, try editing the music differently or choose a different piece.

But some pieces of music—particularly acoustic and traditional rock—may be too dynamic for your mix, and some compression will be necessary.

- Part 1 of Track 57 is the waltz from chapter 10,[10] compressed to remove some of its schmaltzier expression. The ratio was 8:1, and a threshold of −18 dBFS on this piece gave between −6 and −12 dB reduction on peaks. The attack was 2 ms, and the release about half a second.

- Part 2 is the rock song from that chapter,[11] compressed to smooth out levels in the intro and to take the drums down a bit. Ratio was 10:1, and threshold was −20 dBFS; this resulted in about −12 dB reduction during the intro, and −24 dB on the drum hits. An attack time of 2 ms preserved the front edge of the drums—it could be as slow as 4 ms—and a release time of about 90 ms kept the drums from punching holes in the melody.

Sound Effects

Compressors and expanders or gates are helpful for changing the nature of sound effects, either to achieve heightened realism or to create nonrealistic *designed* sounds.

---

9. Compressing original music is another subject, much too big for this book. Look for a copy of David Moulton's *Total Recording*.

10. "Ranza Waltz" excerpt (arranged by C. Jack/D. Aran), DeWolfe CD 288/26. © DeWolfe Music. This and the following piece are used by permission.

11. "Toot, Root, Shoot" excerpt (A. Hamilton/B. Lang), DeWolfe CD 225/11. © DeWolfe Music.

Track 58 shows how this can work with a recording of a mortar (a type of cannon).[12] Part 1 is the original recording. We're standing fairly close to the mortar, and then we hear a distant echo.

- Part 2 is the mortar, compressed. While the firing sound is the same, it seems to last longer because the initial reverb is increased. The distant echo is boosted to the point that it sounds like the explosion of the mortar hitting its target. The ratio is 6:1 and the threshold is −40 dBFS, enough to cause about 25 dB reduction on the initial firing. The attack is 30 ms, slow enough to retain some crunch; the release is 12 ms so the firing doesn't cause a hole.

- Part 3 is the mortar, downward expanded to keep only the firing sound. Without any echo, it seems more like a drum than a weapon. A fairly high threshold, −6 dBFS in this case, assures that most of the sound will be lost. The floor is a low 48 dB. A very fast attack, 0.01 ms (with look ahead), keeps the initial attack. The release is about 50 ms. You can also hear a tiny hit about 3/4 second after the firing, where the initial echo exceeded the threshold. If this expander had a retrigger time limit,[13] we could have lengthened that setting to avoid the hit. But it's easy to just take out the sound with an edit.

The same principle can also work on background sounds. Track 59 is an interior ambience from a railroad car. With a little dynamics control, you can change its nature to make it easier to mix. Part 1 is the original sound. There are distinct mechanical noises around :05, :07, and :12.

- Part 2 uses a compressor to smooth over those noises. They're still there, but won't distract from dialog now. The ratio was 6:1, and threshold was −8 dBFS, enough to compress about −6 dB at each noise but only have about −1 dB reduction the rest of the time. Attack was 5 ms, and release was 12 ms—timings that could cause distortion on low frequencies, but the noises are midrange. Making sure the noises were caught is more important than avoiding an occasional distortion.

- Part 3 takes a different approach to improving the sound's ability to fit in a mix. A downward expander with a fairly high threshold suppresses most of the train's background and emphasizes the occasional noises. This downward expander would let you mix the effect hotter in a scene with music, or you could carefully cut effects to avoid conflicts with dialog. Threshold was −10 dBFS, floor was −40 dB, attack and release were both 10 ms.

Track 60 shows how dynamics control can change the nature of footsteps.

- Part 1 is a man's footsteps—leather shoes on a pine floor.

- Part 2 uses a noise gate to turn the steps into high heels. Threshold is −8 dBFS, attack is a very fast 0.01 ms (with look ahead), release is 100 ms. A little echo would help the illusion.

---

12. The unprocessed sounds in this section are © The Hollywood Edge, and used by permission.

13. Found in some music-studio gates. Adjusting the retrigggger time limits lets the gate open only on major beats.

- Part 3 is walking on gritty concrete while wearing running shoes.

- Part 4 takes the gritty concrete effect and uses a compressor to make the concrete a lot dirtier. A threshold of −35 dB (it's a soft effect) and ratio of 12:1 results in about −6 dB reduction on each step. An attack of 10 ms lets the initial hit through, and a release of 300 ms lets the gain return toward the end of the step to let us hear extra grit as the sole of the shoe pushes the concrete. A faster release, around 100 ms, could make things even dirtier.

Track 61 is an old production-studio effect that shows how a slow attack time can change the nature of a crash. Part 1 is a cymbal being hit with a stick. Part 2 is the same recording, only now it sounds like the instrument is being rolled with a brush. A compressor extends the original sound by making its envelope more rectangular: ratio is 12:1 and threshold is −30 dBFS (almost −36 dB reduction on the hit); it has a 0.01 ms attack and 300 ms release. Then a gate is set to trigger on the hit (−4 dBFS threshold), but the attack is a full second. This fades up on the cymbal sound instead of letting the hit through. Even though the cymbal is a musical instrument, the gate turns it into an effect. A similar process could be used on any other extended sound when you want to remove the initial hit.

Overall Mix Processing

If all your elements are properly equalized and compressed where necessary, very little overall dynamics processing is necessary for a theatrical mix. On the other hand, mixes for more restricted media—broadcast, generalized Web, and VHS—can often profit from a 2.5:1 ratio and −3 dB gain reduction with a 30 ms attack and about a half-second release. This is gentle enough to keep the dynamics of the mix intact, while bringing midlevel sounds closer to the maximum. If a project is aimed at laptop computers, a 6:1 ratio and -12 dB reduction with those timings can be appropriate.

My favorite process for busy TV commercial mixes—which should be loud, but never sound compressed—is to use a sharp, high-pass filter at 75 Hz followed by a 3-band compressor. The crossover frequencies are set at 200 Hz and 3.5 kHz. Ratio is 4:1 for the bass and 2.5:1 for the mids and highs, with a threshold sufficient for about −6 dB gain reduction during loud passages. Since it's rare that more than one band has that much reduction at any one time, things don't sound squashed. Attack is 30 ms for the lows and 20 ms for the mids and highs; release is 750 ms for the lows and 350 ms for the mids and highs.

It's a good idea to apply limiting to any mix. The threshold is determined by the medium, and can range from −1 dBFS for computer media to −10 dBFS for professional videotape formats. The attack should be as fast as possible, with a release around 30 ms. This is a safety valve, and very little of the mix should ever reach the threshold—if the limiter triggers more than once every half-minute or so, lower the input level. Since there's so little activity except for rare peaks, don't worry about the fast response times causing low-frequency distortion.

Chapter 14

Time-Domain Effects

Remember this:

- A precisely timed delay can drastically reduce dimmer buzz and other power-line noises—but at a cost.

- Delays that automatically vary timing, common in music production, are also useful for soundtrack design.

- Artificial reverb can be an effect, or it can also sound perfectly natural and realistic—once you understand how to control it.

The equalizers and compressors described in previous chapters are primarily corrective devices, and most of the time they are used to subtly enhance a sound rather than call attention to themselves. On the other hand, time-domain effects—long and short delays, and reverberation—are often in your face. You know they're there.

Reverberation is, of course, a natural part of life and art. The ancient Greeks were aware of how it affected intelligibility in their theaters; classical composers wrote differently for small spaces than for giant cathedrals largely because of the differences in echoes.

But artificial reverb had to wait for talking motion pictures. Producers noticed that the close miking necessary with early equipment was unrealistically free from reverb and didn't appear to match the camera angle. So they built large, hard-walled rooms on the lot, fed the dialog to a speaker in those rooms, and picked up the echoes with another mic.[1] These *echo chambers* were used for special effects in radio as well, but because the echo chambers were expensive real estate, substitute echo chambers often had to be improvised. (It's said that when Orson Welles created his famous *War of the Worlds* broadcast, he achieved the echo on some sound effects by having them performed in a nearby tile bathroom.)

---

1. In another Hollywood convention that defied physics, producers of early talkies decided that exterior scenes had to have more reverb than interiors. Why? Because everybody *knows* there are echoes outdoors—even though you seldom hear them, and when you do, they're nothing like what you'd get from a mic in a hard-walled room.

Since echo chambers weren't practical for a lot of situations, they were replaced by suspended springs or thin metal plates that were coupled to a speaker mechanism on one end and a contact microphone on the other. The delay of a large acoustic space was simulated by forcing sound through a very long tube filled with air,[2] recording it and then immediately playing it back on a loop of magnetic tape, or even through a strange electro-mechanical device that stored small chunks of analog audio in a circle of upright capacitors: An arm swept across the top of the device, transferring charges from one capacitor to the next.

Digital reverb was invented in 1959, but only as a lab curiosity. A one-minute piece of audio could take a full day to process. It was another dozen years before practical all-electronic delays were available. These used a chip which emulated the circle of capacitors and rotating arm (the charge coupled device, a variation of which picks up the video in your camera). But delay is only a part of artificial reverb. It wasn't until the mid-70s that the first electronic studio reverb was born, the EMT 250—a hulking device the size of a small file cabinet, with spaceship-like levers on top.

Today, a variety of excellent sounding low-cost delays and reverbs are available as software plug-ins and DSP-driven hardware. Some of the more expensive versions can even analyze a test signal played in a concert hall or shooting stage, and then generate a near-perfect clone of the room's characteristic reverb in software. But even the simpler delays and reverbs that came with your NLE can be useful:

- While boom mic operators are careful to pick up a mix of the room's natural echoes along with dialog, artificial reverb is necessary to make lav or ADR dialog sound right.

- Reverb can be used to spread sounds out in implied physical space—even on a mono track—giving you more ways to keep sounds from competing in a mix.

- Delays can be used as a filter to almost completely eliminate some kinds of noise (though this will damage some of the desired sound).

- Both reverb and delay can be used as special effects, ranging from subtle enhancements that make a sound seem to be moving, to outright science-fiction or underwater effects.

Reverb *versus* Echo *versus* Delay

Reverb, echo, and delay are not the same thing.

---

2. The speed of sound is roughly one foot per millisecond. It takes 1/10 of a second to travel 100 feet, regardless of whether it's across a parking lot or in a coiled garden hose with a speaker at one end and a microphone at the other.

Reverberation is the collection of thousands of random reflections that real-world spaces contribute to a sound, or it's a simulation that includes specific kinds of individual and blurred repeats. As you can guess, good reverb software is very complex.

Echo is a series of evenly spaced repeats that get softer and softer. It doesn't sound like natural reverb. On the other hand, it's very simple to create and might not require specialized software at all.

Delay is a simple, single repeat of a sound. With some tweaks and additional functions, it can be an incredibly useful effect.

The Short Delays

A single repeat of a sound, about 20 ms shorter than the original, may not get heard as an echo at all. Instead, it can blend with the original and change it in interesting ways. By constantly changing the exact delay time, mixing it with other delays, and letting the delay repeat (by routing some of its output back to the input), we can create a family of fascinating effects.

Comb Filter

Imagine a sine wave at a fixed frequency. If you mix it with a delayed version of itself, precisely one-half cycle later, the delayed version will be positive while the original is negative. It will cancel itself out. Figure 14.1 shows how this could happen with a 1 kHz wave and a version delayed one-half millisecond later. On the top is the original signal; in the middle is the delayed version; the sum of the two is on the bottom. Except for that first half cycle before the delayed version starts, the result is silence.

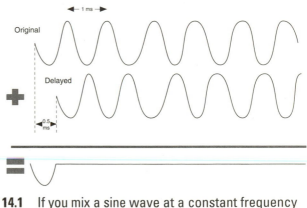

14.1   If you mix a sine wave at a constant frequency with a version that's been delayed one-half cycle, the result is silence. Only the first half-cycle, before the delay is added, is left—and that's usually irrelevant.

The interesting thing about this effect is that it works for any regular signal, even ones that are rich with harmonics. The delay effectively creates a series of nulls and boosts, extending across the audio band. Figure 14.2 is a spectragram of *pink noise*, a random air-rushing sound that has equal energy in each octave and is frequently used as a test signal. On the left side of the figure is the original noise. On the right, I've mixed in a 5 ms delayed version of the noise. The dark lines are the frequencies that have been completely filtered out.

14.2   Pink noise on the left; the same noise combined with a 5 ms delayed version of itself on the right. You may notice that the pattern of this supposedly random noise seems to repeat every half second. Many digital noise generators do that to save computing power

These lines appear to get closer as the frequency increases, but that's only because the spectragram has a logarithmic scale. If you match the lines to the numbers, you'll see that they're every 200 Hz (starting with 100 Hz). If the frequency scale were linear, they'd be as evenly spaced as the teeth of a barber's comb—and that's how this filter got its name.[3]

The location of a comb filter's notches can be predicted with grade-school math. The first notch is at a frequency equal to one-half of the delay in seconds. For our five millisecond example, that's 1/0.010 (one millisecond = 0.001 second, in case you'd forgotten), or 100 Hz. Every subsequent notch is spaced twice that frequency higher. Twice 100 Hz is 200 Hz, so the next notches are at 300 Hz, 500 Hz, 700 Hz, 900 Hz, and so on.

Hum elimination using a comb

Unlike a traditional equalizer, a comb filter can be sharp without doing damage at other frequencies (except the sound of the delay itself may be audible). This can make it useful for getting rid of constant pitch, harmonically rich signals, such as power-line or dimmer buzz under dialog. These annoying noises have lots of upper harmonics from the 60 Hz line frequency, but a notch every 120 Hz can nail them. You could create those notches by mixing the signal with a delay of

---

3. Not as an abbreviation for "combination filter," as I've heard some people insist.

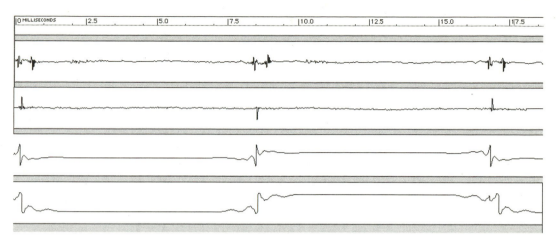

14.3 Power line related buzzes can look like these waves. They'll always repeat every 16.66 ms, with a subpattern halfway between.

8.333 ms. The first notch would be at 240 Hz. There often aren't any components at lower frequencies; but if there were, you could get rid of them with a parametric equalizer.

The problem is a comb's notches are so narrow that absolute precision is necessary when setting it. Most desktop software won't let you specify a delay setting to the thousandth of a millisecond. On top of that, there can be tiny variations in the camera's or NLE's sample rate which would affect the frequency of the buzz. So it's unlikely you could turn a desktop delay into a comb that would eliminate the buzz. But there is a workaround:

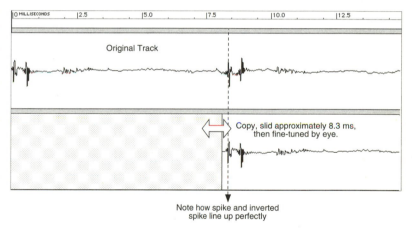

14.4 Using two tracks of an audio program to simulate a comb filter, you can tune exactly to the power-line frequency.

1. Open the noisy track in a multi track audio software.

2. Select and copy the entire audio, and paste it onto a second track.

3. Zoom in on both tracks until you can see individual waves of the buzzing. Depending on the nature of the noise, the waves may be a wide repeating pattern, or they may just be periodic spikes. But you should see some feature repeating just about every 16 ms, with a similar feature facing the opposite direction halfway in between. Figure 14.3 shows some examples.

4.   Slide the second track about 8.3 ms. Then adjust its position by eye, so the inverted feature lines up precisely under the noninverted one (Figure 14.4). Dropping a marker across both tracks can serve as a guideline.

5.   Mix the two tracks together at equal volume. If you've done step 4 properly, the hum should virtually disappear—as it does in Track 62.

The process isn't perfect (which is why it's always better to eliminate buzzes before you shoot). The 8.3 ms delay is almost long enough for the ear to hear as an echo, and it adds a metallic hollowness to the track. You can reduce the hollowness, if you're willing to put a little of the buzz back, by lowering the delayed track –3 dB before you mix. By the way, you'd do the same steps in countries with 50 Hz power—but look for patterns repeating every 20 ms and slide the copied track 10 ms.

🎵 *Hear for yourself* _____

Track 62 is an interview track with considerable dimmer buzz—it's actually the clip shown in Figure 14.4—before and after applying the comb, and then with the comb lowered –3 dB.

Flanger

Imagine a comb filter where you could constantly vary the delay. The notches would keep moving, imparting a *swooshing* to the audio. In fact, you've heard this effect countless times in pop music and science-fiction films (and you can hear it again on part 3 of Track 63).

The effect predates digital delays by close to 20 years. It was originally accomplished by using two identical tape recorders. Professional tape decks have a separate playback head after the record head, so the engineer can monitor the quality of a recording. Since the two heads can't occupy the same space, there's a slight delay in the monitor output while the tape travels between the heads, between 60 ms and 400 ms, depending on the model and tape speed. Of course, changing the speed changes the delay.

The same signal would be sent to the two recorders, and their monitor outputs were then mixed. Then an engineer would drag a few fingers on the outer flange of only one of the tape reels. The more pressure on the flange, the more that recorder would slow down, and the delay would get longer relative to the other recorder. By varying the pressure, the engineer could make the comb slide up and down the band. It added an extra moving tonality to the sound without changing the pitch. Logically enough, the technique came to be known as *flanging*.

Figure 14.5 shows a modern flange effect. The solid lines are audio paths; the dashed ones are the control. Essentially, the original signal is mixed with a delayed version of itself. One knob lets you set the basic delay time, usually in a range around 0.5–100 ms. The *modulation speed* controls a *low-frequency oscillator* (*LFO*) in a range from about 0.1 Hz (one cycle in ten seconds) to a few hertz. This slow wave modifies the basic delay time in a range set by the *modulation depth* control, usually calibrated in hertz or percent. If the basic delay were 10 ms, the modulation speed were 1 Hz, and the depth were 4 ms, for example, the actual delay time would change once per second from 6 ms to 14 ms and back.

A *mix control* sets the proportion of original signal to delayed, so you can change the depth of the notches. It's usually calibrated from 0 (no delay) through 100 percent (all delay with no original). A *feedback control* lets some of the delayed signal recirculate through the delay, which can intensify the effect. It's often calibrated from –100 percent through zero to +100 percent, because negative feedback—with the waveform inverted—can sound different from positive feedback.

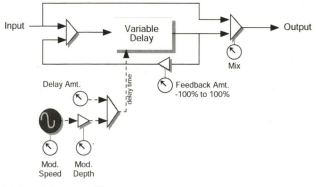

14.5 A flange effect.

Not every *flanger* has all these features, but good ones will have most of them. A few add a switch to control the LFO waveform; a sine wave will have a different sound from one shaped like a square, triangle, or sawtooth. One or two flangers feature an optional second delay to replace the direct path from input to output; this simulates the fixed-speed tape recorder. The flangers supplied with NLEs may have only a limited number of controls,[4] so its worth shopping for additional plug-ins or using an audio program.

Here are some settings to give you an idea of what a flanger can do. All of them can be heard on Track 63. Part 1 of that track is unprocessed voice and music samples for reference.

- To add vibrato to a voice (Track 63, part 2), set the delay to 2 ms, the speed to 6.5 Hz, the depth to 5 percent, and the mix to 100 percent.

- For classic *wooshing* on music or effects (part 3), use a lot of feedback. Set delay to 0 ms, speed to 0.15 Hz, depth to 10 percent, mix to 50 percent, and feedback to 90 percent. Try it with feedback at –90 percent as well.

- A more subtle woosh, with no feedback, can add motion to sound effects. Part 4 of the track is a steady helicopter exterior, with no processing. But with some flanging (part 5), you can make the helicopter move. Settings were 0 ms delay, 0.1 Hz speed, 10 percent depth, 50 percent mix, and no feedback.

---

4. Premiere's factory-supplied Flanger is somewhat stripped of controls. But its *Multieffect* is really a sophisticated flanger.

- To put voices underwater (part 6), use a 4 ms delay, 1.5 Hz speed, 15 percent depth, 100 percent mix, and no feedback. If your flanger lets you select a triangle waveform, use it. A small amount of reverb can heighten this effect.

While these are the settings I used for the CD examples, subtle changes in any of them may produce a sound more compatible with your source material.

 Hear for yourself

Track 63 demonstrates flanging effects on voice, music, and sound effects.

Chorus

Imagine a telescoping trough that lets you change its length, while sending a steady stream of ball bearings into it (Figure 14.6, top). There'll be a delay before the first ball comes out, because it has to travel the length of the trough. Then balls will start coming out at the same rate as they went in, assuming the trough stays the same length. But if you start extending the trough (Figure 14.6, middle), the output slows down because each ball has to travel slightly farther than the ball before it. Once the trough settles at its new length (Figure 14.6, bottom), the output resumes its normal speed.

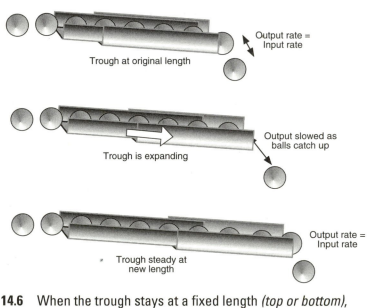

14.6 When the trough stays at a fixed length *(top or bottom)*, balls come out at the same rate as they go in. But while you're expanding the trough *(middle)*, each ball has to travel slightly farther than the one before it—and the output slows down.

Replace the ball bearings with individual samples and the trough with digital memory, and you've got a delay. While you are increasing the length of the delay, output samples slow down and the pitch lowers. If you decrease the length of the delay, each sample has to travel a shorter path than the sample before, and they come out faster—the pitch goes up. That's how the vibrato effect above works. With the mix control set to 100 percent, there isn't any comb filtering, but the LFO constantly changing the delay length makes the voice warble in pitch.

⚠ **Gotcha** _____

Pitch shift? Well then, turn me into Darth Vader... Sorry, Luke. A flanger or chorus-based pitch shift that could smoothly knock your voice down an octave or more would require a constantly growing delay. Your computer would run out of memory. You could get a pitch change by using a sawtooth wave in the LFO: It would stretch the delay length, lowering the pitch. It would snap back to the original length instantly, and then start stretching again. But the snap from long back to short would throw away a lot of samples already in the pipeline, and cause periodic glitches in the signal.

There are ways to avoid this glitching, but that's for Chapter 15.

Take a bunch of flangers, eliminate the feedback loops, and make tiny variations in their LFO frequencies, and you can simulate the tiny pitch variations that happen when a group of people sing the same note. You could turn one voice into many. That's why it's called a *chorus* effect. Figure 14.7 shows one way of putting a chorus effect together (there are other architectures, but they all sound pretty much the same). Each LFO runs at a slightly different speed, partly determined by the master speed control. A *range* control, usually 1–100 percent, sets how much speed variation there'll be. If it's set to a low value, the LFOs all run at about the same speed; at a high value, they can be very different.

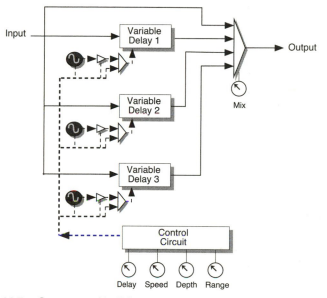

14.7 One way of building a chorus effect.

Here are a few chorus recipes:

- Track 64, part 1 shows a basic chorus effect on speech. You can hear the original voice in the middle with two phantom voices, at slightly different pitches, on the sides. Part 2 is the same process as a mono effect. It sounds something like an echo, but there's still that pitch variation. Part 3 shows the process on music; chorusing is often used to thicken a vocal soloist. The settings were 10 ms delay, 0.16 Hz rate, 10 percent depth, 70 percent range, and 45 percent mix.

- Part 4 could work as the introduction to a dream sequence. It uses more delay and a faster LFO to spread the phantom voices' pitch and timing unrealistically. Set to 100 ms delay,

> ⚠ *Gotcha* _____
>
> *It doesn't sound like a choir to me.* Chorus is a fairly simple process and too unchanging to be absolutely realistic. If you want to make one person sound like a real crowd, you also have to include random and subtle changes in the pitch and timing of each voice relative to the others. It takes a lot of computing. We'll describe such an effect in Chapter 15.

3.5 Hz rate, 8 percent depth, 15 percent range, and 25 percent mix. Or start with 0 percent mix and gradually raise it as the character goes into his dream.

- While chorus is usually used for music production or special vocal processing, I've found it can be wonderful on steady sound effects. It makes them bigger, without the distancing or blurring that reverb can cause. Listen to part 5 of Track 64. The first sound is the unflanged

💿 *Hear for yourself* ___
Track 64 demonstrates various chorus effects.

helicopter used earlier in this chapter. The second is the same effect with a chorus. Instead of being next to the chopper, the blades now surround us! Use a 2.5 ms delay, 2 Hz rate, 25 percent depth, 20 percent range, and 50 percent mix.

Long Delays

There are actually two differences between the flanger or chorus discussed above, and longer *delays* (also known as *digital delay lines* or *DDLs*). One difference is obviously the length of delay, though the lengths can overlap: The effects in the previous section cover between 0–100 ms, and these delays usually run 10 ms to about half a second. The other difference is architecture. A long delay line

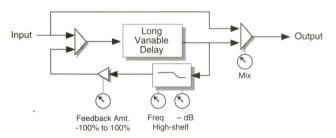

14.8 A delay line. Unlike the previous effects, there's often no LFO. But there is a shelf equalizer to lower high frequencies in the feedback loop.

may or may not have an LFO for modulation, but it should include a high shelf equalizer in the feedback loop. The shelf is usually calibrated between about −36 dB and 0 dB loss, with no boost possible, to simulate the loss to friction as high frequencies travel over long distances of air. Figure 14.8 shows the configuration of most delay lines.

It's the feedback loop that makes a delay useful in computerized audio production (without it, you could accomplish the same thing by simply sliding a copy of the track later). Since delay times are almost always long enough for the output to be heard as separate from the input, feedback lets you keep recycling a sound for multiple repeats. This effect is used a lot in music production, with delay times chosen to match the song's rhythm. Some very long delays are even used for live improvisational music: The performer plays a pattern into a DDL, sets it to keep repeating forever, and then jams over it.

The feedback is calibrated from –100 percent to +100 percent. Negative numbers invert the polarity of the audio, which can change the overall effect when the delayed version is mixed with the input.

- Track 65 part 1 plays our two musical examples through a rhythmic repeat. The delay is about 500 ms (this value works fine for the first song in the montage, but is obviously wrong for the second). Other settings were –50 percent feedback, 85 percent mix, and the filter was –3.5 dB at 15 kHz to prevent hiss buildup.

Infinite, identical repeats are not that useful in audio post; even if they were, it's easy to accomplish them with successive paste operations on a timeline. That's where the equalizer and feedback amount controls come in. You can adjust them so each repeat is a little softer, duller, or both. It's a lot like an acoustic sound bouncing between two distant surfaces. After a while, the repeats become soft enough that they get lost under other sounds.

Delays are useful for creating reverbration for outdoor environments, where there are often a few distinct echoes from large buildings or geologic features, rather than the kind of reverberation you'd hear in an enclosed space. Start with a rough guess as to how far that reflecting surface would be in feet, and dial that number into the delay in milliseconds. If there's also supposed to be a surface behind you, add a little feedback.

- With a lot of feedback and very short times, delays can act as resonant combs. This adds a metallic edge to a voice, much like C3PO's in *Star Wars*. Listen to part 2 of Track 65, and then create the effect yourself with a 10 ms delay, 75 percent feedback, 90 percent mix, and no equalization.

- A properly tuned delay can emulate some of the low-budget attempts at artificial reverb, such as tape-based echo. It was a favorite trick at radio stations in the 60s and 70s, and required a tape deck with separate record and playback heads. A little of the delayed playback would be mixed with the signal being fed to the deck, causing a repeating echo that got softer over time. The sound would also get duller, as high frequencies were lost in the usually misadjusted tape deck. Part 3 of Track 65 shows this effect with a moderately high tape speed; it uses a 95 percent mix, 90 ms delay, 35 percent feedback, and –13 dB loss at 10 kHz. Part 4 is at a slower tape speed; the delay is changed to 180 ms and the equalization to –24 dB at 6 kHz.

Of course, that tape echo doesn't sound like the live reverberation in a concert hall or even the simulation in a good software plug-in. That's because reverb is a complicated process.

Reverberation

You're in a concert hall, perhaps 50 feet from the middle of the stage. A percussionist on the middle of the stage strikes a wood block. We'll round off the speed of sound to keep things simple, and assume it travels 1000 feet per second[5] (or 1 foot per millisecond). So 50 ms later, you hear the *tock*.

But that's not all you hear:

- The sound spreads out from the wood block in all directions. Concert halls usually have reflective walls surrounding the stage area, so the music is focused towards the audience. Perhaps the *tock* hits the rear wall of the stage, 20 feet behind the player, and then bounces back to you. You hear this softer sound 90 ms after it's played—50 ms after you hear the first *tock* (20 ms to the rear wall, then 70 ms from the rear wall to you). The sound also hits the sides of the stage and bounces to you. Maybe it goes a little farther—it's a wide stage—and you hear an even softer *tock* at 115 ms. If you're not standing on the centerline of the hall, you'll be closer to one wall than the other, so there'll be an echo from the more distant stage wall a little later. And don't forget sounds reflected by the ceiling, floor, and walls of the concert hall itself.

- Sounds don't stop at your ear. They continue into the room, where they bounce off other surfaces before returning to you. But by now there are so many different-length paths involved that the reflections arrive too close together for your ear to tell them apart. They merge into a single, long sound. If the concert hall was well designed, the merged sound would be a warm and pleasing one that flatters the wood block.

- Soon, air friction and human bodies in the hall will absorb the sound's energy to the point where you can't hear it any more. That flattering reverberation dies out or is obscured by newer sounds coming from the stage.

The 50 ms it takes the first direct sound to reach you isn't considered part of the sound. While it can be important for video, if there's a tight shot of the wood block and you want lipsync (stick-sync?), it's not something we hear.

But the time between the direct sound and the first reflection—40 ms in this case—gives us a hint of the size of the room. It's called the *initial delay* or *predelay*,[6] and reverb software should give you control over it.

---

5. That's about 10 percent slower than the real speed of sound, a difference you would never hear unless it was a *gigantic* concert hall.

6. The name makes sense if you consider that before digital reverberators existed, initial delay was created by patching a tape-based delay ahead of a spring or plate reverb.

The spacing and volume of all the *early reflections*, in the first 150 ms or so, tells us a lot about the size of the room, and where we are in it. The timbre of the reflections, relative to the direct sound, gives us an idea of the nature of the room's wall surfaces. Better reverb programs let you manipulate all of these factors.

The combined reflections that occur later, merging into a continuous sound, are considered the *reverberation* proper. It's often identified as *late reverb* to avoid confusion. The envelope of this reverb and its timbre are what make a concert hall sound different from a large gymnasium, cathedral, or Hall of Congress. Any reverb program should let you control the decay, known as *reverb time*. Most programs allow some equalization of the late reverb, to simulate different kinds of wall treatments. A few programs give you control over the initial attack, and some even split the reverb into different bands so the envelope can be different for highs and lows.

Waves's TrueVerb does a particularly nice job of visualizing the different parts of reverberation. In the top of Figure 14.9, you can see the single direct sound, a group of discrete early reflections, and the smoother late reverb. (This particular setup simulates a large but somewhat absorbent room.) On the bottom of Figure 14.9 are equalizer controls for both the early reflections and late reverb.

One other control is critical: The *mix*, or how much reverb you hear relative to the direct sound. It's usually calibrated 0–100 percent, but some software gives you separate controls to adjust the level of direct sound, early reflections, and late reverb in decibels. Unfortunately,

14.9 With some plug-ins, like Waves's TrueVerb shown here, you can see where the reflections and reverb will occur.

there's no consistent way to predict where any of these mix settings should be—they depend both on how the software was designed, and how that particular setup has been tuned. You'll have to train your ears by paying attention to echoes in the real world: In most spaces, echoes are not as loud as you'd imagine. Do this ear-calibration live, while you're in various rooms. Don't do this by listening to dialog tracks you've shot.

Unless you're simulating an unusually echoey space or other special effect, reverb levels should be just at the edge of consciousness. You should notice that the reverb is missing when you turn it off, but otherwise you shouldn't be aware of its presence unless you're actively listening for it. Short reverbs can be a little louder than long ones. Closeups should have less reverb than long shots, since we're closer to the subject, but don't change reverb levels with each camera cut. Dialog reverb should be consistent throughout a scene, though if secondary characters appears at a distance, they should have more reverb than the principal.

In standalone audio mixers, reverb is usually patched into an *effects bus*. Each input channel has a separate knob to set how much of its signal will be sent to that bus, and it also has a switch to determine if this *send* is proportional to the channel's level in the overall mix or if it stays constant. The bus goes to the input of a reverb processor; the processor's output is then added to the mix through a separate volume knob. If you're using a setup like this, the processor's mix control should be at 100 percent: early reflections and late reverb, but no direct signal; that's provided by the mixer.

The Acoustic Mirror effect in SoundForge takes a different approach. It relies on samples of reverb recorded in various spaces, and attempts to emulate their decay at various frequencies. This is the same technique used in costly DSP-based *sampling reverbs*, but Acoustic Mirror works on a much simpler level. I don't see it as presenting much advantage over conventional reverb in most postproduction situations. On the other hand, if you're willing to go through the somewhat demanding sampling process at a shoot, you could conceivably use the process to match ADR to location audio.

Reverb and distancing

In real-world interiors, echoes increase as you get farther from a sound source (something you probably learned, to your dismay, if you ever shot dialog with a camera-mounted mic instead of a close-in boom or lav). We usually stand farther away from large noisy objects than we do from small ones, so there's a tendency to associate amount of reverb with size.

Most of the time, this works. If you're mixing a scene set on a factory floor and you want to imply a large machine, feel free to give it more reverb than you're giving the actors. But don't confuse reverb and size: One's related to distance and room construction, and the other is usually reflected in volume and timbre. I've had advertising producers insist I put large, long echoes on their up-close and personal voice-overs to make them bigger. All it really does is destroy the intimacy by moving the announcer farther away.[7]

My personal preference is to avoid reverb any time someone is talking to us from limbo or in front of a drape. That includes voice-overs, of course, but also on-camera spokespeople and demonstrators, and interviews where we're not aware of the questioner or surroundings. This

---

7. One of my mentors taught me how to handle this kind of request: Explain your reasoning, demo it both ways, and then ask if they want to reconsider. If they still insist on doing something that'll hurt the mix, just shrug, do it, and say to yourself, "No problem. I've already got *my* Clios."

keeps their voices in our space, just as the nondescript background suggests they're not in a separate, functional room. But if we can see where they are—if the scene has walls, furniture, or other fixtures—we should hear the rooms echoes as well.

Reverb settings

Most reverb software comes with factory presets, but these are almost always designed for music mixing and emulate large, flattering spaces. They're much too big and wet[8] for the primary use of reverb in video: matching ADR, foley, or dry lav tracks to what we're seeing on the screen. So you'll have to develop your own settings.

Before you grab knobs and start tweaking, think about the space you're trying to simulate. Decide how far the sound source is from the walls, and where we're listening from (usually presumed to be the camera position). Turn feet into milliseconds, and you'll have a good idea of when the early reflections should start. Consider the round trip distance that sound has to travel, and let that influence how the reflections are spaced. Then ask yourself what's in the room to absorb sound; this tells you about the late reverb's timbre and how long it should last.

Track 66, part 1, has two voices close-miked in a dead studio. Part 2 is subtly different: A tight reverb is simulating a large but absorbent room (perhaps a shopping mall blue-jean store, since clothes soak up a lot of echo), with them close to camera. You might have to switch between these two examples a few times to hear the difference, but it's there and can make the voices more realistic.

- For the large and absorbent room in part 2, early reflections started at 40 ms and clustered between the 40 ms and about 100 ms. The late reverb grew quickly, was wide band, and had a 0.3 second decay. For what it's worth, on this software, the mix was set to 40 percent.

- Part 3 is a smaller, but more reverberant room. Early reflections are between 16 ms and 40 ms. The late reverb also grows quickly and has about a 0.7 second decay, though the highs decay a little faster. Since this is a longer reverb, the mix was somewhat less: using the same software as part 2, it was at 25 percent.

Hear for yourself

Track 66 demonstrates the reverb settings in this Chapter.

Larger spaces—theaters, stadiums, cathedrals, and the like—have radically different reverb characteristics from the previously mentioned spaces. But reverb software already comes with plenty of presets for these larger spaces because these presets are also useful for music. Find one you

8. Recording engineers use this adjective to describe a signal with lots of reverb and *dry* for signals without any reverb.

> ⚠️ *Gotcha* _____
>
> *Where's my verb?* Many NLEs apply effects to a clip, and then compute the clip's volume based on a volume line (also known as a rubber band). Good audio workstations and hardware mixers let you put the effects before or after the volume controller. For many processes, the differences are so subtle as to not matter.
>
> But if you're adding reverb to extend a faded note, as in the third tip on the previous page, most NLEs will fade the reverb tail along with the source clip. The effect will be lost. As a workaround, draw the fade but leave the reverb off. Export it as an audio file with the fade, and then use this new file to replace the original on the timeline. Since the file is already faded, leave this version full-up. Add the reverb to it, and it'll be able to continue even after the music stops.

like, tweak at random until you like the sound, and make sure the mix isn't too wet for intelligibility. If you tweak too far, you can always recall the factory preset.

Music reverbs and special effects

Music and large sound effects can sound good with longer and louder reverb than you'd apply to a voice, so factory presets are fine for those sounds. Articulation isn't an issue, and these sounds are usually flattered by warm, long, late reflections.

Unless you're producing original music for your project, chances are the score already has appropriate reverb in the mix. Adding more will just muddy things up. But there are a couple of cases where a bit of controlled reverb is useful on a preproduced music track:

- A medium-length late reverb can help music edits[9] by letting instruments decay naturally over the cut. Part 4 of Track 66 has this reverb. You probably won't even notice it when the music's playing, but you can hear it in two places where the music stops abruptly. Early reflections are within the first 50 ms, then the late reverb builds up very quickly and has a 3.3 second decay. The mix was 35 percent.

- Source music should be run through a reverb set to match the dialog's sound. This overall wash, on top of the reverb applied to individual instruments when the music was mixed, will help place the sound in the room.

- If you have to fade out of a sustained note at the end of a song because the original is held too long for the video, running through a concert-hall preset after the fade can help. It won't sound like the instruments' natural decay, but can add a nice tail that almost suggests the musicians stopped playing. Try to sneak the reverb in gently, a few notes before the end.

_____

9. This reverb won't help music edits that are basically *wrong*. You still have to respect the beat and chords (Chapter 10).

Heavily equalized reverbs, or ones where the decay times are radically different for high and low frequencies, can suggest unusual spaces without having to be so loud that they affect intelligibility.

- Part 5 is voices inside a large steel tank. There are no early reflections, and late reverb starts with a medium-fast attack a few milliseconds after the direct sound. But while high frequencies decay in about two seconds, lows take about 10 seconds to decay.

You can add predelay to suggest immense spaces, even if your software doesn't have controls for the early reflections. Figure 14.10A shows some settings from Premiere's reverb, an oversimplified reverb that doesn't even generate early reflections. So I put a multitap delay (Figure 14.10B) *ahead* of it in the filters list. The result is a reasonably good railroad station announcement, part 6 of Track 66. Add a high-pass filter around 500 Hz to simulate losses in the PA system, and it's near perfect (part 7 of Track 66).

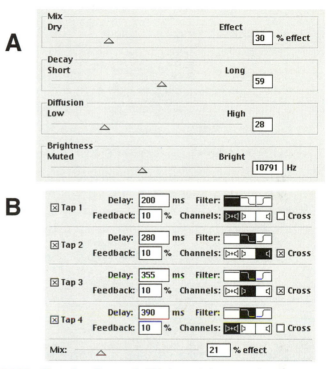

One unworldly effect is the precognitive reverb, which builds up *before* the direct sound:

1. Take an audio clip and add a few seconds of silence to the head.

2. Use a backwards or reverse function in an audio program, or set the clip speed to −100 percent in a NLE.

14.10 Premiere's reverb (A) doesn't have early reflections. So I added some by putting a multitap delay (B) ahead of it.

3. Apply a reverb. In the CD example, the early reflections were within the first 40 ms. The late reverb lasted three seconds, and it was damped with a −3 dB loss at 3 kHz. But since this isn't a natural effect we're creating, other settings can work just as well.

4. Render the reverb, creating a new file that sounds echoey even without a reverb plug-in assigned to it.

5. Repeat step 2. It will now sound like part 8 of Track 66.

6. You can assign the same reverb to the processed track, for a reverb that builds up to the direct sound and then decays after it. The result is part 9 of Track 66.

- The reverb settings for this example were early reflections within about 40 ms, a late reverb time of about three seconds, and about –3 dB loss at 3 kHz.

Reverb as blur?

We started this book by avoiding a philosophical discussion. Let's indulge in one here.

Someone asked me if reverb is the aural equivalent of the *Gaussian Blur* effect found in photo retouching programs and some NLE video filters (Figure 14.11). I don't really think so.

The tool sets for images and audio have to be conceptually different, not only because of how we perceive those functions, but also because the math has to be different. Images require matrix manipulation of a fixed file size. The algorithm needs to know what's above and below a pixel as well as what's to the left or right of it, and that means the width of the image has to be defined at the start. Audio, on the other hand, is a continuous stream of data. There is before and after, but no above or below.

In the very short term (longer than 50 ms but probably not much), distortion that generates additional harmonics could be thought of as similar to a Gaussian blur. In the slightly longer term (maybe 70 ms to 1 second), I'd say a rich chorus is the closest thing to the blur. It can be very hard to pin down the original sound among the mishmash that a chorus creates. Of course that's just my opinion, and I could be completely wrong.

I don't deny that, subjectively, a long late reverb is a blurry thing indeed.

14.11 A moderate Gaussian Blur in the middle; a more severe Gaussian Blur on the right.

Chapter 15

Time and Pitch Manipulation

Remember this:

- You can change the timing of an audio clip, speeding it up or slowing it down to fit a shot, without changing the pitch.

- Or you can change the pitch without affecting the tempo, retuning music and noises, creating cartoon and science-fiction effects, or even changing the character of a voice.

- Both of these processes come with some costs in terms of distortion and other artifacts. Your best chance of success comes from understanding how the processes work so you can choose the best options.

- For the least distortion, change both time and pitch simultaneously.

Back in the days of analog, you'd sometimes hear a radio station run a record at the wrong speed. If it was too fast, the sounds would be jammed together and come out in a little chipmunk voice.[1] If it was too slow, everything would be deep and s-t-r-e-t-c-h-e-d o-u-t. These effects became a comic cliché.

For most of the history of recorded sound, time and pitch have been inextricably linked. You couldn't change one without affecting the other. (In the late 60s, there was a device that used a variable-speed tape recorder with rotary spinning heads to make tapes faster without affecting their pitch. It was expensive and mechanically cumbersome, and it didn't catch on.)

But in the early 70s, digital devices appeared that could change a sound's pitch in real time. The quality was low, and the devices were originally used to raise the pitch of slowed-down tapes for speech research. By the late 70s, they'd made it into recording studios—still with low quality, but useful as a special effect. In the 80s, you could buy a pitch compensator capable of almost a 10 percent shift with acceptable bandwidth and only a few artifacts. The box cost as much as a

---

1. In fact, that's how David Seville created the Chipmunks—Simon, Theodore, and *Alvin!*—in his 1958 hit record and about thirty years of songs and TV cartoons that followed. He recorded his own voice, singing very slowly, and played the tape back at double speed.

small car, but was considered essential in commercial production houses. That's because it could jam 33 seconds of copy into a 30-second spot.

Today, very high quality hardware-based pitch changers with three- and four-octave ranges are standard in most music and audio post studios. They're used to fix out-of-tune singers, create virtual choirs, and—of course—to jam more words into a commercial. They can cost as much as several thousand dollars. But reasonable-sounding time and pitch changers are built into almost every audio program, free, and excellent ones are available as plug-ins. Most can change pitch as much as an octave in either direction without audible glitches, many can compress time as much as 25 percent without losing intelligibility, and a few can slow speech down 25 percent without sounding strange. This is a case where cheaper may be better. Because software-based pitch changers don't have to work in real time and have the option of looking ahead into the file, they can use more sophisticated algorithms than the hardware ones. Only a few programs actually take advantage of this, however.

Speed-based Effects

Despite the ability of today's systems to change time or pitch independently, doing it the old-fashioned way—changing both together—is sometimes more desirable. It's faster and has few side effects that hurt sound quality.

Sample-rate Speed Changes

Believe it or not, you can run a CD or DAT tape at the wrong speed and get exactly the same effect that happened with the phonograph records. Some professional CD and DAT players let you do this by changing their internal sample rate, which makes the sound come out at a different speed. If you play a 44.1 kHz CD at 40 kHz, samples will play about 10 percent slower than they were recorded. The disc will take that much longer to play and be that much lower in pitch. If you play it at 48 kHz, the reverse will happen and the disc will play faster and at a higher pitch. You can do this with files as well, if you manually change the sample rate in the file's header; when a program tries to play the file, it'll use the rate you set. Some audio programs let you do this easily.[2] This speed manipulation is virtually instantaneous, since only a few bytes of the file are changed.

Neither of these techniques affect audio quality. There can be other problems, however:

- In the case of those CD and DAT player vari-speeds, the sample rate on their digital outputs is changed. Some inputs might not accept the new, nonstandard rate.

---

2. Windows users can change the sample rate in the Properties pane within SoundForge and other programs. Mac users will need Tom Erbe's *SoundHack,* essential shareware for anybody doing creative audio on Macs.

- Other devices may lock their internal clocks to the new rate. This can be just as bad. If you speed a DAT up to 50 kHz s/r to raise its pitch, and digitally dub it to a new DAT, the signal might force the recorder to run at 50 kHz as well. When you play the sound back on a standard player—or even on the same player, when its rate isn't artificially raised—it'll slow back down and cancel the effect completely.

The best solution, in the hardware world, is to convert the arbitrary rate audio back to a standard in real time. Sophisticated audio equipment does this by up-sampling the incoming signal to a much higher rate. The equipment repeats individual samples so the pitch and timing don't change. Then it further repeats or skips enough samples to make the signal a multiple of a standard rate, and down-samples to the standard. It's complicated and some data can be lost, but when done right the sound is excellent. Some new chips handle this automatically and are being built into better digital audio equipment.

If you don't have hardware capable of sample rate conversion and want to input a vari-speeded CD or DAT, the only other option is to do an analog transfer, redigitizing at a standard rate. This can result in a slight loss of quality, depending on the equipment you use. But sample rate conversion wasn't available in most equipment a few years ago, and unenlightened engineers may still tell you analog transfers are the only solution.

> ⚠️ *Gotcha*
>
> ***I didn't ask for a sample-rate change.*** One of my clients reported unwanted pitch changes on his high-end NLE, when encoding a video project for the Web. We traced the problem down to a bug in the routine that the editing software used to pass information to a separate data-compression software. Compressing manually in the compression software, rather than calling it from the NLE, fixed the problem.

In the software world, things are only a little different. Most modern computers will do the right thing when playing a file with a changed header, by speeding up or slowing down as appropriate. But some platforms have problems with arbitrary rates, or won't play them at all. Most software can't mix audio files that are at different rates, so these convert the changed files back to a standard rate using a process similar to what's done in hardware. NLEs usually aren't very good at this and may introduce distortion or periodic clicks. If you want to change the speed of a clip by changing the header information, convert the file to a standard rate in an audio program before using it in a video editor. But conversion, in that case, is not worth mucking with the header; most audio programs have a Change Speed function that combines the two steps into one operation.

Speed Changes Using Audio Processing

Changing the speed without changing the sample rate introduces the possibility of distortion, and it does take time, but most audio programs do the processing at a high enough intermediate sample rate that the sound is virtually perfect. Most NLEs let you apply a speed setting to an audio clip, but real time previews are likely to be poor quality, and rendering usually doesn't sound as good as when it's done in an audio program.

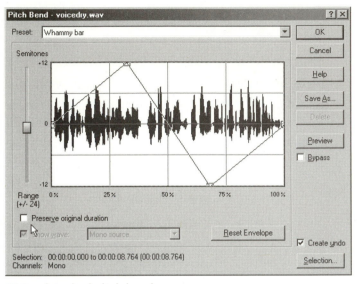

15.1 A typical pitch bender.

Some programs disguise their speed change function or bury it in other processes. Sound-Forge offers a *pitch bender* instead. This is usually used to apply a speed change that varies over time, and it follows a graph you draw. (Figure 15.1 shows a typical pitch bend curve; part 1 of Track 67 plays its effect.) If you want to apply a constant speed change in SoundForge, drag the control points to make a single horizontal line. Peak, a popular editor for the Mac, doesn't have a pitch bender or a speed control; instead, there's a Change Pitch command.

Both these programs have a Preserve Duration check box. Turn it off to accomplish the kind of speed change we're discussing in this section (Figure 15.2). Not only does this keep pitch and time linked together, it's also faster and often sounds better. There's a lot of extra processing necessary to preserve duration, and it can introduce artifacts.

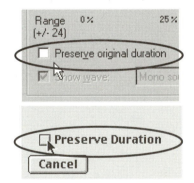

15.2 If you want an old-fashioned speed change, make sure Preserve Duration is turned off.

Hear for yourself ___

Track 67 is the tutorial examples for this chapter.

Making cents of speed changes

Most audio software is intended for music production. Even though you can use a bender or pitch shift to control speed, the dialog box is probably calibrated in musical values, *semitones* or *cents*. (There are two semitones to a whole step, such as from the musical note C to the note D, and one hundred cents in a semitone.) Each semitone has a frequency ratio of 1.05946:1 to the note below it. An octave—a frequency ratio of 1:2—contains 1,200 cents. Cents aren't evenly spaced in hertz because we hear frequencies exponentially. The actual formula to convert speed changes to cents is:

$$cents = 1200 \log_2 (speed_1/speed_2)$$

That roughly translates to 165 cents for a 10 percent change or 17 cents for a 1 percent change.

Pulldown

Film usually runs at 24 frames per second; NTSC video is at about 29.97 frames per second. Chapter 7 covers the implications of this in a section on timecode. Briefly, if you're editing traditionally shot film as video in a NLE, it's often necessary to apply a speed correction of −0.1 percent when transferring location audio from DAT, MiniDisc, or CD. If you don't, sync can drift 1.8 frames for each minute of a continuous take.

Professional timecode DAT recorders have a switch to do this automatically. It works by changing the sample rate, so there's no quality lost in the process. The pitch change that results is too small to be heard by even the most golden-eared listener. For best results, transfer digitally through an input that does sample-rate conversion back to standard file rates.

CDs and MiniDisc are more problematic. Even CD players with speed controls don't allow this precise a setting, and I haven't heard of any commercially available variable-speed MiniDisc player. So you have to use a different approach if you've recorded location audio in these formats.

⚠ *Gotcha* _____

They're not really pitch shifters. Shifting all pitches by the same arithmetical amount—say, raising every-thing 300 Hz—is possible, but sounds awful (listen to part 2 of Track 67).[1] We expect frequencies to change in proportion to their pitch, not by a fixed amount.

What the software actually does is *multiply* pitches, changing everything by the same ratio. Raising a 1 kHz tone to 1,300 Hz means multiplying by a factor of 1.3. That same factor would raise a 5 kHz tone to 6,500 Hz which, as we demonstrated in Chapter 2, is heard as the same degree of change. However, these gadgets are always called *pitch shifters* in the industry. So that's the term we'll use here.

_____

1. Done by using a hetrodyne process in hardware.

The most reliable solution would be to get a timecode DAT deck for the transfer session. Dub your CD or MiniDisc to DAT digitally at 44.1 kHz s/r; then flip the pulldown switch and transfer the dub into your computer at 44.056 kHz s/r. Of course, this process doubles the transfer time.

An alternative is to capture the sound normally, then change its speed in an audio program. If your software lets you apply a pitch correction of -1.75^3 cent, things should sync perfectly. If the program accepts only whole cents, –2 cent will keep things within one frame for about five min-utes, probably as long as you'll be staying on one continuous shot. (You can always slide back into sync during cutaways.) Of course, make sure the Preserve Duration function has been dis-abled.

Changing Pitch and Time Independently

Most audio editors come with a pitch shifter that can preserve duration while changing the pitch, or a tempo changer that changes duration without affecting frequencies. Depending on the qual-ity of the software, this can sound good or may introduce periodic glitches. The problem lies in how intelligently the algorithm handles overlaps.

Pitch Shifters

How a pitch shifter works

Remember last chapter's discussion of how a chorus effect affects pitch by working like a trough that keeps changing its length? In the chorus, an LFO constantly telescopes a delay from short to

_____

3. Actually, –1.728 cent. But –1.75 cent is probably more accurate than the crystals in your film camera and audio recorder, which will start to drift on their own before you notice a pulldown error.

long and back again. While the delay is being lengthened, the pitch goes down. While it's being shortened, the pitch goes up.

Imagine the LFO had a sawtooth waveform, which ramped steadily from minimum voltage to maximum and then snapped back to zero. As the sawtooth's voltage grew, it would lengthen the delay. So we could start with a delay being very short, lengthen it to the maximum, then snap back to short and start the process again. Any signal going through the delay would have its pitch lowered while the delay was growing. If the sawtooth ran in the other direction, from high down to low and then snapping back up again, that would raise the pitch.

This is exactly the same phenomenon as the *Doppler effect*. When a sound source is coming toward you rapidly, say a whistle on a speeding locomotive, the distance between you and the source keeps getting smaller. The time it takes the whistle's sound waves to reach your ears keeps getting shorter, effectively shrinking the delay. That's why the pitch of the whistle appears to rise. But when the train passes you and continues moving away, the time it takes those waves to reach you gets continuously longer, lowering the pitch.

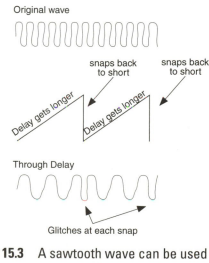

15.3 A sawtooth wave can be used to control the length of a delay for a constant pitch change.

Figure 15.3 shows how a delay can change pitch. A high-frequency wave (on the top) is run though a delay that's modulated by the sawtooth in the middle. While the sawtooth is ramping up, the delay grows and the output pitch is lowered (on the bottom).

There's only one problem with this type of pitch changing: it sounds pretty bad. The problem isn't the pitch shift, which (assuming a well-designed LFO and delay) should be perfect. The problem is the snap: every time the delay jumps suddenly, samples in the delay's memory get thrown away. The result is a sudden jump in the waveform—the glitches on the bottom of Figure 15.3. You can hear it in part 3 of Track 67. The situation is very siimilar if you're raising pitch with an LFO that ramps from maximum to zero. Each time the LFO jumps back to maximum, samples have to be repeated (part 4 of Track 67).

One solution is to have two parallel delays with two separate LFOs at the same speed. The second LFO runs one-half cycle later than the first. When delay A is snapping back, delay B is in the middle of its pitch change. A third LFO (also at the same speed) controls a cross-fade from the output of one delay to the other (see Figure 15.4). If the cross-fade is properly timed, we're always listening to a delay that's got room to change. The result is a smooth pitch change—except once per cycle of the third LFO. In the middle of the cross-fade, we'll hear both delays mixed together. Because it's impossible for the two outputs to be identical, part of the sound will double. Part 5 of the CD Track 67 demonstrates this problem, which I've emphasized by choosing a particularly slow LFO speed.

The cross-fades in practical pitch shifters aren't as obvious as my examples. Commercial units use different cross-fade LFO waveforms and other tricks to hide problems. A few also use extra memory: when a cross-fade is imminent, the pitch shifters compare the two delays and, if necessary, put off the fade until there's a better match.

I've described a simple pitch shifter that works in real time on a continuous audio stream. Others have refinements in how they approach the fade between delays. They may also use a slightly different architecture, with a single memory buffer and three pointers: one pointer writes audio data into RAM addresses, and the other two read that data at a different rate. But the operation is conceptually the same. Part 6 of Track 67 demonstrates a pretty good pitch shifter.[4]

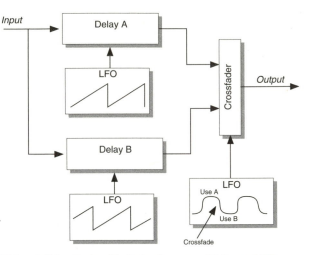

15.4   A "deglitched" pitch changer. All three LFOs are at the same speed. But note how Delay B's LFO is in the middle of its smooth growth while Delay A's LFO is snapping back. A third LFO is timed so that the cross-fader listens to each delay only when they're smooth.

Software-based shifters can work on files much faster than the hardware ones with real-time inputs. The internal processing is virtually identical.

Pitch shifter uses

Obviously, the ability to change pitch without affecting timing can be a cool special effect, particularly in fantasy and science-fiction pieces. The cookbook section at the end of this chapter describes some ways to use this effect, including a few effects you wouldn't think were based on pitch shift.

But pitch shift is also useful as a corrective device. Special shifters are available that analyze singers' voices, spot when they're off-key, and nudge them back. These often have sophisticated controls to preserve some of the natural slides and vibrato that good pop singers produce, and may have the ability to turn one voice into a choir.

---

4. Eventide DSP4000B, a hardware unit. I wrote part of its software. Well, what did you expect?

Some songs change key in the middle, ending a whole step (200 cents) higher than they started. I've found that even the basic shifters found in most audio software can compensate for this by dropping down a whole step, without damaging sound quality. Sometimes, it's the only way to keep both the beginning and end when editing a piece of music.

Shifter limitations

Large pitch shifts can have problems, even if the software does the job without glitches. Changing the key of most musical instruments by more than a few notes doesn't sound like the performer played in a different register; it just sounds wrong. That's because acoustic instruments have fixed resonances determined by their size and shape. When a player changes notes, these resonances—called *formants*—stay put. But when you pitch shift digitally, the resonances change as much as the fundamental and the instrument's timbre doesn't sound natural.

This is particularly a problem with human voices. Vowels are created by taking a buzzing from the vocal folds and filtering it through resonant cavities formed by the tongue, mouth features, and sinuses. This creates vocal formants—harmonics of the buzzing. As you speak, you continuously change the mix of formants; your tongue moves to block some resonances and change the shape of some of the cavities. Because your mouth is a fixed size, the cavity shapes don't change very much.

Most people can sing the same vowel on two different notes at least an octave apart. That means the buzzing frequency is twice as high for the higher note. Since the vocal cavities can't change by that factor, different harmonics of the buzz get emphasized. We're used to hearing this and have no problem identifying the same vowel on different notes. But if the harmonic frequencies were multiplied by the same factor as the fundamental, it would sound like the singer's head suddenly grew or shrank.[5]

Think about this in terms of spoken words as well. Female voices are characteristically at least an octave higher than male ones, though there's a wide variation between voice pitch in either sex. Between the lowest normal male speaking voice and the highest female one, there's got to be at least three and a half octaves of difference. Resonators, including the ones in the human head, work at frequencies directly proportional to their size. If the difference between male and female voices was reflected in formant frequencies, it would mean some men have heads three and a half times larger in diameter than some women! Thickheaded would take on a new meaning.

The difference among voice pitches occurs at a low frequency, the fundamental of the buzz. It's mostly due to differences in the size of the vocal folds and how much tension we apply to those folds. To shift voice pitch realistically, you have to change the fundamental while keeping upper harmonics relatively stable. It can be done.

---

5. That's one reason why a boy soprano has a different sound than a fully grown woman, even when singing the same note in the same style. The boy's resonant cavities are much smaller.

Formant-corrected pitch shifters

The simplest way to shift a voice without destroying its timbre is to split it into two bands with filters, one for the fundamental and another for the vowel formants. The bands are processed separately. This is the approach taken in most software.

But there are a few problems with this approach. Unless you're speaking in a mono-tone, the fundamental frequency changes a lot while you speak. The filters have to be constantly adjusted to sort out the harmonics correctly. This means the software has to detect the lowest frequency, which can take time to do accurately. Also, when the two bands are combined, the harmonics won't have the same phase relationship to the fundamental as they did originally; this can be audible. Any overlap in the bands can cause a flangey smearing, but if the filters are too sharp, they'll add their own phase distortion. Any noise or broadband music in the signal will also be processed and can sound very strange.

A slightly more complicated method involves measuring the lowest frequency, then analyzing whole waves based on the fundamental. The higher frequency harmonics in each wave

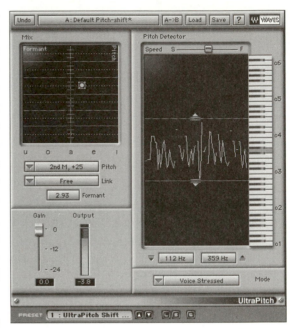

15.5 A formant-corrected pitch shifter, Waves UltraShift.

are captured, then overlaid on a pitch-shifted version of the fundamental. This scheme can also introduce nonspeech strangenesses, but is often fine for background voices.

Both of these methods require accurate frequency detection. To save processing power, most software will ask you to set a frequency range for the detector; the smaller the range, the faster the detector can respond. Male dialog should be set for a range between 60–275 Hz, and female dialog between 100–400 Hz, though of course there are exceptions in both sexes. The frequency detector can be thrown off by low-frequency background noises—even those of a moderately quiet shooting stage—creating even more artifacts.

A different process, brand-new as this book is being written, constantly analyzes the pitch and volume of each of the harmonics as well. Then it generates electronic filters that match those the mouth was making at the time. It applies these filters to a pitch-shifted re-creation of the fundamental buzz. In effect, it creates an electronic model of a specific human's throat and head, and then speaks through it. This has the additional advantage of other vocal characteristics being introduced. Part 7 of Track 67 demonstrates a piece of gender-bending in TC-Helicon's *Voice*

One (www.tc-helicon.com), the first device devoted to this technique. Bear in mind I'm doing some extreme processing in this track, and nobody's had much experience using these techniques for natural speech, as opposed to singing. By the time you read this, newer software for the Voice One, as well as competing units, will probably be available. Or the technology may have been abandoned, replaced by something even better.

Time Changers

Changing the duration of a piece of audio without affecting its pitch is fairly similar to pitch shifting, but you don't have to worry about formants. That's because the final result has the same harmonic relationship as its original. Most software gives you options for setting the time factor; you can enter a percentage (100 percent is the original timing, 90 percent is ten percent faster, and so on) or a new duration for the selected audio. Some let you preview the timing as a real-time vari-speed without additional processing; this is helpful when trying to match musical tempos. A few programs let you select a target area on a timeline and squeeze or stretch the source material to fit.

Most software does time changing as a two-step process: it will vari-speed the selection to the desired duration, and then do a conventional pitch-shift pass to put the frequencies back where they belong.[6] So the pitfalls are the same as with pitch shifting by itself:

⚠️ *Gotcha* _____

Use single-band pitch shift, formant-corrected, or just a speed change? It depends on what you've got to work with and what you're trying to accomplish.

- If the goal is high quality, you don't need more than a tiny amount of shift, and timing isn't critical: use vari-speed. Male voices can usually be lowered 200 cents or raised 100 cents this way. The range for female voices is reversed: these can be raised 200 cents or lowered 100 cents. An example of this would be shifting one or two words to change inflection in a sentence.

- If you're staying within those ranges but timing is critical (as it would be with lipsync) or the original track is noisy, use a conventional pitch shifter. The timbral change will probably be less noticeable than the artifacts from most formant-corrected shifters.

- If you need to change the character of a few background voices to build up a crowd, use any of the formant-corrected shifters. But have some nonshifted voices louder in the mix, to cover the artifacts.

- If you want to change the character of a foreground voice without calling attention to the processing, you'll need a modeling shifter like the Voice One or whatever replaces it in years to come.

- If you're doing other-worldly or cartoon voices, or hiding identity in an interview (obvious processing can be a benefit here), broadband pitch shifting will be fine no matter how much you change things.

- If you're slowing things down, the pitch-shift pass will have to repeat some parts of the waveform. The more radical the change, the more this becomes noticeable.

- If you're speeding things up, the pitch-shift pass has to delete some parts of the waveform. This is usually less noticeable, but can be a serious problem if short phonemes get completely lost.

You can minimize these problems if the software lets you choose the *window size*—how much of the sound it works on at one time. Choose the smallest possible window for speech, between 10–15 ms or so. Use slightly longer times for solo musical lines and the longest times for music with a lot of instruments. Some software disguises this as a mode control, and lets you select for voice or various kinds of music.

You can also minimize the problems by reducing the amount of speed change. If possible, edit as close to the desired length first. Change the length of pauses in a voice-over or during a cutaway, or delete or repeat a bar of music. Skillful editing will always sound better than extreme time-processing.

Part 8 of Track 67 demonstrates a reasonably good speed changer at 75 percent of the original timing, and at 125 percent. When you get beyond that range, some problems usually become audible. The best way to avoid these is to review the processed file. Then make a different processed copy of the original, using a slightly longer or shorter selection, or with a slightly different percentage. The glitches are sure to fall in different places. Edit between the two versions until you've got a perfect one.

Alternative time shifters

A few professional products[7] make tiny edits automatically to change timing, and then apply as little pitch shift and vari-speed as possible. These products will look for individual repeating waves and delete or duplicate them as necessary. Because these changes always happen at zero crossings and no cross-fading is necessary, they don't affect sound quality at all.

How successfully they find places to edit depends on the instantaneous nature of the speech, how radical a change is necessary, and how much of the original they're allowed to look in. If you let them explore a longer time window, the chance of finding good edit points increases—but too long a window can start to distort the patterns of speech because one word may end up with more edits than another. The software may give you just a couple of settings, one that tries to preserve the rhythm as much as possible, and one that compromises rhythm to avoid cross-fades.

---

6. Well-designed software will do this for time expansion but reverse the steps for time compression. The idea is to make the first step one that lowers pitch, either with a speed change or a duration-preserving pitch shift. If the first step raises the pitch, there's a chance of reaching the Nyquist limit.

7. VocALign (Chapter 8) uses this method to match ADR to guide tracks.

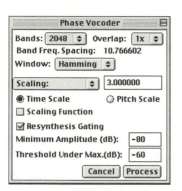

15.6   The phase vocoder in the shareware SoundHack.

The cross-fades are necessary because in sections where there aren't enough repeating waves to make the time change with edits, the software reverts to conventional vari-speed and pitch shift methods.

The *phase vocoder* takes another approach. It continuously analyzes the spectral composition of the source audio, breaking it into small pieces and performing a *Fourier analysis*[8] on each. The pieces run through multiple, sharp filters—as many as a few thousand—and the output at each frequency is mapped. This data is then used to create completely new versions of the sound, timescaled as appropriate. Phase vocoding is processor intensive, but may be found in some desktop software. It's a powerful technique that can have a much wider, glitch-free range than other time manipulation methods, often by a factor of 10 or more.

The success of phase vocoding depends on how the time slices—called windows—are timed and cross-faded, and how closely the filters are spaced. Good software will let you choose from several alternatives for the number of filters and the *window shape*, which affects the cross-fades. If there are more filters, they'll cover narrower frequency bands each and have higher Qs. Window tim-

⚠️ **Gotcha** _____

Specialized time processors aren't just for dialog. We've described these advanced algorithms in terms of speech because they're seldom found in general-purpose (i.e., music oriented) audio programs. That's partly because it takes a very knowledgeable programmer to create them and partially because they're harder to use.

But their principles work just as well for music and sound effects. If you're lucky enough to have them available, try them. You'll probably be pleased with the results.

ing depends on this filter sharpness because higher-Q filters need more input samples to be effective. Counterintuitively, more filters aren't necessarily more accurate. Sharper filters not only slow down the windowing, blurring or phasing the sound at cross-fades; they also add their own distortion. Try different combinations on different source files until you're happy.

---

8. This is named for mathematician Jean Baptiste Fourier, who invented the analysis process about 200 years ago. He proved that any regular wave—no matter how complex or non-musical the waveform—can be broken down into a fundamental sine wave and a number of harmonics of varying amplitude and phase. Physicists used to have to compute these harmonics using slide rules and legal pads. But digital technology made the *Fast Fourier Transform (FFT)* possible and it's used in a lot of audio processes.

Time and Pitch Cookbook

If you're trying to correct a pitch or speed problem, or fitting dialog into a precise time, the recipe will depend on your specific project. Follow the guidelines in the first part of this chapter for using the particular processor.

But often, time and pitch manipulations are used as a special effect rather than a problem solver. This section provides recipes for a few of the things you can do, but feel free to experiment. There are no firm rules for special effects; play around with the settings until you find a sound that satisfies your creativity.

Hear for yourself ____

Track 68 demonstrates most of the effects described in the time and pitch cookbook.

Vari-speed Effects

The lowly vari-speed, simplest of processes, is a powerful tool for creative sound effects work. Most sounds can turn into something completely different when their speed is radically shifted:

- Part 1 of Track 68 is a recording of some boiling water, first at normal speed then manipulated. At half-speed, it starts to sound mechanical. At 20 percent of normal, it's almost completely metallic, suggesting you're standing between two cars on a moving train.

- Part 2 is a mortar fire, completely recognizable at normal speed. At 20 percent, it's a magnum blowing somebody away. But at 300 percent, it could be a single bowling pin being hit.

- Part 3 is an explosion, pretty big by itself. But the second half of part 3 is the same explosion mixed with a version of itself at 50 percent for depth and a version at 200 percent for brightness—much bigger.

- Part 4 shows how vari-speed can add a unique kind of flanging. First we hear a single helicopter effect. Then it's mixed with a copy of itself, offset one frame later with a very slight 106 percent speed increase. Different small speed changes and tiny offsets would have given different effects.

Pitch-bend Effects

Figure 15.7 shows a pitch-bend pattern for the Doppler effect discussed earlier. Note the calibration on the left of the graph; the actual change is only a couple of semitones. Part 5 lets you hear a before-and-after. I also applied a gain envelope[9] similar to the pitch shift. Real-world Doppler

---

9. Called a Graphic Fade in SoundForge, even though it can do a lot more than fades.

effects are usually also coupled with some echo and high-frequency losses that increase with distance.

Try applying pitch bending to a repeating mechanical sound, such as a motor. You'll be able to make it speed up or slow down on command.

Pitch bending can also be applied to steady tones to create a variety of sirens, lasers, and other electronic effects.

Pitch-shift Effects

Pitch shifting is seldom as useful on sound effects as it is on music or voices. I suspect that's because there's less to distract us from the periodic artifacts. On the other hand, it's got more vocal uses than you might expect.

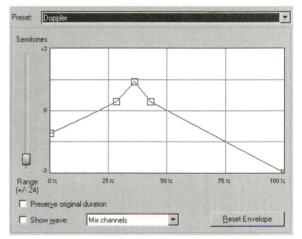

These samples are on voices recorded in a quiet announce booth. Voices with small amounts of background noise or reverb can often be processed in a wideband shifter, though the apparent noise may increase. Noisy tracks are seldom usable in a formant-corrected shifter.

15.7 Basic Doppler is easy with a pitch bender.

Wideband pitch shifting

A lot can be done by mixing a voice with a pitch-shifted copy of itself:

- Part 6 of Track 68 shows how a tiny pitch shift—on the order of 0.15 percent higher, or maybe two cents—isn't heard as a doubled voice. Instead, the subtle timing changes so that the pitch shift algorithm introduces gives a lightly flanged character, almost suggesting a distant voice blowing on the wind.

- Part 7 uses a much bigger shift—a whole step (200 cents). Now we hear it as two people speaking in unison.

- Three isn't quite a crowd, as you can hear in part 8. The unchanged voice is in the center, and two shifted versions are panned about 20 percent, left and right, one up a half step and one down a half step. One of the shifted tracks is delayed by one frame because three people could never achieve perfect unison. Voice doubling, approximately 6 percent or 200 cents down, becomes two people in unison.

- Part 9 could be a small crowd. It uses eight different shifts, ranging between about 70–300 cents, panned across the field. An LFO continuously changes the delay of each shifted output, between 50–200 ms. The original voice is centered and one frame earlier than the shifted voices, to provide an anchor.

- You can take this to the extreme. Start with the processing of part 9, but add a copy of each shifted signal, delayed one frame, and panned elsewhere in the stereo field. A little bit of reverb puts a room around the whole thing. Track 10 shows this effect with the shifted versions added gradually. It starts with a single voice hawking widgets, and smoothly grows to an entire congregation reciting the Acme slogan.

We started this chapter with a footnote reference to David Seville's Chipmunks. Let's hear from the little guys, using three pitch shifts (500 cents, 900 cents, 1 octave). Part 11 brings the Chipmunks in one at a time for each voice. As you can hear, it's more effective on higher voices.

A fascinating class of effects can be created by hooking up a delayed feedback around a real-time pitch shifter. Part 12 gives you a glimpse of this, as an echo that starts on a single word and then spirals up to infinity: 400 cents shift, 75 percent feedback, and a delay timed to the word. Part 13 changes a few settings for a completely different sound, an otherworldly (and possibly underworldly) reverb that would be ideal for a demon's evil laughter: –20 cents shift, 80 ms delay, and about 90 percent feedback.

Formant-corrected pitch shifting

For foreground voices, small shifts—less than 500 cents—seem to work best, and shifts up usually sound better than shifts down. Bear in mind that with few exceptions, these processes don't try to change anything other than pitch. If you want to use them to create new characters or recognizable shouting voices in a crowd, record new lines with a slightly different accent, more or less breathiness, or some other changed vocal characteristic. Then apply just enough pitch shift so the voice itself isn't recognizable. (I deliberately didn't do these things in the gender-bending example, part 7 of Track 67, so you could hear the effect of radical shifts on voice tracks you were already familiar with.)

Despite this, the imperfections of larger shifts can be largely hidden by unshifted foreground voices. Shifts as much as an octave may be acceptable.

I couldn't resist one cookbook example with the Voice One processor, every announcer wannabe's dream: to sound like James Earl Jones. The effect, part 14 of Track 68, is almost believable as a human voice even though I'm starting with the smooth-voiced Acme Appliance recording and have made no attempt to mimic Jones's delivery or talk about CNN or the dark side of the Force. There's a shift of a musical sixth (–900 cents), a slight growl, a facial (mask) resonance added, and the vocal tract lengthened 50 percent.

Time Manipulation Effects

Every program has different limitations of how far you can go with time compression and expansion. It depends on the quality of the algorithm, and also on how fast and how clean the original recording is.

Normal announcer reads can usually be shrunk at least 15 percent and retain intelligibility. Faster settings may be useful for disclaimers at the end of radio spots, but this rarely sounds real. Stretches of up to 25 percent may be usable. In either case, listen to the result, and make sure nothing important has been lost or doubled. It's frequently necessary to do two processing passes and edit together the best from each.

One favorite trick of mine is to stretch individual phrases or the client's name in a voice-over, to give it more emphasis. When edited smoothly into the original, the viewer isn't aware of the manipulation—just that the reading is slightly more expressive. In part 15 of Track 68, you can hear our Acme announcement. But, "earned our place," has been lengthened 20 percent and "top" has been lengthened 25 percent.

Chapter 16

Noise Reduction

Remember this:

- You can often lower the level of perfectly steady, pitched noises (such as lamp dimmer buzz or camera whine) dramatically, and in some cases eliminate them entirely.

- You usually can't get rid of random or unpitched noises (such as traffic or preamp noise) without compromising dialog. The best you can do is make them less annoying.

- Equalizers, expanders, and delays can also be effective noise reducers. Instructions and examples are in previous chapters.

It's Not Really Noise Reduction

Today's sophisticated software and expensive DSP-driven boxes do an amazing job of distinguishing random noise from speech and applying sneaky techniques to make the noise less objectionable.

But make no mistake; if random noise occurs at the same time as dialog, in the same frequency band, you can't get rid of it. At least, not with today's technology.[1] Sorry. No amount of marketing hype, wishful thinking, or impressive prepackaged demos at trade shows will change that fact.

This isn't to say you can't improve most noisy tracks, even on the desktop, by using the right processes intelligently. You can certainly lower noise level in places where it doesn't compete with dialog. But you can only hope the words are loud enough to distract viewers from the noise where it does. If noise isn't too serious and the dialog is otherwise well-recorded, this strategy can be remarkably successful.

---

1. I can see a future device that would use speech recognition and a highly evolved version of the vocal modeling we used in Chapter 15, to synthesize tiny chunks of dialog when noise obscures it. But we're not there yet.

That's what this chapter is about. But you've got to understand the ground rules, and one of the first is that random noise during dialog can never be truly eliminated.

The Reality of Noise Removal

A graphic analogy can help you understand why random noise never really goes away.

Let's assume the DAT recorder in Figure 16.1 is the visual equivalent of well-recorded dialog.[2] Constant random noise, such as the hiss from recording at too low a level, could be equivalent to the dirty gray pattern laid over it in Figure 16.2. This noise is too random to remove with an equalizer or filter any other way because such a filter would also affect the dialog.

But noise-reduction software, properly tuned, *can* tell the difference between the

> ⚠️ *Gotcha*
>
> ***But isn't all noise random?*** I'm using random to mean the sound is of indeterminate frequency, such as electronic hisses, traffic, generator noise, and mumbling production assistants.
>
> Non-random noise, in a technical sense, has absolutely steady frequenices. This includes pure tones and even constant, harmonically rich sounds like dimmer buzz or ground-loop hum. If it's not too loud compared to dialog, this kind of noise may be removable.

recorder and its background. But noise-reduction software, properly tuned, *can* tell the difference between dialog and noise. It lowers the volume when dialog stops, the equivalent of our lightening the non-recorder areas in Figure 16.3. As you can see, the noise over the recorder hasn't changed at all—and we've also lost a lot of shadow variation in the background.

The audio noise gate—for decades, this has been just about the only tool we had for this purpose—works exactly like the graphic one in the figures. It's off when there's no dialog, and it turns on when it hears sound above a preset threshold. Usually there's a floor control which lets

16.1 This clean photo could be an analogy for well-recorded dialog.

16.2 And this dirty one could be the analogy for a noisy track.

16.3 Noise reduction can make the overall picture look better, but the dirt is still there.

---

2. Aptly enough, it's a Tascam DA-P1, a model frequently used for double-system sound at DV shoots.

⚠ **Gotcha** _____

Is noise reduction just for dialog? Current pop music is too broadband for noise reduction software to do an effective job. Other forms of complex music that have some dynamics and spectral movement may benefit from noise reduction if it was badly recorded. But the algorithms can also destroy some musical details, so use them carefully.

Field-recorded sound effects often benefit from noise reduction. This is particularly true of staccato and moderately soft effects such as footsteps, or loud effects with long reverb tails such as gunshots.

We'll refer to dialog noise reduction in this chapter, simply because that's the most common use for the process. The principles are the same no matter what you're trying to clean up.

a small amount of the background noise through at all times—which would account for the reduced but not erased shadow information in Figure 16.3.

Today's noise reduction software is a lot more sophisticated. Systems use hundreds of upward expanders tuned to narrow bands across the spectrum. Noise is allowed through only at those frequencies where there happens to be voice energy. At the same time, noise in other bands is attenuated. Thanks to a quirk in how our hearing mechanism works, this can trick the ear into thinking the noise is completely gone. It's still there; we just don't hear it.

Masking

Our ears are not particularly precise sensors. While each ear has close to 30,000 nerves on the basilar membrane and while these nerves are tuned to respond to different pitches, there isn't a single nerve for each possible frequency in hertz.[3] Neural information gets combined in various ways before it reaches the brain.

When we hear a tone at a particular frequency, a group of nerves centered around that pitch fire. How many nerves will go off depends on the volume of the tone as well as other factors. A loud sound triggers more nerves. These combined nerves are interpreted as a single pitch at a certain volume. But because that loud sound involved a bunch of nerves around its frequency, softer sounds at a nearby frequencies might not be able get through—the nerves or neural pathway that should respond to them are already doing other things.

This phenomenon has been known for years and has been measured across very large populations. It affects the threshold of hearing. The heavy gray line in Figure 16.4 represents that threshold. The decibels are calibrated relative to the frequency where most people's ears are the most sensitive, around 3.5 kHz. You could consider 0 dB on this chart to be true 0 dB SPL—the nominal threshold of hearing—or any other convenient level, depending on the individual.

_____

3. How could there be? The ear's design predates the scientific concept of hertz by at least a couple of years.

The important thing isn't how the vertical axis is calibrated; it's what happens between the center of the band and the extremes. At 3.5 kHz, the short, dark gray bar is louder than the threshold, and it gets heard. But at 50 Hz or 15 kHz, most people won't detect a sound until it gets 40 dB louder. Even though the light gray bars are taller and much louder than the dark one, these light grey ones represent sounds that would get lost.

Unfortunately, that heavy gray line isn't fixed. When something sufficiently loud comes along (dark gray bar in Figure 16.5), it drags the threshold with it. A 250 Hz sound, 25 dB above the threshold, ties up so much neural activity that a simultaneous 200 Hz sound 10 dB softer (light gray bar) isn't heard. The actual amount of masking varies with the frequency, volume, and overall timbre of both sounds, but it's always there to some degree.

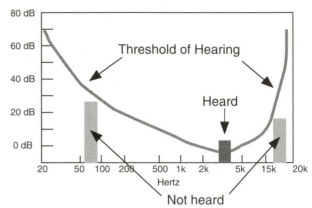

16.4 A typical threshold of hearing curve. Sounds below the gray line are lost for most people.

A similar effect occurs over time, both because it takes a moment for the brain to recognize sounds and because nerves have to recover after being fired. While this effect also varies for different sounds, Figure 16.6 shows a typical *temporal* masking. In this example soft sounds, between a dozen milliseconds before to up to 50 ms after, are masked.

So if we can arrange to have noise only at times and frequencies where it'll be masked by dialog, the noise effectively goes away. A high-precision spectrum analyzer would still see the noise, but we'd never hear it.

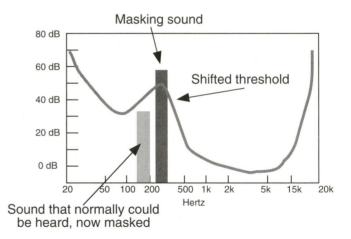

16.5 Frequency-based masking at work. The louder sound moves the threshold above the softer sound.

Masking, by the way, is also the secret behind perceptual encoders like mp3 and AAC. When used properly, these algorithms can shrink an audio file's size by 90 percent with no apparent audible effect,[4] or shrink it even more with minor losses in quality.

Masking is also a reason why it's important not to have elements of a track compete in spectrum or in time. In general, the closer two sounds are in frequency and the farther in volume, the more the softer one will be masked. Masking usually starts when sounds at similar frequencies are within about 10 dB. Loud, low-frequency sounds often mask a wider range than high-frequency ones of the same volume.

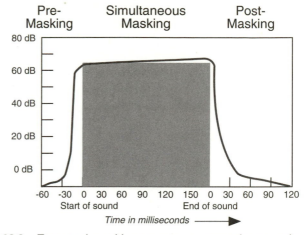

16.6 Temporal masking means you can miss sounds that occur a short time before or after a louder sound at a nearby frequency.

A Few Other Noise Reduction Facts

There are plenty of myths and misconceptions about the process of noise reduction. If you understand what's really going on, you'll usually get better results.

Noise Reduction Without a Noise Reducer

Noise reduction software often attempts to take care of things automatically. This can do more damage, in many cases, than using other techniques manually. If you've been following the examples on this book's CD, you've already heard some fairly effective noise reduction that relies on other kinds of processors.

- Get rid of whistles using the equalization techniques in Chapter 12 and demonstrated on Track 51.

- Tracks 54 and 55 show how downward expansion can improve modestly noisy interview tracks (Chapter 13).

---

4. Some people swear they can always hear *any* encoding. But auditory studies show this probably isn't true. mp3 has gotten a bad rep, primarily because of some awful files on the Web, poorly designed encoders, and people who don't know how to use the technology properly. You'll learn how do it right—and hear how transparent good encoding can be—in Chapter 19.

- Track 62 virtually eliminates dimmer buzz using a comb filter (Chapter 14).

And of course, the ultimate noise reduction for extremely bad dialog recordings is ADR (Chapter 8). These tools are often the first defense, and should be considered before whipping out general-purpose noise reduction software.

Editing can also be used for noise reduction: replace the noisy part with something else. That's one of the principal uses for room tone, though noise-reduction editing can be as subtle as replacing a few waves with clones of adjacent ones. It can even involve changing individual samples by drawing over clicks or other transient sounds with the pencil tool in an audio editing program. A few high-priced DSP-based noise reducers can do these things automatically, though they need precise tuning to sound good.

Nulling noise?

Folks who know a little acoustic theory sometimes ask, "Why can't I create or capture a sample of the noise, invert the polarity, and use that to cancel the noise out?". The idea behind this is basically correct: the comb filter, for example, works by delaying symmetrical noise exactly one-half cycle. This lines up the negative side of the wave against the positive, *nulling* out the noise. But that's a special case, relying on a characteristic of the noise itself and using a precise delay instead of a capture, or copy and paste.

For the sample-and-invert technique to work, the noise would have to be of absolutely consistent waveform and volume, and the sample would have to be pasted back exactly in sync with the continuing noise. We don't have any way to do that with today's technology. If there is the tiniest error in timing or if the noise has changed since the sample, this operation would increase the noise instead of removing it.

There are some noise reduction processes that rely on a sample of the noise, but they're not using an inverted sample. Instead, they take a spectral fingerprint of the noise and use that to control other techniques. Nulling isn't involved.

Dolby noise reduction

The Dolby process revolutionized analog recording, and it is still used in many studios. But it only reduces noise part of the time—just enough to make noisy transmission channels seem quieter.

Dolby A—the original format—worked by breaking the audio into four bands. Each band was then compressed, raising the volume of its soft sounds and decreasing the dynamic range. The four signals were combined and recorded on tape at a high volume. Analog tape adds hiss to a recording. But on playback, the Dolby signal was again split into bands. Each was downward expanded, restoring the dynamic range and—during average or soft passages—lowering the amount of hiss. The combination of compression during record and expansion during playback, is known as *companding*.

During loud passages, no compression or expansion took place. The hiss remained at its usual level, but it was soft enough to be masked by the loud signal. Dolby A used four bands to help the masking; in a single-band system, a loud bass note would momentarily reduce the expansion, letting us hear unmasked hiss in the mids and highs. A newer Dolby format—*Dolby SR*—continuously adjusts the bands based on audio content, helping masking even more. It's used today by music producers who consider analog tape an important step in creating a unique sound.

Consumer Dolby (*B* and *C*), popular in analog cassette decks, also split the signal. But it passed the low frequencies unchanged and only companded the highs. That's because hiss is more of a problem at high frequencies on smaller, slower tape formats. Both versions of consumer Dolby required careful calibration so the compressor and expander would precisely match. If calibration slipped (something common in consumer decks), the spectral balance would be changed. A competing scheme, *dbx*, used a single band with a different companding model that didn't need calibration.

This kind of noise reduction was considered *double-ended* because it used equipment during both recording and playback, specifically to keep tape noise from interfering. Neither system did anything for electronic noise from prior operations or that may have been picked up by the mic.[5] Both Dolby and dbx have since moved on to other things. Current Dolby digital systems don't rely on companding, and dbx is now in the business of making studio compressors and equalizers, as well as single-ended noise reducers.

Double-ended noise reduction isn't necessary in digital production. All of the techniques in this book are single-ended.

Single-ended Processing

The term refers to noise reduction of an already recorded signal, and it can be helpful for noise picked up by microphones as well as noise added by faulty or misused equipment. Unlike double-ended systems, single-ended processes have to be told what's noise and what's useful signal. That's what you're doing when you adjust equalization,

☞ *Rule* _____

Noise reduction works best when there isn't too much noise to begin with. As noise gets louder, noise reduction becomes less successful.

_____

5. Dolby A's four-band decoder could be applied to an unencoded noisy signal and, with careful adjustment of levels, function as a single-ended noise reducer. This use was popular for a while on film mixing stages. But we've got much better tools now.

dynamics control, or comb filters for noise reduction. More complex processes also have to be tuned to the noise. The closer noise gets to signal, in volume or spectrum, the harder this is.

The best way to control noise is to not record it.

Dynamic Filtering

This is a 20-year-old analog technique (still available in some dbx equipment) that works just as well in the digital domain. It's effective against hiss and other random noises that are predominantly high frequency, and it's effective against noise which could be stopped with a sharp, low-pass filter.

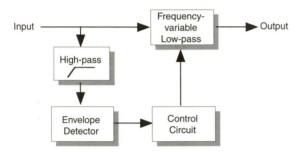

16.7 A dynamic filter changes frequency based on high-frequency level.

Using a normal filter is often out of the question, however, because it would cut important harmonics in the voice and leave the dialog sounding dull and lifeless. Instead, a variable filter is used. Its frequency is controlled by the output of an envelope detector, which is preceded by a fixed high-pass filter. This control arrangement is identical to a de-esser. Figure 16.7 shows the layout.

When there is very little energy in the high frequencies—in dialog pauses, for example, or during the vowel sound in the word *smooth*—the envelope detector has very little output. This swings the filter frequency down, as low as a few kilohertz, reducing the hiss. But as high-end energy increases, the filter frequency rises. During those times, it's more likely there'll be something to mask the hiss. If the action is smooth and fast enough, you're not aware of a timbre shift—just less noise.

An alternative architecture (Figure 16.8) makes it easier to avoid timbral problems, but isn't quite as effective. Instead of a variable filter, it has a fixed-frequency low pass, sometimes as low as 1 kHz. A cross-fader, controlled by the envelope detector, varies the output between the filtered signal and the unprocessed input. When there isn't much high-frequency energy, the output is only what made it through the filter.

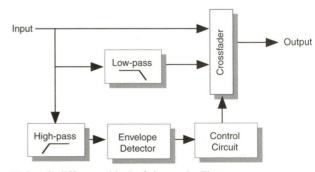

16.8 A different kind of dynamic filter.

But as highs start to appear, more of the unfiltered input is mixed in. When the highs are loud, none of the filtered signal is used at all.

Dynamic filters are often built with only one control, a More knob that sets the sensitivity of the envelope detector. Start with no noise reduction at all; then, while you play the source material, advance the knob until noise is removed but you're not aware of dullness or a swishing sound. These filters are often followed by a downward expander, sometimes in the same unit, with its own sensitivity control. Time constants are usually preset to be very fast.

Dynamic filtering is effective and often implemented in analog systems. A similar algorithm can be found in some multifunction, DSP-based digital processors, and might be available in a well-equipped post suite. For hiss-based noise, dynamic filtering often the least intrusive solution. But I've never seen this technique in desktop software. That's because today's computers are capable of a much more powerful method.

Multichannel Masking

Imagine a bank of hundreds of downward expanders, each preceded by a narrow bandpass filter. Each one would look at a small slice of dialog frequencies, sometimes smaller

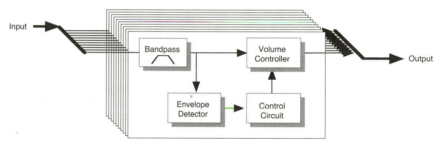

16.9   A multiband noise reducer, simplified.

than a single formant. When there's voice energy in a particular narrowband, the expander would pass it through. Any noise in that band would be masked by the voice. When things are silent in that band, its overall level would be reduced, lowering the noise, even though the voice may be speaking (and masking noise) in other bands. Figure 16.9 shows a simplified version; actual multiband noise reducers often have as many as 512 bands.

While this approach can yield very effective, almost amazing noise reduction, it can also cause problems. Pure tones and narrowband signals can cause a flanging effect in the noise, as single expanders open while their neighbors remain closed. Good noise reducers include a way to partially link adjacent bands, so each expander responds mostly to its own energy but also considers the state of the expanders around it. However, this linking can't be too complete or else masking will be compromised. Time constants are also important. If the release time is too fast, you'll hear a chirping artifact as bands respond to transient sounds. If it's too long, noise can remain after the masking sound is gone. Both attack and release have to consider the frequency of the band as well, to avoid distortion.

This could present the user with a nightmare of controls. Or a manufacturer could preset most of them for average noise—whatever the programmer thinks that is—leaving the system less effective on other tracks. Arboretum's Ionizer plug-in for Mac and Windows (Figure 16.10) seems to make the best compromise; Sonic Foundry's Windows-only Noise Reduction software is a close second. In both, attack and release time, and the amount of linkage between bands (*correlation* or *overlap*) is adjusted globally, and each band's threshold and floor can be automatically fitted to a sample of the noise or adjusted manually. Ionizer also lets you adjust the knee for each band.

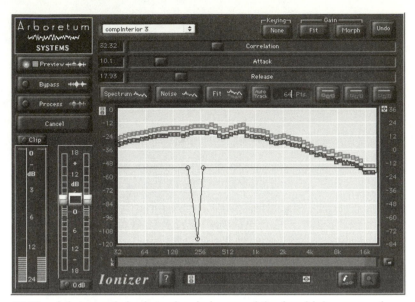

16.10 Arboretum's Ionizer plug-in is one of the few high-powered noise reducers that combines a full set of user controls with mostly automatic setup.

Adaptive Filters

It's a movie cliché that before two spies have an important conversation, they turn on radios and start the shower going. All that extra noise is supposed to defeat hidden microphones. But a powerful noise-reduction technique, *adaptive filtering*, can actually sort music and random noise from speech. It's used to clean up airplane black box recordings, make wiretaps more understandable in court cases, and—yes—catch spies.

A great freebie! Audacity is an open-source, freeware audio editor for Windows, Macintosh, and Linux. Among its features is a fairly good noise reduction processor.

The program has some limitations (as of version 1.0), including the inability to preview effects. So if you're going to use the noise reduction, be prepared to do lots of tests and undos. On the other hand, being open-sourced, it's sure to pick up new features quickly. There's more information at http://audacity.sourceforge.net.

Adaptive filtering relies on statistical models that predict speech and has grown out of the same research that originally made it possible to carry intelligible conversations over the miniscule radio power of an analog cell phone. There are two basic forms of this filter, one that uses a sample of the noise you want to get rid of, and one that can guess what's noise based on what it knows about speech.

Unfortunately, adaptive filters haven't yet reached the sophistication where they can smoothly clean up a voice without leaving flangey, metallic artifacts. This isn't a problem in forensics, where the technology's benefits outweigh this disadvantage. But it makes adaptive filters unsuitable for video and film tracks, and they're seldom found in the post suite.

Declicking

Back before compact discs, sound recordings were released on vinyl discs with an analog groove on each side: the *phonograph record*. The tiny sides of the groove moved in and out in an exact analogy of the sound waves it represented. The disk would spin, and a needle riding in the groove would wiggle with the groove's undulations. That wiggle was picked up by a device that worked similarly to a microphone, which created a voltage that reflected the original sound wave. (I never thought I'd have to explain that process in a book. But filmmakers are getting younger and younger, and it's likely this book will be picked up, some day, by someone who was still a little kid when CDs took over.)

The groove walls were delicate, and vinyl isn't particularly strong. If you accidentally dragged a pencil, fingernail, the pickup needle, or even the wrong kind of dirt across the grooves, you'd indent the walls. This would cause a spike in the audio, which repeated every time the disk came full circle. By the time a much-loved record had been taken out of its protective sleeve and played a few hundred times, it could have a collection of rhythmic ticks and pops as an unwanted rhythm section.

This was a serious problem. By the 80s, a couple of analog processors appeared that could detect the steep rise of an unwanted tick and muffle the sound just long enough to smooth over the problem.[6] They weren't perfect, but could salvage a modestly scarred disk without too much damage to the music.

What irony. Now that we have click-free recordings, we've also got the technology to remove clicks painlessly. There are a number of plug-ins that do this fairly well. Most emulate the click detection scheme of a good analog processor, looking for sudden jumps in the waveform that

---

6. One of them, the Burwen TNE, actually performed as advertised. We kept one in each studio of a multiroom facility. If you're into vinyl and manage to locate a used TNE, you'll find calibration instructions and a schematic on my Web site, courtesy of Dick Burwen.

subside quickly and couldn't be a part of music or speech. Then they replace the click with a wave that's averaged from the ones around it.

Click removal is included in some CD burning software (for those converting their vinyl record collection), in some audio editors, and in reasonably priced plug-ins. It can also be useful for removing some clicks caused by digital audio sync problems.

Lower-end click removers usually have a single sensitivity control; play the source file and slide the control until clicks are controlled but you don't hear too much distortion where they used to be. Better ones, such as Sonic Foundry's (Figure 16.11), give you additional settings. *Shape* or *frequency range* tells the click detector what to look for. The clicks in old 78 RPM recordings were often bassier than the crackles in 33 RPM; optimize this setting so the detector doesn't get confused by transients in the sound. A low *noise level* setting tells the algorithm to completely ignore parts of the track that don't have any clicks, which avoids any chance for artifacts in those sections.

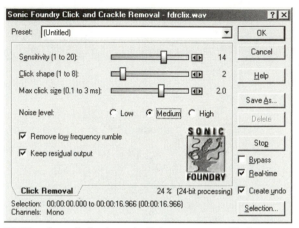

16.11   A well-designed click remover will give you lots of control over the settings.

When click removal is too aggressive, percussion instruments and even stop consonants can get distorted. The best way to avoid these problems is to preview with the Residual Output or Calibrate switch turned on. This lets you listen to only the output of the click detector. Adjust the controls until you hear only clicks and none of the desired audio. Then turn the calibration switch off, and process the file.

Noise Reduction Examples

I can't provide a cookbook for this chapter because every noisy recording has its own unique problems. Instead, I'm providing a few examples of real field recordings, showing the basic steps to clean them and playing the results. Use these as a benchmark for your own efforts.

 ***Hear for yourself*** _____

Track 69 plays before-and-after sounds for the noise reduction example.

⚠️ **Gotcha**

There's a lot more in the arsenal. If you've jumped to this section to solve a particular problem and haven't read the rest of this chapter, you may be missing some major noise-reduction techniques.

Check Chapters 12–14 to learn about noise reduction using equalizers, expanders, and delays. In many cases, these can remove noise with fewer artifacts than specific noise-reduction software.

Moderate Interior Noise

Part 1 of Track 69 is the original track of an interior interview. There's some room rumble and HVAC hum, which we'll remove in Ionizer.

16.12   The first step is to analyze a short sample of the noise.

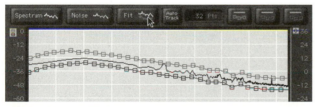

16.13   Step 2: Fitting 32 expanders around the noise.

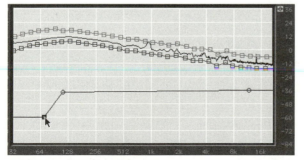

16.14   Step 3: Drawing a floor for the expanders.

The first step is to select a short slice of the noise during a pause. Look for a place that doesn't include breathing or other noises that don't occur during the rest of the track. Make sure you haven't included any of the subject's voice. In this case, I found about 20 frames around 12 seconds from the start.

Open Ionizer and press the Spectrum button. The software quickly analyzes the noise you selected, creating a graph of level versus frequency as in Figure 16.12.

Then cancel Ionizer—it remembers its settings after you close—and select the whole clip. Open Ionizer again and press the Fit button to create 32 downward expanders around the noise's spectrum. This looks like Figure 16.13. Each square is a potential control point. The top line shows the expanders' thresholds; they're just above the noise so that anything softer than the threshold will be reduced in level. The bottom line is where the expanders have a full cutoff. The area between the lines is the expanders' knees. I used only 32 relatively wide bands, even though the software is capable of 512 narrow ones, to avoid filter distortion and other artifacts.

Then draw a floor for the expander. In Ionizer, the numbers to the right of the graph (Figure 16.14) show attenuation. In that figure, there's a floor of -36 dB for most of the noise, but it goes considerably deeper below 100 Hz to reduce rumble. Part 2 of Track 69 plays the result—the noise is almost completely gone. In fact, it was too clean and sounded unnatural.

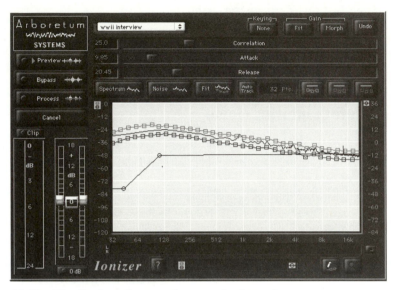

Raise the floor somewhat. Figure 16.15 shows the final settings, including correlation and time constants. Part 3 plays the result.

16.15 The final settings to clean up the interview.

Constant, Loud, Mechanical Noise

Part 1 of Track 70 is an interview recorded on a motorboat. The motor is almost as loud as the voices and is at many of the same frequencies. The best you can hope for in a situation like this is to improve the intelligibility. (Besides, people looking at the shot can

Hear for yourself

Track 70 is the before-and-after for motorboat interview example.

tell it's on a moving motorboat, so the noise won't seem out of place.) I decided to process it in SoundForge, using Sonic Foundry's separate Noise Reduction plug-in.

The first step is to help things along by knocking down noise at frequencies where the voices aren't very active. In theory, this shouldn't do much at all—the motor isn't competing with the voices there. But in practice, lowering the overall noise helps viewers concentrate on the dialog. So apply an equalizer which draws the graph in Figure 16.16. The low-frequency cut hurts the voice fundamentals, but the motor is too darned loud there; I decided the formants would be sufficient. The midrange dip is because spoken voices are typically weak there. But of course, you can turn Preview on and do the tweaking by ear (as you should always tune *any* equalizer).

Then apply noise reduction. Sonic Foundry's is very similar to Ionizer, and the process is the same; sample some noise by itself, fit the expanders to it, select the entire clip, and process. The sequence is slightly different and you don't leave the plug-in to select the whole clip; click the plug-in's Help button for details. Figure 16.17 shows the settings; part 2 of Track 70 plays the result. Because extreme processing was necessary, the voice is left with an echoey artifact. But it's much better than the unprocessed file.

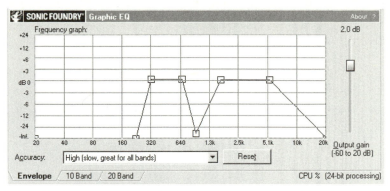

16.16 The background was just too noisy to process directly, so the first step was to equalize it.

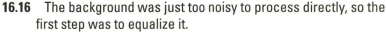

16.17 These are the Noise Reduction settings for the equalized file.

Moderate Exterior Noise with Whine

If the noise has any constant-pitch elements, pre-equalization will always make noise reduction work better. Part 1 of Track 71 is an exterior interview with fairly loud traffic and a machine whine. The whine competes with, and is almost as loud as, the subject's voice; standard noise reduction techniques won't be able to do much.

Hear for yourself

Track 71 is the whiny exterior before processing, using just a noise reducer, and using a parametric equalizer before the noise reducer.

Part 2 plays the interview after being processed with Ionizer, but with no separate equalization. It's an improvement, but there's still noise. Worse, the expander makes the whine pulsate in step with the voice.

In part 3, the unprocessed interview is run through a parametric first, tuned to eliminate the whine (using the sweeping technique in Chapter 12). Then it's analyzed and noise-reduced by Ionizer. The whine isn't part of the noise print any more, so the spectrum doesn't have big jumps. This means that expanders are less likely to interact with a flangey sound, and I can lower the floor. Listen to all three tracks. Compared to part 3, part 2 seems hardly noise-reduced at all.

Click Reduction

Part 1 of Track 72 is a badly damaged 78 RPM phonograph recording, originally recorded in 1933—probably a lot worse than anything you're likely to encounter. Figure 16.18 shows the settings to clean it up in Sonic Foundry's Click and Crackle remover. This is a powerful plug-in, with lots of options. Read its online Help file; the settings in that figure wouldn't be best for a more modern recording.

Hear for yourself _____

Track 72 is a segment from Franklin Delano Roosevelt's first Inaugural Speech. This 70-year-old recording has plenty of clicks, which are easily removed in part 2 of the track.

_____

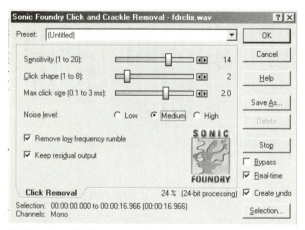

16.18   Declicking a particularly bad 78 RPM in Sonic Foundry's Click and Crackle remover.

Part 2 plays the result. Clicks, particularly during pauses, are seriously reduced. They're also reduced during speech, but because so much processing was necessary, they're often replaced by distortion. However, without those high-frequency clicks, you can apply some creative equalization to improve intelligibility. I'll leave that as an exercise for you.

Chapter 17

Other Effects

Remember this:

- There are lots of ways to turn a mono sound into simulated stereo, but only one works really well. Fortunately, it's easy and doesn't require an expensive plug-in.

- A similar technique lets you change the width of a stereo image, or even eliminate the vocalist from many pop recordings.

- Manipulating a sound's harmonic pattern can produce amazing results, including giving it human vocal characteristics or making it sound like it has bass deeper than a viewer's speaker can carry.

- Equalization, compression, and other basic effects are important—but the real power comes when you use them together.

It's a lot of fun being a sound designer. Among other things, I get to design new processes to solve problems or create new sounds. Other designers and I share these techniques at industry meetings, and then the techniques become part of the standard repertory—at least, among the sound-designing crowd.

Unfortunately, this stuff doesn't fall into standard categories like equalizers or compressors, and there are no textbook algorithms for them, so they seldom appear in NLEs and audio editors. When they do, they're often poorly implemented. If you want to use these effects, you have to get third-party plug-ins or hook up multiple processors yourself. Believe me, it's worth the effort.

In this chapter, we'll cover:

- turning monaural sounds into something very close to stereo;

- supressing or completely eliminating the soloist in some music recordings;

- making existing stereo recordings seem wider;

- adding intelligible vocal characteristics to sound effects and music (how about a doorbell that rings, "hello"?);

- processing tricks to make small playback speakers sound better, without muddying the sound when it's played on good monitors; and

- simulating some everyday sound textures, such as long-distance telephone conversations.

Throughout this chapter, you'll find both explanations of these effects and cookbook demonstrations of how they can be used. Ideally, it'll inspire you to create your own combinations.

Stereo Simulation

Stereo creates a soundstage along a horizontal line between the two speakers (and sometimes beyond). Any individual source in the track, such as one instrument in an orchestra or a single car horn in a cityscape, can come from any point along this line—even though there are only two speakers. Our mind creates intermediate locations by interpreting a sound's subtle volume and timing differences as it comes from the two speakers.[1] When we listen to a well-recorded stereo track, it appears to come from a myriad of locations.

But if a track is recorded in mono, or a stereo mix is converted to a mono file, those volume and timing differences are lost. All the elements that make up the sound—instruments in an orchestra or falling debris in an explosion—are lumped together in one place. Play the track through both speakers at the same volume, and it appears to come from only one point, halfway between the speakers. Add a tiny delay to just one speaker or change its volume, and the sound moves somewhere else—but it still comes from a single point.

That single-point mono sound often can't compete in a finished track. Ambiences, large sound effects, and scoring that's been recorded in mono doesn't sound wide enough next to stereo sounds. While we can't recover the original positions of each element in a mono clip, there are a variety of ways to make it wider. Most ways can be used in theatrical, kiosk, or other situations where you control the listening environment. But only one is appropriate for broadcast TV, VHS, or Web use, so we'll discuss this one first.

Stereo Simulation with Comb Filters

One goal of all broadcast and Web mixing is mono compatibility. You can do whatever you want with stereo effects, but the track still has to make sense to a viewer who has a mono set[2] or a

---

1. Most pop music recordings are a sort of semistereo, where volume differences alone are used to distribute instruments across the soundstage. The timing differences you'd hear in an orchestral recording—or a good recording of a background—are missing. This can actually be to your advantage, as you'll learn later in this chapter.

2. Before you send me email about the prevalence of two-speaker TVs and stereo VHS hi-fi decks, reread the first section of Chapter 6.

computer with a single speaker. Most stereo simulation techniques actually interfere with the sound when played in mono. But this one is a nifty trick that creates a wide image that is completely compatible with mono listening. Furthermore, it's one of the few techniques that actually spreads the original sound across the soundstage. The placement is based on frequency rather than the original source's location, so it's not true stereo. But it can sure be big.

This stereo simulation relies on two processing techniques. One is the comb filter, described in Chapter 14. It combines a signal with a slightly delayed version of itself to cut regularly spaced notches in the spectral distribution of a sound.

Phase or polarity inversion

The other technique is polarity reversal. If you flip the polarity of a signal, formerly positive voltages are now negative and vice versa. This flipping is often called *phase inversion,*[3] and it's easily done in hardware by changing the connection to an op amp, or in software by multiplying every value by –1. If you have a facility with balanced wiring, you can invert phase simply by exchanging the two conductors in a cable or on a patch cord.

In Chapter 14, we made a comb filter by mixing a signal with a delayed version of itself. If we had inverted the delayed version before mixing, it would also create a comb—but the peaks would be at frequencies where the first comb had notches. You can see this effect on pink noise in a spectragram (Figure 17.1). On the left is noise mixed with a 5 ms delay. It has the expected notches at 300 Hz, 500 Hz, and on up. On the right is the noise mixed with the same delay, but inverted. While it's got as many notches, these are halfway between the ones on the left: 400 Hz, 600 Hz, and so on.

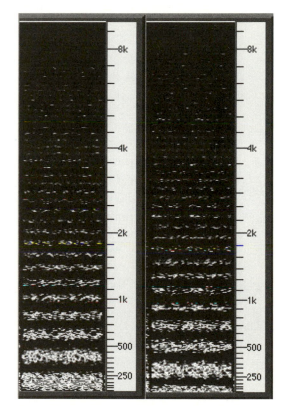

17.1 Pink noise through two comb filters based on a 5 ms delay. The notches are at different frequencies because the one on the right used a phase-inverted delay.

---

3. Actually, phase has nothing to do with it because there's no delay involved. But the effect is exactly the same as a 180 degree phase shift at all frequencies, and *phase inversion* is the way most audio engineers and software refer to the process. So while it's technically imprecise, that's what we'll call it here.

If you mix both of these comb-filtered signals together, each delay precisely cancels the other. You get the original, unfiltered pink noise back. This is just simple math:

```
  pink noise + delay
+ pink noise - delay
= pink noise
```

The simulator

You can take advantage of this cancellation to make a basic mono-compatible stereo simulator.

1. Run a mono signal through a single delay, around 6 milliseconds.

2. Mix the delay's output with the original and call it the *left* channel.

3. Mix an inverted version of the delay's output with the original and call it the *right* channel. You're done.

Figure 17.2 shows the schematic. Frequencies are distributed to the left or right depending on where they fall on the comb. A mono TV plays the two channels equally, canceling the comb and leaving nothing but the original mono signal.

Because most natural sounds are rich in harmonics, it's likely that part of their wave will go to the left, part to the right, and part in between. The result, with most sounds, is a full and wide stereo-like soundstage. You can hear its effect on pink noise in part 1 of Track 72; first the unprocessed noise, then through the 5 ms complementary combs.

 ***Hear for yourself*** ———

Track 72 includes examples of various kinds of stereo simulation and other phase-based tricks.

Combs from a fixed 5 ms delay can cause problems with some source material, so a good simulator lets you vary the delay between a couple of milliseconds and about a dozen milliseconds. The

17.2 A basic stereo simulator, using one delay, a phase inverter, and two mixers.

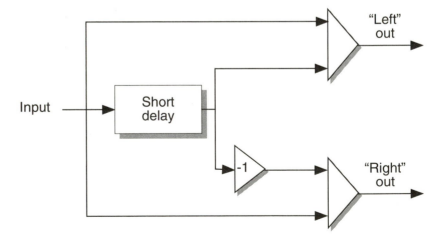

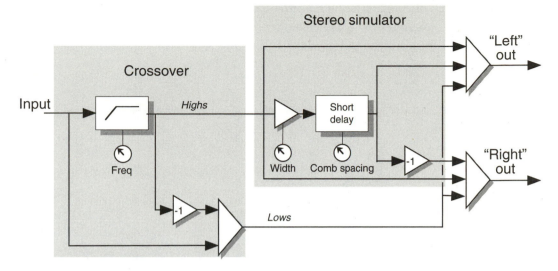

17.3   A complete stereo simulator.

depth of the combs can be made adjustable by putting a volume control on the output of the delay; this lets you adjust the amount of stereo so things don't get too wide.

Simulator improvements

There's one slight problem with this stereo simulator. If one channel gets lost, the low frequency notches can make things sound thin. This would also affect people sitting much closer to one speaker than the other. You can resolve this by adding a *crossover*, which splits the signal into two bands at a preset frequency. The lows go directly to both outputs; the mids and highs are fed to the complementary combs. Since bass notes aren't very directional, the effect still sounds like stereo.

You could build a crossover with matched high-pass and low-pass filters, but it's more elegant to use a single high-pass filter and that same phase inversion technique we used for the combs. The same math applies: if you invert the high-pass filter's output and mix it with its input, the highs are cancelled and only the lows are left. If you combine the unprocessed bass with the two combed mid and high signals—the way a mono listener would—the high-pass filter is cancelled and any phase distortion or other problems it may have caused go away. Figure 17.3 shows the completed stereo simulator, with an additional control to set the crossover frequency.

While this kind of stereo simulation is available in standalone analog and digital hardware processors, and included in good broadcast audio workstations, I have never seen it implemented in desktop software. So I did a version myself, which you're welcome to download from my Web site. Go to www.dplay.com/dv, and look for the entry June '02 (that's when I wrote this chapter). You'll find StereoSim, a preset file for SFX Machine. That's a remarkably versatile and dirt-cheap audio processor available as a Premiere-format plug-in. Instructions for getting SFX Machine are also on that page. Or download Stereoizer from the same place. It's a tiny Windows app contributed by *DV* magazine reader Timothy J. Weber, after I wrote a column about stereo simulation. It uses a similar algorithm and seems to work pretty well. Figure 17.4 shows both programs and their controls.

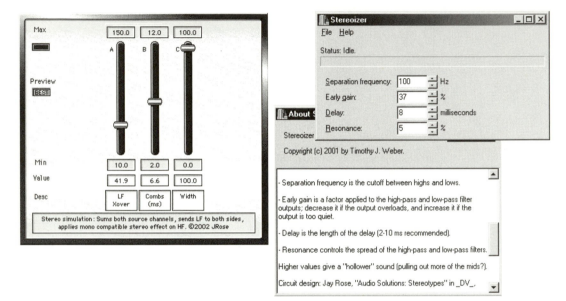

17.4 You can download either of these stereo simulators from my Web site. They're free, but if you want to use the Mac version *(left)*, you'll have to get SFX Machine, an incredibly cheap and versatile audio processor plug-in.

If you're using the preset I wrote, you'll need an audio editor that has SFX Machine installed. Open your mono track and convert it to 2 tracks, using a Mono to Stereo function or by manually adding a second track. There must be two tracks, or else the preset has nowhere to write its two channels of output. (You may copy the original mono sound to both tracks, but it's not necessary; one track can be silent.) Then open SFX Machine, apply this preset, preview and play with the settings until you like the sound, and process. Timothy J. Weber's Stereoizer is a standalone app that doesn't require any other editor or plug-in. It doesn't have a preview function, but runs quickly so you can try multiple passes until you get the results you like. Depending on the original source material and how you set the controls, either method will create stereo-like files with a full and rich sound.

Part 2 of Track 72 lets you hear an example of this processing using voice and music examples. You'll notice a couple of things.

- The voices are somewhat wider, but they no longer seem as focused. That's why dialog is rarely run through a stereo simulator. On the other hand, this effect can be a nice sound design trick for dream sequences and other altered points of view.

- The synthesized music is spread only a small amount. That's because its simple "instruments" don't have many harmonics.

- The orchestral music is spread a lot. Acoustic instruments are generally rich in harmonics, and each instrument's can fall in a different range. Note how the high brass seems to wander slightly from midleft to center, as it plays different notes.

- The pop vocal stays relatively centered, compared to the strings backing her up, because the string choir is harmonically richer.

- The rock band changes width on each beat, in time with the highly processed lead guitar. Guitar fuzz boxes, an essential component of rock and roll, distort the signal to add more harmonics.

Compare these with the original stereo recordings on Track 42.

Other Stereo Simulation Techniques

Reverberation

The most common way to turn mono sources into stereo during the mix is to *pan* them, placing each at a specific point in the sound field and then adding stereo reverberation. This approximates what happens when performers are spread out on a stage, and is perfectly appropriate

---

⚠ *Gotcha*

Completely noncompatible stereo simulation. A few benighted audio applications and some older, low cost keyboards generate stereo by sending a mono signal to one channel, with a phase inverted version of it going to the other. This does make the sound wider—and as you might guess, this also makes it completely disappear for mono listeners.

Or it might not disappear. Some TV stations use *phase chasers* which assume this condition is operator error, and automatically compensate by inverting one channel. If you've run a mixed mono track through a phase-inverting stereo simulator, the chaser fixes things so that mono listeners can still hear the track. Stereo listeners will also hear the track—in mono. But if you've run only one predominant element through the simulator, both mono and stereo listeners may hear other elements completely disappear.

Things get even weirder for viewers with Dolby Surround, which interprets material that's equal, but opposite, on the two channels as something intended for the surrounds. If a phase chaser doesn't turn on, elements or possibly the entire track will end up *behind* the viewer, and in mono.

when mixing individual instrumental tracks into a piece of stereo music. Multitrack audio programs, which are music-centric to begin with, usually have this facility built in. You can do something similar (though with generally poorer-quality reverb) by using a clip's pan line and assigning it a reverb in a NLE.

Unfortunately, the technique isn't as effective on mono recordings of full musical ensembles. That's because if the original mix is panned to just one point, it sounds like all the musicians are jammed together in one spot on the stage. It's also of dubious usefulness on sound effects. Nearby explosions, crowds, and traffic loops *are* big, not a point source with an indoor reverb. Decide for yourself. Part 3 of Track 72 lets you hear this effect with mixed music and sound effects.

The reverb doesn't go away for mono listeners, either, and might be too much on their sets. You can make a reverb effect that disappears in mono, if you have a versatile multitrack audio program or a hardware mixer. Pan the original signal where you want it and also send it to a reverb. Mix both channels of the reverb's wet or 100 percent output, with none of the original signal, and pan to just one side. Then route the reverb's output through a phase inverter and pan it to the other side. For a mono listener, the two reverb signals will cancel each other out, leaving just the dry original. Interestingly, listeners with Dolby analog surround will hear the dry signal in the front of the room, and the reverb coming from the rear. This can be effective.

Delays

A more appropriate alternative for crowds and other backgrounds is to use a long delay—on the order of half a minute or so. You can do this by copying, rather than by using a delay effect. Pan the original mono track midway between the center and the left speaker. Make a copy of the track, offset by at least thirty seconds, and pan it to a similar spot on the other side. Unless there's a memorable shout or other identifiable element in the source audio, nobody will notice the repeat. Play with the pans until the background is as wide or narrow as you want. If you keep things very wide, the background will be easier to mix with mono dialog because none of it will be in the center. Part 4 of Track 72 demonstrates the technique with a mono crowd loop.

Other Phase-inversion Tricks

You can also use the cancellation effect to reduce or completely eliminate the soloist in a lot of pop music, or to control the width of a conventional stereo recording.

Solo Elimination

When mixing a multitrack master of a song down to stereo, the lead vocal is often panned to the center of the soundstage. This means the vocal is equal on both the left and right channels. If you phase invert one channel and then mix the two channels together, the voice cancels itself out.

That's the basis of the vocal elimination technique, which has been around almost as long as multitrack recording.

You can sometimes hear this effect if you have a defective headphone cord plugged into the jack on a portable CD player. If the plug's tip and ring are making a connection but the sleeve isn't, signals that are exactly the same on both channels won't be heard at all. (It may even be worth buying a cheap headphone extension cable and cutting the ground conductor so you can hear this effect yourself. Noted audio educator[4] David Moulton recommends this technique as one of the ways to analyze what's going on in a music mix.)

Vocal elimination destroys any instruments that have been recorded in mono and panned to the center, not just the vocalist. That usually includes the bass and kick drum—important elements in a music mix. With half the mix inverted, some other production effects can disappear. And since you've mixed the channels together, it's now in mono.

Sophisticated solo eliminators partially solve these problem with two techniques. First, both incoming channels have crossovers set just below the lowest fundamental in the singer's voice. The low frequencies are sent, with no cancellation, directly to left and right outputs. The highs are phase inverted on one channel only and then mixed to cancel anything in the center. Sometimes, there's a variable bypass to control the degree of rejection. The mono output of the mixer is finally routed through a stereo simulator. Figure 17.5 puts it all together.

This technique is often used in radio stations to produce song parodies. It can also be helpful in a mix to lower the melody line in preproduced music so dialog or voice-over can show through. Or you might just enjoy turning pop music into karaoke versions for parties. Part 5 of Track 72 applies this effect to our two vocal samples. First you'll hear the unprocessed music, then with partial solo removal, then with maximum solo removal.

⚠ Gotcha

It doesn't always work! The solo elimination technique has its limitations.

- You can't use it to reduce a centered soloist in acoustic recordings (including most jazz and classical music, and live pop performances) because room acoustics and multiple mics introduce differences between the channels.

- It usually won't work on soloists who have been double tracked or had other studio tricks done to their tracks.

- It doesn't eliminate stereo reverberation that might be applied to a mono soloist. In that case, you'll hear the solo go away, but it'll leave a ghostly image of the solo's reverb.

    Still, when it works, it's amazing.

---

4. And tech editor of this book.

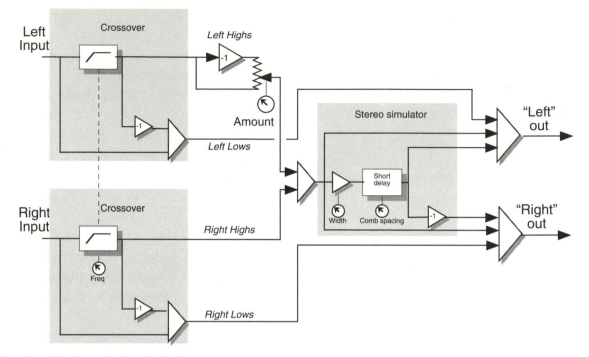

17.5   A sophisticated solo eliminator.

Band elimination?

Audio novices sometimes ask if this trick can also be used to isolate a solo line. Their logic is, "Well, the original is band-with-soloist, and the processed version is band-without. If we invert the band-without and mix it with itself, the band will cancel and leave just the soloist."

Unfortunately, this doesn't work. Since the solo-removed version has half the band's polarity reversed, the result is not what you'd expect. Check the math:

Solo zapping:

```
    Left
  - Right
  = L-R (no soloist)
```

Band zapping?:

```
    Mono mix      or      L+R      or      L+R
  - Solo zapped         - (L-R)         + (-L+R)
      ??                   ??               2R
```

Width Control

As the previous math shows, solo elimination creates an L–R signal. At the same time, we can mix left and right together to create an L+R signal. Having these two signals at the same time can be handy.

- L+R is equivalent to mono, with every part of the sound coming from one place. This is actually what stereo FM and TV stations broadcast as their main channel, and it's all that mono receivers are capable of picking up.

- L–R is sometimes known as *difference* and contains only those sounds that aren't common to both channels. Stations broadcast this signal at a higher frequency for stereo sets. The receivers knock the frequency back down, apply some simple math to it and the main channel, and recover the stereo information.

- L+R is also sometimes known as *mid* because it's what a mic facing directly into the middle of the soundstage would hear.

- L–R is sometimes known as *side* because it's what a figure-eight mic—placed close to the mid mic but facing towards the left side—would hear.

M/S technique

Midside miking (m/s) is a popular technique for recording acoustic music and is occasionally used in Europe for documentary dialog. Many field mixers and some recording consoles have built-in decoder circuits to turn m/s into standard left/right stereo. It's a simple circuit. Mix the mid and side signals together equally, and R cancels to give you just the left channel. Invert the side signal and mix with the mid, and L cancels leaving just the right.

M/s miking has the advantage of being inherently mono compatible. Once decoded, combining the left and right channels cancels the figure-eight mic completely. Other stereo miking techniques can have phase problems when combined to mono, if sounds have had to travel different distances getting to each mic.

M/s miking also lets you vary the width of the image by raising or lowering the volume of just the side channel. This gives you greater control than just panning the signals closer together because you can make the signal wider than it was originally. It's so handy, it's often used as a separate effect on normally recorded stereo signals. A *shuffler* converts the signal to m/s using the technique at the top of this page, has a volume control in the side signal, and then converts things back to left/right. Figure 17.6 shows such an arrangement.

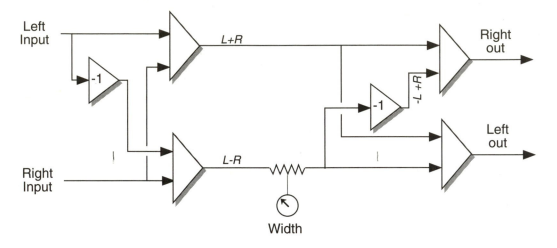

17.6 A stereo width control, or shuffler, turns left/right into mid/side and back again.

Width processing

SoundForge includes this technique in its Pan/Expand process. Figure 17.7 shows it set up so the L-R information will start fairly loud, dip almost to nothing, and then increase to twice its normal loudness. Applying this to the stereo helicopter gives us an interesting effect (part 6 of Track 72): a chopper that fills the field, contracts to the center, and then expands and gets softer. Try combining this with Doppler and some overall panning. As the chopper contracts and expands, it seems to come towards us and then recede. That's because a lot of stereo we

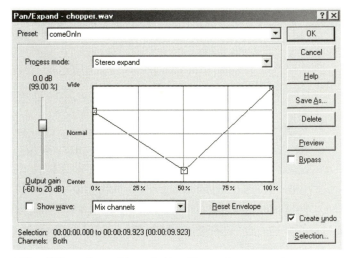

17.7 When SoundForge's Pan/Expand process is set to Stereo Expand, the graphic display works like the volume knob in Figure 17.6.

hear in the real world is reverberation, giving us cues to how far away a sound source is.

If you're building a processing chain like this out of patched-together hardware, or in a DSP program like SFX Machine, try inserting delays, pitch changers, and other effects in the side channel.

M/s can also help if you have to run the left and right channels of a stereo signal through slightly different signal chains (for instance, if you're using two analog equalizers with separate controls).

Normally, this could cause problems when the signals are combined to mono. Instead, turn left/right into an m/s signal first, run mid and side through the dissimilar chains, and then decode. The differences between processors will be averaged across the two channels.

Modulation and Harmonics

Another kind of processing controls the spectral balance of a signal, either modulating it to match the balance of a different signal, or generating harmonics that weren't in the original. The former can be useful in sound design; the latter in improving what the viewer hears.

Modulation: the Vocoder

Vowels and voiced consonants are made by buzzing the vocal folds and then filtering that buzz through resonating cavities in the mouth and sinuses. This creates the vocal formants. Unvoiced consonants are made by applying similar mouth filters to the hissing of air being forced through a small area. This idea of a human voice as a generator and filters was radical in the late 30s, when it was proposed by Homer Dudley of Bell Labs. His goal was to break speech sounds into standard components—buzzes, hisses, and formant volumes—which could be analyzed at one end of a telephone wire and re-created at the other. The data flowing over the wire would consist of the voltages for each critical frequency and a buzz/hiss switch. That's a lot simpler than a voice, so lower-quality connections could be used and more conversations could be carried on long-distance cables.

To prove his thesis, Dudley invented the *vocoder*. It had banks of filters at formant frequencies and measured the energy in each formant during speech. Another circuit detected whether the sound was voiced or unvoiced. The information was passed to a speech synthesizer, consisting of a buzz or hiss source and a bank of matching filters. Volume controllers on the output of each filter would open and close in response to the formants in the original voice. The gadget worked! Unfortunately, it also turned the voice into a depersonalized monotone, and the phone company had to look for other ways to save money.[5]

People started playing with vocoders outside the lab. If you replace the buzz with orchestral chords and vocode a voice, the orchestra seems to sing the words you're saying. In fact, any sound can be used as the *carrier*, so long as it's got enough energy at the formant frequencies. You don't even need a voiced/unvoiced detector if the vocoder has sufficient bands.

---

5. Today, with computerized pitch recognition, the monotone effect can be solved. Vocoder technology is now used in some low bitrate voice compression schemes, including digital cell phones.

When you think about it, a vocoder's construction is very much like the multiband noise reducer in Chapter 16. The only significant difference is that each band has two filters, one for the input (known as the *modulator*) and one for the carrier. Figure 17.8 shows a typical construction.

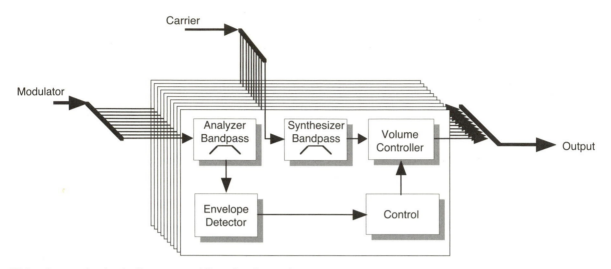

17.8 A vocoder is similar to a multiband noise reducer.

In fact, Arboretum's Ionizer noise reducer has a *keying* switch that lets it function as a vocoder. It assigns one channel of a stereo pair to control filter levels—the modulator—while the other channel acts as the carrier. Opcode's fusion:Vocode uses a similar algorithm, but since it's dedicated to vocoding, the controls are simpler (Figure 17.9). It also has a way to mix the modulator into the output for more intelligibility. The carrier can be a separate sound file, or you can create chords on a built-in synthesizer.

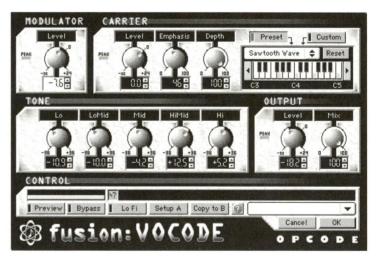

17.9 A vocoder with a somewhat simpler interface, fusion:Vocode.

Vocoder tricks

- If you run dialog through a vocoder and use a single, harmonically rich tone as the carrier, the results can sound robotic. That's because normal inflection is replaced by the fundamental of the carrier tone.

- If you use a synthesizer playing chords as the carrier, you'll get an electro music effect that sounds like the 80s band Kraftwerk (part 1 of Track 73).

- You can also use sound effects as the carrier. Broadband howling wind, for example, can create a ghostlike effect.

 ***Hear for yourself* ___**
Track 73 has demonstrations of modulation-based effects.

> ⚠️ **Gotcha** _____
>
> **Vocoder in wetware.** You don't need special software to create some vocoder effects. You already have the appropriate filters—in your mouth.
>
> Every now and then, pop music rediscovers the *talk box* effect. This is a loudspeaker inside a wooden box, with a funnel directing its output to a flexible plastic tube. The other end of the tube goes in a performer's mouth. You play an instrument through the speaker, and make normal speech movements with your mouth around the tube. The instrument replaces the normal buzz of a vocal fold, and the tongue and mouth movements apply the formant filters. A mic, close to the mouth, picks up this acoustically vocoded speech.

Part 2 of Track 73 shows a powerful application for the vocoder in sound effects processing. First you hear my voice, slowly enunciating a sports cheer. It's followed by some crowd roar from a hockey game. Then I join the two in Ionizer, using the crowd as a carrier; the result seems to be the entire crowd shouting my cheer. It sounds slightly artificial, but a little equalization and sweetening with recognizable solo shouts would make it usable in a mix.

Another Modulator Effect

There are enough formants in well-recorded speech that you can often select the ones that work best for musical reasons. This is what's behind an effect I call "Talking Harp." It's not a true vocoder because there's no carrier.

Instead, it uses a bank of sharply tuned band pass filters. Their Q is set very high (100), just under the point where they'd start to oscillate from random electronic noise. At bandwidths like this, filters are highly efficient resonators. They have almost a bell-like sound and continue to ring for a moment after the sound source goes away. In Talking Harp, the filter frequencies are computed on the fly, multiplying a root frequency by chord intervals stored in a lookup table. A button lets you change chords as desired.

Part 3 of Track 73 plays our test voices through the Talking Harp. It's an odd effect. So far, I've found only one production where I could put it to use.

Harmonic Exciters

There's a style of architectural painting that can make a flat exterior wall look like it's got doors, windows, balconies, and other features. Artists call it *trompe l'oeil*, French for "mislead the eye." One class of audio effect achieves a sort of *trompe l'orielle*, fooling the ear into hearing sounds that aren't there.

Bass Extension

We're so used to harmonics in everyday sounds that when we hear tones in the right relationship, we assume they're harmonics of a fundamental we're hearing—even if the fundamental isn't there. You can use this phenomenon to make a small speaker or other band-limited medium sound like it's handling more bass than it really is.

Waves' MaxxBass plug-in is one of a couple of bass harmonic generators available. It takes parts of the signal below a preset frequency, generates an artificial harmonic exactly an octave above, and mixes it back in with the original. If you choose a frequency at the lower edge of a system's capability, this harmonic can imply a fundamental that's actually been cut off.

Figure 17.10 shows MaxxBass in use. I've chosen a cutoff frequency of about 160 Hz. The dark gray area on the left of the graphic display represents bass energy in the input that the processor will work on. It's not removed by the process, so better playback systems can still reproduce it. But it's also fed to the harmonic synthesizer. The light gray area on the right of the graphic display shows where the harmonics would fall, an octave above the original. The software also lets you compress the harmonics' volume, to help them be heard.

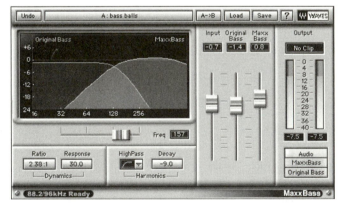

17.10 MaxxBass widens the perceived frequency range by adding bass harmonics.

Part 1 of Track 74 consists of the voice/music demo, twice. The first pass has no processing. The second is through MaxxBass, using the settings in Figure 17.10. While there's a slight difference between these two passes, it's subtle. This is what a listener with a full range system would hear.

Part 2 of Track74 is the same as part 1, run through a sharp high pass at 175 Hz to simulate a poor loudspeaker. You won't hear much difference between its two halves in the female voices or the brass because they don't have much low-end energy to begin with. But in the second half, with MaxxBass turned on, the male speaking voice seems a little fuller. And the synthesized music and both pop songs now have a pulsing bass that's totally lacking from the unprocessed version.

⚠ **Gotcha** _____

That darned dirt! Harmonic extension is an extreme distortion. If it creeps into the midband, it can hurt intelligibility or make a music recording sound bad. Processors like MaxxBass limit themselves to the lowest notes.

Harmonic extension is better than equalization for improving perceived bass. Merely boosting the lows would make the track sound muddy on a good system and wouldn't be much help at all if a transmission medium cut off the frequencies you'd equalized. Like most effects, bass harmonics can fatigue the ear if overused. The process is most appropriate for kiosks, laptops, telephone transmission, and other situations where you know exactly what'll be lost by the system.

High Frequency Enhancement

A related process can be used to improve existing recordings that lack highs. In this case, some of the upper frequencies, a half-octave or so below where the recording falls off, are run through a harmonic generator. A small amount of the generator's output, an octave higher, is mixed with the original signal. This doesn't exactly replace high frequencies that were lost to a bad recording process; those are gone forever. But because many rich sounds have harmonics similar to the ones being generated, it can fool the ear into thinking the original highs are still there.

17.11   A general-purpose sound restorer with high frequency enhancement, Arboretum's Realizer Pro.

Figure 17.11 shows a general-purpose sound restorer that includes this function, Arboretum's Realizer Pro. This software is designed primarily for improving poor music recordings and has some other functions including a bass extender, stereo simulator, and compressor.

Part 3 of Track74 demonstrates only Realizer Pro's HF enhancement; the other functions have been turned off. It uses the voice/music demo rolled off at 4 kHz to simulate a bad recording. You'll hear only the filtered version first, then the filtered version with enhancement added. As you'd expect, the voices aren't too badly harmed by the filtering; the extra harmonics on the second pass seem almost out of place. On the other hand, the music is definitely helped by enhancement. Lowering the crossover frequency—an option in hardware-based enhancers—could make this effect work better on dialog.

Enhancement shouldn't be used at very high frequencies, where its harmonics might exceed the Nyquist Limit and cause aliasing distortion. But the technique can add a little sparkle to an otherwise dull recording, if it's not overused. (By the way, this is not the same as high frequency equalization. If we'd attempted to fix the dull first half of part 3 by applying a boost above 4 kHz, all we'd accomplish is an increase in the noise level.)

High frequency enhancement can also be a useful step in hiss reduction. Apply a sharp low-pass filter at 10 kHz to remove some of the hiss. Then use enhancement to restore harmonics that the filter destroyed. If you then want to apply multiband noise reduction, the noise reduction can be less aggressive and produce fewer artifacts.

Cookbook: Creating New Effects by Combining Old Ones

Almost every program lets you apply effects in series, with the output of one processor being the input for another. In many NLEs, you can stack multiple audio filters[6] on a clip and have them work that way. If you have no other way to use multiple effects on a single clip, look into an effects shell like Bias's Vbox. SFX Machine lets you go even farther by combining up to eight basic effects in any way imaginable, including having the audio output of one change the settings of another.

This is the place to get creative—and have fun—with processing. You can design sounds that go far beyond what an effect's programmers ever expected. Think of this cookbook's recipes as desert.

A few tips for chaining effects:

- Tune the first effect close to where you want it, before you assign the next one in the chain. Then tune the second, and work your way up. If your effects have bypass buttons, use them to check the sound of individual processors.

- Think about what order you'll be applying the effects. In general, apply equalizers and filters before dynamics controllers; that way, compressors won't react to the level of sounds that are subsequently filtered. Reverbs and delay effects can be either before or after a dynamics controller, depending on whether you want to affect the original sound or the processed one.

---

6. The term usually includes compressors and delays, as well as equalizers, in the NLE world.

- Make sure each effect's output is at a good volume. If the effects have their own meters, use them. If not, test the output volume of an effect before you add the next. It's very easy for things to get too loud or soft inside the chain. This will add distortion or noise, even if the last effect in the chain restores the original volume.

- Chaining can take a lot of processing power. If you hear stuttering or other problems while in preview mode, use the bypass buttons to turn off all but the first effect. Render it, remove that effect, and turn on the next. Keep rendering and shortening the chain until it plays smoothly.

- Make sure you can undo both the settings and the actual processing. Always keep a copy of the unprocessed original. If at all possible, save intermediate renderings as well. Once you've tweaked an effect the way you want it, save its settings as a preset, or make notes in a text editor. That'll make it easier to restore the settings if you have to revise part of the track—or if you like the effect so much, you want to use it again.

As an example, we'll combine some effects to create three sound textures that have been lost in the digital world: a movie's optical soundtrack, an old AM radio, and an analog long-distance connection. The challenge in all of these is to make a sound that's true to the original, and yet painted with a broad enough brush that the effect is immediately recognizable through a TV's small speaker.

Some notes on the ingredients

If you're not sure about any of the processes below, review the chapters on each kind of processing.

Filters and equalizers   Filters are the most important tool for simulating old media, but they must be true cutoff filters—ones that can reject sounds beyond a preset frequency. Ordinary graphic or parametric equalizers are too gentle to do the job. Effects filters should have at least 12 dB per octave rejection. You'll need both a low-cut and a high-cut to do most effects right; if you have only one good filter, use it for the lows and apply a standard shelving equalizer to the highs.

But don't throw away your parametric equalizer. Early analog media could be very resonant. Almost any old-time effect can benefit from a sharp peak or two, usually around 500 Hz to 1.5 kHz.

Dynamics processing and deliberate distortion   Most analog signal chains used a lot of compression so loud sounds wouldn't produce distortion. Set yours for a fairly low threshold, high ratio, and fast attack and decay. This will add distortion to low frequencies, so be prepared to back off slightly.

Some distortion was inevitable in early analog systems, particularly those aimed at the consumer. Unfortunately, it isn't the kind a badly tuned compressor makes. But you can simulate it on your desktop by hacking the digital signal so it runs out of bits. (It's not exactly the same sound, but close enough for these purposes.) Start with a well-recorded sound that completely fills the waveform—you'll probably have to use a Normalizing function to do this. Then amplify the file about 18 dB. Do this as a file process, not just by cranking up a volume control; it might take two or three passes. Then lower the amplified file by about 3 dB, so it doesn't crackle on playback.

If you look at the distorted file, the audio envelopes should have turned into a rectangle. On playback, it will be fuzzy but understandable. Experiment with different amplifications until you like the result.

Delay   If a phonograph or tape player wasn't properly engineered, with every mechanical bearing perfectly rounded and the record's hole exactly in the center, you'd hear tiny speed variations—flutter—as things turned. You can duplicate this effect with a modulatable delay effect, found in some delay effects and most flangers or choruses. As the delay time changes, it affects the sound the same way an out-of-round bearing did.

Noises   Movie projector shutters, phonograph groove noise, and telephone cross talk can be mixed in from other sources to make the effect more authentic. If the noise isn't already mangled, mix it with your main signal and apply the filters and distortion effects to both at the same time.

The Recipes

I'll take time with the first one to show the thinking that goes into designing a convincing effect. It can be important to understand what made an old-time communication channel sound like it did, before you try to simulate it. The bulleted paragraphs are the "thinking" part. The paragraphs immediately below them explain how to accomplish each part of the sound.

Movies

A lot of projects need to turn modern DV into old-fashioned cinema—anything from a torn, dirty classroom film to a Hollywood classic. On the video side, the usual formula is to remove chroma, add some scratches and dirt, and make a few tiny jump cuts to simulate spliced repairs. (This combination is so common, it's a preset in many video programs.) But it's not a true film look, as many videographers have discovered. It's a parody, emphasizing film's limitations to broaden the gag. You can parody a film's track as well. Optical recording, used for virtually every soundtrack until a couple of decades ago, had plenty of limitations to exploit.

What makes the characteristic sound of a film?

- The projector has to hold the film perfectly still at the lens, 24 times a second, so individual frames can be projected. A few inches away, the film has to be moving smoothly at the sound head to create a continuous track. The two motions are isolated by a shock-absorbing loop of film. But the isolation was never perfect, and some of that 24 frame-per-second flutter would always sneak in.

- In badly maintained projectors, the mass of the film reels can influence the speed. If the mass isn't perfectly balanced—as can happen when the reels are warped—the speed keeps changing as the reel moves.

Frequency modulate the signal with a 24 Hz sine wave (flutter) combined with about a 0.2 Hz sine wave (*wow* or slow rhythmic speed variations from a 1,200 foot reel of 16mm film). The easiest way is to mix two oscillators and apply the result to the modulation input of a delay at around 40 ms. As the delay changes, it forces the pitch up

> ⚠️ **Gotcha** _____
>
> **This side of parodies...** The steps in this section are designed to simulate old, mistreated film. It's not the same as trying to make a track sound like a modern theatrical feature.
>
> If you want to mimic the sounds of today's Hollywood blockbusters, record all your elements properly. Then apply the non-parody techniques that fill the rest of this book. Believe me; the folks in L.A .don't do anything we haven't talked about here.

and down. This delay also knocks the track one film frame out of sync, which may add to the humor of the effect. If you don't like it, set the delay to exactly 33 ms and slip the entire track one frame earlier to compensate.

As an alternative, you can use two flangers in series, one with a 24 Hz modulation and the other set for 0.2 Hz.

- Film projectors also had a characteristic hum. The lamp that pours light through the optical soundtrack needed a pure DC voltage, but this could be hard to maintain in an older projector, and some of the power line's AC would sneak in.

Add a 120 Hz sawtooth, at low levels, for this hum.

- The photocell that read the light coming through the optical track had its own random hiss.

Add a tiny amount of white noise.

- Optical sound was not a wide-range medium. Both highs and lows were lost in the process. Bad projector maintenance could destroy the highs even more.

Band pass everything between 250 Hz–7.5 kHz. The lower filter should be fairly sharp. The upper one depends on what you're trying to simulate. Well-maintained movie theaters running 35mm tracks could start to fall off around 12 kHz, but a sharp 7.5 kHz filter will make sure the effect is immediately recognizable to an audience, when they see your video. Classroom projectors ran at a slower speed, were not high fidelity to start with, and lost treble when they got out of alignment—you could use a filter that starts a gentle roll off around 2.5 kHz.

- It isn't really part of the track, but the clicking noise from a projector's gate is part of the cliché.

Get one from a sound effects library—or do it yourself with a 12 Hz square wave, high-pass filtered very sharply at 5.5 kHz. Modulate the frequency slightly with the 0.2 Hz sine wave you're using for wow, and it's surprisingly realistic.

For the ultimate illusion, use a pitch bender to ramp both speed and pitch up from zero to normal over about three seconds when the clip starts, and back down to zero as it's ending. Classroom projector motors had to fight a lot of mass and always got off to a slow start.

Don't forget to add a click, and delete a few frames of sound, each time you have a jump cut in the picture. If you want to be accurate, the audio jump should be a second after the picture jump; that's just about how long it took the splice to get from lens to sound head in a 16 mm projector.

- Giant movie palaces had a sound of their own. A 75-foot-deep auditorium had a distinct echo from the rear wall, about 2.5 frames after dialog left the speakers. Every theater was slightly different, and the echo varied, depending on where you were sitting.

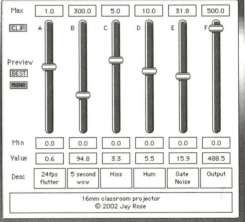

17.12 A SFX Machine preset with most of the functions in this section.

Use a reverb with a short, diffuse characteristic. Set the time before the first reflection to about 100 ms, and bunch the other early reflections together. If your software doesn't let you control the initial time, use a delay line ahead of the reverb.

Part 1 of Track 75 lets you hear this effect the way I implemented it on a powerful DSP-based hardware processor. If you have SFX Machine, discussed earlier in this chapter, you can download a 16 mm projector preset for it from my Web site, www.dplay.com/dv, entry for June '02. As

Hear for yourself

Track 75 lets you hear some of the combination effects described here.

you can see from Figure 17.12, it has almost all of the features above. (I ran out of processing power before I could add the pitch bend and reverb.)

Radios

Broadcast radio's quality changed as the years went by, but a low cutoff between 120–500 Hz, and high cutoff between 4–8 kHz is a good place to start. Use lots of compression and a little distortion. Mix in some square wave or sawtooth at 120 Hz; the harmonics simulate AM radio's power-line interference.

Police and CB radios had much more distortion, a bandwidth as narrow as 400 Hz to 2.5 kHz, and hiss. For an even better simulation, cut the hiss off whenever the voice pauses. Two-way radios did this automatically.

Older AM and shortwave radios had a squeal as you tuned them. You can simulate it with a sine wave sweeping from 8 kHz down, reaching its lowest frequency as you center on the desired station. Single-sideband shortwave—a common form of transmission—would shift the voice frequencies up and down slowly. You can simulate this with a delay line heavily modulated with a sine wave around 0.3 Hz (but to do it right, you need a heterodyne frequency shifter, seldom found in desktop software).

Phonograph

The distortion and band limiting for phonograph was similar to radios, but most players also had tiny pitch variations, repeating at the speed of the turntable; modulate a delay at 1.3 Hz for 78 RPM records, 0.75 Hz for 45s, and 0.55 Hz for 33s. If the record was warped, this modulation could be very deep. Add continuous groove noise and occasional ticks that also repeat in the same rhythm.

Telephone

Local calls are easy to simulate. A low cutoff around 380 Hz and a high one at 3 kHz are a little more extreme than modern phones, but work nicely in production. Add compression and distortion before you filter. Local calls also had some hiss, but that's rarely necessary in the mix.

Old-fashioned long distance calls had a few additional wrinkles. A lot of your voice would be reflected back from the other end of the call. Telephone calls move at the speed of light, but over cross-country distances, it would create a noticeable echo. A 6,000 mile round trip takes about 1/30 second—just like the acoustic slap you get from the back wall of a medium-sized room. Mix in a small amount of the original signal, delayed between 20–120 ms, to simulate a variety of distances and line conditions.

In those predigital days, long distance also suffered from cross talk as other conversations leaked into your call. Match the sound by adding another track of different voices, with a low-cut around 500 Hz, mixed about 30 dB below the main track. If you flip the second track so it plays backwards, the cross talk will sound foreign and not be as distracting.

Part 2 of Track 75 lets you hear a full-bore old fashioned long distance simulator. The cross talk is actually the main voice, delayed, pitch shifted, broken into chunks, and reversed. This lets me apply the effect in real time, without needing a separate track for cross talk.

The Mix

Actually, just about everything in the past six chapters relates to mixing. Equalization, compression, and other processing generally shouldn't be applied until the mix because that's the first time you'll be able to hear how the processed sound relates to other elements in a track. It also may be the first time you can hear the project as a whole, rather than as individual elements or sequences, and feel how the track flows from beginning to end.

If you edit and mix on different setups, this might even be the first time you can hear the track on good monitors. It's foolish to make processing decisions without them. If you're mixing at an audio post facility, their processors will probably be a lot better than what's available on your desktop. It makes sense to wait until you've got access to them.

There are usually only two times where you might want to apply processing before the final mix:

- Clips that are candidates for noise reduction should be tested before you start editing, to make sure you'll be able to get them clean enough to use. You may want to apply some noise reduction over the entire clip to make its dialog easier to edit. But apply the absolute minimum you can get away with, to minimize artifacts. If you need more processing, you can do it at the mix. You might decide the clip doesn't need it, when you hear it in context with other sounds and music.

- It may be necessary to do a little tweaking when creating a temporary mix for client approval. It's a good idea to remove this processing and start fresh at the final mix. (A good strategy here is to warn clients that they're listening for content approval only. Tell them the track will be much more polished after a real mixing session. This also leaves them one more part of your work to appreciate at the final screening.)

This chapter deals with the nonprocessing aspects of a mix: the techniques involved, and how to keep sounds in a proper relationship with each other.

⚠️ **Gotcha** _____

Why not mix while you're editing? On the face of it, this should save time. As you assemble things in the NLE, you can apply filters and adjust the volume of each track. When you finish the last scene, the project will have already been mixed.

Unless a project is very simple—one or two talking heads, a voice-over, and maybe music at the head and tail—this usually leads to an inconsistent track that's hard to listen to. It's nearly impossible to produce a smooth sound when each mix decision is separated by long periods of editing.

What a Mix Needs

Obviously, you can't start without picture and individual tracks, software that's capable of mixing, and probably some processing plug-ins. But a few other things—operating methods as well as hardware or software—can make the difference between a polished, professional track and one that shouts "video amateur."

Know the elements

Learn what sounds are on the timeline and how they relate to the story. It's one thing to see a clip marked, "car start," but to mix it properly, you need to know *how* it starts. Is there a long turnover that gets ridden under other sounds, or does the engine catch immediately? Does the engine then idle, or is it put in gear immediately and the car drives away? You also need to know what's supposed to happen at the end of the sound: Does it cross-fade to a tracking car, drive off, or cut to another scene?

You should know where tweaks are necessary in production dialog and where ADR or other effects will need processing. You should have an idea of how music should segue from one track to another and where it should be faded.

Most importantly, you should understand how the track has been designed. Dialog usually dominates, but there are places where sound effects or music may rise above dialog levels. Know which subordinate elements are most important. In one scene, music might exist simply to punctuate sound effects; in another, effects may be barely audible under the score. It depends on what you're trying to convey from moment to moment.

If you edited the project and are doing the mix yourself, you're probably on top of all this. If you're mixing someone else's film, or they're mixing yours, a track chart—described at the end of this chapter—can help. But even if there's a chart, mixer and editor or director should walk through the project and understand how elements are supposed to fit together.

Know the audience

New clients are often surprised when I ask them how a piece will be shown—not what tape format will be used, but where the audience will be sitting.

If that surprises you as well, go back and read the first section of Chapter 6.

Organize the tracks

Nothing is harder to mix than jumbled tracks. It's tempting to drop sounds on the first available track while you're building a project, and it can save time during the edit. But if the same track has dialog, spot effects, and music at different times, it'll slow down the mix because you don't know what's coming next. Keeping similar elements on the same track also means you can save time by applying effects globally instead of on individual clips.

Have a consistent track layout. In almost every project I edit, the tracks are laid out like this:

- The top track is reserved for principal dialog or narration, whichever drives the show.
- Other dialog is on the track or two below, depending on how much splitting or ADR is used.
- Spot sounds are on a couple of tracks under that.
- Backgrounds are under the spot sounds.
- Music is on the bottom.

This arrangement has a couple of ergonomic advantages in my setup. Since dialog is usually the most important element, it's right at the top of the screen where my eye can bounce between it and the picture monitor above. Other voices are next to it, so I can compare waveforms easily to see if an upcoming clip will need to have its level trimmed. Spot sound effects are often the most actively mixed elements in a track and have to be constantly adjusted. On my setup, this puts their faders right in the middle of the console, where one hand or the other can reach them quickly.

The other advantage is consistency. As I move from project to project, I can pay more attention to content because I don't have to worry about where to find things.

Your setup may be different, you might not have as many tracks to work with, and you might be working with virtual faders rather than real ones. Even so, a consistent track layout will save time and psychic energy, letting you concentrate on the sound rather than having to guess what's coming up and where. If your tracks aren't organized, take a few minutes to swap things around before the mix.

Take a break

In Hollywood, editing and mixing might be days apart and are almost always done in separate studios by different people. It's a good idea to take a similar approach, even if you're doing everything yourself on a single computer.

Editing and mixing are different. One has to be analytical, dealing with discrete units of time. The other is organic, concerned with how elements interact and flow. Even if you're schizophrenic enough to bounce between the two functions quickly, it's hard to keep a sense of perspective about the track if you're also editing. If you've just perfected the cutting in a particular part of one track, it's likely you'll make that track too loud unless you take a break.

I'm frequently hired to both edit and mix. On short corporate and commercial projects, this may be part of the same half-day session. But unless the edits were trivial, I insist on taking a breather before mixing. I declare a lunch break, or stop the clock (so they're not paying for the time) and walk out of the room for a few minutes. When reasonable, I set things up so I can edit in the afternoon and mix the next morning. My clients put up with this because it means they get a better product, often for less money.

The alternative—mixing as soon as you've finished elaborate editing—almost always means remixing a few days later, after you've had a chance to put individual elements in perspective.

Monitor properly

Mix at a consistent level on the best speakers you can get[1]. Both of these factors are critical.

If you don't mix on good speakers, you can't make good equalization decisions. In most cases, you can't even make good level decisions because poor speakers won't give you an accurate balance between voice and music. (You can't even predict how they'll distort the balance. Some poor speakers have a narrow bandwidth and emphasize voice; others hype the extremes of the band and distort the middle, making music seem louder than dialog.)

Without good speakers, you can also miss problems. I was recently asked to remix a TV spot. It was a simple voice-over with an elaborate score, so the producer originally asked the composer

---

1. If you're not building a new facility, you may have skipped Chapter 3 (acoustics and monitoring). If so, go back and read about monitors—particularly the sections on choosing a monitor, the perils of real-world speakers, and metering. Your mixes will be better for it.

to record the voice and mix it. While the composer was gifted, he couldn't afford the best equipment. His microphone preamp had a deep hum, and his speakers weren't good enough to reveal it. His music clients tolerated the hum on acoustic instruments—if they noticed it at all—because it was constant throughout a song and most of his scoring was synthesizer-based. But voice-overs ride above the music and are opened up and slid to match video. This made the hum click in with each edit, and the effect was obvious on the client's home-theater system—to the embarrassment of the producer. I equalized the voice track and applied low-frequency noise reduction before remixing.

Mix with consistent monitor levels   The relationship between the volume coming out of your speakers and the level on a track should always be the same. In other words, don't mess with the monitor volume control.

This is critical because we hear timbre and dynamics differently as sound levels change. There's a natural temptation to raise the monitor level as a session wears on and your ears get tired. Resist it. You'll be able to hear the mix more accurately if you take a short break instead.

Don't crank the monitors to hear soft sequences, either. The audience doesn't have that opportunity, so they'll hear a completely different perspective.

Professional monitoring setups are usually calibrated so that –20 dBFS pink noise coming from any one speaker results in 85 dB SPL at the mix position. You might not need that kind of precision, but it's still important to have a standard level when you mix. Find a position on the volume control that works well for you and reflects a typical viewing level for your audience, mark it with tape or grease pencil, and *leave it there*.

Learn what your monitors sound like when you play a good mix through them at the chosen volume. Start with other people's mixes you respect, in the same medium. If you're making narrative films, there are plenty of great examples for rent. If you're doing documentaries or commercials, tape them from a large network (cable and local shows often have less-than-perfect mixes). Pay particular attention to the ratios between voice, music, and sound effects, and to how natural the dialog sounds.

I haven't included example mixes on this book's CD because there are so many different styles and purposes for a track. If you want to hear what I consider good, check some of my recent short-form projects at www.dplay.com/movies. I won't be upset if they're nothing like the way you want your mixes to sound. This is a book about technique, not creative judgement.

What about smaller speakers?   It's always a good idea to check mixes on a small, TV-like speaker if your mix is headed for that medium. (It's not a good idea to mix on one, for reasons explained in Chapter 6.) Interestingly enough, if you consistently check on small speakers and pay attention to how the balance is different from your main monitors, you'll soon learn what kind of mixes work best on both sets of speakers.

Auratone 5-C Sound Cubes are the standard for small speakers in professional post rooms. They cost about $350 a pair—considerably more than comparably sized units from a hi-fi dealer. The reason they're preferred is consistency—every nearfield 5-C sounds like every other, no matter what studio you're in—and relative freedom from distortion, rattles, and other problems. If you're doing professional audio post for multiple clients, they're a necessity. If you're mixing your own projects on a desktop, they're overkill.

If you want a TV-like monitor for checking mixes, you can get one at an electronics chain. Look for something with a single loudspeaker inside, since TV sets rarely have separate low- and high-frequency drivers. Also, crossover issues in small, dual-speaker systems can affect dialog. Avoid the tiny satellite-type speakers with separate subwoofers; they won't tell you anything useful about a TV mix. Radio Shack sells an acceptable cheap TV speaker, #40-5024, for under $25. It's nowhere near as good (or consistent) as an Auratone, but the money it saves can go toward better main speakers.

In my experience the Yamaha NS-10, a standard reference monitor in music studios, isn't very good for judging video mixes.

How about headphones?   Mixing on headphones is useful if—and only if—you're sure the viewers will be wearing them. Otherwise they give you a distorted picture of the sound field and dynamics, and trick you into making subordinate elements like music or backgrounds much too soft.

Visual monitoring   No matter how good your speakers are, you can't rely on them as an absolute indicator of volume. Too many things, including your own fatigue level, can make a particular volume level seem right one day and wrong the next. Because mixing involves combining multiple tracks, you can't just look at the waveform of individual tracks on a timeline and guess how loud an overall mix will be.

Some NLEs don't provide a master meter for the mix. This is a major failing. But there are a couple of workarounds:

- One strategy is to mix the piece in the NLE so it sounds good. Then play it back in an audio editor with a level meter. If the maximum volume is within a couple of decibels of where you want it, and never hits 0 dBFS, apply gain or normalizing to get to the proper level. But if it's more than 12 dB too soft, or reaches 0 dBFS at any point, it's probably infected with noise or distortion. Go back to the NLE and mix again.

- Get an external meter and connect it to the output of your NLE. The meters on most video decks are adequate for this, once you've calibrated them by playing a tone at your nominal level and adjusting the recorder's input controls. You can also use one of the hardware meters mentioned at the end of Chapter 3.

If you're mixing in an audio program or a hardware mixer, it most likely already has a meter. Glance at it while you're mixing, both to check for problems and to make sure the level is consistent from the start of the program to the end. Watch it carefully on playback. Most programs give a low priority to the meter, and it can miss momentary peaks during record because the software is busy doing complex processing or mixing.

Many professionals also keep a *spectrum analyzer* handy. This is a row of vertical volume meters, each with a band-pass filter, so it responds only to the energy in one octave (or sometimes, in one-third of an octave). Some software does spectrum analysis on an entire file; that's not the same thing as having a real time analyzer available while you mix or listen.

A spectrum analyzer can teach you a lot. Play some good mixes through it. If the sequence is dialog driven, most of the energy will be below 3 kHz and very little will be above 10 kHz. If it's orchestral music, you might see heavy activity up to about 6 kHz. Only a few pop music styles have significant energy above 10 kHz; for radio and club purposes, music is specifically mastered with an every-frequency-loud-all-the-time philosophy.

> ## ⚠ Gotcha
>
> **Beware the master.** When you mix tracks together, their volumes can add up to be more than 0 dBFS. But no digital system can faithfully reproduce signals above zero, so the result would be distortion. You can usually avoid this by keeping an eye on the master level meter.
>
> But the meter only reads volume after the signal has gone through the master fader. If the fader has been pulled partially down, the meter may show an acceptable level—even if the combined volume exceeds 0 dBFS and is distorted internally![1]
>
> If you're mixing in a digital system, leave the master at 0 dB so you can trust the meter. Turn the master down only when you want to perform a smooth fade on an overall scene.
>
> A similar thing happens in analog mixers, though a different kind of distortion can be introduced. Depending on the manufacturer, there'll be a 0, dot, or U marking the proper position for the master.
>
> ---
>
> 1. At least one professional audio workstation lowers individual signal levels during the mix to prevent this from happening. It adds additional bits to the audio words so the lowered levels don't have increased noise. Then, after the master fader, it raises the level again and dithers back to the original bit depth. You're not likely to encounter this in desktop software. I point it out here because it's a darned clever approach, and maybe some programmer will decide to put it into an NLE.

Don't equalize your mixes to look like someone else's on the spectrum analyzer. Your source material isn't the same, and tweaking it to fit some other source's spectral balance will make it sound bad.

Instead, use the analyzer to make sure the average spectral balance is appropriate for the medium, to verify what you're hearing, and as a quick diagnostic for problem tracks—particularly at the extremes of the range. It's also handy to know, if you've got a head cold, that the lack of highs is in your head and not on the track.

An analyzer doesn't have to be elaborate, since you're using it to look at trends rather than making critical measurements. In my last studio, I had a $100 graphic equalizer/spectrum analyzer from a surplus consumer electronics dealer (Figure 18.1). The equalizer part was worthless, but the analyzer portion made up for it. I wired it in parallel with my mixer's main outputs and left it on all the time.

18.1 This $100 graphic equalizer was too noisy to pass signal through, but its spectrum analyzer was certainly handy.

These days I rely on a software-based analyzer with a couple of extra features. This program, SpectraFoo,[2] includes an accurate digital level meter with peak and averaging readouts, spectragrams (three-dimensional analyzers that show relative level at different frequencies over time), and stereo analysis tools. It's also got two-dimensional spectrum analyzers, but I find the spectragram more useful. The program takes its signal directly from the AES/EBU input card in its computer and is as accurate as external test equipment.

Figure 18.2 shows SpectraFoo in use. It's a visual nightmare, particularly in black and white. But in color, if you understand what you're looking at, it has you all you need to know.

Have locked picture

It's easy to go into a finished video and remove a couple of problem frames or stretch the video a tiny bit longer. Often, all you have to do is rerender a small section and print the whole thing back to tape.

It's next to impossible to add or subtract a couple of frames from a finished soundtrack, unless the section is strictly dialog. If there's an underscore, walla, or other continuous element, the edit will likely disrupt it. You often have to remix the entire sequence from the start of that element to the end, and then edit the new version into the old mix—a time-consuming affair.

---

2. www.mhlabs.com; Macintosh only.

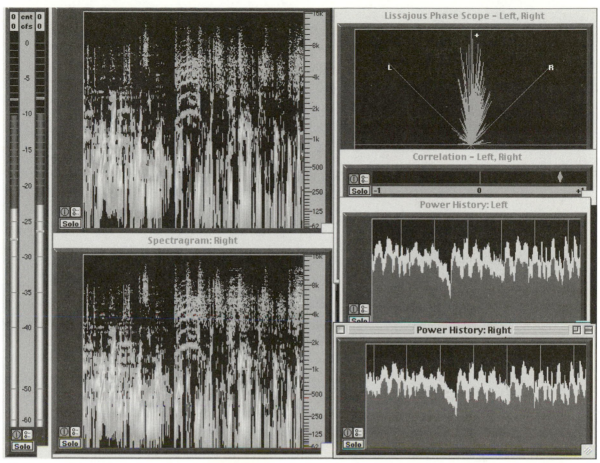

18.2 A software-based audio analysis suite, SpectraFoo. From left to right, peak and averaging level meter, spectrograms for both channels, stereo phase and correlation meters to measure mono compatibility, and relative volume over the past ten seconds. There's also a spectrum analyzer, but I find the spectrogram more useful.

It's wasted effort to mix a track before the picture is *locked* and thoroughly finished. Occasionally, you'll need to mix while still waiting for an artist to complete animations or graphic sequences. This may be acceptable if you know exactly how many frames the missing sequence will take, and you have the timeline with a "missing clip" message or other *slug*[3] of the same length. If the sequence will need audio sweetening timed to animation, you'll have to go back and add that to the mix. This is also time-consuming, but not as drastic as having to change a scene's length.

---

3. The term comes from film-based editing, where scrap film or leader of the precise length was inserted as a placeholder. They got it from typesetting, which used pieces of lead to fill missing text in a column.

Controlling levels

Different systems have different ways to let you control individual track levels during a mix.

- *Keyframes* are dots that you apply to a volume line in the middle of a clip in the timeline. Once you've done so, the volume line hinges there. You can grab on either side of the line with a mouse and bend the volume up or down. (The volume line is often called a *rubber band* for this reason.) It's awkward and a time-consuming way to mix, but may be the only method available in a particular NLE.

- Many NLEs and most multitrack audio programs have *on-screen mixers*. This is a graphic representation of a studio hardware mixer, with sliders you can move with a mouse. Despite the pretty user interface, this mixer is also time-consuming and can lead to compromises in a mix.

- *Hands-on control surfaces* with real faders, instead of pictures of them, are used by post-production professionals. They're fast and flexible, and let you concentrate on the sound.

Which one you use depends on how sophisticated your setup is, and you might not have much choice in the matter. I'm including all three in this short section so you can see what other options may be available. Depending on the software you use, you might even be able to upgrade your existing system to a hands-on system without spending too much.

Changing levels with keyframes

Most NLEs include volume lines or rubber bands. Figure 18.3 shows a music track being faded with a rubber band down before dialog starts.

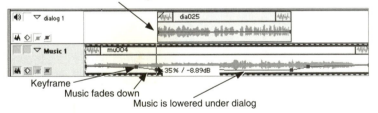

18.3   A rubber band, fading the music track under dialog.

This scheme is one of the easiest for a programmer to implement but unwieldy for all but the simplest mixes. Each fade requires at least two mouse clicks. Because you can't hear the effect while you're drawing it, you then have to preview[4] it (and usually do additional mousing to fine-tune).

---

4. Interesting use of language: When you finish setting up a effect in an NLE, you want to *review* what you've done. But the program calls it a *preview*, since it's prior to rendering the final output.

☞ *Note*
_____

You can speed things up slightly by zooming out on the timeline. Draw all the fades necessary in the section of the track that's visible, without scrolling. Preview that whole screen's worth, note which fades have to be changed, make adjustments, and preview again. When that screen sounds right, scroll on to the next.

While you can try to develop rules for how much to lower one track when another comes in, the right fade always depends on the specific sounds involved. So you can't manipulate rubber bands without previewing afterwards.

Moving On-screen Faders with a Mouse

Rubber-band based mixing is so cumbersome that many NLEs, and all good multitrack audio editors, put an automated mixer on the screen. This usually emulates a hardware mixing console with vertical faders for each track and other track controls above (usually a *pan-pot* to adjust left/right balance, a *mute* to silence the track, a *solo* to silence every other track, and some automation switches). These software mixers often add something you don't find on most hardware mixers: a volume meter for each track, right next to its fader. Figure 18.4 shows the mixer in Premiere.

Mixing this way is easier because you can change things while a track is playing and hear the effect in realtime. But since you have to grab individual controls with a mouse, you can change only one thing at a time. That's where the automation comes in. If you want to cross-fade between two tracks, you set automation to Write and pull one track's fader down as you listen. Then you can jump back to before the fade, switch the automation on that track to Read, start playing, and push the second fader up at the appropri-

18.4   An on-screen automated mixer.

ate time. As you do, the first track's fader goes down, following the move you originally made.

The automation is actually putting keyframes and rubber-band changes on the timeline as you do them in the mixer. In most programs, if you go back to the timeline after a write pass, you can see what you've done as a wiggling rubber band and adjust it manually.

Good programs automate the process even further, letting you select an update mode where faders normally read data but switch to write as soon as you move them. You can do a first rough pass with every track set to write, getting faders approximately where you want them. Then you can do successive passes, fine-tuning only those faders that need to change.

Hardware Controllers

Mixing with a mouse is like trying to write a book by pointing to letters on a screen. I'm a touchtypist and want to use both hands.

It's more than a matter of preference. For the best mixes, you have to be able to move multiple faders simultaneously. The way one track comes up and another comes down depends on the combination of sounds at a given moment. You need to constantly adjust both levels, if you want to smoothly catch some parts of one and lose parts of the other. This means one hand for each fader, something you can't do with a single mouse. (Experienced mixers often manipulate multiple tracks with individual fingers.)

Every professional audio workstation now comes with a hands-on controller, either as an option or as the main control system. Most workstations also put editing controls on the same surface because using dedicated buttons is always faster than searching for a window and mousing. Figure 18.5 shows the system in my studio, an Orban Audicy. Faders are on the left, under a computer monitor with SpectraFoo. Edit controls are on the right, under the track display monitor. (A separate production monitor, above the two computer screens but not in this picture, shows synchronized video.)

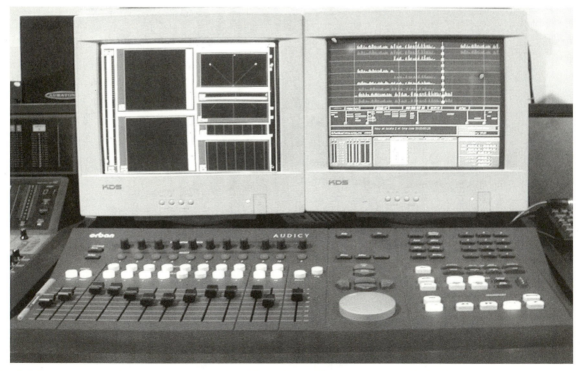

18.5   A hardware controller lets you control multiple channels simultaneously, fading some while raising others.

While the controller looks like a mixer, no audio passes through it. Instead, it's sending automation data to the computer, which performs the fades in software. Some systems also create editable rubber bands on the tracks in response to your real-world fader moves.

Mixing this way has so many advantages that third-party hardware controllers are available for multitrack audio programs (and even a few NLEs). They communicate with the host program via USB. Controllers range from a few hundred to several thousand dollars, depending on their complexity. If you're doing sophisticated mixes, they'll pay for themselves in the time they save.

Putting Things in Perspective

In a traditional mixing console, each channel goes through some processing and has its volume adjusted by a volume fader and pan-pot. The audio is then fed to a pair of electrical busses, where it's combined with other channels to create a single stereo pair. Software does just about the same thing, but uses internal math for processing and bussing.

18.6   A stereo film mix creates a horizontal plane, starting on a line between the speakers and extending behind the screen to infinity. You can put elements anywhere on that plane.

Please don't think of your mix that way. Forget faders, pan-pots, and busses for a moment.

The *human* act of mixing assigns each sound a place in an imaginary two-dimensional sound field. The field is roughly a rectangle, parallel to the floor, at the height of the screen. It's bounded on the front by a line between the two stereo speakers, and on the sides by the speakers themselves. The rear is behind the screen, away from us, almost at infinity. Figure 18.6 shows how it can be visualized.

If you're working in surround, the front boundary doesn't exist. You sit in the middle of the horizontal field, and it stretches behind you as well as behind the screen. Some surround formats, such as the 6.1 used in IMAX, add a slight sense of vertical as well.

Different media have limitations, as discussed in chapter 6. If you're mixing for broadcast television, home VHS, or classroom use, the horizontal plane still exists. But you can't use it as complexly as you would for theatrical film. Usually, no more than three dis-

18.7 A stereo TV mix has to be simpler, with only three distinct distances from the screen, if you want to get your message across.

tinct distances from the screen, or *layers*, are appropriate: close, middle, and farther away. Figure 18.7 visualizes this simpler plane.

For mono listeners, everything is on a single line, starting at the center of the screen[5] and running away from it, behind the screen to infinity. There may be a sense of spaciousness imparted by the natural reverb of the viewing room, but every element still stays on that one line. See Figure 18.8.

18.8 A mono listener will hear everything squeezed into a single line.

---

5. Assuming the speaker is properly located.

⚠️ *Gotcha*

Nobody listens in mono, man! Want to bet? While you and your friends may have elegant stereo or surround setups, simple economics dictates that much of the TV world will hear a production in mono.

• Low-cost TVs, 19 inches or smaller, usually don't have stereo capability. They may have two speaker grills in front—it makes them look more impressive—but will lack the circuits to drive them properly. Profit margins on these sets are incredibly low: The couple of extra chips stereo requires could make a 10 percent difference in the product's bottom line.

• Low-cost VHS Hi-Fi recorders are stereo; it's part of the spec—but only if you hook up through the RCA jacks on the back. The antenna connection, which most people use, is almost always mono. It's a bottom-line thing as well.

• Smaller cable systems have been known to run satellite channels through mono modulators rather than stereo ones. Care to guess why?

Unless you're mixing exclusively for theatrical use, kiosks, or other situations where you can control the playback, mono is very much alive.

Tools for Placing Sounds

The idea of sound field as horizontal plane isn't just film school theory. When we hear real-world sounds, we're very conscious of location. We compare a sound's loudness, amount of reverberation, and (to lesser extent) timbre, with what we'd expect for similar sounds. That gives us a sense of how far away the source is. We compare how the sound differs in volume and timing at our two ears, and we know what direction it's coming from.[6] Those two factors, distance and direction, tell us where the sound is originating

Direction

The primary tool for setting direction is the pan-pot. It might appear in software as a knob or as a secondary rubber band in a timeline. You can place it in any position between left and right, and the sound will come from a matching location between the two speakers.

Panning only makes sense for mono signals. Multitrack audio software and some NLEs treat every signal as mono. When you import a stereo file, it goes on two different tracks which can be panned separately. Usually, you'll pan one to the extreme left and the other to the extreme right, but other arrangements might be appropriate. For example, if the man riding the elephant on the right of Figure 18.6 had been recorded in stereo, you'd still want to keep them on the right side

---

6. We also listen to very subtle differences in how parts of each sound reach us, because of the way they're affected by the shape of our heads and outer ears. That tells us if a sound is above, below, or behind us. But this kind of manipulation is rarely used in stereo mixes.

of the screen. But you could give them a sense of width by panning one channel to the *center* and the other to the right.

Some NLEs import stereo files as a single clip on the timeline and don't let you pan it. If you have to deal with the elephant rider or something similar, there's a workaround:

1. Copy the clip onto a second track, in sync with the first.
2. Apply the Take Left or similar command to the original clip. This turns it into a mono sound using just the information on the left side. The panning rubber band will reappear, centered.
3. Apply Take Right to the copy.
4. Pan the copy to the extreme right. Leave the original in the center.

If you're working in surround, panning works on the same principle but the interface is a little different. Most surround software lets you call up a panning window for each track, with the sound source indicated as a mark in the center of a circle. This puts the source in the middle of the field, being sent equally to the four corner speakers. Grab the mark and move it to where you want it, and the window will direct the right proportions of the sound to the proper output channels.

In the real world, timing is also a component of direction. A sound coming from the right will reach our right ear sooner than it reaches our left one. The sub-millisecond it takes a sound to cross the width of our head helps up paint a more accurate picture of the world around us. But this is usually ignored when mixing mono sources into a stereo or surround track.

Precedence effect   A similarly short delay can sometimes fool the ear about the direction a sound is coming from. If we hear the same sound panned to two different points in the sound field, but one is delayed by a millisecond or so, we'll believe that it's coming from only the earlier location—even if the later sound is almost as loud. This *precedence* or *Haas effect* is noticed most on sounds with sharp attacks, such as gunshots or piano notes.

If you're mixing a theatrical track, you can use the precedence effect when a loud sound has to match a visual on the side of the screen. Just panning to that side wouldn't be fair to viewers on the other side of the house, who wouldn't hear it as loud as it should be. Add a delayed version on the opposite side. Everybody will hear it loud, but the source will stay with the picture. Don't do this if the track is destined for TV, though: When the channels are combined to mono, the delay will turn into a comb filter.

Visual anchoring   Our aural sense of direction can get overwhelmed by an image, particularly if it's an immersive image like a movie screen. Imagine a race car zooming across from left to right and then off the screen. At the same time, we hear its sound Doppler pan from left to right and then fade out. Most people will swear the sound continued to move to the right, beyond the sound field—even though there's no speaker there to reproduce it. The visual is enough to steer our perception.

On the other hand, if a film is projected on a widescreen, there has to be at least an attempt to match a sound's panning with the on-screen source. Most people start to feel uncomfortable if an important sound is coming from a direction more than about 15 degrees different from where they see it. Dialog, which by convention always comes from the center, is an exception.

This match between visual and acoustic direction isn't as important in television, both because of how people watch and the need for mono compatibility. Documentaries and other nonnarrative projects—even those destined for a big screen—frequently ignore specific sound placement as a convention of the medium.

Distance

The principal tools for establishing a sound's distance are the volume control and reverb.[7] Don't forget there's much less reverb outdoors, and it's almost always less complex than indoor reverb because there are fewer surfaces to bounce off of.

Volume as distance   The effect of a volume control is obvious; all other things being equal, louder sounds are perceived as being closer. Of course, things are seldom equal. Soft sounds are boosted when they're recorded, and loud ones lowered, to get the best recording quality. So you can't simply use the fader position as a distance gauge.

In most scenes, dialog is the most important element. Set its volume first, based on the nominal level for the medium. (If you're mixing on a NLE, dialog peaks should come to between −12 dBFS and −6 dBFS, depending on if sounds louder than voice will be added to the mix.) Once dialog is set, imagine how loud each other sound should be, compared to the voice, at the distance you want to simulate. Then move its fader to match. This procedure becomes intuitive after very little practice.

Ultimate volume   Broadcast projects are usually specified with an average level of −20 dBFS and peaks at −10 dBFS; other shows might be mixed much louder. This is not the time to worry about that. Mix at a level that gives you the best compromise between headroom and noise on your equipment; often it'll be in the range −12 dBFS to −6 dBFS.

Once the show is mixed, you can adjust the overall level to whatever spec is appropriate before making the master.

---

7. Timbre can also imply distance, as high frequencies are lost to air friction. But this doesn't happen until very large distances are involved.

Reverb as distance: dialog   Reverb takes a little more thought. That's partly because most people aren't conscious of how much reverberation surrounds us, until they walk into a nearly anechoic space like a good voice-over studio. (Even then, the usual reaction is, "How quiet," not "How echo-free.")

Actors should sound like they look, at least in terms of their distance from the camera. A close-up should have very little reverb. A long shot will have more reverb, particularly indoors. The actor's volume should also change with distance. But volume changes due to distance aren't as big in a film as the inverse-square law dictates in the real world—dialog has to stay intelligible.

Don't switch reverb or volume with each new camera angle in a scene. We don't hear anything equivalent when listening to conversations in the real world, so it would be disorienting. Find a perspective that works for most of the scene and stick with it.

The type of reverb depends on the space. Most reverb presets in software are designed for music recording, and simulate much larger spaces than appropriate for a film. Chances are, you'll have to work up your own settings using the tips in Chapter 14.

The amount of reverb depends on both how dialog was recorded and the visual distance. That's because some of the location's natural reverb is picked up by the mic:

- Production dialog shot with a properly used boom will have a small amount of echo, just enough to suggest the room. It's usually not necessary to add more, unless a character is far away from us or the presumed setting is much more echoey than the location was.

- Production dialog shot with properly rigged lavs is usually too dry. While there'll be a tiny amount of reverb, it's never enough to match the camera angle. Add a little more in the mix. Documentary interviews shot with lavs will also be dry, but that's accepted in this context.

- ADR, when properly recorded, is dry as a bone. When combining it with production dialog, follow these steps:

1. Set the volume of the ADR track to match the dialog track.

2. Tweak the equalization to make the timbre match. If ADR was recorded with the same kind of mic as production audio and at the same distance, this might not be necessary. Otherwise, you'll almost always need to dip the low frequencies and usually boost the high mids. Then fine-tune the volume because equalization affects it.

3. Add reverb, but not too much. Remember the production mic should have been only a foot or so from the sound source. In most cases, you should just notice the reverb when the ADR track is soloed and not be aware of it when effects and music are added.

⚠ *Gotcha* _____

Wide 'verb, narrow mic. The natural reverb picked up in production tracks is mono,[1] usually centered on the screen. Artificial reverbs in audio programs and hardware have stereo or surround outputs.

- If you're adding reverb to match an ADR insert to production dialog, collapse it to mono. Otherwise the perspective will be wrong. This happens automatically in most NLEs, if you apply the reverb as a filter on a mono source clip.

- If you're adding reverb to increase the apparent size of a room, it can be stereo or surround.

_____
1.   Except in those very rare cases where production dialog is shot m/s.

Reverb as distance: sound effects   In the language of film, foley effects belong to the dialog track. Treat them with a similar reverb, including how the reverb is applied in stereo. A little equalization is almost always necessary, too: When small effects are recorded close to a mic, their low end gets boosted. Use a shelf to turn things down. In general, foley usually should be mixed a little softer than you'd expect; its purpose is to fill a track and add naturalness, not call attention to how good the foley artist was.

Hard effects are often recorded fairly dry. If you're adding them to an interior shot, reverb will help. Large hard effects, such as explosions, usually have their own reverb; adding more isn't necessary unless the explosions are very far away. Gunshots seem to come either wet or dry, depending on the whim of the recordist. A gunshot without reverb sounds wrong.

Good ambiences are recorded in stereo or surround and include natural reverb. Adding extra usually makes things sound artificial. If you've added walla or stingers to improve a background, give it some reverb to match the background recording.

Reverb (and other tricks): source music and on-screen loudspeakers   Source   or   diegetic music is supposed to be coming from the film's world, whether it's a radio on a character's desk, or an off-screen band at a party. As such, it should have a fixed place on the sound field. The same thing is true of disc jockeys on a radio, newscasters on a TV, intercoms, and any other electronic voices in the scene.

- Narrow the stereo width of source music. If the source is a loudspeaker, it should usually be mono. If the plot calls for us to admire a character's expensive stereo, it should still be much narrower than the full sound field.

- If there's any excuse, add a lot of room reverb. The sound should be far more echoey than a studio recording would be, because we're listening to the recording with two separate reverbs: the presumed one in the film's scene, and the real one we're sitting in.

- Apply appropriate equalization. Radios, TVs, and even that expensive stereo should have seriously limited bandwidth, with sharp cutoff filters. Dialog in the scene has to sound more real than the loudspeaker. Limit the bandwidth in a public address system as well and add some resonances around 1 kHz. The PA system will also resonate around 100 Hz in very large rooms. If a band is playing at a party, its amps should be adding a thudding bass and overall distortion that wouldn't be present in a studio recording.

- Choose the right music. Radios play vocals, not generic underscores written for narration. Bar bands are usually unpolished and don't have the studio tools you'd hear on a pop CD. Good production libraries have tracks specifically designed as source music.

- Edit it right. Real-world radio stations don't start "our song" the minute two lovers turn on the radio. TV anchors don't wait for a character to turn on the set before they announce a murderer has escaped in the neighborhood. The best strategy is to establish the TV or radio's sound long before its content is part of the plot. Leave it in the background from the start of the scene, and fade it up when it gets important. If you've already shot the lovers reaching for a radio in the middle of the scene, right before their song should start, you can still edit the effect properly. Play some other song softly from the start of the scene, as if the radio were already on. Then start their song a few seconds ahead of the action. It'll look like they were motivated to turn the volume up.

- For a TV or film scene, mix all the elements down to mono first. Then process that mix at once to make it diegetic.

One technique for making a sound more diegetic is *worldizing*. Play it through a cheap speaker, in a real room. Mic the speaker in stereo from a distance. Be aware that mono compatibility will suffer unless you're using m/s miking. The choice whether to worldize or process with effects depends on how big the sound is supposed to be and what tools you have at hand.

Remember, It's a Movie

The idea of the sound field as a flat plane between the speakers, with sound sources at fixed spots on it, only applies to sounds that are supposed to be natural.

Scoring

Underscores don't accompany us in the real world, so they don't need a realistic place on the sound field. Music is usually recorded in wide stereo and there's no reason not to leave it that way. If you're using it in surround, the usual convention is to keep the direct sound in front and put the reverb in the rear. If the music has been recorded in surround, it may already be processed that way. Some surround recordings assume we're sitting in the middle of the orchestra, with instruments all around us. This can be overwhelming during dialog scenes, as we're constantly torn between actors that are front-and-center and music coming from every direction. But in emotional scenes where the score predominates, it can be very involving.

Sometimes, it's appropriate to take music out of the center of the screen, leaving that space for dialog. Use the techniques in Chapter 17.

Everything

As filmmakers, we're allowed to play games with reality if it advances the story. Sound effects, ambiences, and scoring can come closer—that is, louder—when they've got something important to say, and recede when other elements are more important. Sudden sounds like crashes or explosions can jump right in front of us and then slowly fall back as their reverb takes over.

Even if you have the luxury of a theatrical track's many layers, you don't have to use them all. Take advantage of the medium's wide dynamic range, instead. Just a soft hint of foley and one or two voices or other quiet effects at the sides of the screen, can be a powerful reminder of where we are, without interfering with dialog.

Equalization and compression can help define individual sources on the soundfield by giving each source a unique timbral fingerprint. This lets you place them closer together without interfering, a necessity when mixing for TV or other limited media. This kind of processing is more important in mono than in stereo, and even less so in surround: When you've got more physical space to deal with, you don't have to use as many aural tricks.

The Last Step

If you're creating a mix with rubber bands or an on-screen mixer, you've built the final track up from a lot of smaller, disconnected movements. After you've finished, go back and listen to the whole show before considering it done. Make sure the sound is consistent in terms of levels and timbre. Watch for distortion on peaks.

Time-savers

A couple of professional techniques can save time and lead to better mixes.

Build from the Top Down

The human voice is the critical element in most films. It has to be heard and sound natural. Get it right before you worry about other elements.

1. If any equalization or other processing is necessary for dialog or voice-over, make those decisions in a vacuum. Turn off every other track while you fine-tune the principal voice track. It

may need brightening, some low-end roll-off, or a little compression. But make sure it continues to sound natural.

If you can hear music or sound effects while you're adjusting the voice's processing, you're likely to overprocess to make the voice compete. This can make it thin or artificial. It's far better to adjust the other elements and let the voice stay real.

Watch out for a honking around 1–2 kHz on voice-overs, particularly if you've recorded the voice in a studio that usually deals with music. Many of the popular condenser mics for music have a peak in that range, to make up for a perceived loss in the phantom center of a stereo mix.

2. Pan the main voice track to the center, unless you have a very good reason to put it elsewhere.[8] Adjust its volume using a meter: peaks should come to about –6 dBFS in most DV setups, if there aren't going to be other sounds much louder than voice in the mix. This is just a starting volume; you can trim during the mix as necessary to compensate for a dynamic performance.

3. Process and adjust the level of any other dialog or ADR tracks to match.

This is the opposite of how a multitrack music mix is generally done. They start with the bottom: bass and drums. But you're not trying to get people to feel the rhythm. You want them to be absorbed by a human story.

4. Leave the voices up and find appropriate volume and panning for the second layer. It may be music or sound effects, depending on how the scene is designed.

If this second layer seems to compete with the voice when it's at the right level, use an equalizer to reduce its energy at speech frequencies. That's usually around 400 Hz and 2 kHz, but you should fine-tune while listening to both this track and dialog.

5. Repeat as necessary for other tracks.

That sets basic levels, panning, and equalization. Now go back to the start of the scene and mix. If you're working with an on-screen or hands-on mixer, be ready to make continuous subtle adjustments as the scene plays. I usually mix with one finger on dialog and another on the second layer, and trim both a few dB in either direction to emphasize individual words or bring out other elements during pauses.

Starts and Stops

Everybody makes mistakes, and I'm no exception. Sometimes I'll bring an element in at the wrong volume, or make a segue that doesn't sound smooth, or just decide that one word is coming through a little too loudly or softly.

---

8. There aren't very many reasons, particularly in a film destined for broadcast or theatrical release.

As soon as I notice that kind of error, I stop. I back up a few seconds, reset the faders to where they were before the mistake, and start mixing again. I try to lose as little time as possible, so the flow of the scene stays in my mind. It's almost always best to fix mistakes this way, rather than try to patch corrections in later.

Automation software will reset the faders for you when you back up, if you're mixing on a screen or a hardware controller with motorized faders. If you're using nonmotorized faders, you may have to check *nulling* lights on the automation system to make sure levels match as you resume. This can be time consuming. It's better to develop a kind of continuous muscle- and eye-memory for where faders were five or six seconds ago. Then, if you have to stop for a mistake, you can reset things from memory.

 Gotcha

Stop, even if you haven't made a mistake. Ears get fatigued, and concentration wanders. Even if things are going perfectly and you don't need to stop, take a break every half-hour or so. It'll be easier to hear subtle details if you do.

Sometimes, fixing things this way can make a mix disjointed or incoherent. Every transition may be perfect, but there isn't a smooth flow between them. If that happens, save the mix and try again. It may be that the only way to achieve both perfection and smoothness is to keep practicing on an entire segment until you get every move right. I've found this to be more of an issue with short, intense pieces like commercials. Long-form documentaries and narrative films usually have enough going on that they pull the viewer through complex mix segments, making a slightly disjointed mix seem smoother.

Premixing and Stems

It's standard practice in Hollywood to do separate mixes for dialog, hard effects, foley, crowds, and backgrounds. This is because there might be dozens of separate tracks making up each of these kinds of sound. These *premixes* are further mixed at a main mixing session, often with three operators—one concentrating on dialog, one on sound effects, and one on music. Their combined work becomes the master. Each operator's mix is also recorded on separate *stems*—full surround mixes having only one category of sound—for dialog, music, and effects (usually abbreviated DM&E). The M&E stems are used when mixing foreign versions.

Television mixes are much simpler, usually with only one engineer. But premixes can still be a good idea. If dialog is coming from a number of sources including multiple on-camera tracks and ADR, it makes sense to create a single, smooth dialog track. Large sound effects that include multiple sources and a lot of processing should also be premixed, so these can be treated as a single sound. Backgrounds should be reduced to alternating A and B tracks, so you can fade between them easily at scene transitions. If you've assembled a score from library elements, there may be music segues on multiple tracks; premixing those will give you less to worry about.

Some hardware controllers don't include a fader for each track but switch a bank of faders to different tracks as necessary. This can be a cost-saving option, particularly if you're adding a third-party controller to multitrack software. Since you can assign this limited number of faders to different tracks, you can write automation data for each one individually and mix a show that way. But that's a little like mousing on-screen faders in multiple passes to build up a mix. It's far better to do premixes for each kind of sound, reducing the number of tracks to the number of faders. That way, you can concentrate on the overall mix instead of individual moves.

To create a premix in most systems, put a 2-pop right before the sequence starts: a one-frame beep on every track, lined up with a one-frame flash in the picture. Then turn on only those tracks that are involved, write the automation, and save the mix as an audio file. Do this for each group of tracks you want to premix. Save the project under another name—something like MyFilmPremixed—delete all the audio tracks, import the premixes, and line them up using the 2-pops. This procedure shouldn't introduce any audio or sync problems. Keep the original edited project, with its original tracks, as a backup.

Networks often require separate DM&E stems for documentaries and other narrated films they commission. The voice is sent to a translation shop, and the M&E is used to create foreign-language versions. Some sophisticated software and digital consoles let you pull these stems while you're mixing, routing individual tracks to a stem output as well as the main mix. Others can play back automation data while muting dialog tracks to create M&E. While this saves time, it isn't the best way to get stems for this kind of show. That's because you've faded other elements to match the original language. The translation is sure to have different timing, putting the fades in the wrong place. Instead, go back to your premixes and create stems that don't fade at all for the narrator.

This isn't a problem in narrative films because dubbed foreign-language dialog is matched to the on-screen mouth movements. Timing remains the same as in the original version.

Mixing Elsewhere

You may have access to good multitrack music equipment outside your NLE and want to use it for your film mix. Or you might want to take a complex project to a professional who specializes in film and video sweetening, to take advantage of their expertise, creative input, and higher-level equipment (that's how I make my living). In either case, the challenge is getting edited video and individual audio tracks out of a NLE and into another system. It doesn't have to be difficult, or require special software.

Digital audio is self-clocking and will play back at a speed determined by the sample rate. While it's inside your computer, the sample rate should be linked to the video frame rate. You need to establish a starting position, but that's simple if you use the 2-pop described above. Then you need to make sure things stay self-clocked while you export.

- When you dub edited picture to videotape to take to the facility, the tape recorder should automatically lock to your computer. If it doesn't, you'll see problems in the video. When the facility plays that tape, it should be locking the playback to its house sync generator.

- If you're exporting edited picture to a file, to carry on CD or portable hard drive, make sure you've selected 29.97 fps.

As you're dubbing picture, put a rough mix on the videotape or computer file as well. It'll serve as a sync reference if things get lost.

- You can export individual audio tracks with their 2-pops as audio-only files and carry them on CD-ROM, audio CD, or hard drive. Just don't select any kind of sample-rate conversion. When the facility plays your tracks back, locked to its house sync, they should match the video.

- If you have a multichannel FireWire sound output, and your editing software supports it, you can dub eight channels at once to digital multitrack. The recorder is connected digitally; it will lock to your computer as you dub. Otherwise, you should connect the recorder to the same word clock or video sync source as your NLE. The playback deck will be locked to the audio facility's house sync.

Prefades and handles It's likely you've added rubber band fades on scene transitions, or dipped music when a voice comes in. Remove these fades before exporting. The audio facility can do a cleaner job of them. These fades will also cause problems if you want to add processing or fine-tune edits at the mix.

It can be a good idea to extend in- and out-points of clips half a second or so before exporting, if there's room on the track. These *handles* give mixers a little extra time for fades, let them clean up audio edits that might not be exactly on a frame line, and can provide room tone or other valuable audio for fixes elsewhere. Some NLEs let you automatically apply handles when you export.

OMF Avid has promoted an interchange method that exports audio files, picture, and edit information between its brand of NLE and ProTools, a multitrack audio program made by Digidesign, a division of Avid. This *open media framework*, or *OMF*, is supported in various ways by some other NLE and audio manufacturers. In many cases, it's the fastest way to move a project from edit to mix.

But OMF is not quite as open as the name suggests. Even if you're editing on an Avid and you know a facility has ProTools, check with the facility to make sure your things will be compatible. If you or the facility is using other systems, make sure you know how to generate an OMF project the facility can read. A test might be in order, or the facility may prefer a different method of maintaining sync.

> ⚠ *Gotcha* _____
>
> *Got a good one: Sync doesn't have to hurt.* Modern digital equipment is driven by reliable crystals that hold its speed steady, usually to within one frame in twenty minutes or more. This error multiplies if you're using separate equipment for audio and video but should still give you accurate sync over a ten minute period.[1] Very often, a 2-pop is all you need.
>
> - A post-pop at the end of a sequence is good insurance. If things have drifted, you can measure the error and apply a speed correction.
>
> - If your project is longer than ten minutes, consider exporting and mixing in short segments. That's how Hollywood often works. And it'll mean less of a disaster if a file gets corrupted, than if you'd lost the whole show.
>
> _____
>
> 1. Some manufacturers cheat and use sample rates or frame rates that aren't precisely on standard. When you play this media on other equipment, there can be a sync error. In these cases you have to rely on house sync.

Timecode While computer interchange is becoming popular, some facilities still prefer good, old-fashioned SMPTE timecode DATs and DTRS 8-tracks, with matching timecode on the picture. It has the advantage of being consistent, perfectly predictable, and absolutely cross-platform.

Of course, it wasn't very long ago that most facilities didn't have timecode DAT. In 1990, midlevel shops even in big markets had to rely on other sync systems. It may not be long before the DAT is as obsolete as, oh, the center track timecode analog tapes us early adopters were using less than 20 years ago.

> ⚠ *Gotcha* _____
>
> *Don't trust; verify.* While facilities that do a lot of broadcast or film work have interchange standards that preserve quality and sync, music studios and desktop editing systems often don't. Before you move your project to another facility for mixing, talk to the people who'll be doing the work. Not to a sales rep or the traffic department, but to the actual technicians involved. Make sure they and you understand exactly what the process will be.

Track chart If you're giving a film to someone else to mix, it can save time and money to let them know what's coming up on various tracks. A simple chart (Figure 18.9) can help.

Think You're Finished?

If at all possible, review the entire film before leaving the mix facility. It's cheaper to make minor changes now, while everything is set up, than to have to start from scratch in a few days.

18.9 If someone else is mixing sound you cut, give him or her a track chart.

Creative Media Group
Homeowner's Advantage: "Flying Through" Intro Video
5830 TRT 8:14

M:S.F	VO	OC 1	OC 2 / ADR	FX 1	FX2 /Alt Foley	Foley	Ambience	Music
0.01				Woosh				Intro
0.19	Anncr intro							—
5.22		Wow!					Street	—
5.25							—	—
9.18	>			Woosh			>	—
17.17					Cymbal		—	
17.23								>
18.07							—	
20.01							Store	
20.18		Marge					—	
32.13		—	walla	Crash!			—	
34.16		—			"Cleanup aisle 2"<need proc		—	
37.12		—			mop		—	
51.28		—	clerk	cart			—	
59.21		—			cash reg		—	
1:06.17		>					—	Stab
1:11.05						coins	—	
1:16.12							>	>
1:19.05				woosh	Cymbal			>
1:21.12			Philip					
1:37.12			—	woosh				
1:53.19			>		Cymbal			
2:12.05								Music under
2:14.21	Anncr							—
2:25.05	—			Woosh				—

Ask about the facility's archiving policy. A few facilities leave projects on a hard drive for a day or two, as a convenience for client changes. Others archive immediately, and there's a charge if they have to de-archive. Some don't archive at all, unless you request it.

Don't assume an archive made at one facility will be readable at another. There are a lot of different digital audio mixing systems. Even if two facilities use the same brand of workstation, they may have different ways of storing inactive projects.

Layback

A mix doesn't do any good until you marry it with the finished video. If you've mixed on your own desktop system, it should be a simple matter to import the mixed audio back to the NLE and sync it with picture. Otherwise, there are a couple of good options:

- If you've printed your video to a professional format to take to a mix, chances are the facility can *layback* the finished track to that tape, in sync with the existing picture. This then becomes the master. It's a good idea to also ask for the mix on timecode DAT tape as a protection. This can be made at the same time as the layback.

- Or have the facility dub the mix as a file to CD-ROM at the sample rate you've used for the production. You can also use an audio CD if you're working at 44.1 kHz. Open the disc in your workstation and either copy the file to NLE or rip the audio as a file.

- Or have them dub to the DV format you use. Take it back to your desktop, capture the mix via FireWire, and sync it in your NLE. This is more time-consuming since you have to capture in real time. It may also introduce quality loss, unless the facility has a way to dub DV via a digital input.

- As a last resort, have the facility give you an audio CD or DAT to redigitize via the analog inputs to your NLE. This is probably the worst option because you'll have to recalibrate the levels, the CD player can introduce sync errors in long films, and the analog conversion will definitely introduce some loss.

Chapter 19

After the Mix

Your film is done. You've edited dialog to sound completely natural—even though it's assembled from multiple takes. You've cleaned up noisy source material. You've created engaging sound effects. You've found perfect music, cut it precisely to your picture, and made it even more perfect with some processing. And you've put everything together in a smooth, compelling mix.

Your film may be done. You're not.

- You still have to test the track to make sure it's listenable under real-world viewing conditions.

- You also should test to make sure it has the desired effect on the audience.

- It's almost certain, these days, that you'll want to put at least part of it on the Web.

- You might also need to convert it to a format for film or DVD release.

This chapter will help with all of these things.

Testing the Track

I am an avid TV viewer—particularly of my own work. I scan cable documentary listings to see when a project I edited or mixed will be shown, and then I try to catch a few minutes of it on as many different TVs as I can. If I'm in a store or someone's home, and one of my spots comes on, I'm all ears. This isn't just ego, though I have plenty of that. It's professional education.

How Does It Sound?

A lot can happen to a track after it leaves your hands. Some of it is electronic—tapes get badly dubbed, signals get data-compressed for servers or satellite, broadcasters and cable channels add lots of processing, and no two TV models have exactly the same sound. On top of that, a track has to survive echoey environments, bad speaker placement, and competition from every possible type of noise.

That's why I listen to my mixes in the real world. I'm checking for specific things:

- Are the voices clear, crisp, and natural sounding?

- Are music and critical sound effects loud enough without interfering with dialog?

- If it's narrative, does every scene have a sense of place?

- If it's stereo, is there a sense of spaciousness?

- How does this track sound compared to others on the same channel?

Over the years, this kind of listening has altered my views about compression (a lot on the voice, but only through a digital connection). It's convinced me to mix underscores and hard effects a lot louder than I originally thought. It's changed the way I think about reverb, and now I make TV tracks dryer than theatrical ones.

The techniques I've learned have gone into this book. But some of these things are matters of aesthetics and personal judgement. That's why you've got to do your own listening. If your projects are aimed at home or office viewing, check them on every set you own. Then borrow the neighbors'. If your projects intended for sales meetings or other auditorium presentations, show up at the rehearsal or attend the event. If it's CD-ROM or Web video, try every combination of platform and browser you can find, on your own computers, at friends' houses, even at computer stores.

How Does It Act?

Some people in this business believe the soundtrack is a self-contained work of art: "I mixed it perfectly. If you can't hear everything I put in, too bad." I prefer the philosophy expressed in Chapter 6: it's not art until somebody's moved by it. That tree in an empty forest might make a sound, but *who cares*?

Back when I was an unemployed audio artist, my wife was my most important critic—even though she didn't know much about sound or music. I'd ask her to listen to my latest sound sculpture. While she did, I'd watch her. I was looking for involuntary reactions—a smile, a slight nod, even a withdrawal when appropriate. I'd correlate it with what I'd done in the track at that moment and remember it for next time. I was also looking for times her attention wandered. That's when the message was getting lost.

When I started doing sound for a living, I transferred that attention to my clients, employees, and anybody else who had a reason to listen. (I suspect that's a main reason *why* I was able to do sound for a living.)

A living parable

I have two different kinds of advertising clients: agency folks dealing mostly with consumer products, and broadcast promo producers. Their projects are essentially the same, thirty-second spots designed to motivate a particular behavior. The ad agency types don't see sales results until long after a job is produced, and there's usually no way to tell which spot motivated which sales. They can only guess about what works and what doesn't. Their jobs are on the line, but they have no real feedback about how well they're doing. It seems that ad people tend to be insecure and burn out early.

On the other hand, the broadcast promo people get overnight ratings. A day or two after they produce a promo, they know exactly how many people were attracted to the show. They can modify their techniques on today's promo and see if it makes a difference in tomorrow's ratings. They're free to try new things, without worrying they'll make more than one days' worth of a mistake. By and large, it seems these promo producers stay at it for years—and also have lives outside of work. Of course, I could be completely wrong about all this. I'm just the happy-go-lucky sound guy.

Data Compression and Streaming

While audio data is tiny compared to high-resolution video, each channel of a 48 kHz sample rate, 16-bit signal requires more than five megabytes per minute. Much of that bandwidth can be better spent on other things, and so virtually everything you hear on TV or in a movie theater has gone through some kind of data compression. Web audio wouldn't exist without it.

Actually, compression may be the wrong word; it implies expansion might be possible. These algorithms work by reducing data, throwing it away forever. When done right, this data tossing process is fairly benign. Consider how almost nobody can tell the difference between a well-encoded mp3 at 256 kbps (kilobits per second) and the six-times-bigger CD-quality audio file it came from. A lot of what's on FM radio has been reduced to 128 kbps over a satellite or ISDN link. Dolby Digital theatrical tracks have even more data taken away from them, and very few moviegoers complain.

But it is true that the more data compression you apply, the more likely you are to hear problems, and the more careful you have to be during encoding. Dolby Digital tracks are encoded by experts, using very high quality equipment. On the other hand, there are plenty of idiots posting badly encoded mp3 tracks on the Internet (usually from badly written freeware encoders). That's why the format has gotten such a bad reputation. When done right, mp3 can sound very good.

We'll deal with its problems, and how to get around them, later in this chapter. But to understand them, you need to know what's happening inside the encoder.

How They Work

The key to all modern audio data compression is masking, the same phenomenon that powers high-powered noise reduction algorithms. Briefly, a loud signal will hide a softer one at a similar frequency, even if they don't occur at precisely the same time. Chapter 16 explains the process more thoroughly.

To apply masking for data compression, the process first breaks the audio stream into frames, lasting up to a few milliseconds each. The length of each frame depends primarily on the data rate; lower rate files with more compression have longer frames. Each frame is boosted so its loudest wave reaches 0 dBFS, to take advantage of every bit during processing. The amount of boost is noted so the frames can be restored to their original volume on playback.

Then the algorithm measures how much energy the frame has at different frequencies. The number of frequencies is a trade-off: more bands allows tighter masking, but requires sharper filters that respond more slowly. The mp3 format uses up to 512 bands, other compression systems have more or less.

- If a particular band is silent during the frame, the process notes that fact and doesn't waste any more data on the band.

- If a band is loud, it *reduces* the number of bits used for that frame. Normally, lowering the bit depth raises the noise. But in this case, the loud signal masks noise at the same frequency.

- If a band is soft, it's processed with more bits, unless there's a masking sound in an adjacent band (and in some algorithms, in the previous or next frame). Then it assumes this band won't be heard and doesn't waste bits on it at all.

- The resulting audio is run through a data packer similar to WinZip or Stuffit. Normal audio is too complex to compress well in these systems, but the simplified masked audio does.

Speech-only encoding

A different kind of data reduction system, used in voicemail and many cell phones as well as Qualcomm PureVoice,[1] uses the vocoder discussed in Chapter 17. Incoming speech is analyzed to determine what pitch the vocal folds were vibrating at. If no pitch can be found, it's assumed the source was an unvoiced consonant. Then Fourier transforms measure which harmonics of

---

1. One of the algorithms available in QuickTime for Mac or Windows.

that pitch were emphasized by mouth and tongue resonators. None of the actual voice is stored or transmitted, just the pitch and resonator data.

On playback, a vocal-fold buzz or friction hiss is generated electronically. Then digital filters are applied to simulate the resonators, re-creating the speech formants. Essentially, when you listen to a cell phone or check your voicemail, you're probably hearing a robot faithfully mimicking the original voice.

For obvious reasons, vocoder-based compression falls apart on instrumental music. It also distorts if two people are speaking simultaneously, or if there's high background noise, because that confuses the pitch analyzer.

Adaptive Delta

Adaptive Delta Modulation is an early encoding scheme that doesn't rely on psychoacoustic masking. Instead, it makes a mathematical assumption. 16-bit audio is capable of more than 65,000 different values from the most negative to the most positive part of a wave. But this process assumes real-world sounds won't jump that far from one sample to the next.

Instead of measuring each sample and storing the value, Adaptive Delta stores the difference between samples. It assigns 4 bits for this, with additional scaling information every few dozen samples so jumps of more than 16 values are possible. The algorithm is found in QuickTime IMA and Microsoft *ADPCM*—the other three letters are for *pulse code modulation*, the technical name for normal digital recording.

While ADPCM can sound fairly good, it fails on sounds with very fast attacks such as gunshots. These get noisy for the first split second, before the numbers catch up. More importantly, ADPCM is capable of only 4:1 compression—and at ratios like that, masking algorithms can achieve true CD quality. So except for cases where there just isn't enough processing power to encode or play modern formats, it's been largely abandoned.

Making Data Compression Sound Good

The most critical setting in a data compression system, including mp3 encoders, is the bitrate. Lower bitrates mean longer frames, increasing the chance that the masking sound won't be available for the entire length of the frame. The result is noise and a flangey or chirping sound.

What kind of bitrate you consider low, and how much noise or other distortion is acceptable, depends on the application. But if you do things right, broadcast-quality sound can be achieved at 128 kbps. One of the most important factors is which encoder you use. Even in a standardized format like mp3, there are multiple trade-offs that program designers have to make. Commercial encoders are usually better designed in this respect than freeware. Because they've also paid licensing fees to the Fraunhofer Institut—inventors of the mp3 format—commercial publishers may have had more access to inner workings of the system.

It makes sense to use a high-quality encoder. Other things will help as well.

- If you have to encode at a low bitrate, get rid of high frequencies first. Apply a low-pass filter at 8 kHz to 12 kHz (or use a good sample-rate converter to lower the rate to 22 kHz, which filters sounds above 10 kHz). The moderate dullness this imparts will be less objectionable than low bitrate noises.

- *Do not* try to help the high-frequency filtering by boosting just below the Nyquist Limit (this boost is often available as a Preserve Highs option in a sample rate converter). This wastes precious bits on unimportant sounds, increasing the possibility of flanging or chirping.

- *Do not* use extreme level compression, particularly multiband compression. This makes it harder for the algorithm to tell the difference between important sounds and those that can be lost, lowering the overall quality.

- Speech is harder to encode in a masking processor than music because it changes faster. The most common distortion at low bitrates is a reverberation-like noise tail on the words. It can be lessened by lowering the number of bands in the encoder, which raises the internal filters' response times. Most encoders don't let you control the number of filters, but you can choose one that's been optimized for speech.

- Higher background noise levels also increase problems with encoding. Start with the cleanest recording possible.

Other choices during encoding

Processing the source sound and selecting a good encoder and bitrate is only part of the story. A few other decisions can help you get the most from a compression system.

Stereo or joint stereo   Most algorithms expect the left and right channels of a stereo pair to be similar. This is usually true in music. A *joint stereo* mode encodes only major differences between the channels, particularly at high frequencies, freeing up more of the bitrate for better quality. But ambiences and crowd sounds can be very different on the left and right, if the space isn't reverberant and there are lots of spread-out sources. With these sounds, joint stereo pushes things toward the center.

- If this is a problem, choose *true stereo*, an option on many encoders. This halves the bitrate available for other characteristics of your sound, but encodes each channel separately to preserve the stereo image.

- You should also select true stereo when the left and right channels are totally independent, as in a split voice/music track.

Variable bitrate   This option, also known as *VBR*, can both reduce file sizes and improve the sound. The algorithm specifies a different bitrate for each frame, between limits you set. This avoids wasting bits on pauses or easy-to-encode sounds, making the overall file smaller, while making sure bits will be available when needed.

- VBR works best on simpler or slower-moving sources, including a lot of new age or classical music. It presents little advantage on faster and highly processed sounds, such as most pop styles, because the maximum bitrate must be used for most frames.

- Some older mp3 players can't handle VBR. They may produce significant distortion, or not play the file at all.

Encoder engines   Good commercial encoders will give you a choice of algorithms for creating mp3s, including Fraunhofer's, the open-sourced LAME extensions, and possibly one created by the program's publisher specifically for the purpose. Each will sound different. If you have the choice, experiment to see which gives the best results on your source material. Non-mp3 formats rarely give you this kind of choice, and have a single proprietary algorithm.

Ogg Vorbis   Open-source fans might also want to experiment with Ogg Vorbis, a patent-free encoding and streaming technology. It's very similar to mp3, though not compatible with mp3 players. Free or shareware encoders and players are available for every platform at www.vorbis.com.

Multiple generations

Data compression is lossy. When you convert a compressed file back to 16-bit linear audio, something will be missing. If you encode it again, the algorithm has a harder time finding details that can be safely deleted. Noise and distortion build up with each subsequent pass.

- Don't encode more times than is necessary. While it may be tempting to save file space with an algorithm like mp3, always keep backup files and intermediate sources as 16-bit linear. Blank CDs are cheap; noise or distortion is forever.

- If you must go through multiple encodings, stay with the highest bitrates possible. If the final release format will be at a low bitrate, don't apply it until the last step.

- There is some evidence that multiple generations through the same compressor sound worse than the same number of generations through a variety of algorithms.

Streaming

Web formats such as RealMedia, Windows Media, and QuickTime are designed to *stream*, so they start playing before all the data is downloaded. Streams can be played easily in most browsers or free add-ons, and the fast response is gratifying to users. But the biggest advantage may be that most users don't know how to save streams as files; this appeals to the security-conscious.

There are plenty of self-contained streaming formats. Some, such as Macromedia Shockwave, rely on garden-variety mp3 with a slightly different header. But you can stream mp3 files directly with a little extra Web programming. Or you can convert an mp3 file to streaming QuickTime easily, with no quality loss.

Streaming by mime type

Most Web browsers accept a mime type of audio/mpegurl. This is a text file with the extension .m3u, containing a single line pointing to the URL of an mp3 file. Link to the m3u with a standard <A HREF> tag. When the browser loads the m3u file, it passes the URL to an application that can handle mp3 streams, typically RealPlayer. The application loads a buffer and the file starts playing.

A typical m3u might have a name and content like this:

```
Filename:    intro.m3u
Content:     http://64.33.79.241/aes/audio/intro.mp3
```

You can also specify the mp3's location with a domain name, but IP addresses generally load faster. Some older servers may not support this mime type and you'll have to link directly to the mp3 file. Or go to plan B.

Streaming via QuickTime

QuickTime doesn't save mp3 audio—Apple doesn't have the Fraunhofer encoding license—but it can play the files. You can trick the player into streaming raw mp3 by putting it in a QuickTime shell. You'll need Apple's QuickTime Pro, a $30 upgrade to its free Mac and Windows player.

1. If you're making an audio/video movie, save the track as 16-bit linear audio. If it's to be an audio-only file, find the source file and skip to step 3.

2. Export the A/V movie's track as an AIFF or WAV, 16-bit linear file. Leave the original movie file open.

3. Open the audio file and convert it to mp3, using a good encoder.

4. Choose QuickTime's File>New Player command. Then open the mp3 file in that player.

5. Choose the Edit>Select All, and then Copy. This puts the mp3 audio data on the clipboard. If you're making an A/V movie, jump to step 7.

6. If you're making an audio-only movie, select File>New Player again. This creates an empty movie.

7. Click on the original A/V movie or the new player you created in step 6. Choose Edit>Select All, then Edit>Add. The mp3 data is now in the movie. If you're doing audio-only, skip to step 9.

8. Choose Edit>Delete Tracks and, in the window that appears, delete Audio Track 1. This gets rid of the original 16-bit linear data.

9. Chose File>Export. In the window that appears, select Export>Quick Time Movie. Click Options, and in that window, turn on Prepare for Internet Streaming, Quick Start. Click OK, name your movie, and Save.

The QuickTime with its mp3 track can now be put on a Web page with a standard `<A HREF>` command or you can `<EMBED>` the movie.

I use this process on all of my movies, streaming or downloadable, because mp3 sounds better than the other compressors in QuickTime. It's a lot of steps and worth the effort. Maybe some reader will be inspired to write a script to automate things.

Release Formats

In many cases, the physical format of a project won't make much difference in how you treat the sound, beyond the issues discussed in Chapter 6. But there are some technical issues you should be aware of, mostly dealing with data compression.

Web

Apple's QuickTime and Microsoft's Windows Media are the two most common Web video formats at this point. While free players for both are available for both computer platforms, features usually lag behind in the non-native one. The Mac version of Windows Media Player doesn't work as well as the Windows version. The Windows version of QuickTime Player is almost as good as the Mac version, possibly because Apple has to try harder to keep market share.

Some Web sites put video up in both Mac and Windows versions to get around this, or skip the platform wars altogether and use RealMedia instead. However, that Internet pioneer—Real Audio was the first streaming format—seems to be losing ground at this writing. All this may be different tomorrow.

There are also browser issues. The `<EMBED>` tag, which lets you put movie controls on a page in Netscape, has been left out of some versions of Internet Explorer. Other Web features are Explorer-friendly only and don't display in Netscape. And this too will change.

If you're putting video on a page for client approval, the only sensible solution is to ask what format the client prefers. If it's for public consumption, check what leading sites in your industry are using at the time. (I get about 3,000 hits a month for the QuickTime streaming video samples on my Web site. I have no idea why. The hits are certainly not from potential clients.)

Other Internet uses

Email is the most direct way to get samples to a clients, if you're sure their mailboxes can handle the file sizes involved. If not, password-protected Web pages or an FTP site can provide confidentiality. If you don't have access to a server and don't mind the whole world seeing your video, there are advertising-supported sites that'll let you put up large files.

- You can save data by sending progressive mixes as mp3 audio-only files. The client already has the video on his or her desk, so there's no need to repeat that information. If the clients are NLE savvy, it won't take long for them to sync your new track to the picture. If not, Apple's QuickTime Pro for Mac or Windows (described earlier) can do the job. Make sure your track is the same length as the client's video copy before you send it. Then tell the client to do the following:

1. Open the sound in QuickTime Player. Select All>Copy.

2. Open the picture in the Player. Click the left-most button to jump to the beginning of the file.

3. Select Add from the Edit menu.

The movie might now have two soundtracks, your new one and the original. You can play them both to verify sync.

4. Use Enable Tracks, in the Edit menu, to turn tracks on or off. Or use Delete Tracks in the same menu to get rid of old ones.

- Occasionally, mp3 files don't survive the email process. The data gets corrupted or lost entirely (I suspect some ISPs randomly trash enclosures with the extension .mp3). Zipping or Stuffing the file before mailing seems to be the best cure. It doesn't change the file size because mp3 already uses that kind of data packing. But it does provide redundancy and error checking—and changes the extension as well.

Film

Dolby Digital, DTS (Digital Theater Systems), and SDDS (Sony Dynamic Digital Sound) are somewhat similar. All three use some form of data compression. In some cases, the compression is fairly extreme; ratios can be as high as 17:1.

Dolby Digital uses an optical data track in the space between sprocket holes. SDDS runs its data down the edges of the film. DTS puts timecode on the film and runs audio from a separate CD-ROM. While DTS is more work than the other two formats, it provides the highest bitrate and so needs the least compression. All three rely on a stereo analog optical track on the film for backup.

> ⚠ **Gotcha**
>
> **What about THX?** THX (named for its inventor, film sound genius Tomlinson Holman) isn't a format at all. It's a set of specifications for equipment and acoustics in theaters, home setups, and mastering labs; and a certification process to see that users and films meet the spec.

If your project is heading for theatrical release and you want to use any of these formats, it'll be encoded in a lab. The lab will probably want you to provide audio on timecode DTRS tape for multitrack, or timecode DAT for stereo, at 48 kHz sample rate and 16-bit or 24-bit resolution.

DVD

Digital Versatile Disc (almost never referred to by that name) is capable of the three film formats plus noncompressed PCM audio and MPEG encoding. PCM is obviously the highest audio quality, and the format can handle 16-, 20-, or 24-bit resolution at up to 96 kHz sampling on up to eight channels. Extreme sampling is almost never used for multichannel sound because of the high data rates required.

Proprietary DVD surround formats can be encoded on the desktop with plug-ins, but because of licensing fees, this software can get very expensive. MPEG encoders are available for much less. Desktop DVD mastering programs have become popular and range in price from Apple's free iDVD to the thousand-dollar range. The price of desktop DVD burners continues to drop.

DVDs can also be recorded in standalone decks that look remarkably similar to home VCRs. While the product category is new as I'm writing this, recorders are already under $1,000. Because recordable DVD is consumer electronics and takes advantage of computer technology, the decks will probably be priced similarly to good VHS equipment in a few years. Current models aren't capable of multichannel sound, and that's not likely to change because they're aimed at consumer and corporate use.

DVD compatibility can be a dicey thing, and this will probably continue until the format matures. Some combinations of recorder and blank disc won't play reliably in some brands of player. *DV* magazine is keeping on top of this issue, and the latest information can be found at DV.com's Features section and in their Community Forums.

Afterword

I started this book with the assumption that readers are intelligent filmmakers who know what they want their track to sound like but aren't quite sure how to get there. That's why I've stayed away from creative or aesthetic concerns, except where they're thoroughly wedded to the technical.

But over the years, I've adopted a working philosophy that helps my creative side as well as my engineering. It applies to any filmmaking style and to creating visuals as well as soundtracks. While I express it in terms of client and supplier, much of it also applies when you have to wear both hats at once. I want to step beyond the technical, and end this book with this philosophy.

Little things mean everything

Studs Terkel ends the preface of his book, *Working*, by interviewing a stonemason. This man loves his job, and stones are his life. When he's at work, he's totally aware of each piece's different grain and shape. He knows the success of his projects depends on respecting the individual stones. If one wasn't placed perfectly, it will bother him years later.

This is a paradox in any creative craft. The more attention you pay to individual elements—in my case, every syllable and sound—the more you can appreciate the whole. You see the forest better if you know the trees are healthy. For me, this has meant the most enjoyable projects have been with clients who let me fine-tune the details. (In order to keep those clients, I've had to learn to do the fine-tuning quickly and cost-effectively. That's what the rest of this book has been about.)

This attention to detail also keeps you from being bored. It's only human nature to look at each new assignment in terms of what you've done before, because you want to reuse techniques you've already developed. But even the most mundane project has something different about it. It doesn't matter whether that difference lasts only a few seconds on-screen or drives an entire sequence; solving the new problem is what makes it fun. For me, there's genuine joy in discovering new ways to make sounds work together in time or timbre. For you, it might be a new way to move a camera, reveal a personality, or fool the eye. Figure out what's unique about a project, and you've got something to look forward to.

Spread the joy

I learned a lesson early in my career. I was given a hard-sell commercial script to produce, and the copy was one cliché after another. The account executive actually apologized, saying every good creative concept had been shot down and those awful lines were the client's idea. He asked me to just do the best I could. I hired a couple of good actors and presented them with both the script and the story behind it. Big mistake. As hard as we all tried, we couldn't make the readings justify even the poor writing. The actors believed the agency and I didn't care, so despite their professionalism they couldn't care either.

What I learned immediately was to always find some aspect of the job that you can be positive about. If not the script, then the visuals, or the quality of the product, or even the creative challenge of delivering old lines a new way. It will motivate you and the people around you. One cliché wasn't in that awful script, but should have been inscribed on my forehead: "What's worth doing, is worth doing well."

After a few years, I learned another lesson—one the hapless account executive apparently never discovered. The best way to express it may be a saying I developed when teaching at Berklee College of Music. I told students there was a secret key to success in our business, and they should repeat it after me:

- Never give the clients what they ask for.

Of course, everybody in the room started laughing—how arrogant!—but then I told them that was only *half* the rule. They also had to repeat the second part:

- Always give the clients what they want.

If clients knew exactly what to ask for—how to frame a shot, edit a sequence, or mix a track—they could do the job themselves. On the other hand, even the most inept client knows what the message should be, a lot better than we can. Our task is to deliver that message in a way that's memorable and engaging.

So while you can ignore the details of outlandish client requests, you still have to figure out what was in the client's mind when he or she asked for it. Client ideas should only be a starting point. Apply your own creativity and production expertise, and you can turn it into something that satisfies all of you.

If a client doesn't like what you suggest, there's probably a reason—even if they can't express it well. Find a way to satisfy their objection, or drop the concept and move onto something else. Don't expect to win every creative battle. Even if the client rejects all your ideas and insists on doing something you know will be awful, you'll have given it your best effort.

Learn by playing

Almost every mechanical skill from my early career is now obsolete. Clients have absolutely no interest in my ability to edit magnetic film or repair a tubed amplifier. Even my more mature skills—like cutting dialog on a CMX keyboard—have gone by the wayside. But these technologies died because more exciting ones replaced them. Cultivate that excitement; if you let yourself get caught up in the thrill of a new technology, learning how to use it gets easier.

Notice that I said technology and not tool. There are plenty of new production devices introduced every year. Each has its own interface, idiosyncrasies, and power-user tricks. Keeping up with them can be a chore—and an unrewarding one, when next year's hot product makes this year's interface obsolete. But a few times a decade, some part of our industry discovers a radically different way of working. When it happens in your field, you've got the choice of being thrilled or threatened.

Be an early adopter, even if it means making very modest steps. When it first became possible to edit sound on a desktop computer about fifteen years ago, I was thrilled to spend $75 on a little application for my Mac Plus. It was slow and sounded horrible, so I still had to use tape and a razor blade for the real projects. But it was fun, and trying to accomplish things with this awkward new technology forced me to learn more things about digital audio—and become a better engineer—than if I'd started with a powerful workstation.

19.1   One year I decided to pack tapes with balloons instead of bubble wrap. Important words to remember when things seem to go wrong.

You can also learn from your own good efforts. Six months after you've finished an important project, show the tape to someone who hasn't seen it before. Watch his or her reactions. Something magical will usually happen. Between your own hindsight and their body language, you'll notice a few simple changes that would have made a big difference. You can't change the existing tape, but you'll know what to look for next time.

Remember this:

No matter where the technology goes, ultimately you're selling creativity.

What you learned with your first set of finger paints is still true: creating is fun.

Keep that sense of play while you learn the technology and you'll never be bored.

Glossary

Every industry creates its own jargon, mostly to save time when talking about complex subjects. But it can be intimidating to the uninitiated.

Here are some of the audio terms I've thrown around in this book. I've also included a couple of production terms you probably already know, in case sound people are reading this as an introduction to the video world.

ADAT Alesis Digital Audio Tape, an eight-track format using S-VHS cassettes and named for the company that invented it. ADATs were the first practical, low-cost digital multitracks and became a favorite of scoring composers. A similar but more robust eight-track format, Tascam's DTRS (also known as DA8 or DA88), uses Hi8 cassettes. The DTRS format was adopted by Sony and is the standard in feature production, and when supplying D/M/E stems to a network. Both systems allow multiple decks to be linked for unlimited tracks. ADAT and DTRS are not compatible.

ADPCM Adaptive delta pulse code modulation, a math-based audio compression system now largely replaced by more efficient perceptual encoding. See Chapter 19.

ADR Automatic (or automated) dialog replacement, also sometimes known as looping. Production audio can be noisy and, even if recorded on a quiet sound stage, can be inconsistent from shot to shot. ADR systems let actors go into a sound studio, hear short pieces of their own dialog repeated over and over in a constant rhythm, and then recreate the performance—line by line—in sync with picture. See Chapter 8.

AES/EBU Literally, the Audio Engineering Society and European Broadcasting Union. But the combination of initials almost always refers to one of its standards for interconnecting digital audio devices. See Chapter 4.

AIFF Audio interchange file format, the standard for Macintosh audio- and video-editing systems. Different from Microsoft's WAV format. Fortunately, most programs are smart enough to open either, and there are plenty of shareware converters for both platforms.

aliasing   A form of distortion in digital recording that takes the form of annoying whistles accompanying high-frequency sounds. See Chapter 2.

ambience   Background sounds. Usually a track or two of an environment, such as a factory or traffic noises, played under a scene to set the place. Careful choice of ambiences can eliminate the need for a lot of *foley*. Acousticians and music recording engineers frequently use this term to refer to a room's characteristic reverberation, a totally different meaning.

ASCAP   American Society of Composers, Arrangers, and Publishers. A performing rights organization, which collects royalties from broadcasters and others who play music—either live or recorded—for the public. The money is distributed to the writers and publishers of the music, not the performers or record companies.

ATTC   Address track timecode. LTC recorded on a special track of an analog videotape or down the center of an analog audio tape.

auto-conform   In the dark days of analog video editing, each generation would add noise to the soundtrack. Because a video master could be three or four generations removed from the original, the production audio was often treated only as reference. An automatic conforming system (or hapless audio engineer) would use the original field recordings and an edit list, and rebuild the sound. Modern nonlinear and online systems keep audio as 16-bit digital data, so this step shouldn't be necessary. But in professional productions, audio is frequently digitized into a NLE by an assistant editor, using less-than-perfect equipment. So auto-conforming is frequently required. It's

also used in feature productions that work with 24-bit audio for greater dynamic range.

BGs   Another name for *ambience track*, pronounced like the disco group.

BMI   Broadcast Music Incorporated, a performing rights organization. See *ASCAP*.

boom   Literally, a fiberglass or metal stick used to hold a microphone near an actor, just out of camera range. But the term is also used to refer to the mic as well, and to a soundtrack that was recorded with one.

bump   To adjust the timing between sound and picture in precise frame or subframe units, while both are running. While this is most often used to fine-tune lipsync and sound effects placement, bumping a piece of music a frame or two can have amazing results.

burn-in   A videotape with timecode numbers superimposed on the picture.

BWF   Broadcast wave format, an audio interchange format standardized by the European Broadcasting Union. It's similar to Microsoft WAV and can be read by standard audio programs, but software designed for this format also lets you embed sync and other information.

CD-quality   Properly speaking, a digital audio signal or device capable of 20 Hz–20 kHz bandwidth within a decibel, with very low distortion and a 96 dB dynamic range. Many manufacturers use the term improperly to imply a quality that isn't justified by the system's analog components, or to describe any processing they think sounds good. Unless you can verify specifications, the phrase is meaningless.

click track An electronic metronome played into headphones, or a track on a tape with that signal, so that musicians can perform to precise timing.

codec Coder and decoder processes that turn audio or video into a format that can be transmitted or stored more efficiently (such as mp3) and then restored. The term is sometimes used to refer to the data format itself.

cue sheet A document listing music used in a TV production, including information about the composer and publishing company. These are given to the TV station so it can report the usage to a performing rights society (see *ASCAP*). See Chapter 10.

DM&E Dialog, music, and effects; three *stems* commonly provided with a mix for foreign-language dubbing.

DA8, DA88, DTRS See ADAT.

DAW Digital audio workstation. A computer system designed specifically for editing and mixing sound, often in sync with picture. While the term was originally reserved for high-powered and expensive systems with dedicated computers and hands-on controllers, now just about every software publisher calls its multitrack audio software a DAW.

dBFS Decibels referenced to *full scale*, the largest signal that can be expressed in a digital system. See Chapter 4 for discussion of this and the following three decibel standards.

dBm Decibels referenced to 1 milliwatt across 600 Ω. Some manufacturers use this term when they really mean dBu, but 600 Ω hasn't been part of most equipment specifications for more than a decade.

dBu Decibels referenced to 0.775 volts. That's the voltage a traditionally terminated dBm produces.

dBV Decibels referenced to 1 volt.

decibel Also dB. A precise, and often misunderstood, measurement of the ratio between two acoustic or audio signals. See Chapter 2 for an explanation of all these *dB* terms.

dipole speakers Speakers that radiate out of their front and back simultaneously. Sometimes used for surround channels.

distortion Anything that changes the output of an audio system so it no longer reflects the input signal. Noise and changes in frequency response can be forms of distortion, though the term is usually reserved for unintentional, gross changes in the waveform.

dither Specially shaped random noise added to a digital signal to improve its quality at low levels. See Chapter 2.

Dolby Digital A *codec* used in film and DVD sound. See Chapter 19.

dropframe A way of counting timecode so that frame numbers stay, on average, in sync with real-world time. No actual frames are dropped in the process. See Chapter 7.

DTS A *codec* used in film and DVD sound.

dynamic range The range between the loudest signal a system can carry without distortion and its low-level noise that would obscure any softer signals, expressed in decibels. In a purely digital signal, each bit is worth about 6 dB dynamic range. But when you start involving analog circuits, dynamic range gets harder to pin down. Low-level noise is contributed by the electronics itself and distortion increases as the volume increases beyond a nominal value.

foley   Generating sound effects by duplicating the actors' on-screen movements in a sound studio. A team of good foley artists can watch a scene once, gather armloads of props, and then create everything from footsteps to fist fights in perfect sync. *Digital foley* refers to the process of recording the sounds without picture and then matching them in an audio workstation. See Chapter 11.

Haas effect   Also known as *precedence effect*. Part of our hearing that assumes a sound is coming from the direction from which we first hear it. Because of this, it's also a way of fooling the ear into thinking a sound comes from one specific place, when it may be coming from two or more. Used in film mixing, but may not be suitable for broadcast (see Chapter 18).

hard effect   Also known as *spot effect*. Sounds that are impractical to foley (such as telephone bells, explosions, and light sabers) and usually important to the story. These are often drawn from large CD effects libraries, but may be created for the project. In feature film production, the term often refers to *any* sound effects that are in sync with picture.

high fidelity   An ambiguous term. It often refers to somewhere near a 20 Hz–20 kHz frequency range with less than 2 dB variation between sounds of different frequencies, and a dynamic range of at least 60 dB with less than 0.3 percent distortion—but the bar keeps getting raised as technology improves. Has nothing to do with whether a system is analog or digital.

hitting a post   Audio people use this term to refer to the cues within a long sound effect or music track. It's not enough to make a sound begin and end in sync with the picture; you also have to make sure that internal elements match the on-screen actions. A good sound editor will make lots of tiny edits and use other tricks to hit as many posts as possible.

house sync   In large facilities, a single video signal (usually an all-black picture in color TV format) is distributed to just about every audio and video device. House sync is not the same as timecode. See Chapter 4.

ISDN   Integrated services digital network. A way of combining standard telephone wiring with special equipment to create 128 kilobit per second dial-up connections as needed. It's more reliable (as well as faster) than high-speed analog modems, and it's more flexible than other systems like DSL or cable modems. In the world of audio, the term usually refers to realtime transfers and remote recording sessions using ISDN and specialized codecs.

lav   Short for lavaliere, a small microphone originally worn on a necklace (hence the name). Lavs are mounted on actors or interview subjects, often concealed in their clothing or hair, for close-up miking. Lavs are frequently used with wireless transmitters to give the actor freedom of movement, but will sound better if wired directly to the recorder. The term is also used to refer to a soundtrack that has been recorded with a lav.

layback   Copying a finished mix from an audio workstation or separate audio tape back to a videotape master.

layup   Transferring production sound from edited videotape to an audio medium for further manipulation. Networked nonlinear editing systems can make both layback and layup unnecessary.

lipsync   One technical goal of a soundtrack, in which sounds occur at the precise moment we see what's causing them. An example would be actors' voices matched to their mouth movements. If you're having lipsync problems, check Chapters 1 and 7.

LTC   Longitudinal timecode. SMPTE timecode data is actually a biphase digital stream in the audio range, sounding something like a fax machine signal. When it's recorded on an analog audio track it's called longitudinal, since it runs parallel to the tape instead of slanting like a videotape track. LTC also refers to the biphase signal itself, so the wire that plugs into a timecode input is actually carrying LTC—even if the data came from a digital data track or VITC. See Chapter 7.

M&E   Music and effects, a sub mix of a production's soundtrack with no dialog to make foreign translations easier.

masking   A phenomenon where sounds at one frequency make it difficult or impossible to hear other simultaneous (or, in the case of temporal masking, closely occurring) sounds at a nearby frequency. It's the basis behind a lot of noise reduction and every system of perceptual encoding. See Chapter 16.

MIDI   Musical instrument digital interface, a common language and electrical standard for describing events such as the turning on or off of a note.

mid-side (M/S)   Stereo microphone technique with excellent control of width and mono compatibility.

MOS   Scenes that are videotaped or filmed without any audio, usually because the camera setup or location makes sound impractical. The expectation is that a track will be created using foley and other effects. This is often a bad idea in video production, since any track—even one from a camera-mounted microphone far from the action—is better than nothing and may be used for sound effects or a sync reference. Rumor has it, the term MOS originated when an early German-speaking film director wanted to work "mitout sound."

mp3   MPEG II layer 3, the most common file format and data reduction scheme for delivering audio over the Internet.

MPEG   Moving Pictures Expert Group, a standard-setting body primarily concerned with applying perceptual encoding to sound and video.

music library   A collection of music intended for use by film and television producers, written in specific styles but not for a specific project. You can license the music for use in a particular production, usually for considerably less than original music of the same quality would cost. See Chapter 10.

needle-drop music   A scheme for buying library music where you pay very little for the discs—sometimes they're free—but report each use and pay a licensing fee when you do. Needle-drop libraries often offer an annual blanket covering every project a producer does, a bargain for busy filmmakers. Also sometimes known as laser-drop music.

NLE Nonlinear editor. Software, often with dedicated video input and processing cards, for cutting picture and sound. Today's NLEs care capable of a wide range of special visual effects and some audio processing. A few also include automated tools for mixing sound.

noise, pink Electronic noise that averages an equal level of signal in each octave. Since any octave has twice as many frequencies as the octave below it, pink noise is created by filtering white noise, so there's less energy as the frequency gets higher. It reflects how we hear better than white noise does and is used for acoustic testing.

noise, white Random electronic noise that averages an equal level of signal at any frequency. This is the kind of noise commonly generated by analog circuits.

Nyquist A mathematical proof that digital sample rates must be more than twice as high as the highest frequency a system will be called on to carry. The *Nyquist Limit* is that highest frequency. See Chapter 2.

octave the musical interval of 12 semitones, or a frequency ratio of 2:1.

offset The difference in timecode between any two tapes. Video editors typically start their programs at 1:00:00:00 (one hour; no minutes, seconds, or frames) to allow for color bars and slates. If an audio operator decides to start that same program at 00:01:00:00, the sound would have a –59 minute offset. Some digital audio processors introduce delays to handle the sound more intelligently, so small offsets are sometimes necessary.

perceptual encoding An audio data compression scheme that relies on the masking phenomenon. Also known as psychoacoustic encoding. See Chapter 19.

phantom image A location where sound seems to be coming from in a stereo or surround setup, even though there's no speaker there. A good mix can have a lot of these, depending on which medium the project will be shown in. See Chapter 18.

production audio Sounds recorded in the field while the picture is being shot, usually dialog. It may be recorded directly on the videotape, or as *double-system*.

public domain music Legally, a composition that has fallen out of copyright, usually because of its age. But that refers only to the notes on paper. Recordings, even of public domain pieces, are almost always protected by other copyrights. Not to be confused with *royalty- free music*.

R-DAT Exactly the same as a standard or timecode DAT tape. When R-DAT was first invented, some digital audio systems used stationary heads (like an analog audio tape deck) and others used rotating heads (like a helical-scan video deck).

royalty-free music A scheme for buying library music where you pay a premium for the discs but then can use the music as many times as you wish without extra fees. Also known as buyout music. See Chapter 10.

s/pdif A standard for interconnecting stereo digital audio devices, similar to AES/EBU but using a lower-cost wiring scheme and carrying information that's appropriate for consumer audio. See Chapter 4.

SDDS Sony Dynamic Digital Sound, a *codec* used in film and DVD sound.

sibilance A speech sound with considerable high-frequency energy, which can often distort in a system. A de-esser can control them. See Chapter 13.

slate A board with handwritten scene and take information, photographed at the beginning of a scene. Often has a hinged, wooden stick that can be slapped against it, so that sound and picture can be precisely matched. Modern ones display timecode as well. The term also refers to a human voice calling out scene and take information, to identify sound recordings.

SMPTE Usually short for SMPTE timecode, the frame-accurate time data recorded on video and audio tapes to control editing and keep elements together. It stands for the Society of Motion Picture and Television Engineers, who invented the format, and can also be used to refer to the organization itself.

sound designer Someone who creates special sounds or sound effect montages for a project and often oversees dialog and music as well. Usually a person with both engineering and musical experience. But there's no reason the sound designer can't also be the producer/director/editor.

spotting Going through an edited film to find places where music would be appropriate, and deciding what kind of music to use there. See Chapter 10.

stem A stem is a fully mixed and processed version of a soundtrack, but containing only one category of sound, such as music. See *DM&E*.

sync license The right to use a piece of music in a production. See Chapter 10.

THX A set of specifications for film and DVD speakers, acoustics, and equipment quality, and a program to certify that they've been adhered to. It's not a soundtrack format.

timbre A characteristic of a sound wave that has to do with the number and strength of a wave's harmonics (Chapter 2), and often referred to as its *brightness* or *richness*. Timbre is different from volume or pitch, though an untrained ear can easily be tricked into confusing these characteristics.

timecode See *SMPTE*.

VITC Vertical interval timecode. Time data encoded as a series of dots at the top of each video field. Unlike LTC, it can be read when the tape is paused. This makes it easier to jog a tape to find a specific action, and then match a sound to it. Unfortunately, VITC can't be read when the picture is distorted because of high-speed winding. Most professional analog video systems put identical VITC and LTC data on a tape and choose the most appropriate for the speed.

wet/dry Refers to echoes. Most foley, hard effects, and ADR are recorded dry, without any natural reverberation. Appropriate echoes are then added during the mix, to make the sounds appear to belong to the on-screen environment. But some effects are recorded wet—that is, with natural (or artificial) reverb. These have to be chosen carefully so the echo's quality matches the scene, and they can be harder to edit because you can't cut into the reverberations.

wild   Recorded without synchronization. Sound effects are usually gathered this way and matched up in an editing system. But some things are wild by mistake and have to be carefully resynced. This can happen when a time-code generator or low-end audio workstation isn't locked to *house sync*, or when audio has been stored on an unstable medium such as audio cassette.

XLR   The most popular connector type for high-end analog and digital audio, originally known as Cannon's XLR product line. However, the presence of this connector doesn't guarantee any particular electrical standard. See Chapter 4.

zero level   Literally, a ratio of 1:1 to some specified standard; if expressed in decibels, the ratio 1:1 is 0 dB. In practice, zero level means different things depending on whether you're working in analog or digital. Analog zero is a volume near the system's maximum, but loud sounds are expected to go above it. Digital zero is a mathematical absolute limit, the loudest thing that can be recorded. There is no fixed relationship between any analog zero level and digital zero, but depending on the facility and style of audio mixing, analog zero is equivalent to somewhere between 12 dB and 20 dB below digital zero. See Chapter 7.

About the CD

This is an audio CD, rather than a CD-ROM, so you can play it on the best speakers you've got. The tutorials, of course, should be loaded into your computer.

Tracks that are voice or music demos have been mastered around –2 dBFS, comparable to commercial CDs. Most of the tone-based tracks have been mastered at –10 dBFS, to play at a moderate level on your system. Track 10 includes tone at 0 dBFS as a system check—turn down your speakers before playing it.

Instructions and track identifications on the CD have been sharply filtered, so they're not mistaken for the material being demonstrated.

Track Listing

Track 5   High frequency diagnostic **5:18**

This may be one of the most revealing tracks on this CD. It uses a montage of three well-recorded selections from the DeWolfe Music Library,[1] one acoustic jazz, one classical vocal, and one rock. The montage is played seven times, alternating between full fidelity and through lab-quality filters that remove high frequencies above a precise setting. Each time, the frequency setting is lowered.

If you can't hear the filter switching in and out, you're not hearing anything above the filter setting (hint: listen for the highest percussion). This may be a limitation in your system or just the normal way hearing deteriorates with age.

The frequencies are 20 kHz, 17.5 kHz, 15 kHz, 12.5 kHz, 10 kHz, 7.5 kHz, and 5 kHz. Filters were switched on and off in exactly the same place in each example.

Track 6   The envelopes, please **0:18**

The actual sounds whose envelopes are studied in Chapter 2.

Track 7   Low bit depth, low sample rate **0:13**

The organ-like tone from Track 4, recorded with 2 kHz sampling and 4-bits' depth, then converted back to CD format. Details that were lost to the lower standard are gone forever and not restored by the conversion back to 16-bit, 44.1 kHz sampling. But the sound isn't as bad as you'd think; read the text to find out why.

Track 8   Frequency sweep **0:22**

A continuously-rising pure tone to test speakers. It should sound equally smooth across the band. Harshness or rattles indicate a speaker problem. Extra tones moving in the opposite direction are aliasing distortion in your soundcard or CD player.

Track 9   Speaker polarity check **0:22**

This track has 10 seconds of simultaneous low and high frequency narrowband noise on both channels. Then it dips momentarily. When it comes back, one of the channels has its phase reversed.

Sit between the speakers and listen through the entire track. If the first half seems to have both bands of noise coming from the same place, and the bass is loud and centered, your speakers are correctly wired. If that describes the second half, you need to change the wiring as suggested in the chapter. If the second half is very soft—or the sound disappears entirely after 10 seconds—you're listening in mono.

---

1. "Swing Out Brother" (J. Trombey, DWCD219/10), "Queen of the Night" from *Magic Flute* (Mozart, DWCD142/2), "Rock Hits" (R. Hardy / B. White, DWCD293/11), from the DeWolfe Music Library. All are protected by copyright and used here by permission. Learn more about this versatile library in Chapter 10.

Track 10   Computer output test 1:35
Play this in your CD-ROM drive as a test for the soundcard. First, there's a pure tone swept from 15 kHz to 20 kHz to check for aliasing. Listen for random whistles whose pitch is moving downward. If you don't hear anything for twenty seconds after the first voice announcement, don't worry: It just means that your speakers—or perhaps your ears—can't carry those high frequencies. (Neither can U.S. analog television, which cuts off at 15 kHz to protect the subcarrier.)

Then you'll hear acoustic music:[2] The guitar should sound natural, with no harshness and no rattles.

Finally, three pure tones to test for harmonic distortion at high levels. First, you hear them at –20 dBFS for reference. Then there's a pause, while you're instructed to turn down the monitor to about one-quarter the volume. Then the tones are repeated at 0 dBFS. They should sound the same. Any harmonic distortion will make the second set of tones sound richer or brighter. This is not a good thing, because it prevents accurate monitoring.

- The second set of tones are the loudest thing on this disc. In fact, they're the highest level a CD can reproduce. If you don't turn down the monitor volume, you may damage your system or your ears.

Note that turning the volume down *in software* invalidates this last test. You need to leave the software and system volume controls at their normal position, and turn down an external monitor amplifier's volume control or the control on powered speakers.

Track 11   Lineup tone: 100 Hz, -20 dBFS 0:30
Use this and the next three tracks for test purposes or to check equalizers and meter calibration. Track 12 is the standard used at the start of professional digital videos, usually in conjunction with color bars.

Track 12   Lineup tone: 1 kHz, -20 dBFS 0:30

Track 13   Lineup tone: 10 kHz, -20 dBFS 0:30

Track 14   Lineup tone: 1 kHz, -8 dBFS 0:30

Track 15   Demonstration of scrubbing algorithms 0:59
Good software will offer at least a couple of these as options.

Track 16   Countdown leader 0:08

---

2. "Finding Your Way" *(C. Glassfield, DWCD226/02).* © DeWolfe Music, used by permission.

Track 17   True stereo **0:15**
In this orchestral selection,[3] you should hear piano in the center, violins to the middle left, and woodwinds to the middle right. If the directions are reversed, check your speaker wiring.

Track 18   Mono on two tracks. **0:15**
The same material as Track 17, with all the directional information removed. If you play it on stereo speakers, the sound should come from a point halfway between them.

Track 19   Record level meter calibration **0:19**
Five seconds of a 1 kHz tone at –20 dBFS, –12 dBFS, and –6 dBFS.

Track 20   A technical nightmare. **1:10**
Samples of analog and digital overload distortion, noise caused by too low a level, thin and dull-sounding dialog, and aliasing. Learning to recognize these symptoms can help diagnose problems in your own system. (This track was recorded at a lower level than others on the disc, for aesthetic reasons.)

Track 21   Microphone directionality **1:06**
A short piece of music,[4] first played as it would sound from the front of a cardioid mic, then from the rear of the cardioid, and then from side and rear of a short shotgun.

Track 22   Material for dialog edit **0:39**
This, and most of the tracks that follow, won't make sense without the book's tutorials.

Track 23   Edit demonstrations. **0:34**

Track 24   Using loops to find an edit point **0:22**

Track 25   Edits constrained by frame lines **0:08**

Track 26   Hearing phonemes in normal speech. **0:11**

Track 27   Two takes, with noise **0:08**

Track 28   Editing unvoiced consonants. **0:09**

---

3. "Voyage of Destiny" (F. Talgorn, DW272/1). © DeWolfe Music, used by permission.

4. "Fingal's Cave" (F. Mendelssohn, DW70/11). © DeWolfe Music, used by permission. Also known as "The Hebrides." Yes, the *music* is public domain—Mendelssohn wrote it in 1830. But the performance is protected, as are most recordings of classical music. See Chapter 10.

Track 29   "Marine Hymn," for counting[5] 0:29
This—and the other musical examples in this chapter—are edited from much longer selections in the DeWolfe Music Library.

Track 30   "Marine Hymn," with counts 0:29

Track 31   Typical corporate theme[6] 0:29

Track 32   Music edit with double note... 0:22

Track 33   Same edit, fixed by rolling.. 0:22

Track 34   Mellower corporate theme[7] 0:30

Track 35   Music edit diagnostics 0:51

Track 36   Rock soundalike[8] 0:31

Track 37   John Williams soundalike[9] 0:31

Track 38   Editing in threes[10]... 0:30

Track 39   Door squeak and close[11].. 0:06

Track 40   Looping a rhythmic sound.. 0:44

Track 41   Using a C-loop.. 1:15

---

5.   "Marine Hymn" (trad, arr J. Howe, DW238/12). © DeWolfe Music, used by permission.

6.   "City Power" (R. Hodgson, D. Molyneux, DW190/1). © DeWolfe Music, used by permission.

7.   "The Main Chance" (R. Hodgson, D. Molyneux, DW190/8). © DeWolfe Music, used by permission.

8.   "Root, Toot, Shoot" (A. Hamilton, B. Lang, DW225/11). © DeWolfe Music, used by permission.

9.   "Epic Movie Adventures" (F. Talgorn, DW272/11). © DeWolfe Music, used by permission. This sounds like the American composer and conductor John Williams. DeWolfe also has pieces that sound like the British guitarist John Williams.

10. "Ranza Waltz" (trad, arr. D. Aran, C. Jack, DW288/26). © DeWolfe Music, used by permission.

11. This and most of the other sound effects on this disc are © Hollywood Edge, used by permission.

---

12. Montage includes some cues credited previously, plus "You Are My Fantasy" and "Hell Child" (both C. Kiddy, DW77/9, DW77/13). © DeWolfe Music, used by permission.

Notes on the CD

Music courtesy of Mitchell Greenspan of the DeWolfe Music Library, 25 West 45th St., New York, NY 10036, 212-382-0220 or 800-221-6713. This is an immense and well-produced library, which I use in a lot of productions. Hear their demos at www.dewolfemusic.com.

Sound effects courtesy of John Moran at The Hollywood Edge, 7080 Hollywood Blvd., Hollywood, CA 90028, 213-603-3252 or 800-292-3755. Not only is it an excellent sound effects company; it's also very generous. As of this writing, legitimate producers can get a free CD of 99 well-recorded effects to use in any productions. Those who don't qualify for the CD can download the effects from www.hollywoodedge.com.

Location audio for noise reduction and other demos was supplied by friends in the Boston production community: Rob Stegman of Bluestar Media, Marc Neger of Creative Media Group, Francine Achbar of High Impact Marketing and Media, and Mike Kuell of Jetpak Productions. I won't identify who was responsible for which noisy track.

Most of the studio voices are me and my wife Carla Rose; we've both done voicing for a living. One track was contributed by popular PBS announcer Don Wescott. The disc was mastered at my studio, The Digital Playroom, primarily on an Orban AudicyVX workstation.

Index

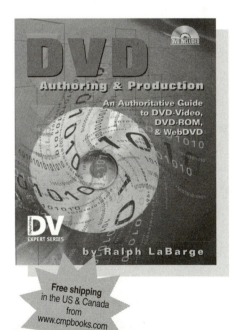

Final Cut Pro 3 Editing Workshop

Second edition

by Tom Wolsky

Master the art and technique of editing with Final Cut Pro 3 on Mac OS X. Thirteen tutorial lessons cover the complete range of tasks—from installing the application to color correction and outputting. All of the ingredients, including raw video footage and tips & tricks, blend to give you a working knowledge of the principles taught in film schools. CD-ROM and KeyGuide™ included, 598pp, ISBN 1-57820-118-7, $49.95

Nonlinear Editing
Storytelling, Aesthetics, & Craft

by Bryce Button

Build your aesthetic muscles with this application-agnostic guide to digital editing so you can excel in the art and craft of storytelling. Take stock of what feeds your vision and develop your abilities in employing timing, emotion, flow, and pace to present your story effectively. Exercises and interviews with the pros help you to hone your skills. CD-ROM included, 523pp, ISBN 1-57820-096-2, $49.95

What's on the Audio CD?

The one-hour audio CD for *Audio Postproduction for Digital Video* features platform-independent diagnostics, demonstrations, and tutorial tracks. You can play the tracks on the best speakers you've got and load them into your NLE. The tutorials, of course, should be loaded into your computer.

Voice or music demos have been mastered around –2 dBFS, comparable to commercial CDs. Most of the tone-based tracks have been mastered at –10 dBFS, to play at a moderate level on your system. Track 10 includes tone at 0 dBFS as a system check—turn down your speakers before playing it.

For more information on the CD's contents, tracks—as well as licensing and copyright information—see the Introduction (page x) and Appendix B beginning on page 415.